C000165274

1,000,000 Books

are available to read at

---◆---

www.ForgottenBooks.com

---◆---

Read online
Download PDF
Purchase in print

ISBN 978-1-332-31163-7
PIBN 10312470

This book is a reproduction of an important historical work. Forgotten Books uses
state-of-the-art technology to digitally reconstruct the work, preserving the original format
whilst repairing imperfections present in the aged copy. In rare cases, an imperfection in
the original, such as a blemish or missing page, may be replicated in our edition. We do,
however, repair the vast majority of imperfections successfully; any imperfections that
remain are intentionally left to preserve the state of such historical works.

Forgotten Books is a registered trademark of FB &c Ltd.
Copyright © 2018 FB &c Ltd.
FB &c Ltd, Dalton House, 60 Windsor Avenue, London, SW19 2RR.
Company number 08720141. Registered in England and Wales.

For support please visit www.forgottenbooks.com

1 MONTH OF
FREE
READING

at

www.ForgottenBooks.com

By purchasing this book you are
eligible for one month membership to
ForgottenBooks.com, giving you
unlimited access to our entire
collection of over 1,000,000 titles via
our web site and mobile apps.

To claim your free month visit:
www.forgottenbooks.com/free312470

* Offer is valid for 45 days from date of purchase. Terms and conditions apply.

English
Français
Deutsche
Italiano
Español
Português

www.forgottenbooks.com

Mythology Photography **Fiction**
Fishing Christianity **Art** Cooking
Essays Buddhism Freemasonry
Medicine **Biology** Music **Ancient**
Egypt Evolution Carpentry Physics
Dance Geology **Mathematics** Fitness
Shakespeare **Folklore** Yoga Marketing
Confidence Immortality Biographies
Poetry **Psychology** Witchcraft
Electronics Chemistry History **Law**
Accounting **Philosophy** Anthropology
Alchemy Drama Quantum Mechanics
Atheism Sexual Health **Ancient History**
Entrepreneurship Languages Sport
Paleontology Needlework Islam
Metaphysics Investment Archaeology
Parenting Statistics Criminology
Motivational

JANE MAXWELL, DUCHESS OF GORDON.
By Geo Romney, R A

THREE GENERATIONS OF FASCINATING WOMEN

and other Sketches from Family History

BY

LADY RUSSELL

WITH ILLUSTRATIONS

SECOND EDITION

LONGMANS, GREEN, AND CO.

39 PATERNOSTER ROW, LONDON

NEW YORK AND BOMBAY

1905

All rights reserved

Br 6050.136.2

✓

HARVARD COLLEGE LIBRARY
FROM THE LIBRARY OF
HAROLD MURDOCK
JUNE 1935

PREFACE TO THE SECOND EDITION

THE kind reception which was accorded to the first edition of the 'Three Generations of Fascinating Women,' &c., has encouraged me to bring out a second, in which I have thought it well to make a few trifling alterations and additions, besides correcting some inaccuracies. For the sake of compactness I have now incorporated in the body of the work much of the information formerly contained in notes in the Addenda, and have also reproduced a photogravure from Romney's beautiful picture of Ann Barbara, sister of Earl Whitworth and wife of Sir Henry Russell, Bart.

The Gunning Pedigree I have revised and brought up to date.

CONSTANCE RUSSELL.

Swallowfield: June 1905.

PREFACE TO THE FIRST EDITION

In offering these family sketches to the limited circle of readers who may be interested in them, I should like to deprecate the obvious criticism that so much of my information has been taken from the letters of Horace Walpole. Owing to his great intimacy with many of the subjects of these memoirs, I have unavoidably drawn somewhat largely on his writings in search of contemporary opinion, but I venture to suggest that the quotations of which I have made use may not prove unacceptable to those readers who, while wishing to know what that brilliant critic of the Society of his day had to say of one particular person, may not have the time or opportunity to wade through all his works and extract these plums.

Many of these very trifling sketches were written several years ago, and alas ! in some cases without noting the sources from which they were taken. For this I must apologise. In daring to publish them, my hope is that they will be found beneath criticism, ' For who would break a fly upon the wheel ? '

CONSTANCE RUSSELL.

CONTENTS

LIST OF ILLUSTRATIONS

THE HON. MARY BELLENDEN.

From a Picture at Inveraray Castle

THREE GENERATIONS

OF

FASCINATING WOMEN

MOTHER, DAUGHTER, AND GRANDDAUGHTER

1

THE HON. MARY BELLENDEN

Now to my heart the glance of Howard flies ;
Now Harvey, fair of face, I mark full well.
With thee, youth's youngest daughter, Sweet Lepell,
I see two lovely sisters hand in hand,
The fair-haired Martha, and Teresa brown ;
Madge Bellenden, the tallest of the land ;
And *smiling Mary, soft and fair as down.*

Epistle to Mr. Pope by Gay.

THE HON. PETER WENTWORTH, in writing to his brother, the
Earl of Strafford, on October 12, 1714, concerning the arrival in
England of Caroline of Anspach, Princess of Wales, says : 'The
Princess landed at Marget, the Prince, Duke of Sommerset,
and Duke of Argile,[1] went in coaches to meet her. The town,
or perhaps themselves, have named four Beautys for Maids

---

[1] The Dukes of Somerset and Argyll were the influential Whig magnates,
and swayed everything from the time that Queen Anne was seized with her last
illness.

1 £

of her Highness, viz. Molly Balliden, Miss Shorter,[1] Miss Hammond and Bell Roe.   If her H—— has any spice of jealousy, some people may be baulk't.'   The first named of these beauties, the Hon. Mary Bellenden—' smiling Mary, soft and fair as down '—was duly appointed Maid of Honour to the Princess of Wales.

The Hanoverians were always glad to secure the allegiance of any scion of well-known Jacobite families of distinction, amongst whom none could claim more distinguished rank than the Drummonds.   As some one has said, their fidelity ran in their blood and was part of their nature, and they were doomed to lose their lives and their fortunes in the Stuart cause.   To this family Mary Bellenden belonged.   She was the only daughter of John, second Lord Bellenden of Broughton and Auchnoule, who was son of William Drummond, second Earl of Roxburghe, the fourth son of John Drummond, second Earl of Perth.   Her father had taken the name of Bellenden as a child, on succeeding to the honours and estates of his cousin, Lord Bellenden of Broughton, in 1671.[2]   Following in the footsteps of his ancestors, he attached himself to the cause of James II.; and for refusing to take the oath of allegiance to William and Mary he was imprisoned in Edinburgh Castle with the Earls of Seaforth and Home, and Paterson, the deposed Archbishop of Glasgow.   In 1692 King William issued an order to the Privy Council of Scotland ' to prosecute Lord Bellenden and the officers sometime in Sir Thomas Livingstone's regiment of

---

[1] Charlotte Shorter, the second daughter of Sir John Shorter, of Bybrook, Kent (son of the Lord Mayor of London of that name), and sister of Lady Walpole. She married, in 1718, Francis Seymour Conway, Lord Conway, by whom she was mother of the first Marquis of Hertford and of Field-Marshal Seymour Conway, who married Mary Bellenden's daughter.

[2] See Addenda, page 333.

Dragoons,[1] who have been too long detained prisoners without being brought to trial.' Lord Bellenden's estates were confiscated, but he was given his liberty, under security of a thousand pounds, on condition that he went abroad and never again engaged in any movement against the existing government. He chose the Low Countries as his place of exile, probably because his father had been in the service of the States, where he had the command of a regiment and acquired the reputation of a brave soldier. Lord Bellenden asked permission to be allowed a month to settle his family affairs, but he was told he must leave as soon as a vessel then loading at Leith was ready. He sailed for Rotterdam in company with the Hon. William Livingstone (afterwards third Viscount Kilsyth) and his wife, who was the widow of Viscount Dundee, 'Bonnie Dundee,' the hero of Killiecrankie. We may conclude also that Lord Bellenden was accompanied by his own wife, Lady Dalhousie, as James, fourth Earl of Perth, his cousin, who followed him to exile in Holland, says, writing from Antwerp, September 17, 1694 : 'We went to The Hague, Lord Bellenden and his spouse, my Lady Dundee and Kilsyth [2] took an ague.' A worse fate soon befell the latter poor lady,

---

[1] Now the Scots Greys. They had been generally known as 'Old Tom Dalyell's Dragoons,' having been raised in 1681 by General Thomas Dalyell of Binns, the fiery cavalier, and were continually under the orders of Claverhouse, then under Lord Dunmore. He was superseded by Sir Thomas Livingstone, of the Dutch fort, a cadet of the family of Kilsyth and long wedded to the Dutch service, but many of the officers were staunch to King James.

[2] Many elegies were written on the charms and sad fate of this lady. The following is part of a long one preserved in the Advocates' Library :

> Who will not grieve for her death, who, when she
> Did live on earth, all others did outvie
> In all the charming attraits of that grace
> Of stately person and most beauteous face ;
> And in proportion to this sacred shryne,
> The Gods did make her spirit all divine.

she and her infant son William being killed by the fall of a
ceiling in an inn at Utrecht, which buried them in its ruins.
Her husband, who was reading a letter at the window, sprang
out of it and was saved, though much hurt.   It was said that
the beams of the room were purposely cut so as to kill Kilsyth
and Lady Dundee and the Jacobites who came to see them (see
Napier's 'Memoir of Dundee'); but a letter which has lately
come to light from a Mr. Stewart, who was on the spot and
wrote a graphic account of the catastrophe two days after it
occurred, clearly proves that it was an accident caused by the
overloading of a loft above with 300 tons of turf fuel.   When
extricated, the bodies of the mother and child were carefully
embalmed and sent to Scotland, where they were interred in the
church at Kilsyth.   In 1795, close upon a hundred years later, a
leaden coffin was there opened and their bodies found in an extraordinary state of preservation, the beautiful auburn hair and fine
complexion of Lady Dundee occasioning in the crowd of onlookers
a sigh of silent wonder, so says a contemporary account.[1]
That Lady Dundee's happy second marriage should terminate
so briefly and so terribly was supposed to be the verification
of a prognostic at the time of her engagement.   When, as
a young widow, she was met and wooed at Colzium House,
Stirlingshire, by William Livingstone, he gave her a ring
having for its posy 'Zours onlly and Euer' (Yours only and
ever).   She lost it in the garden ; and though every search was
made she never got it back, and this was considered at the time
an ill omen.   Strangely enough, just a hundred years later the
ring was dug up in a clod of earth, and it is still preserved at

---

[1] A Mr. Watts made a drawing of Lady Dundee in her coffin, which was
engraved for Dr. Garnett's *Observations on a Tour through the Highlands*,
published in 1800.

Colzium House by the present proprietor of the Kilsyth estates, Sir Archibald Edmonstone of Duntreath.

After four or five years spent in Holland, Lord Bellenden obtained his pardon on condition that he took no part against the Hanoverian King. He returned to Edinburgh, and was present in Parliament in 1696. He lived in the Canongate, in a house called Golfers' Land.[1] He had very little means ; and in 1700 the Duke of Queensberry,[2] writing to Mr. Carstares,[3] says : 'I must entreat of you to speak to the King in favour of my Lord Ballantyne ; he has continued very firm to his Majesty's interest, though there has been great pains taken to make him otherwise. He has a numerous family and not much to support it, and because I knew he was a little straightened, I have given him £100, for which I desire a warrant payable to me.' As one of the results of this application, we find that Lord Bellenden was in 1704 appointed Governor of Dumbarton Castle.

Lord Bellenden died at his house in the Canongate in 1706, aged forty-five, and was buried at Holyrood Abbey on November 3 of that year.[4] His wife survived him many years ; she was Lady Mary Moore, daughter of Henry Moore, first Earl of Drogheda, by Lady Alice Spencer, daughter of Lord Spencer of Wormleighton, and she had been married previously to William Ramsay, third Earl of Dalhousie, and

[1] Also known as 'John Paterson's House.' Soon after the Union the 'Golfers Land' became, as it is now, a habitation of the lower orders.

[2] The Duke of Queensberry was sent to hold a Parliament in Scotland in 1701.

[3] The Rev. Mr. Carstares, a Scotch minister, had an extraordinary share in the management of Scotland at this time, and was greatly in King William's confidence ; his correspondence was printed in 1774, and he is styled there Confidential Secretary to King William.

[4] The following invitation to attend the funeral of Lord Bellenden is rather curious : 'The honour of your presence to accompany the corps of My Lord Bellenden, my father, from his lodgings in Patersan's Land, near the Cannongate foot, to his burial place in the Abay Church, upon Sunday the 3rd instant, at 8 of the clock in the morning, is earnestly desired by John Bellenden.'

always kept his name.[1]   Lady Dalhousie must have had a great share of beauty, judging by the portrait of her, painted by Sir Peter Lely in brown and red draperies, which hangs in the saloon at Inveraray Castle.   She came of a good-looking stock ; her grandmother, Lady Penelope Wriothesley, was the daughter of Henry Wriothesley, third Earl of Southampton, the patron of Shakespeare, and reckoned the handsomest man at Court.

By Lord Bellenden she had five sons and one daughter. John, the eldest, born in 1685 at Dalhousie Castle, succeeded his father as third Baron Bellenden, and in 1709 sold his manor of Whitehill, near Musselburgh, to Sir David Dalrymple, Bart., ancestor of the present Sir Charles Dalrymple, who still holds it, though the name was changed to Newhailes about 1738.   The central part of the present house is probably the same as it was when Lord Bellenden sold it.   In 1710 a memorial was presented to the High Treasurer in favour of Mary, Countess of Dalhousie, and her son Lord Bellenden, praying that the salary of the latter as 'Usher to the Exchequer in Scotland' might be settled.   This post, the salary of which was only £250 a year, was hereditary in the Bellenden family.   In 1565 Sir John Bellenden of Auchinowe obtained the office, and had a charter under the Great Seal 'to himself, his heirs and assigns, de toto et integro officio custodiæ portæ sive ostii Domus Reginæ Scaccarii deverus ad idem pertinens.'   All the Lords Bellenden held it in turn.   It was apparently a sinecure, as the third Lord Bellenden [2] lived entirely at Westmill, a small

---

[1] Her eldest son, George, fourth Earl of Dalhousie, was killed in Holland by a Mr. Hamilton in 1696 ; her second son, William, fifth Earl, also died unmarried.

[2] The third Lord Bellenden married in 1722, at Radwell, Herts, Mary, daughter, of John Parnell of Baldock, Herts, and had six daughters : (1) Hon. Jane Bellenden married in 1741 Ephraim Miller of Hertingfordbury ; (2) Hon. Caroline Bellenden, married in 1760 John Gawler of Ramridge, Hants, and of the Inner Temple, and had two sons, John Bellenden Gawler, 2nd Life Guards (who in 1804 assumed

R LELY, *pinx*.

MARY, COUNTESS OF DALHOUSIE.

village in Hertfordshire, where he is buried with many members of his family.

Of the four remaining sons, one only was well known—Sir Harry Bellenden, who was Usher of the Black Rod. He is often mentioned by Horace Walpole, who thus alludes to his death, which took place in 1761 : 'Poor Sir Harry Bellenden is dead ; he made a great dinner at Almacks for the house of Drummond, drank very hard, caught a violent fever, and died in a few days . . . though but six hours in his senses, he gave a proof of his usual good humour, making it as his last request to the sisters Tufton, to be reconciled, which they are. His pretty villa in my neighbourhood, I fancy he has left to the new Lord Lorn.'[1]

The only daughter of John, second Lord Bellenden, was Mary, the subject of this sketch. At an early age she removed from Edinburgh to London ; her mother, Lady Dalhousie, being appointed Keeper of Somerset House, where she was given apartments in the east side of the Palace, and it was here that Mary Bellenden spent a great part of her youth.

the name of Ker Bellenden), and Henry Gawler of Lincoln's Inn ; (3) Hon. Diana Bellenden, married John Bulteel of Flete ; (4) Hon. Mary Bellenden, married John Eaton of Cambridge, and died at Egham in 1805, æt. 80 ; (5) Hon. Alice Bellenden, died unmarried at Westmill in 1796 ; (6) Hon. Henrietta Bellenden, died unmarried.

[1] Horace Walpole quotes the following 'Anacreontic' written by Lord Middlesex upon Sir Harry Bellenden :

> Ye sons of Bacchus, come and join
> In solemn dirge, while tapers shine
> Around the grape-embossed shrine
> Of honest Harry Bellendine.

> Pour the rich juice of Bordeaux's wine,
> Mix'd with your falling tears of brine,
> In full libation o'er the shrine
> Of honest Harry Bellendine.

> Your brows let ivy chaplets twine,
> While you push round the sparkling wine,
> And let your table be the shrine
> Of honest Harry Bellendine.

Somerset House was then, as it had long been, a royal palace, the dower-house of the Queens of England, and it continued to be so till the time of Queen Charlotte. Henrietta Maria made very pleasant additions to it when she took up her residence there in 1662 ; and it is said that this Queen, inheriting the practical taste for architecture which had caused her mother, Marie de Médicis, to design with her own hand the Luxembourg Palace, had made original drawings for all the buildings she added to Somerset House. Anne of Denmark and Catherine of Braganza both successively held their Courts there, and it was called Denmark House after the former Queen. We have an account of it as it was when Mary Bellenden lived there. Her mother's rooms extended across what is now part of King's College as far as Strand Passage, and adjoining them was a 'pleasance' which opened on to the extensive terraced gardens with their straight gravel walks and avenues of trees. From these gardens descended a handsome flight of stone steps, at the bottom of which was the Thames ; and there was always moored there a sort of house-barge called 'The Folly,' and a kind of wherry like a gondola, for the use of the inhabitants of the Palace.

Mary Bellenden first entered upon her duties as Maid of Honour at Hampton Court Palace, then the principal residence of George I., where apartments were provided for the Prince and Princess of Wales and their suite. The Court life at this time appears to have been extremely dull. Pope, writing to Teresa and Martha Blount[1] in 1717, says: 'I went by water to

---

[1] Teresa and Martha Blount were daughters of Lister Blount, Esq., of Mapledurham, by Mary, daughter of Anthony Englefield of Whiteknights. Teresa, born in 1688, died 1759 ; Martha, born in 1690, died in 1763. Pope gave Martha a fan on which he had painted a design of his own from the story of Cephalus and Procris with the motto 'Aura veni.' This fan was afterwards in the possession of Sir Joshua Reynolds. After Pope's death Horace Walpole writes to Lady Ossory: 'I was standing at my window after dinner in Summer, in Arlington St., and saw

Hampton Court ; met the Prince with all his ladies on horse-back coming from hunting. Mrs. Bellenden and Mrs. Lepell took me into their protection (contrary to the law against Papists) and gave me a dinner with something I liked better, an opportunity of conversation with Mrs. Howard.[1] We all agreed that the life of a Maid of Honour was of all things the most miserable, and wished that every woman who envied it had a specimen of it. To eat Westphalia ham in a morning, ride over hedges and ditches on borrowed hacks, come home in the heat of the day with a fever, and (what is worse a hundred times) with a red mark on the forehead from an uneasy hat . . . then they must simper an hour, and catch cold in the Princess's apart-ments, from there, as Shakespeare has it, to dinner with what appetite they may, and after that till midnight, work, walk, and think, which they please. I can easily believe no lone house in Wales with a mountain and a rookery is more contemplative than this Court, and as a proof of it I need only tell you Mrs. L. (Lepell) walked with me three or four hours by moonlight, and we met no creature of any quality but the King, who gave audience to the Vice-Chamberlain all alone under the garden wall.' [2]

Patty Blount with nothing remaining of her immortal charms but her *blue eyes*, trudging on foot with her petticoats pinned up, for it rained, to visit *blameless Bethel*, who was sick at the end of the street.'—H. W. vol. ii. p. 254, Letters to Lady Ossory.

  [1] Henrietta Hobart, daughter of Sir Henry Hobart, and sister of John, Earl of Buckinghamshire, married the Hon. Charles Howard, afterwards ninth Earl of Suffolk. She was Bedchamber Woman and Dresser to the Princess of Wales.

  [2] Many months later than the date of this letter we find Pope writing to Lady Mary Wortley Montagu the same thing with a curious variation ; he says to her, ' No lone house in Wales, with a rookery, is more contemplative than Hampton Court : I walked there the other day by the moon, (no companion mentioned !) and met no creature of any quality but the King, who was giving audience all alone to *the birds* under the garden wall.'

Molly Lepell, here mentioned by Pope, the beautiful and witty daughter of Brigadier-General Nicholas Lepell, was one of the Maids of Honour to the Princess of Wales, and the bosom friend of Mary Bellenden, with whom her name is constantly associated. In Gay's poem, 'Damon and Cupid,' the God of Love says :

> So well I'm known at Court,
>   None ask where Cupid dwells,
> But readily resort
>   To Bellenden's or Lepell's.

'Sweet Lepell,' as Gay calls her elsewhere, married John Hervey, and three of her sons became Earls of Bristol. The writer has a medallion with miniature portraits of Mary Bellenden and Molly Lepell on either side. 'Bella Dine' and 'Tom' were the pet names by which they addressed each other.

When the quarrels between George I. and his heir culminated in the expulsion of the latter from St. James's Palace, a new era opened for the Maids of Honour. The Prince and Princess and their household took refuge at first in Albemarle Street, where Lord Grantham,[1] Chamberlain to the Princess, lent them his house.

> Then up the street they took their way,
>   And knocked up good Lord Grantham,
> Higledy Pigledy they lay,
>   And all went Rantum Scantum.
>   *The Excellent New Ballad.*

Mary Bellenden's sprightly demeanour on this occasion is thus specially alluded to in the same ballad :

---

[1] Henri de Auverquerque, Earl of Grantham, had been Keeper of the Privy Purse to King William III.

THE HON. MARY BELLENDEN.

> But Bellenden we needs must praise,
> Who, as down the stairs she jumps,
> Sings ' O'er the hills and far away,'
> Despising doleful dumps.[1]

Shortly after, the royal fugitives moved to Old Leicester House, at the north-east corner of Leicester Fields, which the Prince bought for £6,000. Here the Princess had her Court for the next ten years ; she held a Drawing Room every morning, had a reception at night twice a week, and on other nights went with her ladies to masquerades, concerts, operas, and to the theatre.

The gaiety of the Court life at Leicester House naturally had its effect on general society, and Lord Chesterfield at this time writes to Bubb Dodington : ' As for the gay part of the town you would find it much more flourishing than when you left it. Balls, Assemblies, and Masquerades have taken the place of dull, formal visiting days, and women much more agreeable trifles than they were designed. Puns are extremely in vogue and the licence very great.'

Even when the Prince and Princess moved to Richmond Wells, as it was then called—where the Prince first rented and then bought the Jacobite Duke of Ormond's ' White House,' which he named ' Richmond Lodge '—the gay life continued. We read of the Maids of Honour accompanying the Prince and Princess to Penketham's playhouse on the Green, where Mr. William Penketham, the popular actor celebrated by Steele, delighted them with his low comedy. Lady Bristol, one of the Ladies of the Bedchamber, writes that she had no patience to see a play of Mr. Addison's (who had just died) burlesqued, as it was,

---

[1] ' O'er the hills and far away ' is a line of a song called ' Distracted Jockey's Lamentation,' which was in considerable vogue at the beginning of the eighteenth century.—*Pedlar's Pack of Ballads and Songs.*

for the entertainment of their Royal Highnesses. The play was
' Cato ; ' and she adds, ' their audience was too good for them, for
there was a great many people of quality.'

Then there were innumerable water-parties ; and on warm
evenings, Lady Bristol says, the Court often walked on the
terrace, ' to hear the fine musick the Prince has taken for the
summer.' On other nights they had Mrs. Robinson to sing
to them. This exquisite singer was the celebrated Anastasia
Robinson, afterwards married to the great Lord Peterborough.
The Princess of Wales, being a woman of considerable attainment, and fully appreciating wit and talent in others, welcomed
most of the celebrities of the day, amongst whom were Pope,
Swift, Gay, Steele, Addison, Congreve, Rowe, Tickell, Prior,
Atterbury, Arbuthnot, Marlborough, Lord Peterborough, John
Duke of Argyll, Harley, Bathurst, Sir Robert Walpole, Lord
Chesterfield, Bishop Berkeley, and a host of others.

Shortly after her arrival in England she received in her
own apartment Sir Isaac Newton, then an octogenarian, who
expounded to the Princess and her ladies his system of
philosophy ;[1] but we can fancy that Mary Bellenden and Molly
Lepell were more interested in 'The Beggar's Opera,' which
Gay read to them, or with ' Gulliver's Travels,' with which we
are told Swift delighted them.[2]

' The apartments of the Bed-Chamber Women,' says Horace
Walpole, ' became the fashionable evening *rendez-vous* of the
most distinguished wits and beauties, and above all for universal
admiration Miss Bellenden, one of the Maids of Honour. Her
face and person were charming, lively she was, almost to

---

[1] It was at her suggestion he wrote his *Abstract of a Treatise on Ancient
Chronology*.

[2] It is said by Swift that the Princess sent nine times for him before he came
to Leicester Fields ; but Croker says he was several times at Richmond Lodge.

MARY BELLENDEN—Daughter to LORD BELLENDEN—Married to
JOHN CAMPBELL—Afterwards DUKE of ARGYLL—

THE HON. MARY BELLENDEN.

étourderie, and so agreeable she was, that I never heard her mentioned afterwards by one of her contemporaries who did not prefer her as the most perfect creature they ever knew.'

Lord Hervey says : ' Mrs. Bellenden was incontestably the most agreeable, the most insinuating, and the most likeable woman of her time ; made up of every ingredient likely to engage or attach a lover.'

The Prince of Wales frequented the waiting-room, and was much enamoured of her ; but she rejected his attentions with scorn, and indeed treated him at all times with the utmost nonchalance.   His avarice disgusted her ; and Horace Walpole tells us that one evening, when the Prince was counting and re-counting his money, Miss Bellenden, losing all patience, cried out, ' Sir, I cannot bear it !   If you count your money any more I will go out of the room.'   On another similar occasion she seems actually to have carried this threat into execution, and as the Prince was counting his money, shook his arm, and, whilst the coins were sent flying all over the floor, left the room in peals of laughter.   She herself tells us, in one of her letters, that she was in the habit of standing before him with her arms folded, and that when he asked her why she did so, she replied, ' Because I am cold.'   In the Memoirs of Viscountess Sundon we read : ' This fair and irreproachable young lady divided the Court with Mrs. Howard . . . as she delighted the danglers in the waiting-room with her sallies, yet kept the most audacious of them at a distance by the real innocence of her heart ; . . . her heart was shielded, not only by principle and modesty, but by a true affection.'   The affection thus alluded to was for Colonel John Campbell—' handsome Jack Campbell '[1] as he was

---

[1] Jonathan Richardson painted Colonel John Campbell the year after his marriage.   This picture belongs to Mrs. Campbell Johnston, and has been engraved by James Basire.   He is represented sitting drawing.

called—one of the Grooms of the Bedchamber to the Prince, and in 1720 she was privately married to him ; her friend and co-Maid of Honour, Molly Lepell, also privately marrying the same year.   No doubt the secrecy of Mary Bellenden's marriage was in some degree due to its extreme improvidence ; for, though Colonel Campbell ultimately succeeded to the Dukedom of Argyll, at this time there appeared no chance of such a contingency arising, and he was one of the thirteen children of a poor younger son.   His father, the Hon. John Campbell of Mamore,[1] was a son of Archibald, Earl of Argyll, who was executed in 1685, and had himself been capitally convicted of having joined the Earl in his attempt to invade Scotland.   Sentence of death was commuted to banishment, and this was rescinded in 1689.   He was ultimately given a small post as Surveyor of the King's Works, and died in 1729.   He left his large family destitute, and Queen Anne looked after them.[2]

The announcement of Mary Bellenden's marriage was dated October 22, that of Molly Lepell's October 25, and we know that both were post-dated ; probably, as Croker suggests, the friends agreed to face the storms together, and announced their marriages and consequent resignations just previous to the courtly epoch of the Birthday, October 30, when we find two other young ladies were appointed in their room.   The Prince was extremely angry with Mary Bellenden for not having taken him into her confidence, and vented his annoyance by whispering rude speeches in her ear whenever they met.   However, this did not deter him, on his accession to the throne in 1727, from

[1] There is a portrait of the Hon. John Campbell of Mamore at Rosneath, which is a copy of one in the possession of Sir Archibald Edmonstone, Bt., and there is another which belongs to Mrs. Campbell-Johnston.
[2] See letter of Earl of Islay to Mrs. Howard.

reappointing Colonel Campbell to be one of the Grooms of the Bedchamber.

Soon after their marriage Colonel and Mrs. Campbell went to Bath, which was then rising into fashion; and the following passage, which occurs in one of Mrs. Campbell's letters written thence at this time to Mrs. Howard, points to money difficulties:[1] 'O Gad! I am so sick of bills, for my part, I shall never be able to hear them mentioned without casting up my accounts!' The beautiful Mary's letters, though lively and witty, are unfortunately sometimes disfigured by the prevailing coarseness of the age. But it is fair to say her letters were not intended for publication. This very one closes with the following sentence: 'Don't shew this, I charge you at your peril.'

During their stay at Bath, Colonel Campbell went to London 'on South Sea business.' He appears to have been bitten with the stock-jobbing infatuation which at this time had taken possession of so many persons. His cousin Archibald, Earl of Islay, writes: 'Cousin Jack has got near £10,000 in the Mississipi Scheme, and has lost the half of that sum.' And Mr. John Hervey in his Diary writes: 'I betted Colonel Campbell 100 guineas that ye Mississipi Stock at Paris would not be above 1,000 on that day twelve month, which I won, and he paid me.' After leaving Bath, the beautiful Mary and her handsome husband paid a round of visits. They stayed with Lady Betty Germaine[2] at Drayton, which Mrs. Campbell describes as 'a fine

---

[1] As Groom of the Bedchamber Colonel Campbell received £450 a year, and he also received £400 a year pension; but probably this was the extent of their income.

[2] Lady Betty Germaine, the friend and correspondent of Swift, was a daughter of the second Earl of Berkeley, and married Sir John Germaine, who was originally a Dutch merchant, and so ignorant that it was said of him that he left a legacy to Sir Matthew Decker, as the author of St. Matthew's Gospel; but Kirkpatrick Sharpe, in a letter to Sir Walter Scott, says he was 'more beautiful than an angel,'

place where we live very easily and agreeably ; ' at Knole with
the Duke and Duchess of Dorset ; and at Mereworth with
Colonel Fane, afterwards seventh Earl of Westmorland. From
Knole she writes to Mrs. Howard that she is ' in dread of the
plague ; ' and says, ' Pray let me know what your opinion is about
it, and if you are afraid. I reckon you know what is proper to
be done on that occasion, and I expect you will communicate
your knowledge for the good of the public.' [1]

Mrs. Howard appears to have recommended smoking, an
idea then being prevalent that this was a deterrent. Hearne
wrote in January 1720–21 : 'I have been told in the last great
plague at London, none that kept tobacconists' shops had it, and
I remember that I heard Tom Rogers say that where he was that
year when it raged, a schoolboy at Eaton, all the boys of that
school were obliged to smoke in the school every morning, and
that he was never whipped so much in his life as he was one
morning for not smoking.'

While staying at Knole Mrs. Campbell obtained, through
the interest of the Duchess of Dorset, who had been Mistress of

so his comparatively low birth and ignorance did not prevent him from doing well
in the matrimonial line. He married firstly Lady Mary Mordaunt, Duchess of
Norfolk, who left him the estate of Drayton, which he in turn left to his second
wife, Lady Betty, who devised it to Lord George Sackville. The latter was son of
Lionel, Duke of Dorset, nominally by the Duchess, his wife ; but according to many
statements Lady Betty was his mother, though the Duchess pretended he was
her child. In the letter alluded to above, Kirkpatrick Sharpe says that the Margravine d'Anspach, who was Lady Betty's near relation, declared this to be the
case ; and Sarah, Duchess of Marlborough, writes of Lionel, Duke of Dorset : ' Such
a wretch as he is I hardly know, and his wife—whose passion is only for money—
assists him in his odious affair with Lady Betty Jermyn, who has a great deal to
dispose of.'

[1] In 1720 the plague devastated Marseilles ; and in 1721 an Act was passed by
the English Parliament for the building of pest-houses, to which not only the
infected but the healthy members of an infected family were to be removed, and
round every town visited by the plague, lines were to be drawn which no one was
to pass. This pestilence did not, however, come to Great Britain.

the Robes, the post of Maid of Honour for her niece, Elizabeth Hawley, daughter of Lord Hawley; [1] and shortly after she writes : ' I had a letter from Margaret [2] last night, which informs me of Madam Hawley having been at Richmond (at the Court) and her great fright thereat. I beg you will let me know how she looked and behaved, and if she is likely to take with their Royal Highnesses. I hope you will put her a little in the way of behaving before the Princess, such as not turning her back, and then some sort of warning as to Claton [3] (I cannot spell her name) and gaming.'

In April 1722 Mrs. Campbell was settled at Combe Bank, near Sundridge, Kent,[4] which her husband had bought. She writes at this time : ' Nothing can make me unhappy while John lives and is good to me, which, hitherto, I have no reason to fear will ever be otherwise.' She appears to have been interested in their little farm. The following year she writes to Mrs. Howard : ' I have nothing better to entertain you with, but to tell you the news of my farm. I therefore give you the following list of the stock of eatables that I am fatting for my private tooth. It is well known to the whole county of Kent that I have four fat calves, two fat hogs for killing, twelve promising black

---

[1] Mary Bellenden's half-sister, Lady Elizabeth Ramsay, married Lord Hawley. She died in 1713.

[2] The Hon. Margaret Bellenden, her niece and a Maid of Honour; she is frequently alluded to by Mrs. Delany, and appears, like her aunt, to have been celebrated for her wit. She probably lived with Lady Dalhousie after Mary Bellenden's marriage. Mrs. Pendarves, writing in 1728 from Somerset House, says Mrs. Bellenden (Miss Peg) is a very agreeable neighbour. She was living at Beaconsfield in 1734, and eleven years later Mrs. Delany visited her there with the Duchess of Portland, and writes that she uttered many a droll thing.

[3] Mrs. Clayton, *née* Dives, afterwards created Viscountess Sundon, was Mistress of the Robes, and ruled the Princess at this time.

[4] Combe Bank was part of the estate of the Isleys, by whom, at the end of Elizabeth's reign, it was sold to the Ash family. The last of them, William Ash, sold it to Colonel John Campbell.

pigs, four white sows big with child, for whom I have great com-passion,[1] two young chickens, three fine geese sitting with thirteen eggs under each (several being duck's eggs, else the others do not come to maturity). All this with rabbits and pigeons and carp in plenty, beef and mutton at reasonable rates.'

In 1730 Mrs. Campbell was appointed Keeper of Somerset House Palace in succession to Lady Stanley, who had succeeded Mrs. Campbell's mother.[2]

This same year we read of her being at Tunbridge Wells for her health ; and in 1736 she died, aged forty-one, to use Dr. Doran's words, 'as good and true a wife as she had been a fascinating maiden.' She was buried at St. Anne's Church, Soho, where her mother, Lady Dalhousie, had been buried eleven years before. No sign of any monumental slab or inscription to their memory is now to be seen at St. Anne's, but the name of ' Mrs. Mary Camble ' appears in the registry of deaths.

In Sundridge Church, which she regularly attended when at Combe Bank, there is a bust of her, executed by her grand-daughter, Mrs. Damer.

Mrs. Campbell left four sons and one daughter : (1) John, who succeeded his father as fifth Duke of Argyll, and married the beautiful Elizabeth, Duchess of Hamilton and Brandon, *née* Gunning. (2) Henry, A.D.C. to Sir John Ligonier ; was killed at the battle of Laufeldt in 1747.[3] (3) William, R.N., who married

---

[1] 'A fellow-feeling makes one wondrous kind' !

[2] In the King's Warrant Book XXX., page 20, is a Royal Sign Manual, directed to the Attorney or Solicitor General, for the preparation of a Bill to pass the Great Seal for the grant to Mary Campbell of the Office of Keeper of Denmark House, *alias* Somerset House, *alias* Stroud House, in like manner as the same was granted to Dame Anne Stanley, deceased, given at the Court at Windsor, June 24, 1730.

[3] Laufeldt, or Lauffeld, near Maestricht, in Holland, where the allied English, Austrian, and Dutch armies were defeated by the French under Marshal Saxe. The English were commanded by the Duke of Cumberland.

GAINSBOROUGH, pinx

JOHN, 4TH DUKE OF ARGYLL, K.T.

Miss Sarah Izzard of Charleston, South Carolina, of which he was the last Governor. (4) Frederick, who married Mary, widow of the mad Lord Ferrers, who was hanged at Tyburn for murdering his steward. And Caroline, afterwards Countess of Ailesbury.

Colonel Campbell survived his beautiful and fascinating wife thirty-four years, and died on November 9, 1770, in the seventy-seventh year of his age, having succeeded to the Dukedom of Argyll on the death of his cousin Archibald, third Duke, in 1761.[1] Mary Bellenden's great-great-grandson, the present Duke of Argyll, has four portraits of her (one by Sir Godfrey Kneller), and a lock of her hair, inscribed by her husband 'My Angel's Hair.'

[1] He was painted, when about 70 years of age, by Gainsborough.

CAROLINE, COUNTESS OF AILESBURY

Mild as a summer sun, serene,
In dimpled beauty next be seen,
Aylesbury, like hoary Neptunes Queen.
' The Beauties,' an epistle to Mr. Eckhardt, the painter.
Written by Horace Walpole.

CAROLINE CAMPBELL, the only daughter of Colonel John Campbell of Mamore and his wife, *née* Mary Bellenden, was born in 1721, and received her name from her godmother, Caroline, Princess of Wales. She was scarcely fifteen years of age when her mother died; and Colonel Campbell being continually abroad on active service, it became important to find her a husband early, and thus provide her with a home, the more so as her father's circumstances were the reverse of affluent. It was not therefore surprising that when, three years later, Lord Bruce proposed for her hand, her friends, notably Lady Suffolk and Lady Westmorland, prevailed upon her to accept him, although he was a widower and older than her father. Mrs. Delany thus alludes to the engagement : ' Miss Campbell is to be married to my Lord Bruce, her father can give her no fortune, she is very pretty, well-behaved, and just eighteen, has £2,000 a year jointure, and £400 pin money. They say he is cross, covetous, and three-score year old,[1] and this unsuitable marriage is the admiration of the old, and the envy of the young.'

[1] As a matter of fact, Lord Bruce was fifty-seven when he married Miss Campbell.

HON. HENRY SEYMOUR CONWAY, AND CAROLINE, COUNTESS OF AILESBURY,
(*in Fancy Dress*), AND THEIR CHILD, ANNE SEYMOUR CONWAY.

The marriage took place on June 13, 1739; and Mrs. Delany mentions seeing Lady Bruce shortly after, at a party given at Norfolk House by Frederick, Prince of Wales, ' in lemon-colour, richly embroidered with silver and colour.' Two years later Lord Bruce succeeded his father as third Earl of Ailesbury and fourth Earl of Elgin, and became the possessor of great wealth and vast estates, including Tottenham Park and Savernake Forest, Wilts. He did not, however, live long to enjoy his fortune, for he died on February 10, 1747, leaving his widow with one daughter, Lady Mary Bruce. To his wife Lord Ailesbury left a jointure of £3,000 a year, his fine house [1] in London, and half his jewels, which were considerable. The other half he left his daughter, as well as £30,000. Thus Lady Ailesbury found herself a rich widow, free to indulge her own taste, at the early age of twenty-six. She was not long in bestowing her affections, and on December 19, 1747, she was married at the private chapel at Somerset House to the Hon. Henry Seymour Conway, second son of Lord Conway and brother of the first Earl of Hertford. This event seems to have been foreseen by Horace Walpole, who in the previous July writes of Mr. Conway, then in Flanders with the Duke of Cumberland's forces : ' Harry Conway, whom nature always designed for a hero of romance, and who is *déplacé* in ordinary life, did wonders . . . but was afterwards taken prisoner, is since released on parole, and may come home to console his fair widow.' Lady Ailesbury's second marriage, according to all contemporary accounts, seems to have been one of almost unalloyed happiness : nor is this surprising, as husband and wife were alike conspicuous for fascination combined with the highest principle.

---

[1] Savile House, Leicester Square ; afterwards occupied by Frederick, eldest son of George II., and pulled down in 1791.

Mme. du Deffand [1] writes : ' Miladi Ailesbury est certaine-
ment la meilleure des femmes, la plus douce, et la plus tendre.
Je suis trompée si elle n'aime passionnément son mari, et si elle
n'est pas parfaitement heureuse; son humeur me paraît très égale,
sa politesse noble et aisée ; elle a le meilleur ton du monde,
exempte de toutes prétentions ; elle plaira à tous les gens de
goût, et ne déplaira jamais à personne. C'est, de toutes les
Anglaises que j'ai vues, celle que je trouve la plus aimable, sans
nulle exception.' The devotion to her husband, of which
Mme. du Deffand here speaks, was certainly bestowed upon
a man worthy of possessing it ; for, apart from his handsome
exterior and his distinction as a soldier, he was endowed with
qualities of heart and mind which endeared him to all with whom
he was brought into contact. Horace Walpole says : ' Mr.
Conway is deservedly reckoned one of the first and most rising
young men in England. He has distinguished himself in the
greatest style both in the army and in Parliament, and has the
finest person and the handsomest face I ever saw.' In later
life, when field-marshal, he was generally called ' the divine
Marshal.'

Mr. Conway and Lady Ailesbury commenced their long and
happy married life at Latimers, in Bucks, which they rented for
three years from Lord George Cavendish. Their first visitor
was Horace Walpole, whose friendship with his cousin, Henry
Conway, lasted from their boyish days at Eton till Marshal
Conway's death, and was extended to Lady Ailesbury and her
children. In describing his first visit to Lady Ailesbury, he
writes : ' Latimers is large and old, but of a bad age, finely
situated on a hill with a river at the bottom and a range of hills

[1] The celebrated correspondent of Voltaire and Walpole, Marie de Vichy-
Chamrond, born 1697, died 1780, leaving all her manuscripts to Horace Walpole.

PARK PLACE, HENLEY-ON-THAMES.
From an old Print.

and woods on the opposite side belonging to the Duke of Bedford.'[1] The house he lamented over as having 'undergone Batty-Langley discipline.'[2] When the tenancy of Latimers came to an end in 1751, Mr. Conway was ordered to join his regiment, the 29th Dragoons, of which he had the command, at Minorca. He left Lady Ailesbury with her father at Combe Bank, near Sundridge, the home of her childhood, but she seems never to have been out of his mind. He corresponded with her as often as it was possible, and sent her home presents by every opportunity, one being a 'jeriboo,' which must have been a jerboa, probably the common jerboa of Northern Africa (*Dipus ægyptius*), a beautiful little animal.

Soon after his return from Minorca, Colonel Conway became the purchaser of Park Place, Henley-on-Thames, a place justly celebrated for its lovely situation.[3] It had been the residence of Frederick, Prince of Wales, for nearly twenty years, his Royal Highness having bought it from Lord Archibald Hamilton.[4] Colonel Conway had hardly completed his purchase when he was ordered to join his regiment, the 13th Dragoons, then quartered in Sligo. Thither Lady Ailesbury accompanied him, leaving their little girl, Anne Seymour Conway (afterwards Mrs. Damer), now about eight years of age, at Strawberry Hill, under the care of Horace Walpole. Colonel Conway and Lady Ailesbury remained in Ireland four months, and at the end of this time

---

[1] Latimer, as it is now called, is at present the seat of Lord Chesham.

[2] Batty-Langley was a popular architect who endeavoured to reconcile Greek with Gothic architecture, and introduced five new orders into his art. His mixed style went by the name of 'the Batty-Langley manner.'

[3] There is a picture representing Park Place in 1748 at Buckingham Palace.

[4] Lord Archibald Hamilton bought Park Place from Mrs. Elizabeth Baber; it was then called 'Park's Place,' having previously belonged to one 'Park.' Before that it went by the name of 'Strode's,' from the former possessors. Richard de la Strode owned the whole of Remenham, of which this formed a part.

established themselves at Park Place. In August 1752 Horace Walpole writes : 'I have been at Park Place, where I saw the individual, Mr. Cooper,[1] a banker and lord of the manor of Henley, who had those two extraordinary forfeitures from the executions of the Misses Blandy and Jefferies.' The allusion made here is to two somewhat similar murders that had been recently committed ; the one perpetrated by Miss Blandy having taken place in the immediate neighbourhood of Park Place only a few months before, and at the very time of General Conway and Lady Ailesbury's taking possession of that place. This murder caused immense excitement, owing to the social position of the persons incriminated and the peculiar atrocity of the crime ; and we are induced to allude to it at some length, as Park Place indirectly played its part in the tragedy and the instigator of the crime was related to Lady Ailesbury.

Mary Blandy was the only daughter of Mr. Francis Blandy, a solicitor and the Town Clerk of Henley, a man of old family, possessing some means, and much respected ; and her mother was a daughter of Mr. Serjeant Stephens, of Culham Court, Henley. She was a rather good-looking girl with dark eyes, of a lively and agreeable disposition, highly educated, of considerable capacity, and reputed to be a large heiress, her father being apt to boast unduly of her fortune. In 1746, when she was about twenty-seven, she, with her father and mother, dined at the house of General Mark Kerr, a cousin of Lord Lothian, who was then renting a house at Henley. There she met Captain the Hon. William Henry Cranstoun, a cousin of General Kerr, who was recruiting in Oxfordshire. This gentleman was one of the twelve children of the fifth Lord Cranstoun. His father was unable to leave

---

[1] Gislingham Cooper, Esq., who lived at Phyllis Court, Henley, which he bought from his brother-in-law, Bulstrode Whitelock.

him more than £500, and at this time Captain Cranstoun was reduced to great straits. Though by no means good-looking, being described as diminutive in stature, disfigured by smallpox, blear-eyed, and of mean appearance, he was possessed of talent and said to take generally with the fair sex. Certain it is that he managed to fascinate both Miss Blandy and her mother ; and he also succeeded in insinuating himself into the good graces of the father by pandering to his weakness for great people. Captain Cranstoun never failed to make a parade of his noble birth and of all his ancestors and connections. His mother was a daughter of the Marquis of Lothian, his grandmother was a daughter of the Earl of Argyll, and he was nearly connected with half the aristocracy of Scotland.

He stayed frequently with the Blandys during the next year, and seeing the impression he made on the whole family, especially on the young lady, declared himself as a suitor for her hand. This miscreant had, however, at the time a lawful wife and child in Scotland, having married, two years earlier, Anne, sister of Sir David Murray, Bart., of Stanhope.

General Mark Kerr, suspecting the state of affairs, communicated with Lord Mark Kerr, Captain Cranstoun's uncle, who informed Mr. Blandy that his nephew was already married. On Mr. Blandy asking Captain Cranstoun for an explanation, the Captain pretended that he was not legally married, and that the contract, such as it was, would be put aside by a decree of the Supreme Court of Sessions. This explanation seems to have satisfied the Blandys more or less, and Miss Blandy declared she would wait for him. Captain Cranstoun then wrote an artful letter to his wife, enclosing another for her to copy, disowning her marriage, as he said he could not procure advancement in the army if it was known he had a wife and child. At first she refused to do this; but at his repeated request she reluctantly complied, copied his letter by which she disowned herself as his wife, and subscribed it with her maiden name. The villain then sent copies of her letter both to her relations and his own, which alienated them from her and reduced her to the utmost poverty and distress. At the same time he commenced an action to prove the illegality of his marriage, producing her letter as evidence. This at first went against her, until she came forward herself with the original letter in her husband's writing, when the judges gave a verdict against Captain Cranstoun and confirmed their marriage. Captain Cranstoun still did not give up Miss Blandy. He went to Henley and tried by specious eloquence to put things on the same footing as before; but though the young lady stuck to him, Mr. Blandy would no longer receive him. Before he left Henley for the last time, Captain Cranstoun made an assignation with Miss Blandy to meet him in the grounds of Park Place, which had long been their trysting-place; and here it was that, in a walk which still goes by the name of 'Blandy's Walk,' he first broached his diabolical plan. He told her that he would send her some powders which, if she gave them to her father, would act as a love philtre, and that by their help he should get back the love of Mr. Blandy.[1] He added that to prevent suspicion they should be labelled 'Powder, to clean the Scotch pebbles,' he having presented her with an ornament of this nature.[2] Accordingly Miss Blandy did on several occasions administer these powders to her father in his food, with the result that he

[1] In former years in Scotland many persons believed in the efficacy of love philtres. Bothwell, in the remarkable paper which he left, in which he maintained Queen Mary's innocence and also his own as to Darnley's murder, stated that he owed his influence over her to the use of philtres.

[2] Ornaments of Scotch pebbles were the extreme of fashion in the year 1750.

MISS MARY BLANDY IN PRISON.
From an old Print

succumbed, after much suffering, on August 14, 1751, the powders containing arsenic. Up to the end, though he knew what his daughter had done, the doting father treated her with the utmost love and tenderness, exclaiming when he was first told the cause of his illness, 'Poor love-sick girl! What will not a woman do for the man she loves!' And he went on to say, 'I always thought there was mischief in those cursed Scotch pebbles.'

When suspicion was aroused, Miss Blandy threw Captain Cranstoun's letters, together with the packet containing the remainder of the powders, into the fire; but a maid who saw her do it, instantly put some large lumps of coal upon the fire, and, when Miss Blandy left the room, removed the coal and found the packet with the powder, only partially consumed. It was sent to Reading to Dr. Addington (father of Lord Sidmouth), who declared it to be white arsenic. Miss Blandy endeavoured to escape, but was arrested and placed on her trial at Oxford before Baron Legge, when she was found guilty, and hanged a month later, in April 1752. An account of her proceedings from the time of her commitment to Oxford Castle till her execution says : 'Her imprisonment was indeed rather like a retirement from the world than the confinement of a criminal. She had a companion and servant, or rather two servants, to attend her, the best apartments in the keeper's house at her command, and during a long confinement was indulged to an unparalleled degree ; for no person, without her previous consent, was permitted to see her, tho' very extraordinary sums were daily offered for that purpose. . . . For some time Miss was without fetters, but when it was discovered that an escape was intended, orders were given to have her fettered. . . . On her trial, which lasted near thirteen hours, she never once changed her countenance . . . and when the verdict was given in, she seemed to smile.   When she went from the bar to return to prison, she stepped into the coach with as little concern as if she had been going to a ball, and when she came into the castle, finding the family in some disorder, the children being all in tears, said very cheerfully, "Don't mind it ; what does it signify ?   I am very hungry ; pray let me have something for supper, as speedily as possible."   Accordingly mutton chops were dressed, of which, and of an apple pye, she eat very heartily.   On the Friday she diverted herself for some hours in reading fables, and then went up several times into the rooms facing the Green to see the great concourse of people collected to be spectators of her execution, a report having been spread that it was to take place that day.' She asseverated to the last her ignorance of the nature of the powders ; but all the evidence adduced at the trial points irresistibly to the conclusion that, even if at the outset this may have been the case, she must have become cognisant of their true character when she witnessed their effect, not only upon her father, but upon two servants who accidentally partook of food containing a portion of them, notwithstanding which she still went on giving the powders to her father.

Many, however, believed in Miss Blandy's innocence, and Lady Ailesbury, it is said, used all her influence to obtain a pardon.   General Conway had had considerable communication with Mr. Blandy in relation to the purchase of Park Place, of which he was a trustee, which increased her interest in the case. Miss Blandy was buried at one A.M. in the chancel of Henley Church, in the same grave as her parents, her funeral being attended by an immense number of spectators.   Meanwhile, a writ had been issued against Captain Cranstoun, who was living at Berwick.   But he managed to hide himself for six months in

CAPTAIN THE HON. WILLIAM HENRY CRANSTOUN,
AND HIS FUNERAL PROCESSION.

Scotland, and at the end of that time escaped to Boulogne, where he found out a Mrs. Ross, a distant relation, who, out of regard for his family, promised to serve him to the utmost of her power. She made him change his name to Dunbar, which had been her maiden name, and for a time he thought himself safe ; but some of his wife's relations, happening to be living in Boulogne, threatened revenge whenever they should light on him, so that he had to secrete himself there, and soon moved, first to Ostend and afterwards to Furnes, a town in Flanders, then in the jurisdiction of the Queen of Hungary. Here he lived in a miserable condition, without being known by any one, dependent wholly on the goodness of his brother, who was not obliged to allow him more than £25 per year ; for the Lords of Session in Scotland had ordered £50 to be paid annually to his wife, who, with her child, went to live with some relations at Hexham in Northumberland.

In December of the same year Mr. Cranstoun fell ill, and after nine days' illness he expired in the most agonising torments, showing all the symptoms of poison, and some said raving mad. Shortly before his death he became a Roman Catholic, and he was buried in great solemnity in the cathedral church at Furnes, the whole corporation of the town attending the funeral, and a grand mass was said over his body. About a month before he died he made his will and left his fortune of £1,500 to his daughter ; this will, and other papers found in his custody at the time of his death, were sealed up and sent to his brother in Scotland. It was said that in one of them he stated that he had privately married Miss Blandy.

This horrid story was, of course, long the talk of the neighbourhood. In November of the same year Horace Walpole wrote to Mr. Conway : 'Have the Coopers seen Miss Blandy's ghost, or have they made Mr. Cranstoun poison a dozen or two more private gentlewomen ? ' This was no doubt an allusion to the rumour that Mr. Cranstoun was also answerable for the death of Mrs. Blandy, who had died very suddenly, a year and a half before her husband, in great agonies ; and also for that of a Mrs. Pocock. Even a year later we find Horace Walpole writing : ' The town of Henley has been extremely disturbed with an engagement between the ghosts of Miss Blandy and her father, which continued so violent that some bold persons, to prevent further bloodshed, broke in and found it was two jackasses which had got into the kitchen.'

In the autumn and winter of 1755 Lady Ailesbury was living at Dublin Castle, General Conway having been appointed Secretary to Ireland to assist the Lord Lieutenant in restoring tranquillity to that ever-troubled kingdom.

General Conway and Lady Ailesbury seem from the commencement of their occupation of Park Place to have taken a great delight in it, and were continually carrying out alterations and improvements, both in the house and grounds. One of the attractions of Park Place was the Druid Temple which was presented to General Conway by the inhabitants of Jersey on his resigning the governorship of that island. It had been discovered buried under a tumulus on the top of a hill near St. Helier, and consisted of forty-five granite stones averaging seven feet in height, arranged in a circle sixty-five feet in circumference ; and this ' little Master Stonehenge,' as Horace Walpole called it, was re-erected at Park Place by General Conway, stone for stone as it had been found.[1]

[1] The following is the inscription which the Council of Jersey sent over to General Conway with the Druidic temple :
> Pour des siècles caché aux regards des mortels
> Cet ancien monument, ces pierres, ces autels,

Lady Ailesbury and General Conway gave great attention to tree-planting at Park Place, and planted cedars, firs, and pines ; and the first poplar-pine (or, as it has since been called, Lombardy poplar) planted in England was at Park Place, on the bank of the river. It was a cutting brought from Turin by Lord Rochford, and was planted by General Conway's own hand. Lady Ailesbury took a special interest in the lavender farm which they established on a large scale, the fame of which seems to have given an impetus to the culture of lavender elsewhere.

Lady Ailesbury entertained many distinguished as well as fashionable visitors at Park Place. Lady Mary Coke, her cousin, who was one of its *habitués*, writes : ' The company there is the most agreeable I know ; ' and she tells us, in that wonderful Journal of hers, about the expeditions by river and road, the fishing, the games of bowls, at which she herself excelled, and the long walks, though of those she complains that ' the hills are steep,' and says ' one must be a good walker to keep company with Mr. Conway and Lady Ailesbury.' And amongst the indoor recreations she mentions the games of ' Pope Joan ' and ' Whisk.' Horace Walpole was constantly there, and we have a graphic description of an expedition to Caversham Park, near Reading, when he read out loud in the coach, as they drove there, his new play, ' The Mysterious Mother.' This was in July 1768. Caversham Park then belonged to the second

Où le sang humain offert en sacrifice
Ruissela pour des dieux, qu'enfanta le caprice ;
Ce monument sans prix par son antiquité
Témoignera pour nous à la postérité
Que dans tous les dangers Césarée eut un père
Attentif et vaillant, généreux et prospère,
Et redira, Conway, aux siècles à venir,
Qu'en vertu du respect dû à ce souvenir,
Elle te fit ce don, acquis à ta vaillance,
Comme un juste tribut de sa reconnoissance.

Lord Cadogan, the uncle of the third Duke of Richmond, who married Lord Ailesbury's daughter; and the romantic story of the alliance between the Cadogan and the Richmond families is too interesting to omit.

William, first Earl of Cadogan, to cancel a gambling debt which he owed to Charles, first Duke of Richmond, engaged to give his daughter and co-heiress, Lady Sarah Cadogan, in marriage to Lord March, the Duke's eldest son. At the time of the wedding the bride was only thirteen years of age, and the bridegroom a few years older. She was amazed and silent; but the juvenile husband exclaimed, 'Surely you are not going to marry me to that dowdy!' After the ceremony, his tutor took him off to the Continent, and Lady Sarah went back to her mother. Three years after, Lord March returned from his travels; but, having such a disagreeable recollection of his wife, was in no hurry to join her, and went to the theatre the first evening after his arrival in London. There he saw all eyes turned upon a lady in a box, whom he thought so beautiful that he asked who she was. 'The reigning toast—the Lady March,' was the answer he got. He hastened to claim her, and they remained throughout their lives the most devoted of lovers. Indeed, it was said she died of grief within a year of his death. They had a very large family, of whom twelve survived; one of them was the celebrated Lady Sarah Bunbury, and one was the mother of Charles James Fox.

Another expedition from Park Place to which Horace Walpole alludes, was to Whiteknights, then the property of Sir Henry Englefield. This afterwards became the property of the Duke of Marlborough, at whose death it was sold, when many of its art treasures were bought by Sir Henry Russell and are now at Swallowfield. It has since been cut up into villa residences.

Lady Ailesbury also took Horace Walpole to see Harley-ford, Mr. Clayton's place, which Lady Mary Coke, who was one of the party, describes as 'one of the prettiest places she ever saw.' It is now the property of Sir William Clayton. Though some of Lady Ailesbury's friends enjoyed those expeditions, she and her daughters appear to have been too energetic for Gray, the poet, who writes in 1760, on returning to Cambridge from Park Place : 'For me, I am come to my resting place, and find it very necessary after living for a month in a house with three women that laughed from morning to night, and would allow nothing to the sulkiness of my disposition. Company and cards at home ; parties by land and water abroad, and (what they call) " doing something," that is racketting about from morning to night, are occupations I find that wear out my spirits, especially in a situation where one might sit still and be alone with pleasure, for the place is a hill like Clifden, opening to a very extensive and diversified landscape with the Thames, which is navigable, running at its foot.' Horace Walpole, alluding to this visit of Gray's, says : 'Lady Ailesbury protests he never opened his lips but once, and then only said, " Yes, my lady, I believe so." '[1] And still Lady Ailesbury appears to have tried to suit her habits to her company. When Princess Amelia, that inveterate gambler, stayed with her, which she often did, 'Pope Joan' and 'Whisk' were the order of the day, combined with even less intellectual pleasures. For instance, we find that the Princess was much diverted by 'a set of Morris dancers with a fool at their head, who appeared upon the green before the windows and performed exceedingly well.' When

---

[1] Horace Walpole himself said 'Gray is the worst company in the world,' although he was very angry with Dr. Johnson for saying, 'Sir, he was dull in company and dull everywhere.'

Lord Camden, the Lord Chancellor, and Lord Lyttelton, the historian, were her guests, Lady Mary Coke tells us, 'Conversation is kept up extremely well and we have no cards since this company has arrived.'

In one of Lady Mary's accounts of the proceedings at Park Place she gives a curious description of a panic in the neighbourhood caused by an outbreak, real or imaginary, of rabies. She says : 'During the Winter [1771] above forty people were bit by mad dogs and cats at Henley. They all took some medecine and were likewise sent to the sea,[1] but one of the women, who was bit by a cat, was taken ill at the last change, mew'd like a cat, and endeavoured to scratch and bite everybody that came near her. Upon this Mr. Conway ordered Sir George Cobbe's[2] medecine[3] to be given, (the Musk, &c.) which had a

[1] The belief in the efficacy of salt water as a cure for rabies, which was general at that time, was of old standing. In *A Mechanical Account of Poisons*, by the celebrated Dr. Richard Mead, printed in 1702, we read : 'The greatest and surest cure [of rabies] is frequent submerging, or ducking the patient in water. The first mention of this is in Cornelius Celsus, and not improbably he got this from Asclepiades, who discarded all inward medecines for the hydrophobia. This practice was revived by the ingenious Baron Van Helmont, who, having in his own country seen how great service it did, has at large set down both the manner of the operation and shewn the reason of its good effects. Since him Tulpius, an observer of very good credit, takes notice that tho' he saw many, yet that never one miscarry'd where it was in time made use of. We need go no farther to fetch the reason of the great advantage of this method than to the pressure of the water upon the body of the patient : when the fermenting blood stretches its vessels the exceeding weight of the ambient fluid resists and represses this distension. For this reason the salt water of the Sea is especially chosen for this business because of its greater gravity. This we may do without having recourse to the fright and terror with which this method (when practis'd by keeping the party under water for a considerable time till he is almost quite drowned) is usually accompanied.'

[2] Sir George Cobbe, Bart., of Adderbury, Oxon. He married Ann, daughter and co-heiress of Joseph Langton of Newton Park, widow of Robert Langton. He died in 1762, aged ninety, from drowning, having fallen into the moat at Bulmersh, near Reading, the seat of John Blagrave, his son-in-law.

[3] The 'Tonquin Recipe,' *i.e.* 'Twenty-four grains of factitious Cinnabar, 16 grains of Musk very well pounded and mixed together in Rum or Brandy. If very bad repeat in one hour, at all events to repeat for 14 days.'

most surprising effect, and there is great reason to believe she will perfectly recover. This is so strong an instance in favour of that medecine that I think it may be of use to be known.' Unfortunately, Lady Mary writes a few days later, ' Mr. Conway has had a bad account : the poor woman had mew'd again, and attempted to scratch every body that came near her.' Amongst Lady Ailesbury's guests at this time was her dear friend Lady George Lennox, with her young son of seven years old. When hearing of the panic [1] caused by the dread of this dire disease, how little did Lady George think that she should live to mourn over the agonising death of that son from the same terrible malady forty-two years later !

The royalties were very fond, in Lady Ailesbury's time, of paying impromptu visits, which often created consternation in domestic households. There are accounts of some of these royal raids amongst the manuscript papers of Hardwick House, which Mrs. Climenson of Shiplake has lately edited. She gives us a graphic description of one which took place at Park Place, where, without any warning, a party arrived one day when General Conway and Lady Ailesbury were at their dinner— and arrived not only to dine, but to sleep ; the party consisting of the Princess of Hesse,[2] Count and Countess Zekany, and

---

[1] This panic was not confined to Henley, and commenced in London ten years before. The Common Council of London, in August 1760, issued an order for killing all dogs found in the streets or highways, and 2*s.* 6*d.* was given for every dog's head that was brought to the Mansion House ; but after paying 438 half-crowns the Mayor repented of his zeal ! Horace Walpole writes this same year : ' In London there is a more cruel campaign than that waged by the Russians, the streets are a very picture of the murder of the Innocents, one drives over nothing but poor dead dogs. The dear, good-natured, honest, sensible creatures.' No doubt, then as now, many a long-suffering animal paid the penalty of the ignorance and rapacity of official underlings.

[2] Princess Mary, fourth daughter of George II. ; married, in 1740, Frederick II., Landgrave of Hesse-Cassel. This Prince separated from her soon after their

Count Khevenhüller.[1] 'Luckily,' says the narrator, 'Lady Ailesbury's two daughters were with her, and as all spoke French and Italian, the visit passed most agreeably.' The two daughters here mentioned were Mary, her only child by her first husband, Lord Ailesbury, who had married in 1757, before she was seventeen years of age, Charles, third Duke of Richmond ; and Anne, the only child of her second marriage, who had married in 1767 the Hon. John Damer. Horace Walpole, writing at the time about the former of these marriages, says : ' The Duke of Richmond has made two balls for his approaching wedding with Lady Mary Bruce. It is the prettiest match in the world ; youth, beauty, riches, alliances and all the blood of all the Kings from Robert Bruce to Charles II. They are the prettiest couple in England, excepting the father-in-law and mother.' The following year the Duke of Richmond, at the early age of twenty-three, commanded the 72nd Regiment and accompanied the Duke of Marlborough's expedition to the coast of France. During his absence the Duchess resided with her mother, chiefly at Park Place, but paid constant visits to Horace Walpole. He writes about this time : ' Strawberry Hill is grown a perfect Paphos, it is the land of beauties. On Wednesday Lady Ailesbury and the Duchesses of Hamilton and Richmond dined there, the two latter stayed all night. There never was so pretty a sight as to see them all three sitting in the shell.[2] A thousand years hence, when I begin to grow

marriage, and when remonstrated with, said that he had understood from George II., when he married the Princess, that he need only be her husband for a few weeks. He died 1771. The late Duke of Cambridge was her great-grandson.

[1] Count Khevenhüller, made a prince in 1763, died 1776 ; married Caroline, daughter of Count von Metsch. He was Grand Maître to the Emperor.

[2] The Shell was a large seat carved in oak in the form of a shell, from a design by Mr. Bentley, placed at the end of a winding walk at Strawberry Hill.

ANGELICA KAUFFMANN, *pinx.*

MARY, 3RD DUCHESS OF RICHMOND.
(DAUGHTER OF THE EARL OF AILESBURY)

old, if that can ever be, I shall talk of that event, and tell young people how much handsomer the women of my time were than they will be then. I shall say women alter now. I remember Lady Ailesbury looking handsomer than her daughter, the pretty Duchess of Richmond, as they were sitting in the shell on my terrace with the Duchess of Hamilton, one of the famous Gunnings.' [1]

Later in the same year Horace Walpole writes : ' I passed all the last week at Park Place, where one of the bravest men in the world who is not permitted to contribute to our conquests, was indulged in being the happiest, by being with one of the most deserving women, for Campbell goodness no more wears out than Campbell beauty. All their good qualities are hucka-back.' Lady Ailesbury and her cousin, Lady Strafford (daughter of John, Duke of Argyll), preserved their beauty so long that Horace Walpole called them ' Huckaback beauties that never wear out.' [2]

Any account of Park Place and Lady Ailesbury's intimate friends would be incomplete without an allusion to General O'Hara, who was at one time an habitué of that house, and whose name is associated with one of the saddest love affairs— ' For of all sad words of tongue or pen the saddest are these : It

---

[1] Elizabeth, Duchess of Hamilton, had been married only a few months to Colonel John Campbell, Lady Ailesbury's brother, who became fifth Duke of Argyll in 1770.

[2] Just a hundred years later, when a great-great-granddaughter of Mary Bellenden, on her first appearance in London society, was presented to Mrs. Norton, the latter said to her : ' My dear, I cannot do better than repeat to you what my grandfather [meaning Sheridan] said to your mother when she was pre-sented to him. " The beauty of the Campbells is like huckaback and never wears out." ' It is clear that the expression is used by Horace Walpole and Sheridan in a different sense. Horace Walpole intended to say that the ladies of the Campbell family preserved their beauty very long ; whilst Sheridan of course meant the strain of beauty lasted long in the Campbell family.

might have been '—a love affair which took its rise there under the direct auspices of Lady Ailesbury. Lady Theresa Lewis tells us that General O'Hara ' was a cherished friend of Marshal Conway and Lady Ailesbury, and was on terms of almost brotherly affection with their daughter, Mrs. Damer,' and she quotes the following character of him which is introduced in the novel of 'Cyril Thornton,' which may account for that enthusiastic love which he inspired in vain and never really lost—' his appearance, indeed, was of that striking cast, which, once seen, is not easily forgotten. General O'Hara was the most perfect specimen I ever saw of the soldier and courtier of the last age, and in his youth had fought with Granby and Ligonier, &c. . . .' At Park Place he constantly met Mary Berry, the eldest of the two celebrated sisters, whom Horace Walpole described as ' angel both inside and out,' and towards the end of 1795, whilst staying there, they became engaged. His wish was to marry her at once, as he had to leave for his military duties at Gibraltar and hoped to take her with him ; but though most deeply in love, for some unaccountable reason and from a mistaken sense of duty, she declined marrying him till his return. In making this arrangement she wrote, ' I think I am doing right, I am sure I am consulting the peace and happiness of those about me and not my own.' They never met again. In April 1796 the engagement was finally broken off and General O'Hara remained on at his post at Gibraltar till 1802, when he died there. Forty-eight years after the correspondence between General O'Hara and Miss Berry terminated, the latter reopened the packet of letters that passed at this time, and ere she closed it again attached to it the following touching little record : ' This parcel of letters relates to the six happiest months of my long and insignificant existence, although these six months were accompanied by fatiguing and

'Conway House, Warwick Street, London.

unavoidable uncertainty, and by the absence of everything that could constitute present enjoyment. But I looked forward to a future existence, which I felt for the first time, would have called out all the powers of my mind and all the warmest feelings of my heart . . . a concatenation of unfortunate circumstances—the political state of Europe making absence a necessity, and even frequent communication impossible, letters lost and delayed, questions unanswered, doubts unsatisfied. All these circumstances combined in the most unlucky manner, crushed the fair fabric of my happiness, not at one fell shock, but by the slow mining misery of loss of confidence, of unmerited complaints, of finding by degrees misunderstandings, and the firm rock of mutual confidence crumbling under my feet, while my bosom for long could not banish a hope that all might yet be set right. And so it would had we ever met for twenty-four hours. But he remained at his government at Gibraltar till his death in 1802, and I, forty-two year afterwards on opening these papers, which had been sealed up ever since, receive the conviction that some feelings in some minds are indelible.—M. B., Oct. 1844.'[1]

In the middle of the eighteenth century the neighbourhood of Spring Gardens was a charming locality, and the Conways (as Lady Ailesbury and her husband were generally called), when in London, lived there for many years, in old Warwick House, situated at the end of Warwick Street. They spent a great deal of money on it, and relaid the court which contained some trees, and they re-christened it 'Conway House.'[2] No sooner had they

---

[1] Mary Berry died in November 1852, surviving her lover to whom she ever remained faithful fifty years. She is buried in Petersham Churchyard, in the same grave as her sister Agnes, who died a few months earlier.

[2] After Field-Marshal Conway's death it became the property of the Earl of Jersey, when it was called Jersey House, which name it retained till it came into the hands of the Prince Regent. It was then for some time occupied by his

completed their improvements than the house was set on fire, and considerable damage done to it, besides their lives being endangered. The incendiary was General Conway's secretary, who carried off £900 and then tried to hide his theft. The crime was brought home to him ; he confessed, and was sentenced to be hanged. When the King heard the story he said, ' Now I am sure that when this man is condemned Conway will be teasing me to pardon him, but I am determined to hang him.' General Conway did try to save the man, but in vain ; and hanged he was.

It was in Conway House, Warwick Street, that Lady Ailesbury gave her constant card-parties. Card-playing was, at this time, one of the vices of the age, and Lady Ailesbury was certainly not exempt from it ; she played high stakes almost nightly, Princess Amelia,[1] that inveterate gambler, frequently forming one of the party.

'Gaming,' writes Seymour, the author of 'The Court Gamester,' ' had become so much the fashion that he who in company should be ignorant of the games in vogue would be reckoned low-bred and hardly fit for conversation.' Loo was the favourite game at this time, and Lady Ailesbury was reputed to be very lucky. Not so her cousin and great friend, Lady Mary Coke, who usually played at her table. The latter in her Journal tells us how she got carp bones (the palate) to bring

---

secretary, Thomas Tyrwhitt, Esq. ; but when a separate establishment was assigned for his daughter, Princess Charlotte, this house was given for her residence, and was then and afterwards again known as Warwick House.

[1] Princess Amelia Sophia, second daughter of George II., was born in 1711. The Dukes of Newcastle and Grafton were said to have been rivals for her favour, and the latter to have had the greater success. The ' Little Miss Ashe ' so often alluded to by Horace Walpole was her reputed daughter ; her father said to be Lord Rodney. Miss Ashe married Captain Falkner, R.N. In later life Princess Amelia held a sort of court of her own in her house in Cavendish Square, the corner of Harley Street. She died in 1786, aged seventy-five.

her luck at cards. 'I lost,' she writes, 'fifteen guineas, though the carp bone lay upon the table, but I fear the Princess has taken away the virtue, for she unfolded the paper, took it out and called it an old tooth, which diverted the company more than it did me, for from that time I lost. At cards I am superstitious, and as it is only at play, 'tis pardonable.' Another day she says 'The carp bones are intolerable ; in the evening I lost eight and thirty guineas and I have thrown one in the fire.' Lady Mary always spells the game 'Lu,' giving as her authority Pope, who so wrote it in 'The Rape of the Lock : '

> E'en mighty Pam,[1] that Kings and Queens o'erthrew
> And mow'd down armies in the fights of Lu.[2]

Gambling by no means engrossed all of Lady Ailesbury's time. She read much and enjoyed discussions on the books she read, and had the courage of her opinions, notably with Hume, who acted as secretary, first of all to her brother-in-law, and afterwards to her husband when he was Secretary of State. Hume, she tells us, was not a great admirer of Shakespeare. Gray, with whom she also had literary talks, on the contrary loved Shakespeare, who, he said, had several souls to his own share.

Hume thus alludes to his intercourse with the Conways, writing to Blake in 1767 : 'My way of life here is very uniform and by no means disagreeable. I pass all the forenoon in the

---

[1] 'Pam' was the knave of clubs and ranked above the court cards of the trump suits.

[2] Apparently there is authority for both spellings, as the original name is said to be 'Lanterloo,' from the French 'Lanturelu' (nonsense, fudge), the refrain of a famous vaudeville of the time of Cardinal Richelieu. It appears under the title of 'Lanterloo' in *The Compleat Gamester* of 1674.

Secretary's house from ten till three, where there arrive from time to time messengers that bring me all the secrets of the Kingdom and indeed of Europe, Asia, Africa, and America. I am seldom hurried, but have leisure at intervals to take up a book, or write a private letter, or converse with any friend that may call for me ; and from dinner [1] to bed-time is all my own. If you add to this that the person [General Conway] with whom I have the chief, if not only transactions, is the most reasonable, equal-tempered, and gentlemanlike man imaginable, and Lady Ailesbury [the General's wife] the same, you will certainly think I have no reason to complain, and I am far from complaining. I only shall not regret when my duty is over, because to me the situation can lead to nothing, and reading and sauntering and lounging and dosing, which I call thinking, is my supreme happiness, I mean my full contentment.'

After Hume's occupation as secretary came to an end, he continued his friendship with the Conways.   In 1771 he writes : ' I am assured that Lady Ailesbury and Mr. Conway are to be with the Duke of Argyll this summer, which will oblige me to leave the Town for a fortnight and go to Inverara.'   From there he writes to upbraid his publisher for not having sent Lady Ailesbury 'a new edition of my history and essays.'

Lady Ailesbury was also acquainted with Rousseau, who arrived in England from Paris in 1766 with Hume ; and it was General Conway who procured Rousseau his pension of £100 a year.   Amongst other literary celebrities with whom she was intimate were the poets Thomson,[2] Shenstone, Gray, and Mason, Gibbon, Hannah More, and the Miss Berrys.   She and General

---

[1] Three o'clock was the usual fashionable dinner hour at this time.
[2] Thomson she often met at Hagley, Lord Lyttelton's place in Warwickshire.

Conway visited Shenstone at Leasowes soon after their marriage. In his 'Pastoral Ode' he thus alludes to them :

> Here too shall Conway's name appear :
> He prais'd the stream so lovely clear,
>   That shone the reeds among ;
> Yet clearness could it not disclose,
> To match the rhetoric that flows
>   From Conway's polished tongue.

> . . . . . .

> But what can courts discover more
> Than these rude haunts have seen before,
>   Each fount and shady tree ?
> Have not these trees and fountains seen
> The pride of courts, the winning mien
>   Of peerless Aylesbury ?

Hannah More, writing in 1787, says : 'I spent a day at Lady Ailesbury's. In the evening there was a concert ; it was quite "le temple des beaux arts." Lady Ailesbury works portraits as Raphael paints them ;[1] and there was Mrs. Damer to remind us of her famous dogs of exquisite sculpture, and there was my Lord Derby to talk about his company of Richmond House Comedians, and there was General Conway, poet to the ducal theatre.' The Miss Berrys were introduced to Lady Ailesbury in 1789 by Horace Walpole, and from that time became constant visitors at her house both in London and at Park Place, and continued to be ever after the dear friends of herself and her daughter.

Lady Ailesbury was a great patroness and admirer of the

---

[1] The practice of executing pictures in needlework was greatly in fashion at this time, and Lady Ailesbury excelled all competitors in this art, and showed, as Horace Walpole says, 'a wonderful genius for it.'

fine arts. Sir Joshua Reynolds, who often entertained her and General Conway at his parties, said that Angelica Kauffmann [1] owed her introduction in London in 1766 to the Conways, they having been greatly struck with her portrait of Garrick, painted in Rome and exhibited at the Society of Arts in Maiden Lane in the preceding year. Lady Mary Coke writes : 'Went to Lady Ailesbury ; found Mr. Conway and her going to a Paintress who is just arrived from Italy, brought over by Lady Wentworth. Went with them to see a picture she was painting of Miss Conway (now 18) ; 'tis like and appears to me well done, but much too large, you would take it for a big woman !' Angelica Kauffmann painted Miss Conway several times, as also Lady Ailesbury's eldest daughter, Mary, Duchess of Richmond, and various other members of the family ; and Lady Ailesbury induced her sister-in-law, the beautiful Duchess of Argyll, *née* Gunning, to sit to her in a group with her two daughters. [2]

Lady Ailesbury loved music even more than painting. She seldom, when in London, missed any representation at the New Opera House, where Box No. 3 was held in her name ; the other occupants being Lady Mary Coke, Lady Strafford, General

[1] Sir Joshua was said to have been in love with her. In his Life (Leslie and Taylor) we are told that there are frequent entries of ' Miss Angelica ' in his pocket-book, and sometimes ' Miss Angel,' and once there is the suggestive addition, ' Fiori.' Anyhow, he was her steady friend, and aided her in procuring the dissolution of her marriage with a swindler, the valet of Count Horn, who, arriving in London with his master's stolen wardrobe and credentials, had figured successfully for a time in the character of the Count, and as such had wooed and won the fair Angelica. She married Antonio Zucchi, who was elected A.R.A. in 1770. It is a curious coincidence that the real Count Horn, personated by the impostor who married Angelica Kauffmann, was a nephew of Lady Ailesbury's first husband, his mother having been Lady Charlotte Bruce, daughter of the second Earl of Ailesbury by his wife Charlotte d'Argenteau, Comtesse d'Estieux.

[2] This lovely picture, as well as the above-mentioned portrait of Miss Conway, is now in the possession of Mrs. Campbell Johnston, whose husband was great-nephew of Lady Ailesbury.

Conway, Lord Hertford, and Horace Walpole. Lady Ailesbury gave musical parties in London, and at Park Place she constantly enjoyed the good music of her dear friend, Lady Cecilia Johnston,[1] who was one of the finest amateur musicians of the day and generally called 'St. Cecilia.'

Lady Ailesbury was devoted to the drama, and she lived in a good time for those who had that taste ; for the stage was then adorned by Garrick, Kemble, Barry, Sheridan, Foote, Quin, Macklin, Bannister, Mrs. Siddons, Peg Woffington, Mrs. Pritchard, Kitty Clive, Mrs. Abington, Mrs. Cibber, Mrs. Pope, Mrs. Yates, Mrs. Bellamy, Miss Farren, and many other bright stars. 'The Queen of Tragedy,' Sarah Siddons, owed her first footing in London to Lord Ailesbury. When acting at Cheltenham,[2] quite unknown, he saw her and was struck with her beauty and grace in 'Rosalind.' On his return to London, meeting Garrick at the Conways, he extolled her so enthusiastically that Garrick sent down two emissaries to see her, the result of their reports being that she was engaged for Drury Lane at £5 a week.

Miss Farren's first patronesses in London were Lady Ailesbury and her daughter, Mrs. Damer. The Duchess of Leinster, who was sister-in-law of Lady Ailesbury's eldest daughter, knew something of the Farren family in Ireland, and asked Lady Ailesbury to do what she could for Miss Farren. When the latter had reached her fame, Lady Ailesbury became one of the *habitués* of Miss Farren's celebrated supper parties

[1] Lady Cecilia Johnston was daughter of John, first Earl De la Warr, by Charlotte, daughter of Donough MacCarthy, fourth Earl of Clancarty. She married General James Johnston, Colonel of the Inniskilling Dragoons.

[2] Shortly before, as Sarah Kemble, she had been lady's maid in the family of the Greatheads of Guy's Cliff, who were great friends of the Conways, and quitted their service to be married to Mr. Siddons.

and constantly met Kemble and Mrs. Siddons there. John Riddell in his MSS.[1] says : 'I have often heard of these charming suppers from the late Lord Berwick, the diplomatist,[2] who used to say, "Oh ! those charming suppers at the bow window in Green Street, Grosvenor Square, where I was admitted when I was a very young man, and where one used to meet General Conway, Lady Ailesbury, Mrs. Damer, the old Duchess of Leinster,[3] and the Ogilvies,[3] General Burgoyne,[4] Fitzpatrick, your father, and all the pleasantest people in London."' It was through Lady Ailesbury that Miss Farren became acquainted with Lord Derby, whom she afterwards married.[5] Kitty Clive, of course, the Conways constantly met at Strawberry Hill ;[6] and they were very intimate with Garrick and his charming wife, who stayed with them at Park Place more than once, and with whom they often dined in London.

There were amateur theatricals, too, in those days, of a very high order. In March 1751 all the fashionable world in London went to see 'Othello' given in Drury Lane by the Delaval family—Sir Francis taking the part of 'Othello,' and his sister, afterwards Lady Mexborough, that of 'Desdemona.' The rage was so great to see this performance that the House of Commons adjourned at three o'clock to enable the members to go to it ! Then there was the Scotch company formed by Lady Dalkeith, Lady Ailesbury's cousin, who acted at a theatre in Queensberry

[1] John Riddell MSS., in Advocates' and Signet Libraries.
[2] William Noel Hill, third Lord Berwick ; died 1842 at Red Rice, near Andover.
[3] The Duchess of Leinster, daughter of the Duke of Richmond. She married secondly William Ogilvie, by whom she had two daughters.
[4] General Burgoyne, author of *The Maid of the Oaks*.
[5] Lord Derby's first wife, Lady Betty Hamilton, was daughter of Lady Ailesbury's sister-in-law, the Gunning Duchess of Argyll.
[6] Kitty Clive lived close to Horace Walpole, in a house which he called 'Cliveden,' afterwards known as 'Little Strawberry Hill.' In 1791 it became the residence of the Miss Berrys and their father.

House. Amongst the performers were Sir Harry Bellenden, Lady Ailesbury's uncle, and Frederick Campbell, her brother, then 'a most beautiful youth.' Lady Ailesbury says that their acting of Otway's ' Orphan,' a good deal clipped and pared, was such a success that Frederick, Prince of Wales, asked for an extra performance for himself and the Princess and the audience they chose to nominate. But first of all in her affections were those theatricals originated by her son-in-law, the Duke of Richmond, at Richmond House, Whitehall, where her daughter, Mrs. Damer, took a distinguished part, and where Lord Henry Fitzgerald, the Duke's nephew, acted so finely as to make Horace Walpole say he preferred him to Garrick ! ' The World ' newspaper of January 4, 1783, states that on one occasion a motion in the House of Commons was postponed in order to enable Mr. Pitt to be present at these theatricals.

This rage for amateur theatricals led to some disastrous results. Professionals helped the amateurs, and more than one fair lady of the aristocracy fell in love with a handsome actor. The most notable of these cases was that of Lady Susan Fox-Strangways, Lord Ilchester's daughter and a cousin of the Duke of Richmond. When she eloped with O'Brien, the actor, in 1764, a post was provided for him in America, where they remained eight years. At the end of that time he returned to England ; and on his refusing to go back, General Conway, who was looking into all the abuses of the Board of Ordnance, dismissed him from his post. Lord and Lady Holland and Charles James Fox tried to make the General alter his decision, but he refused ; and it has been suggested that this was a proximate cause of Fox's withdrawal from the Administration and his becoming in permanent opposition to the Court.

The Margravine d'Anspach, formerly Lady Craven, both wrote plays and acted them, and her theatricals at Brandenburg House in later years became very celebrated. She was first cousin of Lady Ailesbury's son-in-law, the Duke of Richmond ;[1] and Lady Ailesbury was very intimate with her. Her 'Memoirs' are amusing, if only for the extraordinary conceit which they display. She mentions that her portrait was painted by Sir Joshua and also by Romney, but that neither painter did her justice, one failing to represent the beauty of her face, and the other that of her figure ; nor did Mme. Vigée le Brun's portrait please her more. The Margravine says that Sheridan, under pretence of writing an epilogue for her play, 'The Miniature Picture' (which was first performed at Newbury for charity), borrowed it and brought it out against her will at Drury Lane ; but she adds, 'Yet enraged as I was, by the persuasion of Lord Orford and the Duchess of Devonshire and Lady Aylesbury in whose box I sat, I went to its last representation.'

Amongst the many celebrities whom Lady Ailesbury mentions as meeting, was that singular creature, 'Le Chevalier d'Eon,' or rather we should say 'La Chevalière d'Eon,' as when Lady Ailesbury knew him he was passing as a woman. She met him at a party at the Cosways' in 1786 and at dinner in September 1789, and also at a supper given by Mr. and Lady Cecilia Johnston, the rest of the party being composed of General Conway, Mrs. Damer, the Farrens, and Lord Mount Edgcumbe. The latter said, 'Mlle. d'Eon is her own widow.' Lady Ailesbury found her 'entertaining and witty.' Twenty-five years before, D'Eon had been A.D.C. to the Comte de

---

[1] The Margravine was a daughter of the Earl of Berkeley, and her mother was a daughter of the first Duke of Richmond. The Margrave was a nephew of George II.'s queen.

Broglie, and fought in the French army against the Anglo-Hanoverian army, the centre of which was commanded by General Conway! He died at the age of eighty-three, having lived forty-nine years of his life as a man and thirty-four as a female. Beaumarchais, the author of 'Le Mariage de Figaro,' proposed marriage to D'Eon. A notability who was often entertained by the Conways was Louise de Stolberg, Comtesse d'Albanie,[1] the widow of Prince Charles Edward Stuart. She arrived in England in 1791, and Lady Ailesbury gave several parties in her honour, as she was great-niece to Lady Ailesbury's first husband. Horace Walpole, who calls her 'the Pinchbeck Queen,' says 'she had not a ray of royalty about her;' and Lady Ailesbury thought her 'the image of Hannah More.'

In 1785 Lady Ailesbury met Mme. de Genlis and 'Pamela'[2] for the first time. They were staying in Portland Place, at a house taken by the Duc d'Orléans, and were on their way, accompanied by Wilkes's daughter, to Oxford, where Mme. de Genlis was about to take her doctor's degree.[3] Lady Ailesbury never had any doubt as to the paternity of Pamela; and many years after, Mme. de Gontaut told her that she herself had been present when the Chevalier de Grave, premier écuyer de M. le duc d'Orléans, first arrived with her, and Mme. de Gontaut added: 'Nous cherchâmes un nom de famille, et

---

[1] Louise, daughter of Prince Gustavus Adolphus of Stolberg Gedern, and great-granddaughter of the outlawed Earl of Ailesbury, who died at Brussels. She was married to Prince Charles Edward at Macerata in 1772. It was said that she married Count Alfieri, the poet, after the Prince's death.

[2] Pamela ultimately became a connection of Lady Ailesbury's, as Lord Edward Fitzgerald was nephew of the Duke of Richmond, Lady Ailesbury's son-in-law.

[3] H. Walpole. See his *Letters to the Countess of Ossory*, vol. ii. p. 232, Letter cclxxvii.

celui de Seymour fut choisi et proclamé.'[1]   Mme. de Gontaut
also told Lady Ailesbury that, although in early youth she
had been fascinated by Mme. de Genlis, she had been equally
disgusted in later times at seeing her in a tricolor dress with
Paméla coiffée du bonnet rouge, 'dancing to the horrible air
of "Ah ! ça ira." '[2]

Sir William Hamilton was a great friend of Lady Ailesbury's
family ; and after he made the beautiful Emma Harte his

[1] In Mme. de Genlis' *Mémoires* she says : 'Je lui [Lord Edward Fitzgerald]
montrai les papiers qui constataient sa naissance ; elle était fille d'un homme
nommé Seymours, qui avait de la naissance et qui épousa une personne de la classe
la plus inférieure qui s'appelait Mary Syms et qui l'emmena à Terre-Neuve dans
un lieu appelé Fogo. Paméla y naquit, on la nomma Nancy. Son père mourut
et sa mère repassa en Angleterre avec l'enfant âgée de 18 mois. Elle s'établit
à Christchurch. Ce fut là que quatre ans après passa M. Forth, chargé par M. le
du d'Orléans de nous envoyer une petite Anglaise après l'avoir fait inoculer.'
This statement does not coincide with Mme. de Genlis' other declarations. In
Pamela's marriage contract (1793) she had her put down as 'Citoienne Anne
Caroline Stéphanie Sims, fille de Guillaume de Brexey' ! This was signed by
Philippe Egalité. In the *Masonic Magazine* for January 1793 the marriage was
announced of 'The Hon. Lord Edward Fitzgerald to Madame Pamela Capet,
daughter of his Royal Highness the ci-devant Duke of Orleans.' Mlle. d'Epinay,
daughter of the Baronne d'Epinay, one of Pamela's intimate friends, said she had
heard Pamela express her belief that she was the daughter of Madame de Genlis,
and a French writer talks of her astonishing resemblance to the Duke's children.

[2] Mme. le Brun, in her *Souvenirs*, writing in 1789 of the first terrors of the
Revolution, says : 'Nous passions devant la grille des Invalides où se trouvait
une foule immense composée de vilain monde avec des piques effrayantes, et j'avais
une telle peur que je reprenais le chemin de la maison, quand nous vîmes arriver
une jeune personne à cheval . . . à l'instant l'horrible bande forme la haie de
deux côtés pour laisser passer la jeune personne, que suivaient deux piqueurs à la
livrée d'Orléans. Je reconnus cette belle Paméla que Madame de Genlis avait
amenée chez moi. Elle était alors dans toute sa fraîcheur et vraiment ravissante,
aussi entendions-nous toute la bande crier : "Voilà celle qu'il nous faudrait pour
reine !" Paméla allait et revenait sans cesse au milieu de cette dégoûtante populace, ce qui me donna bien tristement à penser.' Miss H. Bowdler, writing to Miss
E. Ponsonby from Bath in 1793, says : 'I am greatly shocked at the account I hear
from various quarters of Madame de Genlis and Pamela. Can it be possible that
that lovely form really contains the mind of a fiend? I hear that when every one
else put on mourning for the unfortunate Louis XVI., she wore red ribbons, which
she said were "couleur du sang des aristocrates," with many other circumstances
too shocking to repeat.'

wife he brought her to see the Conways, whom she delighted with her 'Attitudes.' Lady Ailesbury remarks that, though Lady Hamilton had such consummate art in the management of her draperies on these occasions, her taste in ordinary dress was atrocious. One night she was in a box at Drury Lane near Lady Ailesbury, who noticed her rapt gaze at the actress, Mrs. Powell, as she came on the stage. It was afterwards explained to Lady Ailesbury that Mrs. Powell [1] had been under-housemaid in Doctor Budd's house at Chatham Place, Blackfriars, at the same time that Emma Harte had been nurserymaid there.

General Conway was much thrown with most of the politicians of the day of every party, and when he was in office Lady Ailesbury entertained some of the foremost men of the time ; but Horace Walpole tells us that she ' seldom thought of politics and understood them less.' She, however, felt most bitterly when, in 1764, her husband was not only dismissed from being Equerry to George III., but had the command of his regiment taken from him, in consequence of his voting in the House of Commons against the Ministry at the time of the prosecution of Wilkes. On this occasion Lord Hertford, the Duke of Devonshire, and Horace Walpole pressed General Conway to receive from them a sum equal to what he was losing ; but he refused all these offers, and said he should wait till ' one day the great political wheel that is always in motion should turn him up, fly that he was, upon it.' He had not long

[1] Harriet Powell, a celebrated singer and actress, whose portrait was painted by Sir Joshua, Catherine Read, and William Peters, is said to have been married to Kenneth Mackenzie, Earl of Seaforth, whose first wife died in 1767. She herself died in 1779. Lady Louisa Stuart, in one of her letters to Sir Walter Scott, says : ' Mrs. Powell had caught the voice, tone, and manner of Mrs. Siddons so exactly that I was more than once surprised into thinking, " How comes Mrs. Siddons to act so ill to-night ? " '

to wait for his turn on the wheel of fortune; in about a year's time he was Secretary of State and leader of the House of Commons. Lady Ailesbury shows in all the letters she wrote to her relations at this time how proud she was of her husband. Burke's laudation of him made her very happy. It was in his celebrated speech of April 19, 1774, that he said of General Conway, who was then leading the House of Commons : 'We all felt inspired by the action he gave us. I remember, sir, with a melancholy pleasure, the situation of the honourable gentleman who made the motion for the repeal, in that crisis, when the whole trading interest of this empire crowded into your lobbies with a trembling and anxious expectation . . . when, at length, you had determined in their favour, and, your doors thrown open, shewed them the figure of their deliverer in the well-earned triumph of his important victory, from the whole of that grave multitude there arose an involuntary burst of gratitude and transport. They jumped upon him like children on a long absent father. All England, all America joined in his applause, nor did he seem insensible to the best of all earthly rewards, the love and admiration of his fellow citizens. "Hope elevated, and joy brightened his crest." I stood near him, and his face, to use the expression of the Scripture, was as if it had been the face of an angel. I do not know how others feel, but if I had stood in that situation, I never would have exchanged it for all that kings in their profusion could bestow.'

Lady Ailesbury was very fond of visiting foreign countries, and took every opportunity that offered itself of accompanying her husband abroad. Though travelling was a somewhat serious undertaking in those days, its difficulties never seemed to deter her. In 1758 she went with him to Sluys, where he was sent ' to settle a cartel with the French.' Colonel Conway in describing their journey says : 'We crept over the sea in four tedious days, and from thence stepped immediately into a bilander, which bilander is a certain vast fresh-water machine answering one's idea of the ark, fitted with just such a motley complement, Dutch, English, German, Flemish, Civil, Military, male, female, dogs, cats, &c., but all, in appearance, of the unclean kind. In this agreeable conveyance we were dragged by two lean Flanders mares up a narrow canal, and then a melancholy flat to Bruges. . . . The next day, we changed our amphibious vehicle for its counterpart upon wheels, very improperly called a " Diligence," which brought us five or six leagues in twice as many hours, to Ghent.'

In 1761 Lady Ailesbury's husband, now a general, was sent to join the British army serving with Prince Ferdinand of Brunswick, and commanded the centre. On Lord Granby's return to England, General Conway was left in charge of the English army and took up his winter quarters at Osnaburg, where he was joined by Lady Ailesbury. This same year she went to Holland with him, and stayed at the Hague and at Amsterdam. Lady Ailesbury's constant companion there was Lady George Lennox, whose husband was also with the army in Holland. She was a daughter of Lord Ancrum, afterwards fourth Marquis of Lothian, and two years before had eloped with Lord George to Gretna Green, where they were married by the blacksmith,[1] Lord Ancrum having refused his consent. The marriage turned out thoroughly satisfactory, and their son became fourth Duke of Richmond. The Conways did not return to England till the conclusion of the peace in February 1763.

---

[1] They were also married in the orthodox manner at Dumfries. Lady George Lennox survived till 1830, when she died, aged ninety-four, clever and sharp to the last. She was then called Lady Louisa Lennox.

Some of the more prudish ladies in London society disapproved of these devoted wives following their husbands. Mrs. Scott, the sister of Mrs. Montagu, the blue-stocking, writes at this time as follows : ' Report says that the Duchess of Richmond and some others, whose husbands are going or gone to Germany, are going there likewise, and are to lie at Brunswick. I much question whether their husbands will rejoice in their company, but certainly Prince Ferdinand will not be fond of such auxiliaries. It is the oddest party of pleasure I ever heard of. Diaforus, who invites his mistress to the lively amusement of making one at a Dissection, would be an agreeable lover to these ladies. . . . Perhaps they think Germany may afford them more of their husband's company than they can obtain in England, for some among them would think that a valuable acquisition, and possibly they may not be mistaken, for a drum that leads to battle may not be so powerful a rival to a wife as one that leads its followers only to coquetry.' This, however, was not applicable either to the Conways or to the George Lennoxes, both couples being proverbially attached to each other.

Lady Ailesbury's first visit to Paris was in 1774–75, when she passed the winter there. In Mercy-Argenteau's letters to Marie Thérèse, he tells us masked balls were given by Marie Antoinette at this time every Monday, when country dances took place in Norwegian and Lapland dress ; amongst the dancers was ' Milady Elsbury,' otherwise Lady Ailesbury. She was accompanied by her daughter, Mrs. Damer, and Lady Harriet Stanhope, and was joined by General Conway. The latter had been spending the months of July and August in Germany, whither he went for the purpose of attending some of the reviews of Frederick the Great. On his way he stopped at Celle to pay his respects to the unfortunate Queen Matilda of Denmark.   In writing from Potsdam to his brother, Lord Hertford, General Conway describes his interview with Frederick.   He says : ' The King gave me a most flattering audience of more than half an hour and talked on a great variety of things with an ease and freedom the very reverse of what I had been made to expect. His music still takes up a great share of his time.   On a table in his cabinets there, I saw, I believe, twenty boxes with a German flute in each ; in his Bed-chamber and Cabinet three arm-chairs in a row for three favourite dogs, each with a little stool by way of step that the getting up might be easy.[1]   I saw the Foot-guards exercise, especially the splendid First Battalion ; I could have conceived nothing so perfect and so great as all I saw : so well dressed, such men, and so punctual in all they did.'   A month later he describes to his brother the manœuvres near Breslau.   He writes : ' The beauty and order of the troops, their great discipline, &c., almost pass belief.   I can't say how much I am obliged to his Majesty for his extraordinary reception and distinction shown me throughout.   Each day after the manœuvre he held a little Levée at which I can assure you it is not an exaggeration of vanity to say that he not only talked to me but literally to nobody else at all.   He also called me up, and spoke to me several times on horseback when we were out, which he seldom did to anybody.'

Lady Ailesbury and her husband became great favourites in French society, and made many friendships.   Mme. de Deffand, whose flattering opinion of Lady Ailesbury we have already given, writes of the General: ' Savez-vous combien il connaît déjà de personnes dans Paris ?   Quatre-vingt-six !   Il

---

[1] The last thing the great Frederick said shortly before his death was to tell an attendant to throw a covering over one of his dogs who appeared to be cold.

n'est nullement sauvage.' Lady Ailesbury, who, we know on
Horace Walpole's authority, had a great love of dress, writes
a most amusing account of the extravagant lengths, or rather
we should say heights, that the Parisian fashions had reached.
There was a story current at the time that Lady Ailesbury on
her return to London found that the Duchess of Devonshire
had still the highest feathers ; upon which she tried to get one
higher, without success, till she luckily thought of sending to
an undertaker. He sent word that his hearses were all out,
but they were expected home in a few days, and then he hoped
to accommodate her ladyship.

Many of Lady Ailesbury's French friends visited England,
and all were cordially welcomed and hospitably entertained by
her and General Conway ; and she also met them at the house
of her son-in-law, the Duke of Richmond, who had been
Ambassador at Paris. In 1783 Lady Ailesbury says there was
an ' Anglomanie.' The attractions of Newmarket brought over
that year the Ducs de Chartres, de Coigny, de FitzJames, and
de Polignac. The Duc de Bouillon also came to England
about this time. He called himself Mr. Godfrey and tried to
pass as an Englishman. Horace Walpole said : ' He would do
better to call himself " the Duke of Mutton Broth." ' The
' Anglomanie,' however, began before this. In 1772 Lady Mary
Coke wrote to Lady Ailesbury that a large party had arrived
from France composed of persons of great distinction, amongst
whom she mentions the Duc and Duchesse de Rochechouart
Mortemart, a family celebrated for their wit.[1] The party stayed
in England three months, and went to Bath under the auspices

---

[1] The family of Mortemart, of whom Mme. Montespan was a member, was so
celebrated for keen and polished wit that similar talent was, at one time, universally
called ' l'esprit de Mortemart.'

of Lord March. Mme. de Genlis says : ' Ce furent les philosophistes, et surtout M. de Voltaire, qui répandirent en France l'anglomanie, qui devint si générale sur la fin du dernier siècle . . . les femmes ne portaient plus que des robes à l'anglaise, des popelines, des moires, des toiles, du linon d'Angleterre ; elles vendaient leurs diamans pour acheter des petits grains d'acier et des verreries anglaises ; la poterie anglaise faisait dédaigner la porcelaine de Sèvres ; on reléguait dans les gardes-meubles les magnifiques tapisseries des Gobelins pour y substituer du papier bleu anglais ; on renonçait à toute conversation pour passer les soirées à prendre du thé et à manger des tartines de beurre, on culbutait les beaux jardins de La Nôtre ; on contournait nos majestueuses allées, à perte de voie ; on détruisait nos bassins et nos jets d'eau ; on creusait de petits ruisseaux bourbeux, honorés du nom de rivières, on surchargeait nos parcs de ponts, d'ermitages, de mines, de tombeaux ; nos jeunes gens allaient passer huit jours à Londres pour y apprendre à penser.   Le résultat de cette étude était de raccourcir les étriers de leurs chevaux, de hausser le siège de leurs cochers, et, dans la société, de terminer toutes les discussions par un pari.   Enfin, on métamorphosa des champs de verdure en tapis de jeu ; on établit des courses de chevaux, on se ruina, on perdit toutes les habitudes nationales, on se moqua de l'ancienne galanterie, de l'ancienne politesse, on cessa d'être français.'

In the summer of 1787 the charming Princesse de Lamballe[1] came to England, nominally for her health. She suffered terribly from her nerves, and was always trying some new *régime*.   A bunch of violets or the sight of a crayfish, even in a

---

[1] Marie Thérèse, Princesse de Savoie Carignan, born at Turin 1749, married in 1792, when she was seventeen, the Prince de Lamballe, son of the Duc de Penthièvre, and became a widow at the age of nineteen.

picture, made her faint.   Mme. de Genlis,[1] who hated her, pretended that these faints were simulated, and talks most satirically
of the Princess's visit to Mr. Hope's collection of pictures
in Holland, where she fainted at the sight of a Flemish
picture representing women selling lobsters.   Bachaumont says
the Princess came to England to induce M. de Calonne to
withdraw from his ' Mémoires' certain statements regarding
Queen Marie Antoinette ; and this may have been the case, as
not only was Calonne in England at this time, but the infamous
wretch, Mme. de la Motte, his mistress, who had been flogged
and branded for her share in the Collier de la Reine affair, was
also there.[2]

Lady Ailesbury was much with the Princesse de Lamballe
during this visit, and accompanied her on sundry sightseeing
expeditions.   One of these was to see the Royal Military Academy at Woolwich, and a field day of the Royal Artillery ; and
another to go over a man-of-war, the Duke of Richmond (Lady
Ailesbury's son-in-law) conducting the party.   We also hear from
Lady Ailesbury of a sumptuous dinner given to the Princess by
the Duke of Queensberry,[3] to which Lady Ailesbury was invited.

---

[1] Mme. de Genlis was necessarily often in the company of the Princesse de
Lamballe, being *gouvernante* to the children of the Duchesse d'Orléans, her
sister-in-law, the daughter of the Duc de Penthièvre.

[2] Jeanne de Luz de St. Rémy married Monsieur de la Motte ; she called herself Comtesse de Valois, because she was descended from a natural son of Henri II.
She was marked on the shoulder with a ' V,' for *voleuse*, and condemned for life to
confinement in the Salpêtrière, but managed to escape from the latter place and came
to London.   Once when she was playing at piquet with Calonne, the ex-minister
said, ' Madame, vous êtes marquée.'   She took this as a *double entente*, and got into
the most violent rage.   She upset the table, threw herself upon Calonne, and
scratched his face.   Her last days were spent in abject poverty ; and her death,
which took place in London in August 1791, was the result of her having thrown
herself out of the window.   She was buried at St. Mary's, Lambeth.

[3] The Duke of Queensberry was a star of fashion, and his dress, carriages,
&c. considered as models, and he was the best gentleman jockey of his day ; but
he was a notorious profligate, and it is said that when he died, at the age of

In June 1791 [1]. the Princesse de Lamballe came again to England, having settled with her august mistress to do so simultaneously with the flight to Varennes. She arrived in England with her two ladies, Mmes. de Ginestons and de Lâge, and their husbands and one child. Queen Charlotte and the royal princesses received her with gracious cordiality ; and this time, though the Princess went to Bath and to Brighthelmstone for her health, she certainly had an ulterior motive for her visit of paramount importance, which was to try and get the protection of the English Government for the French Monarchy. Her correspondence with Marie Antoinette at this time, in complicated cipher, is all about this confidential mission.[2] Marie Antoinette hated Pitt, and said to Mme. Campan : ' Je ne prononce pas le nom de Pitt que la petite mort ne me passe dans le dos ; cet homme est l'ennemi mortel de la France. Pitt a servi la Révolution française dès les premiers troubles.[3] Je veux essayer de savoir jusqu'où il compte nous mener, et pour cela j'envoie à Londres M——. Il a été intimement lié avec Pitt ; je veux qu'il le fasse parler, au moins autant que peut parler un pareil homme.' Mme. Campan goes on to say that shortly after the Queen said to her that her envoy had returned from London, and that all he had been able to extract from Pitt was that he would not allow the French Monarchy to perish, ' but,' added Marie Antoinette, ' il a gardé le plus absolu silence

eighty-five, his bed was covered with *billets doux* which he had not the strength to open ! Under the name of ' Old Q ' he was the subject of many satires.

[1] It is singular that in Lescure's *Life of the Princesse de Lamballe* the visit to England in 1787 is not mentioned, only the visit in 1791 ; whilst in Bertin's Life the former is mentioned and not the latter.

[2] *Correspondances inédites*, Campan.

[3] And yet in Fouquier-Tinville's speech for the prosecution of Mme. Du Barry he says that ' all the conspiracies of tyrants, nobles, and priests against the French Republic, march under the orders of Pitt ; ' and one of the charges against Mme. Du Barry was living habitually with Pitt, whose effigy she wore on a silver medal.

sur ce qui concerne le monarque.'   The Princesse de Lamballe
was told to cultivate the acquaintance of the Duchess of Gordon,
who was supposed to possess more influence than any woman in
England—in order to learn the sentiments of Mr. Pitt.   It was
to further this mission that the Princesse de Lamballe applied to
the Duke of Richmond.   Lady Ailesbury had her son-in-law to
meet the Princess more than once, but he was unable to help her.
At the end of four months, in October 1791, the Princesse de
Lamballe entreated to be allowed to join the Queen, but Marie
Antoinette always wrote to her not to come.   'Non, encore
une fois non ; ne revenez pas, mon cher cœur, ne vous jetez pas
dans la gueule du tigre.'   The Princess, however, insisted upon
returning, and was one of the first victims.   In August 1792
she followed the Royal Family to the Temple and was massacred
on September 3.

Another Frenchwoman, of a very different type, paid no less
than four visits to England in the years 1791–92.[1]   This was
Mme. Du Barry ; and during one of these visits Lady Ailesbury often met her at public entertainments, such as Ranelagh,
Vauxhall, &c., and she also met her at a 'rural breakfast' given by
Mrs. Hobart, and at a party given by the Duke of Queensberry.
Lady Ailesbury did not admire her looks very much, and agreed
with Horace Walpole, who said she was 'pretty, when you consider her, yet so little striking that I never should have asked
who she was.'   One must remember, however, that Mme. Du
Barry was at the time forty-eight years [2] of age, so that of course
her beauty was on the wane.   Mme. Du Barry came to England

[1] The expenses of Mme. Du Barry's second visit to London, which lasted less
than six weeks, amounted to the large sum of £15,059 8s. 9d.

[2] The following is the entry of her birth in the register of the church at
Vaucouleurs : ' Jeanne, natural daughter of Anne Becu, sometimes called Quartigny,
was born August 19, 1743, and was baptised the same day, &c.   L. Galon, Vicar
of Vaucouleurs.'

to try and recover her jewels of great value, which were stolen from her château of Louveciennes in January 1791,[1] whilst she was attending a grand fête given by the Duc de Brissac in the Rue de Grenelle. The jewels had been taken to London, where the thieves were arrested ; but after a long delay they were ultimately acquitted, the robbery not having been committed within English jurisdiction. The diamonds which were recovered were placed in the bank of Messrs. Ransom, Morland, & Hammersley. Mme. Du Barry never regained possession of them, but it appears from recent investigations that they were removed by some one from the custody of the bankers. According to H. Noel Williams, the author of a 'History of Mme. Du Barry published 1905, the jewels were sold by order of the Court of Chancery at the end of the following year, and the proceeds of the sale, 13,300 guineas, were paid over to Mme. de Boissaisson (her niece) and some creditors.

Mme. Du Barry stayed in Bruton Street from May till the end of August in 1792, and it was during this visit that Lady Ailesbury met her. She paid a fourth and last visit to England in October of the same year, and remained till March 1, 1793. Owing to the recent tragic death of her friend, the Duc de Brissac, who was brutally murdered by the populace at Versailles, she went nowhere, excepting to see some of the *émigrés*, notably M. Crussol, M. de Cahouet, M. de Calonne, M. d'Aiguillon, and the Prince de Poix.[2] Lady Ailesbury also saw her at the funeral service held at the Spanish Embassy Chapel in memory

---

[1] Her jewels were carried off by three German Jews, a Frenchman, and an Englishman named Harris.

[2] The Prince de Poix was son of the Maréchal and Maréchale de Mouchy, who were both guillotined in July 1794. He bribed two members of the Commune, Martin and Danjon, and escaped as he was being conducted to the Abbaye Prison. (Matimer-Ternaux, t. iv. p. 443.)

of Louis XVI., Mme. Du Barry's presence there being one of the accusations brought against her at her trial.   At the end of four months she returned to Paris, notwithstanding the warning of her friends, and six months later she was arrested, though soon set at liberty, and then might have saved her life if she had gone back to England ; but she had now started another love affair, with the Comte de Rohan Chabot,[1] and refused to go.   She was re-arrested, and shortly afterwards guillotined, attaining at her death the unenviable notoriety of having been, it is said, the only woman in those dreadful days who showed abject terror.

Lady Ailesbury had entertained at different times the Vicomte and the Marquis de St. Chamant, the Baron de Montesquieu, the Luxembourgs, the Lusignans, the de Guisnes, Mme. d'Hénin, the Duchesse d'Ayen, the Comtesse de Boufflers, the Duchesse de Gramont, the Duchesse du Châtelet, the Comtesse de Noailles (Dame d'Honneur to Marie Antoinette, who called her ' Mme. Etiquette ') and her husband, the Duc de Mouchy, the Duc de Cossé-Brissac, and the Duc and Duchesse de Biron (better known in England under the name of Lauzun).   All of these perished in the Revolution, and one can therefore well realise how vividly the horrors of those awful days must have come home to her.[2]   She was specially intimate with the Duchesse de

[1] Alexandre Louis Auguste de Rohan Chabot, afterwards Duc de Rohan, born 1761, died 1816, greatgrandfather of the present Duc de Rohan. (See Addenda, p. 334.)

[2] The Maréchal Philippe de Noailles, Duc de Mouchy, his wife, their sister-in-law the Duchesse de Noailles, their daughter-in-law the Duchesse d'Ayen, and their granddaughter the Vicomtesse de Noailles, all perished at the same time. The Duchesse de Gramont and the Duchesse du Châtelet were at first detained in the large hotel kept by the mad doctor, Belhomme, where also were the Talleyrand-Périgords, Mme. la Duchesse d'Orléans, the Rochechouarts, the Nicolaïs, and the Demoiselles Lange et Mezerai, actresses of the Théâtre Français. This was an arrangement of Fouquier-Tinville, who, when the prisons were so gorged with prisoners that they could hold no more, established auxiliary places of confinement for those who he thought could pay for this privilege.

Biron, *née* de Boufflers. This lady had a long illness when paying a visit at Goodwood ; and Lady Ailesbury, as well as her daughter the Duchess of Richmond, assisted by Madame de Cambis, helped to nurse her. When sufficiently well, the Duchesse de Biron insisted, notwithstanding the entreaties of Lady Ailesbury, upon returning to Paris, where she was almost immediately arrested, set at liberty through the intervention of her husband,[1] re-arrested at the end of 1793 and confined in the Couvent des Anglaises. There she found the old Maréchale de Biron, *née* La Rochefoucauld. After many weeks, an order came for ' Citoyenne Biron ' to appear before the Tribunal. ' Which ? ' asked the gaoler, and he sent up both, and both were sentenced and executed. The Duchess's worthless husband became an avowed Republican, but was afterwards suspected, seized by the Convention, and ordered to execution. He was allowed an hour's respite, and,

Both he and Dr. Belhomme found it a very good speculation as every one tried to get there. As long as they were able to pay the exorbitant prices their lives were safe, but as soon as they came to the end of their resources they were transferred to the common prisons and soon condemned. 'En vérité,' Mme. du Châtelet said one day to Belhomme, 'vous n'êtes pas raisonnable et il m'est, à mon vif regret, impossible de vous satisfaire.' 'Allons, ma grosse,' answered Belhomme, 'sois bonne fille, je te ferai remise d'un quart ;' but even this she and her friend the Duchesse de Gramont could not pay ; they had to leave the establishment, and a few days after were guillotined, Belhomme remarking 'que ces dames périssaient victimes d'une économie mal entendue.' The Duchesse de Gramont behaved heroically ; she never tried to defend herself before the terrible Tribunal, but only thought of Mme. du Châtelet, whom she had advised to return to France. She replied to her judges : ' Je ne veux pas me défendre, mais cette ange qui est auprès de moi n'a pris aucune part aux affaires politiques, sa vie et son caractère suffisent à la justifier : condamnez-moi et laissez la vivre.' ' N'as-tu pas envoyé de l'argent aux émigrés ? ' demanda un des juges. ' Je pourrais dire non,' answered the Duchesse, 'mais ma vie ne vaut pas un mensonge.' The two friends perished the same day.

[1] At the end of 1790 the Duchesse de Biron was at the play in Paris, when a song applicable to the Queen was encored ; she applauded with her fan on the box, and was pelted with a shower of apples, and a penknife with them, that nearly hit her. She brought it away and sent it to La Fayette, telling him to lay it on the altar of Liberty.

on returning to his dungeon, sent for oysters and white wine, and drank to the health of the turnkey and the executioner when they came to tell him they could wait no longer.

Some of Lady Ailesbury's French acquaintances were wise enough to take refuge in England, and in 1791–92 there was quite a colony of them established on Richmond Green, where she often went to visit them. Mme. de Cambis remained there till her death in January 1809.[1] She was a most delightful and attractive woman, and often stayed at Park Place, and, as Horace Walpole says, 'doted on Lady Ailesbury and her daughters.' Sir Gilbert Elliot, writing in 1793, says: 'Paid a visit at Richmond to Mme. de Cambis, an old lady of high rank and a remarkably sensible and agreeable woman, whom I saw every morning for six months at Mme. du Deffand's when Douglas and I were together at Paris.' Amongst the fugitives were the Princesse de Poix, the Princesse d'Hénin,[2] Mme. de Fleury, Mme. de Coigny, Mme. de Simiane, the young Duc de Richelieu, the Comtesse de Boufflers and her daughter-in-law, Comtesse Emilie de Boufflers. Sometimes Lady Ailesbury remained the evening with them, to play 'Loto' and listen to Comtesse Emilie's harp-playing. The following year—1793—many more *émigrés* of distinction arrived in London, amongst whom Lady Ailesbury mentions the Comtesse de Montault-Navaille and her daughter Joséphine, accompanied by M. de St. Blancard; Vicomte de Gontaut-Biron (whom Mdlle. Joséphine

---

[1] Gabrielle Charlotte Françoise, Vicomtesse de Cambis, was a sister of the Prince de Chimay and of the Prince d'Hénin. Horace Walpole describes having seen her at the Convent of St. Cyr in 1769, 'beautiful as a Madonna.'

[2] Etiennette de Montconseil, daughter of the Marquis de Montconseil (married in 1766 to Charles, Prince d'Hénin, captain of the Bodyguard to the Comte d'Artois), was Dame du Palais to Marie Antoinette. She was rescued from Paris by Mme. de Staël and sent to an hotel in Downing Street. Lally-Tollendal was supposed to be privately married to her.

married during their stay in England), the Comte de Noé, the Duc de Gramont, M. de l'Aigle, the Prince de la Trémouille, Comtes Boson and Archambaut de Périgord, and the Prince and Princesse de Léon. The latter, who was a very hand-some woman, held a salon, which was largely attended by the English *élite*; and Lady Ailesbury was often there, where she met the Beauvaus,[1] M. d'Haussonville and his friend M. d'Aramon, the FitzJameses, Mortemarts, and the Duc d'Harcourt.[2] The Princesse de Léon was not the only *émigrée* who entertained. 'On riait au nez de la fortune,' as Chateaubriand said; and many of them, after working for their bread during the day, met together in the evening and danced. The Duchesse de St. James entertained all the best company, and when any one was invited to dine with her it was an understood thing that they left three shillings in a cup which was on the mantelpiece! At other dinner parties each of the guests brought a dish, and at a tea party every one brought their own sugar.

In '93 Lady Ailesbury became acquainted with Mme. de Staël, but did not appreciate her, and said that she well understood a *bon mot* of Talleyrand which was often quoted at this time: ' Il faut avoir aimé Mme. de Staël pour connaître le bonheur d'aimer une bête.'[3] Mme. de Staël was now at the head of another colony of illustrious French exiles, established at Juniper Hall, Mickleham, near Dorking, Mr. Jenkinson's house. These were 'les Con-stitutionnels,' and included M. de Lally-Tollendal, Mathieu

---

[1] Marc Etienne Gabrielle de Beauvau, Prince de Craon, and his wife, Natalie de Mortemart, took up their residence at King's Wick, Sunninghill; and here their son, Charles François Victurnien, was born, March 7, 1793.

[2] All of these were living at Staines and in the neighbourhood. M. d'Hausson-ville taught Latin to the children of his friend the Duchesse de Mortemart.

[3] He had been on intimate terms with Mme. de Staël, and had given up her society for that of Mme. Grandt, who was quite a fool. M. Grandt was a native of Lausanne.

Duc de Montmorency, M. de Jancourt, Guibert, the Vicomte and Vicomtesse de Narbonne,[1] the Marquise de la Châtre,[2] M. de Girardin, and General d'Arblay ; and M. de Talleyrand[3] often visited there.   Juniper Hall was very near Norbury Park, the owner of which—Mr. Locke,[4] a man of great taste and cultivation —was most hospitable to the French refugees ; and a daily inter- course took place between the two houses, one result of which was the happy though highly improvident marriage[5] of General d'Arblay with Miss Fanny Burney, the authoress of 'Evelina,' who spent a great deal of her time with the Lockes.

Lady Ailesbury was one of those who, in answer to Mme. d'Arblay's appeal, subscribed for the poor French ecclesiastics, of whom there were 6,000 in England, besides 800 in Jersey, in utter want.[6]   She also took part in getting up a bazaar for the benefit of the poor French ladies, and, indeed, she never lost an opportunity of showing her sympathy with the French in their terrible time of trial.   On April 8, 1795, she was present at the funeral service for Marie Antoinette which took place at the Spanish Ambassador's chapel in Manchester Square.

[1] The Vicomte de Narbonne was son of Comte de Narbonne by Mme. Victoire, daughter of Louis XV.   The Comtesse de Narbonne saved the Princess from disgrace and declared the child was hers.   Mme. Victoire survived till June 1799 ; her last days were spent in anguish.   She and her sister, Mme. Adélaïde, were turned out of Rome and Naples and were obliged to take refuge in a small vessel at anchor.   Mme. Victoire died twenty days after her release.

[2] Mme. de la Châtre returned to Paris, and was guillotined in 1794.

[3] Talleyrand had escaped from Paris in 1792, and came to England accom- panied by the French minister, Chauvelin, and lived in Kensington Square.

[4] Mr. Locke bought Norbury Park in 1774.   There appears to be some mystery as to his parentage, and I believe it was said of him that 'he was every one's father and no man's son.'   Amongst the friends he entertained at Norbury were Dr. Johnson Sir Joshua Reynolds, Burke, and Gibbon.

[5] The d'Arblays could only scrape together £100 per annum, and settled in a cottage in Norbury Park.

[6] Monsignor l'Evêque de St. Pol de Léon was accepted as the primate of the emigrant priests.

The last time we have any account of Lady Ailesbury's appearance at a public function was when she went on April 8, 1795, to St. James's Palace, first to see the procession of the Prince of Wales to the Chapel Royal on the occasion of his marriage with Princess Caroline of Brunswick, and afterwards to the Drawing Room. Lady Ailesbury took with her the Ladies Maria and Louisa Stuart,[1] her cousins, daughters of the first Marquis of Bute. They went in chairs to the Palace a little before seven. At eleven the procession arrived from the Chapel Royal, and after that there was the Drawing Room in the great Council Chamber. Lady Ailesbury says the Princess looked in high spirits, but not so the Prince. The Princess's train was borne by four young ladies—Ladies Mary Osborne, Charlotte Spencer, Charlotte Legge, and Caroline Villiers. Lady Ailesbury particularly admired the latter, whom she described as 'a most beautiful girl.' She little thought that the said young lady would ultimately, *en secondes noces*, become the wife of her nephew George, Lord Lorne, afterwards sixth Duke of Argyll. After the Drawing Room, Lady Ailesbury and the Ladies Stuart supped at Mrs. Herbert's, the Bedchamber woman ; Lord and Lady Carnarvon, Lady Jane Herbert, Lord Porchester, Mr. C. Herbert, Lady Townshend, Lord Malmesbury, and Miss Bruhl making up the rest of the party. Lady Ailesbury did not get home till one, rather a long outing for an old lady of seventy-four.

Although, on the whole, the life of Lady Ailesbury was a happy and prosperous one, she had some great troubles. Her son-in-law, Mr. Damer, as the sequel of a short and dissolute life, shot himself in a tavern. She had the sorrow of losing her charming eldest daughter, Mary, Duchess of Richmond, in

---

[1] Lady Louisa Stuart has been brought before the public of late by the publication of her clever letters.

1796 ;[1] and she also survived Marshal Conway, who died at Park Place very suddenly in 1795,[2] thus losing a husband who, in the words of Horace Walpole, 'living and dying thought only of her.' Without him the joys of Park Place were gone, and Lady Ailesbury sold it the following year to Lord Malmesbury, and subsequently made her home with her daughter Mrs. Damer. Two years later Lady Ailesbury had to mourn over the loss of her lifelong friend, Horace Walpole. Still she lived on into the next century, 'the picture,' as Miss Berry writes in 1799, 'of what an old woman ought to be and so seldom is.' She died on January 17, 1803, at her daughter's house in Upper Brook Street, after a few days' illness, in her eighty-third year.[3] Mrs.

[1] Horace Walpole writing in November 1796: 'I had loved the Duchess of Richmond most affectionately from the moment I first knew her, when she was but five years old ; her sweet temper and unalterable good nature had made her retain a friendship for and confidence in me that was more steady than I ever found in any other person to whom I have been the most attached. It is a heavy blow. I had flattered myself the last time I saw her, five months ago, for she came to me twice when I was so extremely ill last winter, that she would recover. She has languished ever since, suffered terribly, as much as could be discovered under her invincible patience and silence ; but she is gone, and I am still here, though above twenty years older ! The Duke, who is exceedingly afflicted, and retains all her servants, and pensioned them all for their lives, has sent me, as the dear soul had desired him, one of her own rings. I can never put it on my swelled fingers, but I will for ever carry it about me while there is any *for ever for me* !'

[2] Field-Marshal Conway went from his house in Soho Square to Park Place the preceding day, apparently in good health. He was seized at three o'clock in the morning with cramp in the stomach, which proved fatal at five. The following character of Marshal Conway which appeared in Lord Orford's works, but which Miss Berry owned came from her hand, says : 'It is only those who, like the editor, have had the opportunity of penetrating into the most secret motives of his (Marshal Conway's) public conduct, and into the inmost recesses of his private life, who can do real justice to the unsullied purity of his character—who saw and knew him in the evening of his days, retired from the honourable activity of a soldier and of a statesman to the calm enjoyments of private life ; happy in the resources of his own mind, and in cultivation of useful science, in the bosom of domestic peace—unenriched by pensions or places, undistinguished by titles or ribbons, unsophisticated by public life and unwearied by retirement.'

[3] Lady Ailesbury was buried at Sundridge Church, where there is a bust of her executed by her daughter, Mrs. Damer.

FIELD MARSHAL THE HON. HENRY SEYMOUR CONWAY.

Damer writes to Miss Berry the day after her death as follows:
' My dearest, kindest of mothers expired yesterday morning
without a groan, even without a sigh ; her countenance became
placid and her fine features made her beautiful in death.   Such,
I am convinced, can be the end only of one possessing a virtuous
mind and a conscience without reproach, and such a one, I am
proud to think, was my mother !   A scene more affecting, more
impressive than her end it was not possible to see, and much as
I ever thought I should regret this dear mother, I find that
regret deeper and more painful than I expected.   All the
arrangements—every little improvement at Strawberry Hill—
this house, all (sometimes imperceptibly at the moment to myself)
tended wholly to procure her amusement and comforts, and all
these have lost their value to me.   Never more to behold that
benign countenance brightening up at the sight of me : this
does give me the feeling of an almost broken heart.'

LINES UPON THE LATE

COUNTESS DOWAGER OF AILESBURY

Thou Heav'n-born Saint, with ev'ry virtue crown'd
That could adorn thy Sex, and give renown
To polish'd manners, not disgraced by art,
But flowing from the fountain of the heart :
A heart replete with tenderness, tho' firm,
Did all the actions of her life confirm ;
Where gentle sweetness ever was the guide
To Rectitude's unerring, powerful tide :
Blessed with that calm Philosophy to cure
Those ills, by Patience, which we must endure,
Her lively wit with satire ever glow'd,
Tho' check'd by better feelings as it flow'd ;
The scourge of vice alone was sure her aim,
Since unexampled worth secures her fame.

THE HON. MRS. DAMER

David ne'er touched the harp like thee,
Anson ne'er saw thy like at Sea,[1]
Mansfield's eloquence is not like thine,
Edgecumbe, who thinks thee all divine,
Records his passion with this line.
Lord Mount Edgecumbe, on Mrs. Damer.

IF Mrs. Damer did not fully inherit the conspicuous beauty of her grandmother Mary Bellenden, or her mother Lady Ailesbury, she possessed much of their fascination, and certainly exceeded them both in talent and acquirements.

Born in 1748, Anne Seymour Conway passed most of her childhood at Strawberry Hill under the care of Horace Walpole, who bestowed upon her the affection he had always felt for her father, Marshal Conway. She appears to have shown great intelligence at a very early age ; and when she was only four, Horace Walpole writes to her parents : ' I shall tell you some stories of her understanding that will please you.' He took great pains with her education, and she became a most cultivated and accomplished woman. She was thoroughly conversant with the best English, French, and Italian authors, and had a good knowledge of Latin ; Homer, Herodotus, Plutarch,

---

[1] This is in allusion to her conduct in 1772, when the packet in which she was crossing from Dover to Ostend was taken by a French frigate after a fight of four hours. She appears to have shown extraordinary coolness and courage.

THE HON. MRS. DAMER, *née* ANNE SEYMOUR CONWAY.

Cicero, and Livy were amongst her favourite authors. Her taste for letters continued with her to the last, and she eventually possessed one of the best selected and most valuable libraries ever formed by a female collector. When she was eighteen a casual occurrence induced her to take to modelling, for which always after she had a passion. It arose in the following way. She used to be a great deal with David Hume when he was at her father's house acting as his secretary, and notwithstanding the great disparity of their ages, he conversed and reasoned with her on all subjects. One day, when she was with him in her father's library discussing a book in which she was much interested, a little Italian boy, who was carrying about on a board some busts and models made in plaster of Paris, was brought in from the streets by her mother, Lady Ailesbury, who sent the boy into the library to show his busts. Hume, upon speaking to the boy, was so much struck with his vivacity and with the knowledge he showed concerning the manner in which his images were made, that he remained in conversation with him for a considerable time, till the patience of Anne Conway being exhausted, she exclaimed to Hume, 'How is it possible that so great a philosopher as you are should lose so much time in talking to a poor ignorant little boy?' Hume, smiling, replied : 'That little boy, so far from being ignorant, as you suppose, has a great deal of knowledge, and although his parents have not been able to lay out any money upon his education, he is more likely to become a distinguished sculptor than you are to become a distinguished woman, notwithstanding the large sums that have been laid out upon you. Be less severe ; these images were not made without the aid of both science and genius, and with all your attainments, you cannot produce such works.' Soon after, Hume received a head she had modelled in wax and subsequently executed in marble, which evoked his wonder and admiration. From that time she made sculpture her study and delight. She studied anatomy under Cruikshank, and learnt the technical part of working in marble in the atelier of Bacon. She also had lessons from the celebrated Ceracchi,[1] and subsequently worked in Italy.

Among those who sat to her were George III., Queen Caroline, Nelson, Fox, Dr. Darwin, Sir Joseph Banks, Sir Humphry Davy, the Duchess of Devonshire, Lady Melbourne, Miss Berry, Mrs. Siddons, the two Kembles, Miss Farren, &c. She had a singular taste for catching the character of animals, and modelled for her sister Mary, Duchess of Richmond, a group of two sleeping dogs, executed in marble, a beautiful piece of sculpture, now at Goodwood ; also a dog of Queen Charlotte's and two kittens belonging to Horace Walpole, which were so true to life and so characteristic that every one was able to recognise them. She cut the figure of the Osprey Eagle[2] in terra-cotta, which was in the gallery of Strawberry Hill, thus inscribed by Horace Walpole : ' Non me Praxiteles fecit, sed Anna Damer.'[3] And she modelled and executed in Portland stone two gigantic masks, representing Thame and Isis,[4] for

[1] Giuseppe Ceracchi was guillotined in Paris in 1801. Ceracchi executed a statue of Mrs. Damer holding ' Isis ' in her hands. There is a similar one in the British Museum.

[2] *Horace Walpole to Lady Ossory.*—' Mrs. Damer has given me her eagle, which I call *the spoilt child* of my antique one, it is in such a passion. I hope your ladyship will approve of the motto I design for it. Do you remember the statue at Milan, with this legend, " Non me Praxiteles, sed Marcus finxit Agrati "? Mine is to be this pentameter, " Non me Praxiteles finxit, at Anna Damer." ' An osprey eagle was caught at Brocket Hall when Mrs. Damer was staying with Lord Melbourne, and in taking it one of its wings was almost cut off. Mrs. Damer saw it in that momentary rage which she executed exactly.

[3] The nymph's face for Isis was taken from Mrs. Freeman of Fawley Court.

[4] Her ' Cupid catching a Butterfly ' was much admired in the exhibition at Somerset House in 1784.

the keystones of the middle arch of the stone bridge over the Thames at Henley, close to Park Place, her father's residence. She was also a proficient with the brush. There is a picture painted by her at Panshanger, in which portraits of Lady Melbourne, Georgina Duchess of Devonshire, and herself appear.

She was a very clever actress, and as an amateur had few equals. She was one of the leading lights of the Duke of Richmond's celebrated company, and contributed largely to its unequalled success. Miss Farren superintended the rehearsals, and Mrs. Siddons deigned to act with Mrs. Damer. She appeared with unbounded applause in the character of ' Violante ' in ' The Wonder,' when Lord Henry Fitzgerald supported the part of ' Don Felix.' Her ' Mrs. Lovemore ' in ' The Way to keep him,' and her ' Lady Freelove ' in the ' Jealous Wife,' likewise created great admiration. In the ' Auckland Correspondence ' these theatricals are thus described in 1787 : ' The triumphs of the Duke of Richmond's private company in Privy Gardens, which begun in April and May, continued through the season, and were resumed in the winter, divide the attention of the town with the French commercial treaty, Warren Hastings, the Prince of Wales's debts, &c.'

Miss Conway married when she was twenty-one, on June 14, 1767, the Hon. John Damer, eldest son of Lord Milton (afterwards Lord Dorchester). His mother, Lady Caroline Sackville, was the daughter of the Duchess of Dorset, who was a great friend of Lady Ailesbury, as she had been of Mary Bellenden. A letter of Horace Walpole to Sir Horace Mann in March 1767 thus announces her engagement : ' Mr. Conway is in great felicity going to marry his only daughter to Lord Milton's eldest son. The estate in Lord Milton's possession is already £23,000 a year, 7 more just coming from the author of this wealth, an old uncle in Ireland. Lord Milton gives £5,000 a year at present and settles the rest. Miss Conway is to have a jointure of £2,500 and £500 pin money. Her fortune, which is £10,000, goes in jewels, equipages, and furniture.'

Notwithstanding his liberal allowance, Mr. Damer became immersed in debts, and at the end of nine years, his father refusing to pay them, he shot himself at the Bedford Arms, Covent Garden, on August 15, 1776. Horace Walpole, in a letter to Horace Mann on August 20, says : 'On Thursday Mr. Damer supped at the Bedford Arms with four ladies and a blind fiddler. At three in the morning he dismissed his seraglio, ordering his Orpheus to come up again in half an hour. When he returned he found a dead silence and smelt gunpowder : he called the master of the house, who came up and found Mr. Damer sitting in his chair, dead, with a pistol by him and another in his pocket. On the table lay a scrap of paper with these words : "The people of the house are not to blame for what has happened, which was my own act." What a catastrophe for a man at thirty-two, heir to two-and-twenty thousand a year ! We are persuaded that lunacy, not distress, was the sole cause of his fate. Lord Milton, whom nothing can soften, wreaks his fury on Mrs. Damer, though she deserves only pity, and shews no resentment. He insists on selling her jewels. This is all the hurt he can do her.' Mrs. Damer was on her way to London the very day of this catastrophe. Charles James Fox met her and stopped her to prepare her for the dismal event. It gives some notion of the extravagance of Mr. Damer when one reads that after his death his wardrobe sold for £15,000.

Soon after the death of her husband, Mrs. Damer, who was

ANGELICA KAUFFMANN, pinx

THE HON. MRS. DAMER.

then only twenty-eight years of age, went abroad with her aunt, Lady William Campbell, visiting Spain and Portugal, Italy and Paris. The War of Independence was going on, and the Channel was teeming with French and American men-of-war; and on their way to Ostend the packet in which they were crossing was taken by a French privateer after a running fight of four hours. 'La belle Anglaise,' as Mrs. Damer was called, was, however, soon liberated, and she won great *kudos* on this occasion by the intrepidity which she showed. *À propos* of Mrs. Damer's visit to Portugal, Horace Walpole writes: 'Mrs. Damer has been received at Elvas with all military honours and a banquet, by order of Mello, formerly Ambassador here. It was handsome in him, but must have distressed her who is so void of ostentation and love of show.' To Sir Horace Mann Horace Walpole writes to introduce her on her proposed journey to Italy, as follows: 'I will say very few words on her, after telling you that besides being General Conway's daughter, I love her as my own child. She has one of the most solid understandings I ever met, but with so much reserve and modesty that I have often told Mr. Conway he does not know the extent of her capacity, and the solidity of her reason. We have by accident discovered that she writes Latin like Pliny and is learning Greek. In Italy she will be a prodigy.' The celebrated Princess Dashkoff (or Daschkow), who made her acquaintance at Rome in 1780, writes of her as 'so justly celebrated for her skill in sculpture and no less to be admired for her profound information and good sense, which under the veil of a peculiar modesty sought rather the disguise than the display of her acquisitions.' And this same lady writes later from Naples as follows: 'Our morning pursuits were usually concluded in the studio of Mrs. Damer. There we generally found her employed with her chisel ; but this was a sanctum in which she received only her particular friends ; for her character was as devoid as possible of ostentation, and she made so little parade of her talents and learning that I remember one morning she was extremely disconcerted at my having observed a Greek work lying in her room, full of marginal annotations in her own handwriting.'[1]

Mrs. Damer being delicate continued to spend most of her winters abroad, and wrote an account of her travels, which she once thought of publishing, but unfortunately it was left to be burnt with the rest of her papers, so we have to fall back upon her letters. In November 1790 she writes from Lisbon : '. . . Nothing can be more civil and attentive than the people in general are to me here—Mr. Walpole, our Minister, and his wife in particular. On Monday in the evening Mrs. ——, wife of one of the Factory, sees company ; on Wednesday, a Portuguese house, the Marquis D'Abrantes, is open ; on Thursday, Mrs. Walpole ; on Friday, the Long room (an assembly and ball) ; on Saturday, the French Ambassadress ; and on Sunday the opera and a Portuguese play, if one chooses to go : *omnia habes*, except some dinners. . . . Yesterday I went to a concert and ball given by the Duc de Cadaval, the first nobleman of Portugal and a prince of the blood. . . . I have been learning Portuguese, and it only deserves the name of a dialect, and to those who have learned other languages is ridiculously easy.' Of the visit to Paris which she made in 1802 with her dear friend Miss Berry, we know something from private letters to her relations and from that lady's journal. It is curious now to read that ' to go from London to Dover

<hr>

[1] Princess Daschkoff was a good judge of talent and acquirements in others, as she was a most capable and clever woman. She was the friend and correspondent of Diderot, who had a high opinion of her intellect. In 1782 she was made Director of the Academy of Arts and Sciences in St. Petersburg, and she projected and executed the first Russian dictionary.

in one day would, at the best time of the year, be a very long day's journey,' and that they had to sleep at Sittingbourne. At Amiens they fell in with the peace 'négociateurs,' and met Joseph Buonaparte and his 'thin, very ugly, and very vulgar little wife, Maria Julia Clary,'[1] and Lord Cornwallis. Arrived in Paris, Mrs. Damer, who was not at all above caring for dress, and was always reputed to be both smart and well dressed,[2] carried off Miss Berry two days after their arrival to the great dressmaker of that date, Mme. Le Roi. Miss Berry says: 'She was very civil, and not at all pert ; but if she had anything pretty, treated us as *dames étrangères*, and showed us nothing that I should have liked to have worn, not on account of its singularity or youthfulness, but of its common vulgar look.' Mrs. Damer, of course, spent a good deal of time at the Gallery of the Louvre, where she met Mrs. Cosway, whom she knew intimately, and who, as well as her husband, had often painted her. It was equally a matter of course that Mrs. Damer should carry off Miss Berry to all the theatres. They saw Talma, but thought his voice rough, hoarse, and very disagreeable, and his 'squint against him.'

They met many old friends in Paris and brought letters of introduction to others, and received the greatest civility from all. They went into the society of the *nouveaux riches* as well as into that of the old world, and were immensely struck by the

---

[1] Julie Clary was the daughter of a rich tradesman in Marseille, where her father had made his fortune as a soap-boiler. Though of very unprepossessing appearance, she had many virtues and was witty and sparkling. Her sister Désirée, who was as beautiful as she was plain, became Queen of Norway and Sweden. Napoleon at one time wished to marry her, but her brothers said one Corsican in the family was enough !

[2] Mrs. Damer was the first female in England who wore black silk stockings ; for this and other habits she obtained the nickname of the 'Epicurean' in the newspaper epigrams of the day.

superiority of the latter, not only in manners but in dress and
looks.   Soon after their arrival they dined with Mme. Chabot
de Castellane in the Rue Plumet, where they met Mme. de
Beauvau, Mme. de Mortemart, Mme. (Louise) de Talleyrand-
Périgord, Mme. d'Audenarde, Mathieu de Montmorency, and
Mme. de Staël.   The latter had known Mrs. Damer in London,
and she invited her and Miss Berry to dinner to meet the
Neckers, de Saussure, Benjamin Constant, and Mme. de Récamier.
Though incontestably beautiful, Miss Berry does not seem to
have been attracted by Mme. de Récamier.   She describes her as
' thinking much of herself, with perfect carelessness about others ;
her manners *douceureuses*, and dressed with much affectation of
singularity.'   Mme. de Staël entertaining Mme. Récamier forcibly
reminds one of the various *bons mots* related *à propos* of their
friendship—the terrible snub to the *gauche* young man who, sitting
between them, said how happy he was to be between wit and beauty.
' Yes, and possessing neither,' being the retort of Mme. de Staël.
And Talleyrand's answer to Mme. de Staël when she asked him
before Mme. de Récamier, if he found himself on a plank in the
sea with both of them and could only save one, which it should
be.   Turning to Mme. de Staël he said, ' Vous savez nager, je
crois, Madame.'

Another evening Mrs. Damer and Miss Berry went to Mme.
de Beauvau to meet Mme. d'Hénin, Mme. de la Rochefoucauld
(widow of the Duke killed in the Revolution), the Duc de Rohan
Chabot, his nephew the Chevalier Chabot, the agreeable and
witty Henry Luttrell, and Lord Henry Petty (afterwards Lord
Lansdowne), the Mæcenas of his age.   And they attended an
assembly at the Duchesse de Luines's, one of the very few houses
of the *ancien régime* that still received, where they admired Mme.
de Bouillie, Mme. de Chevreuse, and Mme. de Montmorenci.

They also went to two balls—one given by M. de Crillon, whom they thought a perfect specimen of a middle-aged gentleman. He was a son of the Duc de Crillon, and had managed, by remaining at his post, to get through the Revolution better almost than any one else. He still inhabited the same handsome house on the Place Louis XV., and was even waited on by the same servants. The other ball was given by the Russian, M. Demidoff, and was a gorgeous affair. In the antechamber was a *bouquetière* who presented every lady with a large bouquet of beautiful forced flowers, worth, says Miss Berry, 'not less than twelve or eighteen livres apiece, and these bouquets were changed as often as you pleased.' Dancing in those days was an art ; and Miss Berry mentions that at this ball Vestris danced a quadrille with Mme. Hamelin, one of the best dancers in Paris, and also alludes to the dancing of M. Jacques Laffitte, the well-known banker, said to be the best dancer of Paris.

Mrs. Damer and Miss Berry were present at several entertainments given by the Ministers. At Berthier's, the War Minister, they met young Beauharnais, 'good-looking, but by no means distinguished-looking ;' La Place, the mathematician and astronomer ; and Cambacérès. Le Brun (afterwards Duc de Piacenza), who had met Mrs. Damer before, in Paris in 1755, at the sale of the Prince de Conti's pictures, invited her and Miss Berry to a party where they met General Lafayette, 'a gentlemanlike, sickly-looking man, in no sort of uniform, a plain blue coat, round hat, and cropped head.' Mrs. Damer and Miss Berry were presented by Mrs. Cosway to Buonaparte's mother at her house in the Rue Chaussée d'Antin. Miss Berry describes Mme. Buonaparte *mère* as possessing the remains of great beauty, with large dark eyes and an intelligent mild countenance. But Mrs. Damer's great treat was reserved for April 8, when she and Miss Berry went by appointment to the Tuileries and were presented to the First Consul, who spoke to each of them for a few moments.   Mrs. Damer had the greatest possible admiration for Buonaparte, and had come to Paris solely in the hope of meeting her hero.   She and Miss Berry had previously seen him at the famous parade, when the latter lady described him as 'a little man, remarkably well on horseback, with a sallow complexion, a highish nose, a very serious countenance, and cropped hair.'   At the presentation, Miss Berry says : 'His manner was simple and unaffected, his hair very dark [1] and cropped very short, not so little as represented, with good teeth, and his mouth, when speaking in good humour, has a remarkable and uncommon expression of sweetness ; eyes of light grey, and he looks full in the face of the person to whom he speaks.'   Thirteen years later, when Mrs. Damer was in Paris in 1815, she presented to the Emperor Napoleon at the Palais de l'Elysée a bust in marble which she had done of Charles James Fox ; and shortly after she received by the hands of General Bertrand a magnificent snuff-box with the Emperor's portrait surrounded by diamonds, now in the British Museum, to which she left it.

In early life Mrs. Damer took an active part in politics. She was a decided Whig ; and when Westminster was divided by Fox's friends into three districts, Georgiana, Duchess of Devonshire, took the management of one, Mrs. Crewe of another, and Mrs. Damer of the third, and she is said to have canvassed for her favourite with great activity and success.   Charles James Fox was a nephew of Mrs. Damer's brother-in-law, the third Duke of Richmond.

[1] The writer has a large lock of Napoleon's hair given to a member of her family by General Bertrand.   It is not black, but a very dark rich brown, of a most beautiful texture, fine, and very glossy.

Nelson was another of Mrs. Damer's heroes. She knew him well ; and he sat to her, immediately after his return from the Battle of the Nile, in the coat which he wore during the battle and which he afterwards gave her. Mrs. Damer made a bust of him in marble, ' heroic size,' which she presented to the City of London, and it was put up in the Common Council Chamber at Guildhall.

To enumerate even the half of Mrs. Damer's friends would be impossible, but it is scarcely too much to say that she was acquainted with almost every one who was celebrated, not only in the world of fashion, but in the world of letters, science, and art. Among the literary lights whom she knew well, besides those whom we have already mentioned, we find the names of Byron, Scott, Rogers, Campbell, Horace and James Smith, Joanna Baillie, Sir James Mackintosh, Lord Brougham, Lord Jeffrey, Sidney Smith, Burke, and Tommy Moore. Amongst her scientific acquaintances were Mrs. Somerville, John Hunter the surgeon, Sir Humphry Davy, Sir Joseph Banks, and Playfair. The latter in writing to Miss Berry says : ' Among my obligations to you I must not forget the acquaintance of Mrs. Damer : the liberality of whose mind, the good sense, and sound reason that dictates her opinions are not less remarkable than her elegance and taste.' Mrs. Damer was a pleasing combination of intellectual attainment and all the lighter accomplishments. She was a most graceful and finished dancer in those days when dancing was worth looking at, and when she was young she enjoyed going to balls. In 1778, Horace Walpole says : ' The quadrilles at —— were very pretty : Mrs. Damer, Lady Sefton, Lady Melbourne, and the Princess Czartoriski, in blue satin with blonde, and collets montés à la reine Elizabeth ; Lord Robert Spencer, Mr. Fitzpatrick, and Lord Carlisle, and I forget whom, in blue dresses with red sashes, black hats with diamond loops and a few feathers before,' opened the ball.   In Taylor's ' Life of Reynolds ' we read that at the opening of the Pantheon a great many of the ladies chose to adopt male dominoes.   Among the most distinguished of these ' pretty fellows ' were the Duchess of Ancaster, Lady Melbourne, and Mrs. Damer.[1]

Horace Walpole, Lord Orford, left Strawberry Hill and £2,000 a year to Mrs. Damer, who was his executrix and residuary legatee.   She therefore in 1798 took up her abode there with her widowed mother, Lady Ailesbury, going only to London for the winter.   She became thus the near neighbour of her dear friends the Berrys, Lord Orford having left them Little Strawberry Hill.   Mrs. Damer fitted up a small theatre at Strawberry Hill and indulged in her favourite amusement of private theatricals, assisted by the Berrys and other friends.   Miss Berry gives the cast of two plays acted there in 1800 ; and in the following year a comedy in five acts, by Miss Berry herself, called ' Fashionable Friends,' was acted there by Mrs. Damer and her troupe, the prologue and epilogue being written by Miss Joanna Baillie.

Mrs. Damer also gave most popular garden parties, and received many distinguished visitors.   Among those who came most frequently were Mrs. Siddons, Garrick's widow, and Joanna Baillie.   Caroline, Princess of Wales, was also often there, and constantly invited Mrs. Damer to Kensington Palace, Blackheath, or Connaught Place.   This intimacy was brought about in a great measure through the medium of Lady Charlotte Campbell, Mrs. Damer's first cousin, who was for some years Lady of the Bedchamber to the Princess, and stood by her till

[1] By this it must not be understood that these ladies were dressed in male attire, but that they merely put on men's dominoes over their ladies' costumes.

she could do so no longer in justice to her own reputation. Miss Berry describes the Princess's first visit to Strawberry Hill, and says that 'after going over the house, but talking more than looking at anything, she departed with a thousand thanks to Mrs. Damer.' The next day she sent Lady Glenbervie to propose to Mrs. Damer to share with her a box at Covent Garden—that is to say, have it on the Opera nights—to which arrangement Mrs. Damer did not accede.

Queen Charlotte paid Mrs. Damer a visit at Strawberry Hill in 1810. Her Majesty thus alludes to it in a letter to one of her children : 'We dined [at Strawberry Hill] at 3 and had, to the honour of Mrs. Damer's housekeeper and cook, as elegant and good a dinner as if a Cordon Bleu had directed it ; we were very chearfull and a little after 4 we drank Coffe' (*sic*). Queen Charlotte much admired the flowers at Strawberry Hill. Mrs. Damer was a great gardener and worked herself amongst them. Miss Berry writes in 1799 : 'Mrs. Damer chips away at her marble one half of the morning and trots about the grounds the other half, in all weathers, and is much the better for this variety of exercise.'

In 1811 Mrs. Damer resigned Strawberry Hill in favour of the then Countess Dowager of Waldegrave, in whom the remainder in fee was invested. At first she went to a house of Lady Buckinghamshire's at East Sheen, and in 1818 she moved to York House, Twickenham, which she bought from her friend Prince Stahremberg, the late Austrian ambassador.[1]

---

[1] Count Stahremberg used to play a great deal. His English was not so good as his luck. Playing one night at trente-et-un, his Excellency, who was not very nice in his person, kept proclaiming the state of his hand by saying, 'I am dirty ! I am dirty !' At last, when he had achieved the best possible hand, he almost embraced Lord Barrymore, exclaiming, 'I am dirty ! I am dirty one !' Barrymore, who had no liking for the nasty embrace, said : 'Damn it, so you are ; but that's no reason why I should be dirty too !'

York House had formerly belonged to the great Lord Clarendon, who gave it to James, Duke of York (afterwards James II.),
when he married his daughter, Anne Hyde ; and it contains the
state room in which Queen Anne was born, though it has been
so often erroneously asserted that she was born at Swallowfield, near Reading, the seat of her uncle, the second Earl of
Clarendon.

For the remainder of her life Mrs. Damer lived at York
House during the summer, and in winter at her house in Upper
Brook Street, where she died on May 28, 1828, aged eighty, of a
gradual decay.[1]   She lost her sight for a few previous hours, but
retained her hearing and other faculties to the last moment.
Her deathbed was attended by George, sixth Duke of Argyll,
her first cousin, and by Sir Alexander Johnston, who had married
her cousin, the daughter of Lord William Campbell.   She was
buried at Sundridge Church, near the married home of her
grandmother, Mary Bellenden, her working tools and apron, by
her express desire, being buried in her coffin.[2]

About a year before her death the Duke of Clarence,[3] on
becoming Lord High Admiral of England, was anxious that

---

[1] In 'The Creevey Papers' there is a letter of Mr. Creevey's written in February
1821, in which he says : 'As soon as Brougham was ready, we set off to pick up
Mrs. Damer, who was to dine also with the Queen.   And here let me stop to
express my admiration for this extraordinary person.   You know she is Field-
Marshal Conway's daughter, cousin of Lord Hertford, &c.   She is the person who
paid all her husband's debts, without the least obligation upon her so to do, and
she is the person who renounced all claim to half of Lord Clinton's estate when
she was informed that by law she was entitled to it.   She is seventy years of age
(as a matter of fact she was seventy-three) and as fresh as if she was fifty.'

[2] There is an inscription in Latin to her memory on the south side of the
church.

[3] Mrs. Damer had made a cast of Mrs. Jordan's leg, for which H.R.H. the Duke
of Clarence sent a note with his own and Mrs. Jordan's thanks ; and at the death of
Sir Joshua Reynolds, who had the cast, the Duke of Clarence applied for it in form
to Burke, as one of the executors, and the latter sent it to H.R.H.

SIR JOSHUA REYNOLDS *pinx*.

THE HON. MRS. DAMER.

Mrs. Damer should execute for him a bust of Nelson in bronze. Notwithstanding her great age, Mrs. Damer began the undertaking at once; and, in spite of her infirmities and weakness, succeeded in finishing it, to her great satisfaction, a very few days before her death. Lady Johnston, her cousin and residuary legatee, shortly after took the bust to the Duke, at the same time presenting him with the coat which Nelson wore at the Battle of the Nile and which he sat in to Mrs. Damer and afterwards gave her. The Duke of Clarence ultimately gave the coat to Greenwich Hospital, where it was deposited in the Painted Hall.

Mrs. Damer left York House to Lady Johnston, whose daughters sold it to the Duc d'Aumale for the Comte de Paris, who lived there till after 1891. She also settled all her busts, and the paintings worked by her mother, Lady Ailesbury, as heirlooms upon Lady Johnston and her daughters; the last of these ladies died unmarried in 1880, when Mrs. Damer's possessions passed into the hands of their brothers, in whose families they now are.

Mrs. Damer was painted twice by Sir Joshua Reynolds, three times by Cosway, and more than once by Angelica Kauffmann, all of whose portraits have been engraved. She was also painted by Romney. The following is a description of her by a contemporary: 'She was fair, with luxuriant hair; her face a perfect oval, her features marked yet delicate; her nose aquiline; her mouth shewed strong decision of character, being firmly closed, though with a merry smile; her eyes full of thought and spirit; her head well set on a long neck. She was gay and witty in society, and had most fascinating manners.' In moral character she was irreproachable, and there was never even a breath of slander raised against her fair fame.   Princess Elizabeth of Hesse wrote to Lord Harcourt in 1795 : 'Mrs. Damer's engaging and enchanting manners must please everybody &c.'

Anne Seymour Damer may surely take her place in this family group of three generations of fascinating women.

A GIPSY PREDICTION FULFILLED

ONE summer's day in the year 1752 four or five young ladies, accompanied by their respective chaperons and attended by some gay gallants, were wending their way through the fashionable crowd down the Mall in St. James's Park. The young girls were cousins—some were Cholmondeleys and some were Merediths[1]—lately arrived from Cheshire on their first visit to the metropolis. They had just partaken of the syllabubs, which was the fashionable thing to do,[2] and were about to return home when a swarthy woman came out from a booth and begged to tell them their fortunes. Some of them at once put out their hands, but Mary Meredith drew back and said she had no faith in such nonsense. The gipsy then shook her fist at the pretty girl, and screamed out, 'You think yourself very clever, but you'll marry a man who'll be hung, and you yourself will never die in your bed.'

That evening this young lady, who had probably almost forgotten the episode of the morning, met her fate. Laurence, fourth Earl Ferrers, made her acquaintance at an assembly, followed her to the country, and after spending a few days in her company at

---

[1] Henrietta Meredith, who married the Hon. Frederick Vane, son of Lord Darlington ; and Elizabeth Meredith, who married William Bankes of Winstanley Hall, Lancashire.

[2] The last remains of the Milk Fair were cleared away in September 1885.

Henbury, the house of her brother, Sir William Meredith, became engaged to her, and shortly after, on September 16, they were married.

Now, if poor Mary Meredith's father or mother had been alive, they would probably have made some inquiries respecting this suitor for the hand of their young and innocent daughter, and they would have ascertained that his antecedents were not satisfactory. Though of a very ancient and noble family, many of whose members were well known to fame, on one side he came of what Horace Walpole calls 'a very frantic race.' His uncle Henry, Lord Ferrers, whom he succeeded, was a lunatic, and died in a *maison de santé* at Kensington Gore ; and his aunt, Lady Barbara Shirley (as well as another one, 'Lady Betty'), was out of her mind.[1]   Lord Ferrers himself, as a boy, was strangely moody and passionate, and had since taken to drink, and though in many ways he was exceedingly intelligent, in others he showed marked signs of insanity.[2]   The poor young wife was not long in finding this out ; for, from the commencement of her married life, he cruelly ill-treated her, and she was soon obliged to leave him, being in terror of her life.   He always took pistols to bed with him and threatened to kill her before the morning,

---

[1] See evidence given on trial.   Several other members of this branch of the family were merely eccentric, and, like Lady Selina Shirley, gave forth their erratic energies in a good cause.   Lady Selina married the Earl of Huntingdon ; she was a fervent disciple of the celebrated Whitfield and the St. Theresa of the Methodists, and was, as Lord Dover says, the peculiar patroness of enthusiasts of all sorts of religion.   Her chapels are to be found all over the kingdom, and Lady Huntingdon's name is looked upon with much veneration by some sectarians. Whitfield in his will says : 'I leave my house in Georgia with all my negroes and everything of which I am possessed to that elect Lady—that mother in Israel, that mirror of true and undefiled religion, the Rt. Hon. Selina Countess Dowager of Huntingdon.'   Horace Walpole says : 'With all his madness, Lord Ferrers was not mad enough to be struck with his Aunt Huntingdon's sermons.'

[2] Dr. John Monro, a specialist for lunacy, gave evidence at the trial to this effect, having treated him when under the influence of lunacy.

and he also beat her. She was separated from him in 1758 by an Act of Parliament, which appointed Receivers of his estate in order to secure her allowance. This angered Lord Ferrers greatly ; however, he named his steward, Mr. John Johnson, a very worthy, honest old man, as one of the Receivers. Lord Ferrers now left his family place, Stanton Harold, and went to live at Muswell Hill, near Highgate, with a Mrs. Clifford, by whom he had four daughters. Whilst here, we are told, he was in the habit of mixing his beer and porter with mud, and he habitually shaved only one side of his face. His relations discussed the question of shutting him up, but no steps were taken to carry this plan into effect.

At last, in January 1760, the climax came. On finding that Johnson had paid Lady Ferrers £50 without his knowledge, Lord Ferrers, who was then at Stanton Harold, took a sudden determination to kill him. There was some method in his madness, for on the fatal day he not only sent Mrs. Clifford and her children away, but also his only two menservants. When Johnson arrived in answer to Lord Ferrers's invitation, the latter locked the door and ordered him to sign a paper confessing that he was a villain. This the steward refused to do ; upon which Lord Ferrers forced him to kneel down, and there shot him with a pistol. Johnson did not die at once, and Lord Ferrers sent for a surgeon and also for the poor man's daughter. Johnson was conveyed to his own house during the night, and died the next day. Lord Ferrers was taken to Leicester Gaol, and a fortnight after was brought up to London under a strong guard, but in his own landau drawn by six horses. On this occasion, we are told, he was dressed like a jockey. Arraigned before the House of Lords, he was committed to the Tower, and two months later was again brought up for trial at the bar of the House of Peers. He cross-examined the witnesses himself with great clearness, and, as Horace Walpole said, ' it was a strange contradiction to see a man trying, by his own sense, to prove himself out of his own senses.' And ' it was moving to see two of his own brothers[1] brought to prove the lunacy in their own blood in order to save their brother's life.' Lord Talbot prophesied that, ' not being thought mad enough to be shut up till he had killed somebody, he will then be thought too mad to be executed.' This prophecy, however, was not realised ; for the trial, which lasted three days, resulted in Lord Ferrers being sentenced ' to be hanged by the neck till he is dead, and that his body be dissected and anatomised.' His mother presented two petitions to the king without avail, and he himself wrote to the king to beg that he might suffer where his ancestor the Earl of Essex had suffered, and hoped to obtain that favour, as he had the honour of quartering part of the same arms and of being allied to his Majesty.[2] All the concession granted was, ' in conse-quence of his rank,' a few days' extension, and the privilege of having a special scaffold. Lord Ferrers retained his composure to the last. The night he received sentence he played piquet with his warders ; and the evening before his execution he

---

[1] The Hon. Robert and Walter Shirley.

[2] Sir Henry Shirley, second baronet, married in 1615 Lady Dorothy Devereux, daughter of Robert, Earl of Essex. It is by this alliance that the Earls Ferrers quarter the arms of France and England with their own ; the Earl of Essex being maternally descended from Richard Plantagenet, grandfather of King Edward IV., and also from Thomas Plantagenet, youngest son of King Edward III. *A propos* of this, James, Earl of Charlemont, tells the following story, which he said was characteristic of the French. 'General Flobert, when on parole, was breakfasting with me, when some one came in and told me that the day was appointed for the execution of Lord Ferrers. I saw his surprise, and upon the departure of the gentleman he eagerly said, "Mais, comment ? est-ce vraiment un milord qu'on va pendre pour avoir tué un bourgeois ?" To increase his wonder, I replied, "Oui, vraiment, et non seulement milord, mais parent du roi." "Pardieu, dit-il, cela est singulier, et cependant, cela est beau." '

THE EXECUTION OF EARL FERRERS AT TYBURN.

made one of his keepers read 'Hamlet' to him after he was in bed, and half an hour before the sheriffs fetched him, corrected some verses he had written in the Tower in imitation of the Duke of Buckingham's epitaph ('Dubius sed non improbus vixi') :

> In doubt I lived, in doubt I die,
> Yet stand prepared the vast abyss to try,
> And, undismay'd, expect eternity.

He was visited by the Bishop of Rochester, by Whitfield, and by his aunts Lady Huntingdon and Lady Fanny Shirley.

At his particular desire, Lord Ferrers went to Tyburn in his own landau drawn by six horses, and he was then dressed in his wedding suit of white and silver. He was preceded and followed by an immense procession, consisting of constables, 'horse grenadiers,' and 'foot soldiers,' which moved so very slowly that it took two hours and three-quarters in getting from the Tower to Tyburn. It is said to have passed by 'many hundred thousand spectators,' and Lord Ferrers appears to have met with universal sympathy. He was accompanied by Paul Vaillant, the Sheriff of Middlesex,[1] as well as by Mr. Humphries, the chaplain. The sheriff told Lord Ferrers that it gave him 'the highest concern to wait on him upon so melancholy an occasion, but that he would do everything in his power to render his situation as easy as possible, and hoped that whatever he did his lordship would impute to the necessary discharge of his duty'! Lord Ferrers thanked him, and asked him if he had ever seen so great a concourse of people before ; and upon the sheriff answering that he had not, said, 'I suppose it is because they never saw a lord hanged before'! The chaplain took occasion to observe that the world would naturally be very inquisitive concerning the

---

[1] Paul Vaillant, a French bookseller in the Strand.

religion his lordship professed, to which Lord Ferrers answered
that he did not think himself at all accountable to the world for
his sentiments on religion, but that he had always believed in and
adored one God, the Maker of all things; that whatever his
notions were, he had never propagated them, or endeavoured to
gain any persons over to his own persuasions; that all countries
and nations had a form of religion by which the people were
governed, and that he looked upon whoever disturbed them in
it as an enemy to society; that he very much blamed my Lord
Bolingbroke for permitting his sentiments on religion to be
published to the world; that the many sects and disputes which
arise about religion have almost turned morality out of doors.
Concerning the unfortunate Mr. Johnson, he declared most
solemnly that he had not the least malice towards him.   When
they approached the place of execution, Lord Ferrers told the
sheriff that there was a person waiting in a coach near there for
whom he had a very sincere regard, and of whom he should be
glad to take his leave before he died; to which the sheriff
answered that if his lordship insisted upon it, it should be
arranged, but that he wished his lordship would not do so lest
the sight of a person for whom he had such a regard would
unman him, and disarm him of the fortitude he possessed.   To
which his lordship replied : ' Sir, if you think I am wrong, I
submit.'   And upon the sheriff telling him that if he had anything
to deliver to that person he would faithfully do it, his lordship
delivered to the sheriff a pocket-book, in which was a banknote,
a purse with some guineas, and a ring.   On the scaffold Lord
Ferrers with an audible voice repeated the Lord's Prayer, and
afterwards, with great energy, the following ejaculations : ' O God,
forgive me all my errors—pardon all my sins.'   Lord Ferrers,
then rising, took his leave of the sheriff and the chaplain, and

EARL FERRERS IN HIS COFFIN.

presented his watch to the former, saying, 'It is a stop-watch and a pretty accurate one ; it is scarcely worth your acceptance, but I have nothing else.' He then called for the executioner, who asked his forgiveness ; upon which his lordship said, 'I freely forgive you, as I do all mankind and hope myself to be forgiven.' He intended to give the executioner five guineas, but by mistake giving it into the hands of the assistant, an unseemly dispute arose, which the sheriff instantly silenced. His body was conveyed with the same procession to the Surgeons' Hall in the Old Bailey to undergo the remainder of the sentence. A print of the time shows the corpse as it lay there. It was afterwards delivered to his friends for interment, and was buried privately at Old St. Pancras Church, in a grave dug twelve or fourteen feet deep under the belfry, but was removed in 1782 to Stanton Harold.

Thus was realised the first part of the gipsy's prophecy.

Nine years later, when Lady Ferrers was thirty-two years of age and still a very pretty woman, besides being a most exemplary one, she took to herself another husband,[1] who was as much the opposite of her first as it was possible to be. Lord Frederick Campbell, her second choice, was the third son of John, fourth Duke of Argyll, and his wife the beautiful Mary Bellenden, and was remarkable for his grace and refinement and for the noble and generous qualities of his heart and mind. 'He united much charm of manner with a very handsome exterior ;[2] his manners, noble yet soft, dignified yet devoid of any pride or affectation,

---

[1] Her second marriage took place in March 1769 at St. Martin's-in-the-Fields. The writer has a very pretty pastelle of her, painted about this time, the draperies and the pose being a replica of Rosalba's pastelle of 'Winter' in the Louvre ; and an engraving of her by Sherwin, done in 1784. There is (or was) also a portrait of her at Winstanley Hall, Lancashire, belonging to Meyrick Bankes, Esq., great-grandnephew of William Bankes, who married Lady Frederick's third sister, Elizabeth Meredith.

[2] This is seen in the fine portrait of him painted by Gainsborough.

conciliated all who approached him.'   Such was the description of
him by a contemporary.   Certainly, from all accounts, public and
private, so far as goodness and kindness and charm were concerned,
he appears to have been a very prince among men.   Without any
very shining talent, he held various posts with great credit to
himself and satisfaction to others.   At the time of his marriage he
was Chief Secretary to the Lord Lieutenant of Ireland,[1] and held
the lucrative place of Lord Clerk Register of Scotland, which was
conferred on him for life.[2]

The Duke of Argyll, his father, made over his place, Combe
Bank, near Sevenoaks, to Lord Frederick during his lifetime, and
this became Lady Frederick's favourite residence.   The situation
and neighbourhood were lovely, and the house contained many fine
pictures and interesting *objets d'art* ; but Miss Berry, Lady Mary
Coke, Lady Ailesbury, and Mrs. Damer, all of whom constantly
went thither, describe it as very uncomfortable and very cold.   It
was here that after many happy years poor Lady Frederick came to
her tragic end when she was in her seventieth year.   On June 25,
1807, Lord Frederick went to London ; and that night Lady
Frederick sat up in her dressing-gown, reading, as usual, till a late
hour.   Her maid left her a little before midnight, and this was the
last seen of her.   At five o'clock the next morning smoke was
perceived issuing from the house by a labourer, who gave the
alarm.   It was then discovered that Lady Frederick had not
been in bed ; and on searching her dressing-room, which was
on fire, the remains of her body were found there, literally burnt

---

[1] Lord Townshend.

[2] Lord Frederick was a Privy Councillor, one of the Vice-Treasurers of
Ireland, a member of the Board of Control for Indian Affairs, Treasurer of the
Society of the Middle Temple, at one time Keeper of the Privy Seal in Scotland,
a Commissioner of the Public Records of Great Britain, and a Trustee of the
British Museum, and he sat in Parliament for thirty-eight years.

LADY FREDERICK CAMPBELL.
From a Pastelle at Swallowfield.

GH, *pinx*.

LORD FREDERICK CAMPBELL.

to ashes. It was conjectured either that the unfortunate lady had fallen asleep, or that she had had a fit and so set fire to herself and the room, fulfilling, by this terrible death, the second part of the gipsy prediction.[1]

[1] Lord Frederick Campbell survived his wife nine years, dying in his house in Queen Street, Mayfair, on June 8, 1816, aged eighty-seven, 'elegant and distinguished even in decay.' Edridge did a charming likeness of him in 1812, when he was eighty-three.

MORE ABOUT THE GUNNINGS

So much has been written of late years about the two beautiful Miss Gunnings that it seems almost superfluous to attempt to say anything more on the subject ; and yet, being in a position to add some further details concerning the fair sisters and their family, as well as to correct some erroneous statements which constantly crop up, we venture to produce them, thinking they may interest their descendants, and we must be forgiven if sometimes we necessarily go over familiar ground.

Though generally called Irish, from the fact that their father and three previous generations had lived in Ireland and married Irishwomen, the beautiful Miss Gunnings were of Cornish descent. The name was originally 'Gonning,' the 'o' being turned into 'u' about the middle of the sixteenth century. According to Sir Bernard Burke, 'the family seat was Tregonning in Cornwall, and the senior line became extinct there in 1587, at the death, without male issue, of Sir John Gonning, Kt., of Tregonning.'[1] Be this as it may, it is about a younger branch, which migrated to Somersetshire in the middle of the fifteenth

[1] In an account of that part of Cornwall by W. Penaluna, published in 1819, the author says : 'The highest hill in Breage is denominated Tregoning Hill, from the principal house and estate upon it, once a place of very considerable importance, having a large building and chapel adjoining it.' Leland also says that the hill was called Gonyn. On visiting the spot a few years ago we found a farm called 'Tregonning,' and the name 'Gonning' still existing there amongst the lower orders.

century, that we have to speak. For two hundred and fifty years this branch was settled in the immediate neighbourhood of Bath and Bristol, several of its representatives rising to considerable wealth and becoming merchants of position in Bristol in its palmy days. The first of the name that we find there was William Gonning, son of Thomas Gonning of Tregonning, who married Alice Long, settled at North Stoke, near Bath, and died in 1458. In 1642 when the Speaker of the House of Commons sent a letter to the Mayor of Bristol (John Locke) and Aldermen requesting contributions from the City for the Parliament, John Gonning and his brother-in-law, Edward Pitt, appear in the list of non-subscribers. In 1643 when Prince Rupert invested the City the Council resolved to offer a present to the King 'as a testimony of the love and good affection of the City.' Alderman Gonning and John Gonning, jun., contributed, the latter giving £150. This same year Fiennes levied contributions, and a mandate, which has been preserved, desires John Gonning, jun., to pay forthwith £200, 'which sum in respect of your estate is below the proportion required of other persons of your quality.' In April 1644 Queen Henrietta Maria spent a night or two at Bristol, and the Council resolved that £500 should be presented to her Majesty. Some trouble was found in raising the money, but Mr. John Gonning again came to the fore. In October 1645 the Parliamentary leaders determined upon extensive changes in the Common Council at Bristol and suspended some who were loyally affected during the Royalist occupation. The favour shown to John Gonning is one of the puzzles of the time. He was then nominated Mayor, and in a note to the magisterial records for 1655 we find that 'Mayor John Gonning, a Cavalier, was serving for the second time,' and in 1661 he was reinstated. In 1662 John Gunning, Mayor and Alderman of Bristol, was

H

granted arms : Gu, three guns or cannon barwise in pale, arg ;
Crest, a wheel, gu, between two wings arg (Harl. MS. 1441).
These canting arms are totally different from those borne by his
third cousin, Peter Gunning, Bishop of Ely, which were Gu on
a fess arg, between three doves of the second, beaks and legs or,
claws az, as many crosses patee of the first.   The Gonnings
continued in the neighbourhood of Bath and Bristol till
the end of the seventeenth century, when they became
extinct in the male line at the death of Sir Robert Gunning
of Cold Ashton, who married Ann, daughter of Sir Robert
Cann, Bart., and died without issue.[1]   At the death of Sir
Robert Gunning in 1682 there were many suitors for the
hand of his widow, who besides being very rich was said to be
beautiful.   Of these the one she favoured was Mr. Dudley North.
He was brother of Lord Chief Justice North, afterwards Lord
Guilford, Keeper of the Great Seal, and he himself became Commissioner of the Treasury to King Charles II., but up to this
time he had led an adventurous life abroad and had no abiding
place ; and Sir Robert Cann, Lady Gunning's father, who was
a very crusty morose old gentleman, made objections to the
engagement and said that 'when Mr. North had purchased an
estate in land of three or four thousand pounds a year, whereby
he might make settlements suitable to his daughter's fortune, he
would hearken to the proposition, but none of less estate in land
must pretend to her.'   Then Mr. North wrote a proposition to
settle £20,000 to purchase an estate, &c.   The old man answered
thus, 'Sir, my answer to your first letter is an answer to your
second.—Your humble servant, R. C.'   Mr. North returned,
'Sir, I perceive you like neither me nor my business.—Your

---

[1] His sister Elizabeth (or Hester) Gunning, who died 1704, married Sir Thomas
Langton of Newton Park, *a quo* the present Earl Temple.

humble servant, D. N.' And there ended the correspondence with the father at that time, but in the meanwhile Sir Robert Cann wrote to his daughter to show her 'the precipice she was upon ; going to marry a desperado, not worth a groat, and one that certainly would be hanged.' The old curmudgeon, however, ultimately consented to the match, which we are told 'was solemnised with a very honourable attendance,' and 'he came at last to be very proud of his son-in-law.' This same year Dudley North was knighted, a distinction we are told he would not have accepted had it not been that he could 'not bear separation from his wife, even of names,' and it was considered necessary that as long as he was only Mr. North she should remain 'Lady Gunning.' The marriage was a very satisfactory one. Sir Dudley died in 1691, and she survived him upwards of twenty-five years, and both lie buried at Glemham in Suffolk. Meanwhile, in the middle of the sixteenth century, a younger son of one of these Bristol merchants—Peter, fourth son of John Gonning of Swainswick and Cold Ashton (by his wife Mary, daughter of William Dodington of Dodington)—moved to Kent, and is described as 'of Brookland and of Ash.' He died in 1567, leaving by his wife (Elizabeth Alchorne[1]) a son, Thomas Gonning of Ash, born 1554 and died 1635, who had four sons.[2] The three eldest remained in Kent : (1) Peter, Vicar of Hoo, near Rochester, and Rector of Gravesend ; (2) Thomas of Southfleet ; (3) Robert of Meopham ; and the fourth was Richard, ancestor of the fair sisters. But before we go to him and his descendants, we must follow his elder brother, the Vicar of Hoo. The latter married, in 1612,

[1] Alchornes of Hall's Place, Kent, descended from the Alchornes of Alchorne, Rotherfield, Sussex.

[2] A manuscript pedigree of the Tracy family states that Thomas Gonning of Ash had also four daughters.

Eleanor, daughter of Francis Tracy of Hoo [1] (and aunt to Sir John Tracy, Bart.), and died in 1615, leaving an infant son, Peter, who became the famous Bishop of Ely. Born in 1613, he was sent when very young to the King's School in Canterbury, his father having requested in his will that his wife should bring him up to learning. At fifteen Peter Gunning went to Clare Hall, Cambridge, and when he was twenty he took orders, and very soon became celebrated as a preacher and distinguished himself by his zeal for the Church and King. The Tracy MS. says that at Tonbridge 'he exhorted the people in two sermons to make a charitable contribution for the relief of the King's forces there; which conduct rendered him obnoxious to the Powers then in being, who first imprisoned him, and, on his refusing to take the covenant, deprived him of his Fellowship.' Being thus ejected, he removed to Oxford. During his residence there he officiated two years at the curacy of Cassington, and sometimes preached before the King, for which service he was given the degree of B.D. in 1646. Soon after this he became chaplain to Sir Robert Shirley, who was so pleased with his great worth as well as learning that he settled upon him an annuity of £100 a year. At the death of Sir Robert he held a congregation at the chapel of Exeter House in the Strand according to the Liturgy of the Church of England; yet it is said 'he met with no further molestation from the Usurper Cromwell, than that of being now and then sent for and reproved by him.' On the return of Charles II., he was restored to his Fellowship, and created D.D., having first been presented to a prebend in the church of Canterbury; soon after, he was instituted to the rectories of

[1] Mrs. Peter Gunning, mother of the future bishop, married secondly Edward Henshaw, and died in 1643, having had by her second husband two sons, Tobias Henshaw, Archdeacon of Lewes, 1670, and Bernard Henshaw, living in 1683.

PETER GUNNING, BISHOP OF ELY.

From a Print after the Picture by Loggan

Cottesmore in Rutlandshire and of Stoke Brewerne in Northamptonshire. He was also in the same year made Master of Corpus Christi College, Cambridge, and also Lady Margaret Professor of Divinity, and in a few months succeeded to the Regius Professorship of Divinity and the headship of St. John's College, he ' being looked upon as the properest person to settle the University on right principles again after the many corruptions that had crept into that body.' Dr. Gunning was reckoned one of the most learned sons of the Church, and was one of the Committee upon the revision of the Liturgy, when it was brought into that state of sufficiency where it has rested ever since ; and we must not omit to say that it was he who wrote the prayer ' For all sorts and conditions of men,' originally much longer. In 1669 he was made Bishop of Chichester, and five years later promoted to Ely. He died unmarried in July 1684, aged seventy, and was buried in Ely Cathedral under a monument of white marble, which has an inscription that has often been printed. (See Appendix.)

Both Pepys and Evelyn frequently allude in their Diaries to Peter Gunning. Evelyn writes in 1672 : 'The Bishop of Chichester preached before the King admirably well, as he can do nothing but what is well ; ' and again in 1673 he says : ' Carried my son to the Bishop of Chichester, that learned and pious man, Dr. Gunning, to be instructed by him before he received the Holy Communion, when he gave him most excellent advice which I pray God may influence him as long as he lives.'

Dr. Gunning is described as ' handsome in his person and graceful in his manner.' Baker says of him : ' His looks were the most graceful I ever saw.' As to his character, his life is described as blameless. He was of a very generous and charitable disposition, and gave much during his lifetime towards supporting scholars at the University and adding to the endowment of poor vicarages. Masters in his 'History' says : 'Among the disputed points in his character were, whether his head was as good as his heart, and whether his judgment was as solid as his parts were quick.'

Dr. Gunning was one of those principally concerned in the conference with the Dissenters at the Savoy in 1661, and Mr. Richard Baxter, the eminent Nonconformist, speaks thus of him : 'Dr. Gunning was their forwardest and greatest speaker. . . . He seem'd a man of greater study and industry than any of them ; was well read in the Fathers and Councils, and of a ready tongue, but so vehement for high imposing principles and Church pomp, and so very eager and fervent in his discourse, that he often overran himself.' Burnet says he was a dark and perplexed preacher, and that his sermons abounded with Greek and Hebrew and quotations from the Fathers. He was nevertheless admired by the Court ladies ; the King (Charles II.) said 'they admired his preaching, because they did not understand him.'

We must now return to the Bishop's uncle, Richard Gunning, who was born in 1587. Being a younger son, he determined to become a soldier of fortune and went to Ireland, where he was rewarded, for the assistance he gave Sir Charles Coote in quelling the rebellion, by the grant of a large tract of land in county Galway ; and here he built himself a house close to the village of Fuerty and in the immediate neighbourhood of Castle Coote, Sir Charles's own residence.

John, the eldest of this Richard Gunning's grandsons, was the ancestor of the baronets of that name. Bryan, the youngest (who lived at Holywell, county Roscommon), married Katherine

JOHN GUNNING, ESQ.

From a Pastile by F Cotes, R A at Swallowfield.

THE HON. MRS. JOHN GUNNING, *neé* BOURKE.

Geraghty and had sixteen children,[1] the second of whom was John, father of the beautiful Miss Gunnings—he being described at the time of his marriage as 'a barrister of the Middle Temple.' He married on October 23, 1731, the Hon. Bridget Bourke, youngest daughter of Theobald, sixth Viscount Bourke of Mayo,[2] by his first wife Mary, daughter of John Browne, Esq., of Westport[3] (ancestor of the present Marquis of Sligo). Bridget Bourke was a very pretty woman, with refined features, as may be seen in her portrait by Cotes at Inveraray; and we are told that she was highly accomplished as well as 'gentle and elegant.' In fact, there is no tradition in the family to give colour to the purely imaginative and very ugly word-painted portrait of her as depicted in the pages of a popular modern novelist.

Soon after their marriage the young couple went to live in Huntingdonshire, and there rented for some years the old Manor House (commonly called the Red House) at Hemingford Grey, near St. Ives; the probable cause of their choice of this locality being that their relation, William Mitchell, represented the county of Huntingdon in several parliaments and

---

[1] Of the daughters were (1) Margaret Gunning, who married four times: first to John Edwards of Dublin, secondly to William Lyster of Athleague, thirdly to Captain Francis Houston, and fourthly to Theobald, Viscount Mayo. (2) Elizabeth Gunning, married in 1749 William Mitchell, M.P. for the county of Huntingdon, whose son, Knight Mitchell, married the Hon. Amelia Molesworth. (3) Anne Mary Gunning, married first Kelly and secondly the Hon. Charles Caulfield, and had issue.

[2] Mary Browne's mother was Maud, daughter of Theobald, third Viscount Mayo, so that Bridget Gunning's father and mother were first cousins. This may have had something to do with the consumption which carried off so many of the family.

[3] The title of Viscount Mayo was created in 1637 and ceased in 1767 with Mrs. Gunning's brother, the eighth viscount. The peerage of Mayo was resuscitated in 1781, when John Bourke, M.P. for Naas, a descendant of an old branch, was created Viscount Mayo of Moneycrower *a quo* the present earl.

lived in the neighbourhood. He was Mrs. John Gunning's nephew, and later on became John Gunning's brother-in-law.

Mr. and Mrs. John Gunning lived happily and peacefully at Hemingford Grey for nearly six years ; and here their four eldest children were born, namely : (1) Mary (or Maria, as she is generally called), in 1732, and baptised at the beautifully situated church of Hemingford Grey on August 15 of that year ; (2) Elizabeth, in 1733, and baptised in the same place on December 17 ; (3) Catherine (commonly called Kitty), baptised June 12, 1735 ; and (4) Sophia, born in 1737 and died the same year.[1]

In 1740, John's eldest brother, Bryan Gunning, dying without male issue, the family property in county Roscommon devolved upon him ; and this same year he and his wife and their three young daughters left Hemingford Grey and settled there. Here two more children were born to them—John, their only son, and another daughter, Lissy, who was born in February 1744. She gave signs, it was said, of even greater beauty than either of her elder sisters, but died of consumption on December 31, 1752, aged eight years and ten months. She was buried at Hemingford Grey, where there is a monumental slab to her memory erected in the chancel.

[1] When the two eldest Miss Gunnings were in the zenith of their fame a large wager was laid between an Englishman and an Irishman, each claiming that their country was the birthplace of the beauties, and the dispute actually came into court. Dr. Dickens, the clergyman of Hemingford Grey, was one of the witnesses, and brought with him the parish register. The Solicitor-General Wallace cross-questioned him and tried to confuse him. 'I find, sir,' said Wallace, 'that you call yourself Doctor. Pray what sort of a doctor are you? Are you a horse doctor?' Dickens, who was a man of humour and had been a schoolmaster, replied : 'Non sum doctor equinus, indoctos doceo, docui, semperque docebo.' This produced a loud peal of laughter in the court, in which the Lord Chief Justice Mansfield (who dearly loved a joke) joined. The parson gained the cause. The Englishman won his wager, and the county of Huntingdon won the prize of beauty.

CHURCH AT HEMINGFORD-GREY, HUNTS,
From a Photograph.

In 1747 the John Gunnings and their family were living in Dublin ; and Lady Charlotte Campbell tells us in her Journal that her mother, Elizabeth Gunning, was presented to Lord Harrington, the Lord Lieutenant, at the early age of thirteen. Lady Charlotte says : ' The fame of her sister's beauty and her own had spread to Dublin ; and though I have heard from all relators that her father was the best and the purest of men, his heart was not proof against vanity, and he carried his two eldest daughters at that early age to the Castle at Dublin, where they were presented and followed by crowds of admiring spectators.'

Mrs. Bellamy, the actress, mentions in her Memoirs that about this time the Gunnings had the bailiffs in their house, and that Mr. Gunning being away she received Mrs. Gunning, Maria, and Elizabeth in her house, whilst the three younger children went to their aunt, Miss Bourke, ' a lady of exemplary piety.' This being the financial state of affairs, it is not unlikely that Thomas Sheridan, then manager of the Dublin Theatre, did suggest, as stated by Horace Walpole and by Cunningham, that the fair sisters should go on the stage ; but it is very improbable that Mr. Gunning, who had immense family pride, ever gave a thought to such a plan, and he shortly after left Ireland and settled in England. The Gunnings went first of all to Windsor, then to Edmonton, and then to Enfield, and from the latter place they moved for a time to Sunninghill, which was then a fashionable resort for drinking waters, being more select than Bath or Tonbridge, and which had plenty of music and dancing. One of Richardson the novelist's female correspondents writes to him from Enfield in July 1750 : ' The celebrated Miss Gunnings have for a while left Enfield, the place together with the Assembly not being gay enough to retain them, so are gone in pursuit of more brilliant diversions, and may the Installation, Sunninghill, &c., do more for them than could . . .'

Early in 1751 they settled in London. Horace Walpole first mentions them in June of that year, when he writes to Sir Horace Mann : 'The two Miss Gunnings are twenty times more the subject of conversation than the two brothers and Lord Granville. These are two Irish girls of no fortune, who are declared the handsomest women alive. I think their being so handsome two, and both such perfect figures, is their chief excellence, for singly I have seen much handsomer than either ; however, they can't walk in the Park, or go to Vauxhall, but such mobs follow them that they are generally driven away ; ' and two months later he writes to the same correspondent : ' As you talk of our Beauties, I shall tell you a new story of the Gunnings, who make more noise than any of their predecessors since the days of Helen, though neither of them nor anything about them has yet been " teterrima belli causa." They went the other day to see Hampton Court ; as they were going into the Beauty-room, another company arrived ; the housekeeper said, " This way, ladies ; here are the Beauties." The Gunnings flew into a passion and asked her what she meant ; " that they came to see the Palace, not to be showed as a sight themselves."' Jesse in his 'Memoirs ' says : ' The surpassing loveliness of the Gunnings has almost become a matter of history ; nor perhaps is there any instance of mere beauty having excited so extraordinary a sensation as that produced by the appearance in the fashionable circles of London of these two portionless girls.'

On March 5, 1752, Maria, the eldest, married George William, sixth Earl of Coventry. Directly after the marriage they went to Crome, Lord Coventry's seat in Worcestershire, where the fame of her beauty had already spread ; and soon after

a shoemaker at Worcester got two guineas and a half by showing a shoe that he was making for the Countess, at a penny apiece.

In July, Lord Coventry took his bride to Paris. James Murphy French, writing from the Temple on June 25, 1752, to Mr. Harry Duncombe, says : ' By the bye the sooner you cross the Alps the better. You remember after your first arrival abroad, I informed you I was swallowed up in a terrible earthquake that happened on the appearance of the Miss Gunnings in England ; now I would have you make your escape over the Alps, or else prepare for your descent underground with all expedition. Whether the waves gave us Venus (as the Poets give out) or not, we have certainly resigned her in Lady Coventry to them ; they are now wafting her to the Continent ; Lady Coventry approaches France every moment, and I do not doubt but so polite a nation as France will also entertain her with an earthquake on her landing, and so, dear Harry Duncombe, take care of yourself. In plain English, she is a most beautiful girl and I had rather make the tour of her charms, a thousand times, than the tour of Europe.'

Lady Coventry did not, however, make the same furore in Paris, being, as Horace Walpole tells us, 'ignorant of the world, and not allowed to wear neither red nor powder.' She could not speak French, and the saucy *naïveté* and *gaucheries* of this unsophisticated girl of eighteen ill suited the Court of Louis XV. There were some fireworks at Mme. de Pompadour's, to which she was invited, but she excused herself on the ground of her music-master coming at that hour. Lord Coventry was as *gauche* as she was ; being pressed to remain for the grand fêtes at St. Cloud, he said he would not like to miss a musical meeting at Worcester. The Maréchale de Lowendahl was pleased with an English fan belonging to Lady Coventry, who very civilly gave it to her. Lord Coventry made his wife write for it to be sent back the next morning, 'because he had given it her before marriage, and her parting with it would make an irreparable breach ; ' and she sent an old one instead of it !

Lady Coventry's great want of tact is exemplified in her well-known *mal à propos* speech to George II. When he was quite an old man he was talking to her and regretting, for her sake, that there had been no masquerades. 'Oh ! ' said the inconsiderate beauty. 'As for sights, I am quite sick of them. There is only one which I am eager to see—that is a coronation.' But notwithstanding this, Lady Coventry was a great favourite of the King. Horace Walpole writes that at some masquerade ,when his Majesty sent for her to dance a minuet, 'it was quite like Herodias, and I believe if he had offered her a boon, she would have chosen the head of St. John.' This was in allusion to the young Lord Bolingbroke, with whom she is said to have had a great flirtation. When Lady Coventry told the King that she had been jostled and mobbed by the people in the Park one Sunday evening, he said that, to prevent the same, for the future she should have a guard ; and on the following Sunday evening 'she did actually,' writes Mr. Jenkinson (afterwards Sir Charles) to Mr. Grenville, 'go into the Park attended by two Sergeants of the Guards in front with their halberds, and no less than twelve followed her. The whole guard was ready to have turned out if there had been occasion, and the Colonel of the Guard in Waiting kept at the proper distance ; with this ridiculous parade, she walked from 8 of the clock till 10, and as all this could not prevent the mob from having curiosity, some of Fielding's [1] men that attended took up the most trouble-

---

[1] Fielding, half brother to the novelist, was a police magistrate, and, though blind from his birth, was most active and sagacious in the performance of his duties.

GAVIN HAMILTON, *pinx*.

MARIA, COUNTESS OF COVENTRY, *nee* GUNNING.

some.' The following are two accounts of Lady Coventry's appearance written about this time : 'One Sunday afternoon in November,' says Mrs. Delany, 'a ducal friend brought the famous Countess to see me, to feast me, and a feast indeed she was. Her dress was a black silk sack [*sic*] made for a large hoop which she wore without any, and it trailed a yard on the ground. She also wore a cobwebbed lace handkerchief, a pink satin long cloke [*sic*] lined with ermine mixed with squirrel skins ; that wonderful face was adorned with a French cap that just covered the top of her head, of blonde, and stood in the form of a butterfly with wings not quite extended. The whole was completed by lappets tied under the chin with pink and green ribands. . . . She has a thousand prettinesses in her cheeks, her eyes a little drooping at the corners, but fine for all that ; she has a thousand airs, but with a sort of humour that diverts me.'

Mrs. Calderwood of Polton does not give us such a pleasing portrait in her Journal published in the Coltness Collection, but she often dipped her pen in gall. She writes in 1756 : 'I saw the Countess of Coventry at Ranelagh. I think she is a pert-like husy [*sic*] going about with her face up to the sky, that she might be seen from under her hat which she had pulled quite over her nose that nobody might see her. She was in deshabille and very shabby drest.' At this time William, Duke of Cumberland, was one of Lady Coventry's special admirers. We have an account of a Russian masquerade in 1755, at which he never left her side, when she is described as being 'dressed in a great style and looking better than ever ;' and again the following year, Horace Walpole says : 'The Duke had appeared in form on the causeway in Hyde Park with my Lady Coventry. How happy she must be with Billy and Bully ! I hope she will not mistake and call the former by the nickname of the latter.'   About this time the following lines were written by Soame Jenyns 'On a Nosegay in the Countess of Coventry's Breast : '

> Delightful scene in which appear
> At once all beauties of the year ;
> See how the Zephyrs of her breath
> Fan gently all the flowers beneath ;
> See the gay flowers how bright they glow
> Tho' planted in a bed of snow ;
> Yet see how soon they fade and die,
> Scorch'd by the sunshine of her eye,
> Nor wonder if, o'ercome with bliss,
> They droop their heads to steal a kiss.
> Who would not die on that dear breast ?
> Who would not die to be so blest ?

In 1757 and 1758 she had her third and fourth children ; and Lady Elizabeth Waldegrave writes at this time : 'The height of Lady Coventry's ambition at present is to play at quadrille, at which she plays four hours a day and prefers it to all other diversions.'   Probably the poor giddy soul was warned by her medical advisers not to go out at night, for the insidious disease which was so soon to carry her off must even then have shown some signs, though it had not yet marred her beauty.   In November 1759 she went to the meeting of Parliament, in bitter weather ; and in December Horace Walpole writes : ' The Kingdom of beauty is in as great disorder as the Kingdom of Ireland.   My Lady Pembroke looks like a ghost—poor Lady Coventry is going to be one.'   In the spring, however, she rallied ; and in April 1760 he says : ' At the trial of Lord Ferrars, to the amazement of every body Lady Coventry was there, and, what surprised me much more, looked as well as ever.   I sat next but one to her, and should not have asked if she had been ill—yet they are positive she has few weeks to live. She and Lord Bolingbroke seemed to have different thoughts and were acting over the old comedy of eyes.' In less than six months from this time poor Lady Coventry was dead. She died at the age of twenty-seven, of consumption, as her youngest sister had done eight years before, and as her sister the Duchess of Argyll and her nephew the Duke of Hamilton did some years later. The end came at Crome. She was attended by Dr. T. Wall, who wrote, on August 8 previous, an account of her illness to George Selwyn, who was one of her greatest friends. 'I make,' said he, 'no excuse for being minute, because I believe it would be most agreeable to you that I should be so. I have spent most of my time at this place [Crome] since My Lord went to London, and indeed Lady Coventry has been so extremely ill, so much worse than when you saw her last, that she wanted all the attendance I could give her. . . . Yesterday a letter came from the Duchess of Hamilton directed for Lord Coventry. Lady Coventry knew the hand and unluckily opened it. "Hinc illæ lachrymæ !" The Duchess had too plainly expressed her sentiments of Lady Coventry's condition, expressing her concern as for one already in the grave.[1] You who know how apt Lady Coventry is to be affected, may easily conceive the anguish which such a letter would occasion. Indeed it did almost kill her ; I was called to her and found her fainting and almost dying away. However she soon after recovered and I took my leave, but after I was gone the same scene was renewed and her attendants thought her dying. They despatched an express to their Lord, who

---

[1] The Duchess, who was unable to be with her owing to the condition of her own health, expressed a hope that the Rev. Mr. Brooke, who constantly visited Lady Coventry, should administer the Holy Sacrament to her.

I suppose will in consequence, arrive this evening.' Lady Coventry lived nearly two months after the date of this letter.

The furore she had created in life followed her even to the grave, and ten thousand persons are said to have witnessed her funeral.

The following poem was written on Lady Coventry's death by Mason :

Yes, Coventry is dead. Attend the strain,
Daughters of Albion ! ye that light as air
So oft have tripped in her fantastic train,
With hearts as gay and faces half as fair ;
For she was far beyond your brightest bloom,
This envy owns since now her bloom has fled.
Fair as the forms that wave in Fancy's loom
Float in light vision round the poet's head.
Whene'er with soft serenity she smiled,
Or caught the orient blush of quick surprise,
How sweetly mutable, how brightly wild
The liquid lustre from her eyes !
Each look, each motion waked a new-born grace,
That o'er her form a transient glory cast ;
Some lovelier wonder soon usurped the place
Chased by a charm still lovelier than the last.
That bell again ! it tells us what she is !
Or what she was, no more the strain prolong ;
Luxuriant fancy, pause, an hour like this
Demands the tribute of a serious song.
Mason casts it from that sable bier,
Where cold and wan, the slumberer rests her head.
In still small whispers to reflection's ear
She preaches the sublime sermons of the dead.

Lady Coventry left two daughters and a son : Lady Coventry, aged six ; Lady Anne, aged three ; and Lord Deerhurst two years old. Her first-born child, Elizabeth, had

MARIA, COUNTESS OF COVENTRY.
From a Painting by Liotard, at Swallowfield.

I suppose will, in consequence, arrive this evening.' Lady Coventry lived nearly two months after the date of this letter.

The furore she had created in life followed her even to the grave, and ten thousand persons are said to have witnessed her funeral.

The following poem was written on Lady Coventry's death by Mason :

> Yes, Coventry is dead.   Attend the strain,
> Daughters of Albion ! ye that light as air
> So oft have tripped in her fantastic train,
> With hearts as gay and faces half as fair ;
> For she was fair beyond your brightest bloom,
> This envy owns since now her bloom has fled.
> Fair as the forms that wove in Fancy's loom
> Float in light vision round the poet's head.
> Whene'er with soft serenity she smiled,
> Or caught the orient blush of quick surprise,
> How sweetly mutable, how brightly wild
> The liquid lustre from her eyes !
> Each look, each motion waked a new-born grace,
> That o'er her form a transient glory cast ;
> Some lovelier wonder soon usurped the place
> Chased by a charm still lovelier than the last.
> That bell again ! it tells us what she is !
> Or what she was, no more the strain prolong ;
> Luxuriant fancy, pause, an hour like this
> Demands the tribute of a serious song.
> Maria claims it from that sable bier,
> Where cold and wan, the slumberer rests her head.
> In still small whispers to reflection's ear
> She breathes the solemn dictates of the dead.

Lady Coventry left two daughters and a son : Lady Mary Coventry, aged six ; Lady Anne, aged three ; and Lord Deerhurst, only two years old.   Her first-born child, Elizabeth, had died

MARIA, COUNTESS OF COVENTRY.
From a Painting by Liotard, at Swallowfield

GAVIN HAMILTON,

four years previously, aged three. Lady Anne seems to have had considerable good looks, but both sisters had wretched constitutions. Lady Mary married Sir Andrew Bayntun-Rolt of Spye Park, Wilts, and died in 1784, aged thirty, leaving no male issue. Lady Anne married first the Hon. Edward Foley, and secondly Captain S. Wright. Lady Coventry's only son became the seventh Earl of Coventry, and the present Earl is his great-grandson.

We must now take up the history of Elizabeth Gunning, who was a year younger than her sister, Lady Coventry; but as the commencement of their life was the same and they were never separated till their marriages, which took place within three weeks of each other, we need not recapitulate her early successes.

With regard to the comparative good looks of the two sisters, they seem to have had their fair share of admirers. Lady Charlotte Campbell writes : 'My mother [Elizabeth Gunning] has ever told me that her sister Maria exceeded her in beauty. She was not by an inch or more so tall as my mother, who, without the aid of heels, was at least five foot seven,[1] but Lady Coventry's form was faultless, and her dark eyes and the jet black of her eyelashes, with that animation which conscious beauty gave, rendered her more dazzlingly attractive than her younger sister, whose mild[2] dignified air characterised her beauty. Grand and majestic, her manners checked the passion her charms inspired, and I have always heard that the soft beams

[1] One criticism of Elizabeth Gunning's looks was that she was 'too tall to be genteel, and her face out of proportion to her height.'

[2] Dr. Moore in one of his poems alludes to this characteristic :

> . . . at length he roves
> By princely Hamilton's high-cultur'd plains
> To greet the Lady of those fair domains,
> Whose judging eye each native charm has graced

of her blue eye never were known to give one glance in favour of coquetry.' Though her manners were mild, the Duchess had a strong character and a great deal of spirit, which she exemplified on many occasions. When the Wilkes Riots took place, the mob insisted upon every house being lighted up in honour of Wilkes having been returned for Middlesex at the head of the poll. Lord Lorne was in Scotland, but his wife the Duchess, who was in their house in Argyll Buildings awaiting her confinement, refused to illuminate, though the mob brought iron crowbars, tore down the gates, pulled up the pavement, and battered the house for three hours.

Another example of her spirit is recounted by James Boswell. He accompanied Dr. Johnson on his visit to Inveraray in 1773, and was very out of favour with the Duchess, having been counsel for Mr. Douglas[1] in the celebrated litigation with her son. The faithful biographer gives the following account of the visit : 'The Reverend Mr. M'Aulay, one of the Ministers of Inveraray, accompanied us to the Castle, where I presented Dr. Johnson to the Duke of Argyle ; we then got into a low one-horse chaise, ordered for us by the Duke, in which we drove about the place. Dr. Johnson was much struck by the grandeur and elegance of this princely seat. He thought, however, the Castle too low ; said, " What I admire here is the total defiance of expense." The Duke placed Dr. Johnson next himself at

> With all the polished elegance of taste,
> Mild as her aspect, as her soul serene,
> Pure as her life, which never knew a stain.

The Duchess seems to have had particularly good taste, judging by all the beautiful marqueterie furniture &c. at Inveraray Castle. The finest things there, including the tapestry, were nearly all collected by her and the Duke during their visits abroad.

[1] Dr. Johnson espoused the cause of the Duke of Hamilton in this trial.

table. I was in fine spirits, though sensible that I had the misfortune of not being in favour with the Duchess, who was very attentive to Dr. Johnson ; I know not how a middle-state came to be mentioned, her Grace wished to hear him on that point. " Madam," said he, " your own relation, Mr. Archibald Campbell, can tell you better about it than I can ; he was a Bishop of the nonjuring communion and wrote a book on the subject." [1] We went to tea—the Duke and I walked up and down the drawing-room conversing ; the Duchess still continued to shew the same marked coldness for me, for which, though I suffered from it, I made many allowances. Her Grace made Dr. Johnson come and sit by her, and asked why he made his journey so late in the year (October). " Why, Madam," said he, " you know Mr. Boswell must attend the Court of Session." " I know nothing of Mr. Boswell," said the Duchess, with some sharpness. I felt the Duchess's speech as rather too severe ; but when I thought that the punishment was inflicted by so dignified a beauty, I had that kind of consolation which a man would feel who is strangled by a silken cord. Dr. Johnson used afterwards a droll expression upon her enjoying the three titles, Hamilton, Brandon, and Argyll. Borrowing an image from the Turkish Empire, he called her a Duchess with three tails ! ' [2]

When the Duchess was one of the Ladies of the Bed-

[1] Archibald Campbell was son of Lord Niel Campbell and grandson of the Marquis of Argyll executed in 1661, and his mother was Lady Vere Ker, daughter of the Earl of Lothian. He was made a bishop of the Scotch Church in 1711, but lived almost entirely in London, where he died in 1744. He was a strong Jacobite and Nonjuror. He took part in the Monmouth Rebellion, but escaped to Surinam. His book, to which Dr. Johnson alludes, was called *Some Primitive Doctrines revived : or Intermediate or Middle State of Departed Souls (as to Happiness or Misery) before the Day of Judgment, plainly prov'd by Holy Scripture and the Concurrent Testimony of the Fathers of the Church* (1713). See *Lockhart Papers*, ii. 99–102.

[2] The Duchess's usual signature was ' E. Argyll Hamilton.'

chamber, Queen Charlotte, jealous of her influence with the King, treated her at one time so badly that she contemplated resigning her post.[1] The Duke consented on condition that he might dictate the letter of resignation. The letter was accordingly written; but the Duchess, dissatisfied with the terms, added a P.S. to this effect: 'Though I wrote the letter, the Duke dictated it'! · Ultimately the affair was arranged and the Duchess retained her place.

Lady Charlotte Campbell in her Journal says: 'My mother once told me a little anecdote which I think proves better than volumes the different dispositions of the sisters. For a grand masked ball that was to take place at Chesterfield House, my mother had a magnificent Sultana's dress, sparkling with gold and jewels.[2] She appeared in all that blaze of beauty before her sister, who had not yet attired herself in the habit of a Quakeress which she had chosen, and who no sooner cast her eyes on the brilliancy of the Sultana dress than she became perfectly dissatisfied with her own; my mother saw this and instantly proposed an exchange. As the modest Quakeress my mother became a duchess, for it was that night the Duke of Hamilton proposed to her.' James, sixth Duke of Hamilton, was the only son of the fifth Duke and Lady Anne Cochrane, one of the three beautiful daughters of the Earl of Dundonald. He inherited some of his mother's good looks, but was an inveterate gambler and dissipated in

---

[1] Horace Walpole says the Queen was angry with the Duchess of Hamilton for making friends with the Duchess of Gloucester. This she certainly did; and the author has a pastelle portrait of the Duchess of Gloucester which she gave to the Duchess of Hamilton.

[2] It is said that the funds as well as the time were wanting to procure suitable fancy dresses for both sisters, and that Sheridan, hearing this, immediately went to Peg Woffington and borrowed from her for one of them an Eastern dress in which she acted one of her most effective characters.

every sense of the term. At this time he was twenty-eight years of age; but before he was twenty he had engaged himself to another Elizabeth, the famous, or rather infamous, Miss Chudleigh. She was descended from an old Devonshire family, and her father, Colonel Chudleigh, had a post at Chelsea College,[1] but at his death his widow and daughter were left in poor circumstances. The latter made the acquaintance of Mr. Pulteney, who obtained for her an appointment as Maid of Honour to the Princess of Wales. She soon became distinguished for the brilliancy of her repartee and the extreme vivacity of her nature, and, notwithstanding that she had a violent temper, appears to have been in early life most fascinating. Amongst her many admirers the young Duke of Hamilton was the one she preferred, and he was very fond of her. He obtained her promise that on his return from a foreign tour she should become his wife, and they agreed to write to each other on every opportunity. Miss Chudleigh during his absence went to live with an aunt, Mrs. Hanmer, who immediately set to work to favour the views of another of her admirers, Captain Augustus Hervey. Miss Chudleigh particularly disliked him; but the aunt worked successfully on the pride of her niece by intercepting the letters of the Duke, until at last, piqued by his supposed neglect, she was prevailed on to accept the hand of Captain Hervey, and they were privately married in August 1744 at Lainston, in the county of Southampton, in a private chapel adjoining the country house of Mr. Merrill. She virtually separated from him the day of their marriage, which was kept secret, and they saw little of each other afterwards,

---

[1] This was then quite away from London; and we are told, as an example of the courage of Miss Chudleigh's mother, that she walked thither each evening from London, with a brace of pistols in her pocket as the means of her defence!

she returning to her post as Maid of Honour ; but she had
one son by him, who died an infant. On the return of the
Duke of Hamilton, he again renewed his addresses, and, like
the Duke of Ancaster and others, was rejected. She then
went through a career of pleasure; but the threats of her
husband to disclose their marriage always hung over her, and
at last she thought she would destroy the sole evidence of the
ceremony. The clergyman who married them was dead, and
she obtained access to the register and tore out the entry concerning herself. Some years after, Captain Hervey succeeded
to the earldom of Bristol and a considerable fortune, and his
wife then repented what she had done, and it is said went again
to the chapel where she was married, and surreptitiously paid to
have her marriage re-inserted. After this, the Duke of Kingston
being much in love with her and willing to marry her, she
managed, with the collusion of Lord Bristol (who was now most
anxious to be quit of her), to get a sentence of the court pro-
nouncing the nullity of their marriage ; and in March 1769 she
married the Duke of Kingston at St. Margaret's, Westminster,
by special licence of the Archbishop of Canterbury, she being
called in the licence ' Spinster.' The favours, we are told, were
worn by the highest personages in the kingdom, including the
Prince and Princess of Wales. During the lifetime of the
Duke no attempt was made to dispute the legality of the procedure ; but soon after his death, a woman, who had been present
at Miss Chudleigh's marriage with Mr. Hervey, went to the
relations of the Duke and acquainted them with every fact, the
result being that the Duchess was indicted for bigamy. The
trial, which lasted five days, ended in her conviction, and she
narrowly avoided being branded. She escaped and went abroad,
finally settling at St. Petersburg, where she was well received by

the Empress Catherine. She there bought an estate for £25,000, which she called 'Chudleigh,' and where she erected works for making brandy. Ultimately she returned to France, where she bought more estates, and died there in 1788 at Sainte-Assise.

And now, after this long digression *à propos* of Elizabeth Chudleigh to whom the Duke of Hamilton was once engaged, we must return to Elizabeth Gunning, to whom, as we have seen, he offered his hand and heart at Lord Chesterfield's masquerade eight years later. A month after, they were married at Mayfair Chapel by the Rev. Alexander Keith. The ceremony took place on February 14, 1752, according to the story repeated by Horace Walpole, at midnight, a curtain ring being used on the occasion !

The public crowded to see the Duchess quite as much after her marriage as before. When she was presented at Court in March, Horace Walpole tells us that 'even the noble mob in the drawing-room clambered upon chairs and tables to look at her.' Her sister Maria, Lady Coventry, went about with her until both brides left London, which they did in April. The Duke and Duchess then went to Hamilton Palace. The 'Dublin Journal' for May 2, 1752, says : 'When his Grace the Duke of Hamilton arrived at Berwick with his Duchess on his way to Scotland, all the country gentlemen and persons of distinction in the town assembled to satisfy a natural curiosity of seeing a lady whose superior charms Fame has carried to the remotest corners of the nation without the least exaggeration. His Grace gave a splendid entertainment and concluded the evening with a Ball.' Horace Walpole writes in March : 'The world is still mad about the Gunnings : there are mobs at their doors to see them get into their chairs, and people go early to get places at the theatre when it is known they will be there.' It is actually said to be a fact that the Duchess gave Tate Wilkinson, the actor, benefits at his theatre.   On their way to Scotland the Duke and Duchess of Hamilton stopped one night at an inn in Yorkshire, and no less than 700 people sat up all night to see the Duchess get into her post-chaise in the morning.

During the next three years the Duke, who proved himself a worthless husband, kept the Duchess almost entirely at Hamilton, whilst he devoted his time to hunting, drinking, and low company.   Her justly offended pride ill brooked the mortification she daily endured, but she found a sensible, clever, and sincere friend in Lady Susan Stewart (afterwards Lady Stafford), who was her constant companion during this period ; and the Duchess occupied herself in trying to ameliorate the condition of the peasantry on the Hamilton estate.   She started looms for spinning cotton and linen yarn and making fine Holland cambric and lawn.   In January 1753 she gave birth to her daughter Elizabeth (afterwards Countess of Derby), and in 1755 and 1756 to her sons James and Douglas, both of whom became successively Dukes of Hamilton.   In October 1756 the Duchess reappeared in London, when Horace Walpole writes : 'The Duchess of Hamilton has brought her beauty to London at the only instant when it will not make a crowd . . . so much are we engrossed by this ministerial ferment.'

In January 1758 she became a widow at the early age of twenty-four.   The Duke had increased his natural delicacy by the vicious habits of his life, and he died from internal inflammation, which came on after a 'hunting match' at Great Tew in Oxfordshire, the seat of his uncle, Anthony Tracy Keck, being only thirty-four years of age.   The Duchess spent much of the first year of her widowhood with her three young children at Hamilton Palace, which now belonged to her eldest son, James,

JOHN, 5TH DUKE OF ARGYLL.

From a Painting by Gainsborough at Swallowfield.

seventh Duke of Hamilton, who was barely three years old; then she went to London, where she had a house in Bond Street, opposite the 'Blue Posts,' an inn immortalised by Etherege in his comedy, 'She would if she could'—a circumstance which gave rise to many jokes.

Soon after the year was over, the Duchess married the handsome Jack Campbell, son of Colonel John Campbell and the beautiful Mary Bellenden. He was then only a colonel in the 14th Regiment of Dragoons, but his father was heir-apparent to his first cousin, Archibald, third Duke of Argyll.[1] Horace Walpole, writing to the Hon. H. Conway, says: 'It is the prettiest match in the world since yours, and everybody likes it but the Duke of Bridgewater;'[2] and to Sir Horace Mann he writes: 'The Duchess of Hamilton is going to marry Colonel Campbell, Lady Ailesbury's brother. It is a match that would not disgrace Arcadia. Her beauty has made sufficient noise, and in some people's eyes is even improved; he has a most pleasing countenance, person, and manner.' To another correspondent he says: 'If her fortune is singular, so is her merit. Such uncommon noise as her beauty made has not at all impaired the modesty of her behaviour.' Mrs. Elizabeth Montagu, the celebrated blue-stocking, no mean judge of character, thus announces the engagement in a letter to her husband, now in the possession of the writer:[3] 'Duchess

[1] His father succeeded as fourth Duke two years later, when Colonel Campbell became Lord Lorne, and in 1770, at the death of his father, he became Duke of Argyll.

[2] Francis, Duke of Bridgewater, was desperately in love with the Duchess, who refused him. Lord Chesterfield in one of his letters says that soon after his refusal the Duke withdrew entirely from the fashionable world, and from this ducal Hegira dates the rise of British canal navigation.

[3] This letter, which has hitherto never been published, was given to the writer by Mrs. Climenson, *née* Montagu, who is about to publish a collection of Mrs. Montagu's letters.

Hamilton is going to be married to Colonel Campbell, a young man of good character and heir to the Duke of Argylle [*sic*]. So between her husband's interests in Scotland and her son's she will be queen of Scotland. She is as good as she is fair, and consequently almost an angel : she has behaved with ye decency and dignity due to ye rank to which she has been raised.' Some months after her marriage Horace Walpole entertained the Duchess at Strawberry Hill, when he raved about her beauty, but at the close of the same year he writes that she is much altered, has become a skeleton, and is 'in a deep consumption.' It is possible that the seeds of this insidious disease may have already shown themselves,[1] and we do find that she was ordered abroad for the winter ; but the alteration in her looks was merely temporary, and may have been the result of her grief in losing her sister, Lady Coventry, who died this year, and to whom she was devotedly attached, this trial coming upon her before she had recovered her strength after the birth of her first-born Campbell child. Later, Horace Walpole writes to Horace Mann in Florence : 'I question whether you will see the Duchess : these mails have brought so good an account of her that unless she grows worse they will scarce pass Lyons, where they are established for the winter.' Accordingly we find that she returned to England the following May, apparently quite well, and in July was chosen as one of the two ladies sent to bring over to this country George III.'s bride. In July 1761 Horace Walpole says : 'Lord Harcourt is to go to the Court of Mecklenburg-Strelitz, if he can find it, to arrange the marriage of George III. with Princess Charlotte of that ilk.' The Duchess was made one of the six Ladies of the Bedchamber, and went with the

[1] Gilly Williams, writing to George Selwyn as early as 1765, says of the Duchess of Hamilton, 'She has already begun to cough.'

Duchess of Ancaster [1] to meet her at Stade. When the Princess saw the two Duchesses it is said that she burst into tears and exclaimed, 'Are all the women of England as beautiful as you ?' The voyage back was performed in an Admiralty yacht under the charge of Admiral Kingsmill, and lasted ten days, and the two Duchesses were extremely ill. The royal party landed at Harwich, and they slept that night at Lord Abercorn's house at Witham. The following day they went on to London. When the Princess saw the palace she turned pale, at which the Duchess of Hamilton smiled. 'My dear Duchess,' said the Princess, 'you may laugh ; you have been married twice, but it is no joke to me.' The day after the marriage there was a Drawing Room, and all the ladies were presented to the Princess by the Duchess of Hamilton.

At the coronation, Horace Walpole says, 'the Duchess of Hamilton was almost in possession of her greatest beauty.' On November 26 there was a small private court ball, consisting of not above twelve or thirteen couples, which began at 6.30 and was over by one, and the Duchess of Hamilton was one of the dancers. The King danced the whole time with the Queen. Of the appearance of Queen Charlotte the Duchess of Hamilton gives this unflattering account : 'Niggardly endow'd by Nature with any charms to render her desirable, the stiff German stays added formality to her Majesty's already stiff figure, and her hair which was black and greasy, being drawn tight from the head in an erect dry frize, betray'd the oilyness of the bare skin between every black pin that supported it. . . . At night she insisted on sleeping in her stiff stays—a German

[1] The Duchess of Ancaster ever afterwards was an intimate friend of the Duchess of Hamilton, and she gave her her portrait in pastelle, which is now in the possession of the writer.

piece of prudery to which, I should imagine, the King had no objection.'

In August 1763 the Duchess of Hamilton went to Paris with the Duke and Duchess of Ancaster. Horace Walpole says: ' The French do not arrive in such shoals as we do at Paris ; there are no fewer than five English duchesses there, Ancaster, Richmond, Bridgewater, Hamilton, and Douglas : the two last, indeed, upon an extraordinary lawsuit.' This lawsuit became one of the most remarkable *causes célèbres* ever litigated. In 1761, Archibald Douglas, third Duke of Douglas,[1] having died without issue, the ducal title became extinct. The marquisate of Douglas devolved upon the young Duke of Hamilton, who was then only six years old. The real and personal property went to Mr. Archibald Stewart, his nephew, who was served as nearest and lawful heir to the Duke of Douglas, and in consequence took the name of Douglas and claimed the title of Earl of Angus, as being a title which descended through the women. Mr. Archibald Stewart claimed to be the son of Sir John Stewart, Bart., of Grandtully, by his wife Lady Jane Douglas, sister of the last Duke of Douglas ; but the guardians of the young Duke of Hamilton asserted that he and his nominal twin brother Sholto (who had died an infant) were not the children of Lady Jane, who had surreptitiously procured them in Paris and passed them off as her own, she being at the time in her fifty-first year[2] and the event being attended

---

[1] This Duke of Douglas was a man of ungovernable passions and not of sane mind. He killed a Captain Kerr, who was staying with him, in cold blood because he heard that he wished to marry his sister Lady Jane. He was not prosecuted for the murder in consequence, it was said, of his adherence to the House of Hanover.

[2] Lady Jane Douglas was in her forty-ninth year when she married Sir John Stewart. She died in 1753, and Chambers says her death ' took place under circumstances of great distress in the second flat of a humble cottage at Drumsheigh, entered by an outside stair.'

MARY, DUCHESS OF ANCASTER.
From a Pastelle at Swallowfield.

with many peculiar and suspicious circumstances. Voluminous evidence was taken in France as well as in Britain, and it was to consult with Mr. Andrew Stuart, one of the young Duke's guardians who was living in Paris for the purpose of collecting evidence, that the Duchess came there in 1763. In 1767 the courts of Scotland decided in the Duke of Hamilton's favour. The decision caused great riots in Edinburgh. Seven judges voted on each side, and the Lord President gave the casting vote against the son of Sir John. The judges who gave their decision for the Duke had their windows broken, and seven asses 'in honour of them' were led through the town.[1] An appeal being made to the House of Lords, the first judgment was reversed, and the cause finally determined in 1771 in favour of Mr. Douglas, a judgment in which Lord Mansfield and Lord Camden united,[2] and against which only five of a numerous body entered a protest. Meanwhile, whilst the Douglas case was going on, the young Duke of Hamilton fell ill and died, and his brother Douglas, eighth Duke of Hamilton, became the 'pursuer.'

The death of her first-born son, whom she idolised, was a most terrible and crushing blow to the Duchess. He and his brother had scarlet fever at Eton some two or three years before, when she went there to nurse them. The eldest was never strong afterwards, and outgrew his strength, being 5 feet 8 inches in height when only fourteen years of age. He ultimately showed signs of rapid consumption, from which he died on July 7, 1769, deeply and deservedly regretted by all who knew him. He was

[1] These seven judges were Lords Clerk, Alemoore, Kennet, Barjarg, Elliock, Stonefield, and Hailes.

[2] Lord Monboddo, as the chief pleader on Mr. Douglas's side, was said to have convinced Lords Camden and Mansfield.

singularly handsome—Gilly Williams says, ' the handsomest boy he ever saw '—and he was equally charming, clever, and good. This opinion is endorsed by Dr. Moore, who wrote the epitaph which is on his tomb in the mausoleum at Hamilton Palace.

> All the reflected dignity that shines
> Through the long annals of two princely lines ;
> And all that liberal nature could impart,
> To charm the eye, or captivate the heart ;
> With every genuine mark that could presage
> Intrinsic greatness in maturer age :
> A bosom glowing with fair Honour's flame,
> A love of Science, and a thirst for Fame,
> Adorn'd the youthful tenant of this tomb,
> Torn from his country's hope in early bloom.
> Whoe'er thou art, who view'st this plaintive stone,
> If e'er thy soul exalted o'er a son ;
> If public fame, avowing his desert,
> Echo'd the praises of the partial heart ;
> Though all may mourn, 'tis thou alone can'st know
> The piercing anguish of a parent's woe.

And in one of his works Dr. Moore says of him : ' He was distinguished by more brilliant personal advantages and nobler endowments of mind than I ever saw united at that period of life.' This Dr. Moore who attended him in his last illness, assisted by Dr. Cullen,[1] was, besides being a skilful physician, a

---

[1] Sir James Macintosh writes in 1784 : ' Dr. Cullen was the most celebrated medical teacher and writer in Europe, whose accurate descriptions of disease will probably survive a long succession of equally specious systems. When quite a young man he was first brought forward in the following manner : Archibald, Duke of Argyll, was staying in the neighbourhood of Shotts, where Cullen was practising amongst the farmers and country people. The Duke was engaged in some chemical research for which he wanted some apparatus, and his host, thinking that young Cullen could help him, asked him to dinner, which was the commencement of a lifelong acquaintance with the house of Argyll. After this the sixth Duke of Hamilton had him when he was suddenly taken ill, and was so benefited by his skill and gratified by his conversation, that he obtained for him a place in the

man of great general attainments and an author of some note. His chief work was 'Zeluco,' which at the time met with extraordinary success, and was the professed prototype of 'Childe Harold.'[1] It is curious to find this now absolutely unknown author criticising and advising Robert Burns, who received all his criticisms and advice with grateful humility. We have before us one of Dr. Moore's letters to the poet, in which he says : 'You ought to deal more sparingly for the future in the provincial dialect. Why should you, by using that, limit the number of your admirers to those who understand the Scottish when you can extend it to all persons of taste who understand the English language ? ' And then the Doctor goes on to recommend him how to set to work. Burns writes to him : 'The hope to be admired for ages is, in by far the greater part of those even who are authors of repute, an unsubstantial dream. For my part, my first ambition was, and still my strongest wish is, to please my compeers, the rustic inmates of the hamlet. I am very willing to admit that I have some poetic abilities ; and as few, if any writers, either moral or poetical, are intimately acquainted with the classes of mankind among whom I have chiefly mingled, I may have seen men and manners in a different phasis from what is common, which may assist originality of thought. Still I know very well the novelty of my character has by far the greatest share in the learned and polite notice I have lately had ; and in a language where Pope and Churchill have raised the laugh, and Shenstone and Gray drawn the tear, where Thomson

University of Glasgow, where his talents soon became conspicuous. He afterwards settled at Hamilton, where the celebrated surgeon, William Hunter, was his assistant for three years.

[1] Lord Byron says in his preface : 'Had I proceeded with this poem, this character would have deepened as he drew to the close, for the outline which I once meant to fill up was, with some exceptions, the sketch of a modern Timon, perhaps a poetical Zeluco.'

and Beattie have painted the landscape, and Lyttelton and Collins described the heart, I am not vain enough to hope for distinguished poetic fame.' And in another letter Burns writes to Dr. Moore : 'Pardon my seeming neglect in delaying so long to acknowledge the honour you have done me in your kind notice of me. Not many months ago I knew no other employment than following the plough, nor could boast anything higher than a distant acquaintance with a country clergyman. Mere greatness never embarrasses me, but genius polished by learning, and at its proper point of elevation in the eye of the world, this spectacle I frequently meet with and tremble at its approach. I scorn the affectation of seeming modesty to cover self-conceit. That I have some merit I do not deny ; but I see, with frequent wringings of heart, that the novelty of my character and the honest national prejudice of my countrymen have borne me to a height altogether untenable to my ability.'

The Duchess was inconsolable at the loss of her eldest son, and never went anywhere for three years. To add to her sorrow, her second son, the eighth Duke, also showed signs of a delicate temperament, and at the age of sixteen she had to send him on a lengthened tour abroad, where he remained till he was twenty-one. He was accompanied by Dr. Moore and his son John, with 'a suitable attendance.' The connection with the Duke of Hamilton nearly cost young Moore his life. The Duke, though only sixteen, was allowed to wear a sword. One day, in an idle humour, he drew it, and began to amuse himself by fencing at his companion, and laughed as he forced him to skip from side to side to shun false thrusts. The Duke continued this sport till Moore unluckily started in the line of the sword and received it in his flank. Dr. Moore was speedily on the spot,

POMPEO BATTONI, pinx

and found his son wounded on the outside of his ribs. The incident led to the formation of a lasting friendship between the penitent and his almost victim. The Duchess procured a commission for John Moore as ensign in the 51st Regiment, which he joined at Minorca in 1776, being then only fifteen years of age; and he ultimately became the famous hero of Corunna.[1]

The interests of another child at last roused the Duchess from her grief, and she once more entered the gay world for the purpose of launching into the vortex of fashion her daughter, Lady Betty Hamilton, who made her *début* at Almack's, which was then the most aristocratic and the most autocratic assembly that probably ever existed. It owed its origin to the Duchess. Her maid, who was sister of Dr. Cullen,[2] married one Mackal, a tavern-keeper. He was a clever pushing man, and Lord Lorne, the Duchess's husband, advanced him money to set up this assembly in King Street, St. James's.[3] It was opened in 1765 with a ball, at which the Duke of Cumberland, then called 'the hero of Culloden,' was present, the Duchess having induced him to patronise it.[4] Mackal reversed his name and called himself Almack, and became a large adventurer in clubs. He first formed the club afterwards known as Brooks's, which in the beginning of its career was held at Almack's rooms.

In 1777, on the return of the Duke of Hamilton, the Duchess seems to have had no further cause of anxiety on the

---

[1] In a large picture painted at Rome by Gavin Hamilton, Dr. Moore and his son John are introduced as well as the young Duke.

[2] See p. 126.

[3] Later known as Willis's Rooms. Almack died in January 1781.

[4] Gilly Williams, writing to George Selwyn in 1765, says : 'Our female Almack's flourishes beyond description. Almack's Scotch face, in a bag wig, waiting at Supper, would divert you, as would his lady, in a sack, making tea and curtseying to our Duchesses.'

score of his health, and he had grown into a very handsome young man, as may be seen in Pompeo Battoni's beautiful portrait of him at Inveraray, which was painted in 1775 when he was at Rome ;[1] but the wildness which he inherited from his father soon began to assert itself and gave his mother many a pang. Before he had sown his wild oats he married Miss Elizabeth Ann Burrell, the youngest daughter of Mr. Peter Burrell of Beckenham, Kent, and the sister of his friend Mr. Burrell, who became the first Lord Gwydir.[2] Lady Charlotte Campbell writes of Miss Burrell : ' In her my brother had all with regard to mental and moral qualities that could have yielded him domestic happiness. With respect to her person people's taste differed. She was little, though very well made, very fair in her complexion,[3] and her manners were gentle and reserved.' These last two characteristics seem to show that she was ill suited to brook with her young madcap of a husband. Mrs. Montagu in one of her letters thus announces her engagement : ' Miss Burrell is to marry Duke Hamilton and accompanies him to America, where it is very proper he should go as the amplest field for him to indulge his passion for shooting. He has exercised himself with shooting out of a wind-gun

[1] There is another picture, in which he appears on horseback on the sea-shore. It was painted by G. Garrard and was engraved by W. Ward. Douglas, Duke of Hamilton, was the first who wore his hair short, and set the fashion.

[2] Lord Gwydir married Lady Elizabeth Bertie (sister of the last Duke of Ancaster), to whom, on her brother's death, reverted the barony of Willoughby de Eresby, with the inherited office of Great Chamberlain.

[3] Soon after their marriage Sir Joshua painted Douglas, Duke of Hamilton, and his bride. She is on horseback in a red riding-habit, and he is standing by her side. There is a curious history attached to this picture. After his wife divorced him, the Duke gave it to his mistress, Mrs. Estens, the actress, who afterwards allowed Sir Thomas Lawrence to have it in exchange for a portrait by him of herself. At Sir Thomas Lawrence's death it was sold and came into the possession of Mr. Strutt. The face of the Duchess is very like a miniature of her by Cosway which belonged to the late Mr. William Russell.

ANGELICA KAUFFMANN, *pinx*

LADY AUGUSTA CAMPBELL.

across Hanover Square, to the utter dismay of old Lady West-morland and Sir Thomas Fredericks.' The marriage turned out very badly ; and after sixteen years' matrimony, during which time the Duchess had no child, she divorced him in 1794. Lady Hester Stanhope, in her Memoirs, says : ' The Duke never lived with the Duchess. He was in love with Lady ——, and used to disguise himself as a one-legged soldier—as a beggar assuming a hundred masquerades, sleeping in out-houses, &c. That was the woman F. M—— married. Oh ! there was a man (the Duke) perfect from top to toe, with not a single flaw in his person.' He died in 1799, aged forty-three, a life of constant excesses of all kinds tending to undermine his naturally delicate constitution. Having no legitimate issue,[1] he was suc-ceeded by his father's half-brother,[2] Lord Archibald Hamilton, in all his titles except the barony of Hamilton of Hambledon in Leicestershire, which devolved upon him at his mother's death, and now went to his half-brother the Marquis of Lorne.[3]

The Duchess of Argyll did not live to see the sad *finale* of her son's matrimonial fiasco, but she was doomed to meet with still further disappointments in her family.

In a contemporary magazine of the day we read an account of one of the ' Birthday Balls ' given at St. James's in 1777, in which Lady Augusta Campbell is described as dancing with the Duke of Cumberland, her dress being white satin and boue de Paris, with gold and white trimming, foil, &c. ; and again, in May 1779, the magnificent ball given by the Knights of the

[1] Douglas, eighth Duke of Hamilton, left an illegitimate daughter who was called ' Anne Douglas.' She married in 1820 Henry Robert, third Lord Rossmore, and died s.p. in 1844.

[2] The Duchess of Hamilton remarried, in 1800, the first Marquis of Exeter.

[3] Elizabeth Gunning, Duchess of Hamilton and Brandon and of Argyll, was created in 1776 Baroness Hamilton of Hambledon (Leicestershire) in her own right.

Bath was opened by the Duke of Cumberland and Lady Augusta. Lady Augusta was the Duchess of Argyll's eldest Campbell daughter, and was only seventeen at this time. Though not a great beauty, she had considerable looks ot a most refined and aristocratic nature,[1] and she sang exquisitely. A little later, in 1781, we read that she was present with her mother at the ball given at Windsor to celebrate the Prince of Wales's nineteenth birthday. He was then paying her considerable attention, dancing a great deal with her, and making her sit next to him at supper at one of the three small royal tables. Lady Charlotte says : ' Augusta received for some time, with undissembled pleasure, the addresses of the Prince. Whither my mother's ambitious views tended I cannot attempt to fathom, but a coolness ensued between her and the Queen from this moment. . . .' The Prince sent Lady Augusta a valuable diamond necklace, which, as it was not accompanied by an offer of marriage, was very properly sent back by her mother to H.R.H. ' When all my mother's romantic hopes in this direction were over, Lord Graham, eldest son of the Duke of Montrose, was the next person her eyes were turn'd upon as a proper and eligible husband for Augusta ;[2] the idea pleased my father also, who, tho' never addicted to plans or intrigues in this most

---

[1] Lady Charlotte Campbell had a lovely picture by Angelica Kauffmann, in which Lady Augusta is standing in front of her mother playing the harp. This picture is now in the possession of Mr. Campbell Johnston. Bartolozzi made a three-quarter-length engraving of Lady Augusta from it ; and there is also another well-known engraving of her by the same artist, entitled ' The St. James's Beauty.'

[2] The following is a paragraph from one of the society papers of the day : ' Although the Drawing-room at St. James's on Monday was rather thin, the Ballroom at night was exceedingly crowded. Lady Augusta Campbell danced the 2nd Minuet with the Marquis of Graham. Her dress was a pea-green satin enriched with a gold trimming and a great quantity of artificial flowers. The elegance of this young lady's person, her graceful manner of dancing, and the particular taste of her dress were exceedingly admired.'

LADY AUGUSTA CAMPBELL, "A ST JAMES'S BEAUTY"
From the Engraving by F. Bartolozzi of the Painting by J H Benwell.

innocent sense, still thought such a match desirable for the daughter he adored. My mother, who was very fond of Lord Abercorn, then Mr. Hamilton, made use of him as a tool to bring this matter to bear ; but whatever might once have been Lord Graham's intentions with respect to Augusta, her undisguised passion for the Prince had checked every favourable opinion he might have entertained for her. Indeed, for some time she did not attempt to rouse herself from the state of lethargy and despondency into which she had fallen.' Lady Augusta Campbell remained single until she was twenty-eight, when she married, without her parents' consent, Henry Mordaunt Clavering, son of General Sir John Clavering, K.B., and his wife, Lady Diana West. 'This match,' says Lady Charlotte Campbell, ' had been made from a masquerade after only a fortnight's acquaintance in the Highlands. Though an honourable man in the world's acceptation, Colonel Clavering was of a character little likely to make a woman's happiness and fortune, and splendour lent no brilliant light to gloss over the rude surface with illusion.' The marriage was not a happy one, and after some years both agreed to part. Lady Augusta died in 1831, aged seventy-one, leaving one daughter, Charlotte Catharine Clavering (who married in 1817 Miles Fletcher, Esq., son of Archibald Fletcher the author and a learned lawyer, as Lord Brougham calls him, styled the ' Father of Burgh Reform,' and two sons, Douglas Clavering, who was drowned in the Redwing, and Rawdon Clavering, R.E., father of Sir Henry Augustus Clavering, the tenth and last Baronet.

The Duchess had now deeply felt the hand of adversity, and, considering the dazzling brightness of her morn of life, its noon was scarcely to be envied. The loss of her darling eldest son, the wild life of the second one, and the matrimonial miseries of her daughters, all conspired to prey on her delicate frame, where Nature had already sown the seeds of that fatal hereditary disorder, consumption ; and during the last five years of her life the beautiful Duchess was in a very bad state of health.   She was, however, blessed with the most excellent and devoted husband, which enabled her to bear up against all her trials, and for his sake she was cheerful and beautiful to the last.   Some one had said of her that 'she seemed composed of a finer clay than the rest of her sex,'

> But coughs will come when sighs depart—and now
>   And then before sighs cease ; for oft the one
> Will bring the other, ere the lakelike brow
> Is ruffled by a wrinkle . . .
>   . . . and while a glow,
> Hectic and brief as summer's day nigh done,
>   O'erspreads the cheek which seems *too pure for clay*.

During this time the Duchess was never in Scotland.   She lived mostly very quietly either at Argyll House, the family mansion in Argyll Street, Regent Street,[1] or at Ealing Grove, which the Duke bought as a country residence for her near London.   At both places she had a little *coterie* of relations and intimate friends who were constantly with her.   Lady Charlotte Campbell in her Journal mentions among the *habitués* of this date, Lord and Lady Frederick Campbell, Marshal Conway ('the divine Marshal,' as she calls him) and Lady Ailesbury, Mary, Duchess of Richmond, Lady Mary Coke[2] and her sisters Lady Greenwich and Lady Betty McKenzie, Mrs. Damer, the two Miss Gunnings (daughters of Sir Robert Gunning, Bart., one of whom became Mrs. Digby and

---

[1] This afterwards became the property of Lord Aberdeen, and was pulled down about 1865.

[2] Lady Mary Coke for many years had a quarrel with the Duchess, but became quite reconciled and was very attentive to her in her last years.

ELIZABETH, DUCHESS OF HAMILTON AND BRANDON, AND OF ARGYLL,
AND HER DAUGHTERS,
LADY AUGUSTA CAMPBELL AND LADY CHARLOTTE CAMPBELL.
From a Picture by Angelica Kauffmann, now in the possession of Mrs. Campbell Johnston.

the other Mrs. Ross), General and Lady Cecilia Johnston, Mrs. Grenville, Mrs. French, Lady Dillon, Lady Mount Edgcumbe, the two Miss Berrys, Mrs. Anderson, Lord and Lady Abercorn, Horace Walpole, Sir Andrew Stewart, Sir Robert Keith, and Generals O'Hara, Skene, and Murray.

When cold weather began, the Duke always took the Duchess to the South; and the last time she appeared at any public assembly was in 1785 at Marseilles, where she and her family spent three months. Cradock in his 'Memoirs' says: 'I had the honour of dining with them the day of the Picnic Ball, and the Duchess as soon as possible retired to dress. She came down to coffee in all her splendour: every one was struck with astonishment, and the Lieutenant of Police, who was present, exclaimed, "I have never seen any one so completely beautiful before!"' And this was when the Duchess was fifty-one years of age and in very bad health. Cradock says in another part of his 'Memoirs,' written at Marseilles: 'The Argyle family, affable to all, has greatly contributed to enliven our evenings. There were no cards introduced, but they had frequent concerts, and their own family could always supply excellent catches and glees; but the health of the Duchess rather declined, and though she had her own physician, Dr. Robertson, with her, yet from mere kindness she condescended to call in Dr. Fischer of Göttingen, who gave so much satisfaction that her Grace was pleased to write a letter in his behalf to the Duke of York, who was then resident at Göttingen.'

The winter of 1789 was spent in Italy, whither the Duchess went 'with a great train,' which Horace Walpole says she always loved. Besides her young daughter, Lady Charlotte Campbell, who was only fourteen, she was accompanied by her two married daughters—poor Lady Derby, who was now a confirmed invalid, and Lady Augusta Clavering and her husband—

and other members of her family ; and of course her own doctor went with them. During this winter the Duchess saw a great deal of Sir William Hamilton, who was related to her first husband ; and Mr. Cordy Jeaffreson in his 'Historical Biography of Lady Hamilton,' founded on letters in the possession of Mr. Alfred Morrison, says : 'It is certain that the Duchess's good and numerous acts of kindness were powerful in determining Sir William Hamilton to marry Emma. Many things might be told yet again to Elizabeth Gunning's honour, but of them all, none smells sweeter or blossoms brighter than her brave and sympathetic goodness to Emma Hart.' The Duchess did not return till the summer, and died the following December, being then fifty-six years old, having kept her bed for some days only. She was buried at Kilmun, the burying-place of the Argylls.

The portraits existing of the Duchess are not equal to her beauty. It is very unfortunate that Gainsborough, who painted her husband, did nothing of her·; and apparently Sir Joshua only painted her once (1758-9), and this picture, such as it was, a full-length life-size (in red mantle lined ermine, with two doves), has entirely lost its colours and has a ghastly green hue all over the face.[1] The best portraits of her are by Gavin Hamilton, Francis Cotes, R.A., and Angelica Kauffmann. The full-length by Gavin Hamilton, with the greyhound, is well known· by Faber's mezzotint. In 'Andromache bewailing the Death of Hector,' by Gavin Hamilton, the Duchess appears as Helen of Troy. It is an immense picture, with thirteen figures life-size, and is at Gordonstown, the seat of Sir William Gordon Cumming, Bart. It was engraved by Sir Robert Strange. At Inveraray Castle and at Swallowfield are lovely portraits

[1] This picture was lent by the Duke of Hamilton to the Exhibition at the Grosvenor Gallery in 1884.

ELIZABETH, DUCHESS OF HAMILTON AND OF ARGYLL, *née* GUNNING.
From a Painting by F. Cotes, R.A., at Swallowfield.

CATHERINE READ, pin.

ELIZABETH, DUCHESS OF HAMILTON AND OF ARGYLL, *née* GUNNING.

of her, by Cotes, in pink and green draperies, leaning against a large stone urn with a sunflower turning towards her, painted in 1767. Cotes also did many pastelle portraits of her, and, being a Galway man, took a special interest in depicting all the members of her family. One of his portraits of her, taken at the age of seventeen, is now in the possession of the writer. It is signed and dated (1751), and was engraved by McArdell. Angelica Kauffmann did a very graceful group in which the Duchess is the central figure, seated with Lady Charlotte Campbell, as an infant, on her knee, and Lady Augusta Campbell standing in front of her playing the harp. This picture, with its companion, one of Lord and Lady Derby, formerly belonged to Lady Charlotte Campbell, but they are now in the possession of members of the family of Campbell-Johnston. Miss Berry talks of seeing in Hamilton Palace an unfinished portrait of the Duchess by Gavin Hamilton, in which the Duke thought the likeness so striking that he took it from the painter and never would allow it to be finished. Miss Berry adds, 'Without being a good picture, it gives an exquisite idea of her beauty, and the head greatly resembles that of the Venus de' Medici.' This is now at Altyre, N.B., in the possession of Sir William Gordon Cumming, Bart., and it was photographed by the Loan Exhibition. The portrait of the Duchess in the high cap, painted by Catherine Read, which is at Inveraray, is world-famous from the beautiful engravings taken from it by Lowry and by Finlayson. In the original picture the cap has blue ribbons, and the cloak is black with a white fichu. The Duke survived his wife sixteen years, dying in May 1806, aged eighty-three. He had been created a British peer in the lifetime of his father as Baron Sundridge of Coomb-bank in Kent in 1766, and became Field-Marshal in 1796. He left four children, George William, sixth Duke, who

inherited from his mother the Barony of Hamilton, of Hambledon, she having been created a peeress of Great Britain with that
title in 1776; John Douglas, seventh Duke; Lady Augusta
Campbell, married General Clavering; and Lady Charlotte
Campbell, married Colonel John Campbell.

Mrs. Grant of Laggan, writing in 1773, says: 'I am told
their children (those of the Duke and Duchess of Argyll) excel
in beauty even the Hamilton family. So they should, having a
double claim! their father having been a model of manly grace
in his day. And here I could find in my heart to stop and rail
at the world; one hears so little about him, he is so quietly
passed over to make room for dashers and boasters, and fighters
and talkers. He does not wish to be talked of, 'tis certain, but
then I would not have them quite so complaisant as to give him
all his will in this particular. Seek for a great man's true and
solid praise at his own door, among his tenants and neighbours,
and let it be a material part of his praise, that he has neighbours,
that is to say that he lives at home among them. In this particular the Duke is unrivalled. Every mouth here will tell you
of some of these "quiet waters, soft and slow," that steal silently
on, carrying bounty and beneficence into all the corners of
obscurity. Don't be tired now, for I have a whole volume to
write of this good Duke's worth and wisdom, which improves
and blesses the whole country. . . . Yet I hope when this modest
and amiable benefactor of mankind sleeps with his fathers, and
when the tenants have ceased to say, "He is the best of countrymen," some powerful voice shall say with effect:

> Rise, muses, rise, add all your tuneful breath,
> Such must not sleep in darkness and in death.'

When Elizabeth, Duchess of Hamilton and Brandon and

MRS. TRAVERS, *née* KITTY GUNNING.
From a Pastelle by F. Cotes, R. A. at Swallowfield

of Argyll, died, she was the last of the Gunning sisters ; for Catherine, or Kitty, as she was commonly called, the third sister, had predeceased her by seventeen years. She was born at Hemingford Grey in 1735,[1] being two years younger than the Duchess. She had a very pretty face, but her figure was slightly deformed and she was marked with the smallpox. After her sisters' marriages she lived with her mother at Somerset House till 1769, when she married, at the age of thirty-four, Mr. Robert Travers (or Travis) of Allhallows, Lombard Street, who belonged to a Derbyshire family.[2] He was only twenty-three and had considerable means. For a short time after their marriage they lived in county Cork ; but in 1770, on the death of her mother,[3] she was given the appointment of housekeeper at Somerset House, and removed there, where her eldest daughter, Elizabeth Dorothea, was born the same year. In three years she died herself, aged thirty-eight, leaving a daughter, Brianna, who married the Rev. Nichols Cole Bowen, fifth son of Henry Cole Bowen, Esq., of Bowen's Court, Kildorrery, co. Cork, by whom she had seven children. The writer has a beautiful pastelle of Kitty Gunning, painted and signed by Cotes in 1751, which was engraved by Houston. Mr. Robert Travis married secondly, in 1775, Frances, daughter of James Compton, and sister of Penelope, Lady Muncaster.

The beautiful Miss Gunnings had only one brother, John, who was the youngest of the family. He was educated

---

[1] She was baptised at Hemingford Grey, June 12, 1735.

[2] She was always called ' Kitty Travers,' and the present representatives of her husband's family call themselves Travers, but in the Somerset House Register his name is entered as ' Travis.' He was son of Samuel Travis and his wife Sarah Manlowe, and he was baptised as such at St. Alkmund's, Derby.

[3] Mr John Gunning died at Somerset House in 1767. The writer has a beautiful pastelle of him, signed and dated by Cotes in 1751.

at Westminster School,[1] and went into the Army ; became
Colonel of the 65th Regiment, and in 1775 was serving in
America, and at Bunker's Hill 'shewed the greatest proofs
of military conduct and personal bravery,' and was honourably
mentioned in despatches. He rose to the rank of major-
general in 1787, and was deputy-adjutant-general in North
Britain. He died in September 1797 at Naples.[2] When very
young he had married, in 1763, Susanna, daughter of James
Minifie, D.D., of Fairwaters, Somersetshire, by whom he had
one daughter, Elizabeth,[3] commonly called 'Betty.' The
Duchess of Argyll, who doted on her brother, took his daughter
to live with her in order that she might introduce her to the
great world. The young lady hoped that the luck of the
Gunnings (which in Ireland had passed into a proverb) would
attend her, and that she would make a brilliant alliance ; but as
she was neither handsome nor clever,[4] she failed in her object and
only made herself ridiculous by her manœuvres to entangle
Lord Blandford in an engagement. She began by bestowing
her attentions on her cousin George, Lord Lorne, who was at
this time very young and singularly attractive, and she fancied
herself in love with him—'a fancy too pleasing to be rejected,'
says Lady Charlotte Campbell, who goes on to say, 'My brother,

---

[1] In the *Dublin Journal* for June 29, 1751, we find the following paragraph :
On Tuesday last the celebrated Miss Gunnings visited Westminster School where
their brother is just entered, and begged a holiday for the scholars, which the
Master readily granted, politely observing that nothing could be denied to such
fair solicitors.'

[2] The writer has a pastelle portrait of him, done in 1751 ; he appears to be a
youth of about fourteen or fifteen, but was probably younger.

[3] Not Catherine, as stated by some writers.

[4] All the prints of her make her decidedly very plain, but she was said to have
a beautiful hand and arm, and agreeable manners. She managed to ingratiate
herself into the affections of her aunt the Duchess, and her cousin Lady Charlott
Campbell, who, as a child, was quite devoted to her.

JOHN GUNNING, JUNR., *afterwards* GENERAL GUNNING.
From a Pastelle by F. Cotes, R A at Swallowneld

in the first *éclat* of youth, novelty, and good looks, had little leisure or inclination to think of an ugly cousin at home, but that unfortunate girl chose to imagine otherwise.'   When the beautiful Duchess died in 1790, Betty Gunning went home to her father and mother, who were living in St. James's Street, next door to Brooks's, and it was then that she started the idea that Lord Blandford wished to marry her. Horace Walpole in his numerous allusions to this subject, which he calls ' The Gunninghiad,' christened her ' the Princess Gunnilda.' The origin of this nickname was that in some paper there appeared a notice about General Gunning, in which it said that he was thirty-second descendant in a direct line from Charlemagne, which assertion so tickled the fancy of Horace Walpole that he always after called him the ' Emperor ' or ' Carloman,' and his daughter ' the Princess Gunnilda.'   Ultimately the young lady behaved so badly about this affair, that not only did the Duke of Argyll refuse to receive her in his house, but her own father also declined to have anything to say to her.   She and her mother, who took her daughter's part, went away, first to Dover and then to Boulogne.   There they met Major James Plunkett of Kinnaid, co. Roscommon, whose family had always lived near the Gunnings in Ireland.   He had been seriously implicated in the Irish Rebellion of 1798, and was condemned to death, but managed to escape to France.   After a time Mrs. and Miss Gunning returned to London, where the mother died in Dean Street in 1800, aged sixty, and was buried in Westminster Abbey ; and in 1804 ' Gunnilda ' married Major Plunkett.   Through the Duke of Argyll's influence he obtained leave to return to England, and they settled at Long Melford in Suffolk, where she had some friends, William and John Campbell of Lyston

Hall, cousins of the Duke of Argyll.[1]   She died there in 1823, and her husband some time after received permission to return to Mount Plunkett, his place near Elphin, but died in London.[2] With the death of General John Gunning in 1797 this branch of the family of the Gunnings of Castle Coote became extinct in the male line,[3] though the descendants of the fair sisters are very numerous, especially those of Elizabeth.[4]

[1] Sons of William Campbell (brother of the fourth Duke), who died in 1797 at Lyston Hall, which he bought.   Their mother was Susanna, daughter of Thomas Bernard of Jamaica.

[2] Major and Mrs. Plunkett had five children : (1) James Gunning Plunkett, married Jane, daughter of Major William Kelly of Cloncannon, Galway, and had a son, James Gunning Plunkett, in the Army, and another who was Chief Justice in New South Wales. (2) Coventry Plunkett. (3) Argyll Plunkett, married Miss Lysaght ; they went to America, where he practised as a doctor, as did also his son Nelson Plunkett. (4 and 5) Twin daughters, who went to America, and one married.

[3] Although there are now no Gunnings descended from John Gunning and the Honourable Bridget Bourke, there are Gunnings still in Roscommon who are descended from his father, Bryan Gunning. Mr. Alexander George Gunning, the present owner of St. John's, is a grandson of the Rev. Alexander Gunning who married Miss Hudson of St. John's, a niece of Oliver Goldsmith.

[4] See Gunning Pedigree in Appendix.

THE MAID OF THE OAKS

On April 1, 1797, a handsome man, still in the prime of life, was riding home through one of the charming Kentish lanes on his return from hunting, when he was obliged to draw on one side to allow a funeral *cortége* to pass. Curiosity led him to ask whose it was, and the answer came, the Countess of Derby. He was much moved, as well he might be, when he thought of the bright and innocent girl whose heart he had won before she was out of her teens, and whose life's happiness had been wrecked through his dishonour.

Lady Elizabeth (commonly called Lady Betty Hamilton), the only daughter of James, sixth Duke of Hamilton, and the beautiful Elizabeth Gunning, was born on January 26, 1753, when the latter was only nineteen. At the age of five she lost her father, and the following year her mother married Colonel Jack Campbell (afterwards fifth Duke of Argyll), and shortly after became Lady of the Bedchamber to Queen Charlotte. Lady Betty was brought forward at a very early age; Lady Mary Coke mentions seeing her at Court when she was not sixteen, and talks of her 'fine figure;' and a year later this same writer describes her at Lady Holderness's assembly as 'appearing gayer than was necessary.' The gaiety was supposed to be ill judged, the decision in the celebrated Douglas case having been just given against her brother the Duke of Hamilton.

Lady Charlotte Campbell, her half-sister, thus describes her : 'Though far from a beauty, my sister Betty had the figure of a sylph, the air and step of a Hebe, with all the *éclat* of natural rosy red and lily white, together with a sweetness of disposition and manners that won every heart, and which time, sorrow, and sickness never deprived her of ; but a natural want of solidity of character, joined to a tender and artless disposition, left her an easy prey to folly and to vice.'

John Frederick, third Duke of Dorset, a man of agreeable ingratiating address, and as accomplished in mind as he was in manners, won her earliest affections, and, for a time, paid her the greatest attention ; but this gay Lothario never dreamt of marrying, and, on being appointed to some foreign mission, left her to mortification and despair. Daily and hourly she hoped to hear from him, but he made no signs, and after a while Lady Betty's despair gave place to pique. Lady Charlotte Campbell writes : 'The pride of youth and of woman enabled her to bury her mortification in dissipation and admiration. Among the number of her professed lovers, Mr. Nisbet of Dirleton was one of her best conquests, and I cannot help marking his addresses, because they seemed to flow from dis-interested attachment, as the rest of his life, even to this hour, has ever proved. He went to Inveraray, as I have heard tell, with old Baron Mure (who was a most intimate friend of my father's) merely to stay a couple of days, but love riveted him to the spot for I know not how long—long enough, however, for prayers, entreaties, and ardent passion so far to get the better of Lady Betty's reluctance as to allow Mr. Nisbet strong hopes of success. Possessed of these he set off immediately for Italy, where the Duke of Hamilton was then upon his travels, merely to ensure his consent and hoping to return doubly armed with

GEO ROMNEY, R A., *pinx*

LADY BETTY HAMILTON, COUNTESS OF DERBY.

power to gain the object of his affections ; but " L'amour est en absence ce qu'un feu est au vent : il éteint le petit, il ranime le grand," and my sister's heart was barred against his addresses for ever. To have given hope she could not fulfil appears unpardonable coquetry, yet in the situation she was there are palliations for her conduct that the memory of her many gentle and fascinating qualities makes me take pleasure in discovering. Had she married Mr. Nisbet her fate in all probability would have been far different, but it was otherwise decided.' At this time Lady Charlotte Edwin, an aunt of her father's, and a woman of an intriguing spirit, set to work to arrange a match between Lady Betty and her nephew Edward, Lord Stanley (afterwards twelfth Earl of Derby), and in the event of this marriage taking place she promised to make the Duke of Hamilton heir to her large fortune.[1] Lady Charlotte Campbell writes : ' My mother, imagining that wealth, title, and splendour would suffice the demands of her daughter's heart, gave in to the plan, and though she did not command, yet used every argument and set forth every circumstance likely to win upon my sister's will. Many were the means employed till Lord Derby's constant and assiduous care veiled the ugliness of his person before the idol he worshipped. Time and despair made Lady Betty give a hasty and undigested consent. After a day of persecutions from every quarter, while a hairdresser was adorning her unhappy head she traced the consent with a pencil on a scrap of paper and sent it wet with her tears to my mother. Unhappy, ill-fated haste ! The paper was despatched to Lord Stanley. Everything was shortly settled, and no blandishments that power and passion could bestow were spared to dazzle the

---

[1] Lady Charlotte Edwin died in 1777, and left the greatest part of her large fortune to the Duke of Hamilton.

unhappy victim.'   On June 10, 1774, a great *fête champêtre* was given by the bridegroom at The Oaks, his villa at Epsom.[1]   All the town rang with the magnificence of the entertainment ; everybody was in masquerade, but not in mask.   ' It will cost £5,000,' says Horace Walpole, writing the day before to Mann ; ' Lord Stanley has bought all the orange-trees round London.'   ' A figure habited like a Druid came forth with verses and flowers,' says Lady Charlotte Campbell, ' to strew in the bride's path and flatter her vanity.'   The fête was managed by General Burgoyne (brother-in-law of Lord Stanley), who composed, expressly for the occasion, his once popular piece, ' The Maid of the Oaks,'[2] in which Mrs. Abingdon delighted all London by her wonderful performance of ' Lady Bab Lardoon.'   There are charming pictures at Knowsley representing this fête, which introduce portraits of Lady Betty and Lord Stanley.   They were painted by A. Zucchi, the husband of Angelica Kauffmann, and have been engraved.[3] Even after this, poor Lady Betty made a feeble effort to break off her matrimonial engagement ; but ultimately she was married on June 23, 1774, at Richmond, by special licence, quite privately, very few persons being present.   Lord Stanley would not hear of any delay, and barely allowed time for the settlements to be transcribed, as will be seen in a letter in the Addenda.[4]

A few weeks after her marriage Lady Elizabeth Stanley was presented at Court.   Lady Mary Coke writes : ' 'Tis said she did not look so satisfied a bride as the Duchess of Devonshire—

---

[1] Lord Stanley, when Lord Derby, instituted in 1789 the race called the Oaks, winning it himself ; a year later he founded the ' Derby.'   The first race brought thirty-six entries at fifty guineas each.

[2] Garrick produced this play at Drury Lane shortly after.

[3] One is called ' The Supper Room,' A. Zucchi, 1773 ; the other, ' The Ball Room,' A. Zucchi, 1777.   Both formed panels in Lord Derby's dining-room in Grosvenor Square.   The former was engraved by Caldwell.

[4] See page 339

her dress was approved of and her diamonds are very fine.   She returns no visits, excuses herself upon the account of her going so soon into Lancashire, where she will find a scene very new to her : she goes to " plain work and to purling brooks, old-fashioned halls, dull aunts, and croaking rooks, &c." '   Lord Stanley, however, went to Lancashire by himself; and Lady Betty remained at The Oaks, where she was joined by her mother and her sisters and brothers.   The King and Queen honoured her with a visit there, and Lady Mary Coke writes : 'The Duchess of Argyll and her family seem much in favour at Court.   To-morrow being the birthday of the Princess Augusta, there is to be a supper and some entertainment at Kew House, to which her Grace and Lady Betty are invited though not now in the neighbourhood.'   In the winter Lady Betty came to town, and we read of her giving parties 'to shew her fine house' (No. 4 Grosvenor Square), built and decorated by Robert Adam.

Early the next season the Duke of Dorset reappeared, talked of letters he had never written, messages he had never sent, said her mother had deceived her, poured poison into her soul, vowed over and over all his former professions, and then with affected generosity bade her be happy while life was a chaos to him.   'My unfortunate sister,' says Lady Charlotte Campbell, 'was plunged into a pit from whence she had neither sense nor sound principles enough to extricate herself, and her husband, to whom she avowed the state of her heart, with unheard-of vanity and folly, plunged her deeper in the abyss by perpetual scenes of dissipation and everything that tended to relax principle instead of giving tension to its feeble fibres.' Lady Betty was now to be seen everywhere, and was everywhere admired.   We read in Sir Joshua Reynolds's ' Life ' how ' conspicuous among the beauties gathered in Westminster Hall on the 15th April 1776 to witness the trial of the Duchess of Kingston [1] were the beautiful young Duchess of Devonshire and the still lovelier young Countess of Derby,' [2] 'with their work-bags full of good things,' says Hannah More, ' to sustain nature during the proceedings ; ' and we also hear that she was present at Admiral Keppel's trial, ' looking lovely.' At Almack's, we are told, she was ' one of the stars, brilliant and beautiful.' The painters of the day loved painting her. Sir Joshua's whole-length of her wreathing the altar of Hymen was one of the most admired portraits exhibited by that artist at the exhibition of the Royal Academy in April 1777.[3] Angelica Kauffmann painted her twice ; one of these pictures is at Knowsley, and the other (in which Lord Derby appears) belongs to Mr. Campbell Johnston. Cosway also painted her twice ; and H. D. Hamilton did a pro-file of her in 1777, which was destroyed, but was engraved by George Townley Stubbs. The most charming portrait of all those existing of Lady Betty is the one by Romney, a half-length sitting, which the first Lord Granville bought in Paris, and which the late Lord Granville sold to Sir Charles Tennant. This also has been engraved, in 1770, by John Dean.

In January 1777, in an account of the Birthday Ball at St. James's, we read of 'Lady Derby looking charming ; ' and a little

[1] Lady Betty must have been doubly interested in this trial if she knew, which probably she did, that her father had once been engaged to Elizabeth Chudleigh.

[2] This year Lord Stanley succeeded to the title and estates of his grandfather.

[3] Unfortunately the whereabouts of this picture, if it still exists, which is more than doubtful, is unknown. Mr. Scharf in vain searched for it, and came to the conclusion that it had been destroyed. A fine engraving by Dickinson, however, shows òne what it was. In it appears Sir Joshua's celebrated macaw, concerning which Northcote tells us how the bird used to fly in fury at the portrait of Sir Joshua's housemaid, between whom and the bird no love was lost. Sir Joshua frequently repeated this experiment before Burke, Johnson, Goldsmith, and most of his friends, and it never failed of success, though the macaw took no notice of any other picture.

further on, the account mentions the Duke of Dorset in a gala suit 'gris de Daricé [*sic*] embroidered upon all the seams.' All through this year his name appears wherever she was. In August we hear of a party assembled at Castle Howard (Lord Carlisle's) for York races, 'including Lord and Lady Derby and the Duke of Dorset.' This was one of the last times Lord and Lady Derby appeared in public together. After a few years of splendid misery, writes Lady Charlotte Campbell, 'Lady Derby left her husband, and went to Brighthelmstone early in 1778.' Lord Derby consoled himself in the company of Mrs. Armitstead,[1] and he failed to get a divorce for which he tried in November of the same year.

The instant Lady Betty's flight was known, her mother, who idolised her, followed her to Brighthelmstone, accompanied by her husband, the Duke of Argyll, and by Lady Betty's brother, the Duke of Hamilton. The Duke and Duchess remained on there with Lady Betty, and henceforward the Duchess's chief object in life seemed to be trying to rehabilitate her daughter's lost character. In this, however, she never succeeded. She

---

[1] Elizabeth Bridget Blane, otherwise Mrs. Armitstead, whom Charles James Fox married at Witton, Huntingdonshire, September 28, 1795. In 1799, on his fiftieth birthday, he addressed to her the following lines :

> Of years I have now half a century past,
> And none of the fifty so blessed as the last.
> How it happens my troubles thus daily should cease
> And my happiness thus with my years should increase,
> This defiance of nature's more general laws
> You alone can explain, who alone are the cause.

Mrs. Fox survived her husband many years, and died July 8, 1842, aged ninety-seven. Lord Albemarle visited her, accompanied by the Duke and Duchess of Bedford, at St. Ann's Hill when she was in her ninety-third year, 'but still hale and handsome ;' and, he adds, 'she insisted upon showing us all over the house herself, pointing, among other things, to the tiny table on which Fox wrote his *James II.*' Mrs. Armitstead sat to Sir Joshua Reynolds in 1779 for Lord Derby, and again ten years later.

made Lady Deroy write at once to Queen Charlotte acquainting her Majesty that she had left her husband, and put out a feeler to see whether she would still be received at Court. The following is a copy of the Queen's answer to Lady Derby :

'Madam, your attachment to the King's family is so well known to him and her, that you may rest secure that no apparent want of attention will ever be laid by either of us at your door. I cannot at the same time help adding that I am sensible of your confidence in stating your present situation so frankly to me.

'I shall ever remain, Madam, your friend and well-wisher,

'CHARLOTTE.

'QUEEN'S HOUSE: *May* 31*st*, 1778.'

In consequence of the Queen refusing to receive Lady Derby at Court, the Duchess (her mother) gave up her post of Lady in Waiting. Lady Derby went abroad, where at first she was joined by Mrs. Campbell of Carrick, a cousin of the Duke of Argyll, and was some time at Spa and Nice. She was at Vienna in 1781, where the Emperor made much of her ; and after that she went to Brunswick, where she spent a summer with Augusta, Duchess of Brunswick (sister of George III.), who was always most kind to her. Sir John Stanley (afterwards Lord Stanley of Alderley) was at Brunswick as a youth in 1782, and in his 'Præterita' says : 'Lady Derby came to Brunswick this summer and was paid all sorts of attention by the Court, and fêtes were given on purpose for her. She claimed me as a relation, and said, " Why will you not come and speak to your cousin ?" I knew little of her story, but I think she had a feeling of my keeping aloof from her purposely. She was beautiful, and I have her contour and engaging smiles and manner vividly in my memory at this moment ; but, young as I was, I could observe her unhappiness in the midst of the flatteries she received and the attempt to please and make her happy. The opera of "Pyramus and Thisbe" had been got up at Brunswick, and I was near enough to Lady Derby to see her shed tears when one of the songs was sung. I was quite a child when I saw her first, soon after her marriage; I saw her at Brunswick as fascinating as she had been in her full glory.' The following letter was written by the Duchess of Brunswick to the Duchess of Argyll soon after Lady Derby's departure from that Court.

'Bronsvic: the 11 of Oct. 1782.

'Dear Duchess,—I feel for the happiness of having your children together. I owe a letter to Lady Derby, but would not write by the same post to her. She is still in such a hurry that I cannot expect that her Bronsvic mother should be often thought of; tell her that I love her with all my heart, and that the better she behaves the more she will confound her enemies. I hear the Prince of Wales earnestly beg'd to have Lady Betty permitted to come to Court again; the answer was, if Lord Derby would live with her again she would be admitted.[1] The Prince of Wales, I am told, has behaved vastly well upon the death of his little brother, and has shown great feeling for his parents; that is well, and I am glad to have an opportunity of commending him, tho' I do not dispair of living to see him make a great and good figure in the world. I must recommend the Austrian Ministers wife to you because she has wrote me a fine letter that I shall send the King without any remark. I knew her at Frankfort; she is pretty, but I have heard that in Denmark she has been very coquette—at Frankfort, they had not long been married, and it was a love match, so all was then very proper.

---

[1] Lady Derby would have returned to her husband, but by this time he had become infatuated about Miss Farren, the actress, and refused to receive his wife back.

He I liked better than her.   I must recommend a book to you, but only to you.   Not for youths ; it's " Les Confessions de Rousseau"—one learns to know oneself by reading that book. Compliments to the Duke of Argyll and Hamilton and Lady Augusta, and remain, my dear Duchess,

'Your most affectionate friend,

'AUGUSTA.'

At the end of three years Lady Derby returned to England with a broken heart and a broken constitution, being now only twenty-eight years of age.   For some years she was able to go abroad every winter with her mother and other members of her family, but in 1790 she had the misery of losing that mother, who, however ill judged she had been about her daughter's marriage, had always adored her.   From that date Lady Derby rapidly declined.   She got too ill to leave England, and lived for some time at Teignmouth with her young brother, Lord John Campbell, who was there with a tutor.   The end came when she was in London staying at the house of Mr. J. C. Hamilton, a relative of her father's, in Gloucester Street, Portman Square.   She died on March 14, 1797, and was buried (by her express desire) at Bromley in Kent.   The register there says she was interred on April 1,[1] and an affidavit was made stating that the rule ordering persons to be buried in woollen cloth was remitted.

'Odious !   In woollen !   'Twould a saint provoke,'
Were the last words that poor Narcissa spoke.

The Duke of Dorset must indeed have felt a pang when he met her funeral.   But this episode—which was death, and a sad lingering death, to the woman—as usual did not affect the man's

---

[1] Lady Derby's body was at first placed in the vaults of South Audley Street Chapel.

welfare. She was an exile from society, she was deprived of her children,[1] and forbidden to appear at Court ; but he, her destroyer, was sent as ambassador to Paris, where we hear of him basking in the smiles of Marie Antoinette, one of the favoured few admitted to the celebrated rural fêtes at the Petit Trianon,[2] and on his return he was made Lord Steward of the Household, and he married a beautiful heiress.[3]

Lord Derby, who had been assiduous in his devotion to Miss Farren for so many years[4] that Horace Walpole uses his constancy as a proverb, did not wait long to claim her as his bride. On April 8 she appeared finally in her celebrated part as Lady Teazle, and on May 1, 1797, just six weeks after Lady Betty's death, she became the second wife of Lord Derby.[5]

[1] Lady Derby left three children : Edward, thirteenth Earl, father of the Prime Minister, born 1775 ; Lady Charlotte Stanley, born 1776, who married her cousin, Edmund Hornby of Dalton Hall ; and Lady Elizabeth Henrietta, who married Stephen Cole, Esq.

[2] Mercy-Argenteau tells-us that Marie Antoinette used to walk about during the masked balls at the Opera, attended by an escort of men of distinction, and mentions the Duke of Dorset as one whom her Majesty treated with special favour. The Duke of Dorset remained in Paris as ambassador till 1790, when he was recalled because his liveried servant, who had been seized by the mob, was found to have a letter in his pocket addressed to the Comte d'Artois.

[3] The Duke of Dorset married in 1790 Arabella Diana, daughter and co-heiress of Sir Charles Cope, Bart., of Brewerne, by Catherine, sister of Lord de la Zouch ; these Copes being a younger branch of the Copes of Hanwell, now of Bramshill. Arabella, Duchess of Dorset, married secondly, in 1801, Charles, Earl of Whitworth. Her only son, the fourth Duke of Dorset, was killed out hunting in 1815, when the title became extinct.

[4] Fifteen years, during which time she had the most wonderful influence over him, and quite altered his life. Lord Derby and Charles James Fox seem to have had a great sameness in their tastes as to women, for Fox was also furiously in love with Miss Farren and at one time seemed likely to cut out Lord Derby, but he married instead Mrs. Armitstead, Lord Derby's former *chère amie*.

[5] It may be remarked that the histrionic talent has come out strongly in the second Lady Derby's great-granddaughter, Mrs. Charles Crutchley, generally considered to be one of the best amateur actresses of the day.

A CANNY SCOT

THE Campbells of Ardentinny,[1] afterwards of Skipness,[2] Shawfield, and Islay, are said to be descended from Sir Colin Campbell of Ardkinglas, second son of Sir Colin Campbell of Lochow, ancestor of the Dukes of Argyll.[3] Be this as it may, 'It is (if we may use the old saying in this sense) a far cry to Lochow!'

The motto of Campbell of Ardkinglas, 'Set on,' seems certainly to have been appropriate to some of these offshoots of the Campbell clan, for, like many of their neighbours, they were formerly cattle-lifters, and lived chiefly on their depredations and on the Black Mail they levied. It should, however, be understood that neither of these modes of procedure must be viewed in the light that they would be nowadays. Cattle-lifting was then looked upon in the Highlands as a kind of clan warfare, and came to be considered rather as a gallant military enterprise than a theft, and young men regarded a proficiency in the art as a recommendation to their mistresses.

[1] Ardentinny, or the 'Fire Hill,' at the mouth of Loch Long.
[2] Skipness, also written Skipneis, Skippinche, and Skipnishe, &c.
[3] This descent is given them in Nisbet's *Heraldry* (1742), and by Crawfurd. The bearing of Campbell of Ardkinglas was gironné of eight, or and sable within a bordure of the first. Crest, a lymphad (galley) with oars in motion.
Of Ardentinny, the same, but the bordure charged with eight crescents. Crest, two oars disposed in saltier, motto, 'Terra, mare, fide.'
Campbell of Shawfield, the same as Ardentinny, but crest, a griffin erected holding the sun between his fore-paws, with the motto, 'Fidus Amicis.'

SIR DUNCAN CAMPBELL, LORD OF LOCHOW, AND HIS WIFE, MARJORY,
DAUGHTER OF THE REGENT DUKE OF ALBANY
Date of Monument 1453, at Kilmun, Holy Loch, Clyde, N B

They thought, to use the words of the poet, 'that they should take who have the power, and they should keep who can.' We are even told by Tennant that when undertaking these expeditions the Highlanders prayed as earnestly to heaven for success as if they were engaged in the most laudable enterprise.

'Black Mail,' or 'Watch Money,' was a system of compromise by which honest persons were enabled in some degree to secure themselves against losses. For a number of years the six independent companies of Highlanders commonly called the 'Reicudan Dhu,' or 'Black Watch,' were effective in keeping down the system of cattle-lifting, and when those companies were formed into a regular regiment, the cattle-lifting burst out again with renewed vigour. Mr. Graham of Gartmore, writing on this subject, says that as late as 1745, £5,000 was spent yearly in Black Mail either openly or privately. We read in 'Waverley' that when a raid had been made upon the cattle of the Baron of Bradwardine, his daughter Rose suggested paying Black Mail to Fergus MacIvor for restitution of the same, and that Captain Waverley, on asking if this sort of Jonathan Wild was called a gentleman, was greatly astonished at being told that MacIvor claimed precedence over all the neighbouring lairds.[1]

Cattle-lifting was probably very lucrative in Argyllshire, and no doubt this is the origin of the saying: 'It came in

---

[1] Macdonald of Barrisdale was said to have been the original of the character of MacIvor. He was the last Highland gentleman who carried on the plundering system to any great extent, and it is said that he made a clear £500 a year by Black Mail. He was a man of fine address and person, and had polished manners, was well-read and a scholar. He engraved on his broad-sword the following lines :

'Hæ tibi erunt artes—pacisque imponere morem,
Parcere subjectis, et debellare superbos.'

hides and it will go in latchets,' alluding to the power of the Campbells.

The first of the Ardentinny Campbells whom we find called ' of Skipneis ' was Matthew Campbell, who appears as 'Capetanis Casteli in Skipneis,' with his wife Devorgilla Macalister in a charter,[1] dated December 7, 1576.[2]

Then we find the second Matthew Campbell ' Captain of Skipness,' who died before 1670. Who his father was it is impossible to say with any certainty, but he may have been the John Campbell of ' Skipness ' whose daughter Mary married John Stewart of Ardmoleish, Sheriff of Bute (from whom descends the present Lord Bute).[3]

There is also about this time another of the ' Captains of Skipness ' whom we find difficult to affiliate ; this is Donald Campbell, a well-known character. He betook himself early to the profession of arms and went into the service of Gustavus Adolphus, King of Sweden, in 1629. He was then under the command of General Alexander Leslie (afterwards Earl of Leven), and when that eminent soldier, who rose to be a foreign Field-Marshal, was called to Scotland in 1638 to take the head of the army of the Covenanters, Donald Campbell returned with him to his native country and continued to fight under him, being at the famous camp at Duns Law, where the words ' For Christ's Crown and Covenant ' were written in golden letters over each captain's tent. Wodrow in his

---

[1] In this charter they grant certain lands to Donald, Filius Liberalis of John Campbell, and Moir Macalister, his spouse. Matthew Campbell, Captain of Skipness, also witnessed a marriage contract in 1588.

[2] In this charter they grant certain lands to Donald, Filius Liberalis of John Campbell, and Moir Macalister, his spouse.

[3] This John Stewart was Lord of the Bedchamber to King James VI. He attended the Parliament in Edinburgh as Commissioner for Buteshire in 1579.

'Eminent Men of Scotland,' says of Donald Campbell of Skipness : 'Devotedly attached to the Presbyterian cause, he took a prominent and decided part in the sanguinary struggle between Charles and the Covenanters. His military genius, which shone in many memorable engagements, his firmness and decision in the hour of difficulty and danger, together with his high sense of honour, soon raised him to the distinction of a formidable leader. He particularly distinguished himself in arresting the progress of the forces of Montrose, and was actively engaged at Philiphaugh.'

Donald Campbell met his death in July, 1647, at Dunaverty in Cantire, on an occasion the reverse of glorious to his party, when the Marquis of Argyll and General Leslie, with an army of three thousand, besieged the castle held by three hundred of Alexander Macdonald's men. This castle of Dunaverty was one of the most famous strongholds of the Lords of the Isles, and for a considerable time was very gallantly defended. Several desperate attempts were made to take it, but the assailants were always repulsed with considerable loss, and Donald Campbell, Argyll's Major, was one of the first who fell. At last the garrison was compelled to surrender in consequence of Leslie having cut off their water supply, and they were all killed in cold blood. John Neave,[1] the chaplain of General Leslie's army, was the most bloodthirsty of the besieging party and urged that no quarter should be given, and when they were viewing the bodies after the massacre, Leslie said to him, as he saw his shoes reeking with blood, ' Have you enough of it now, Master John ? ' Sir James Turner, who was with Leslie at Dunaverty, says that he several times spoke to the Lieutenant-General to save these men's lives, and he always assented to it and was unwilling to

---

[1] Sometimes called ' Nevoy.'

shed their blood, but that Mr. Neave ' never ceased to tempt him to that bloodshed, yea, and threatened him with the curses that befell Saul for sparing the Amalekites,' and he goes on to say : ' I verilie believe that this prevailed most with David Lesly, who looked upon Neave as the representative of the Kirk of Scotland— advise him to that act who will, he hath repented it many times since, and even very soone after the doeing it.' [1]   According to tradition there is one bright spot in this ghastly tale : the nurse of the infant son of Archibald Macdonald—whose name will for ever live in that family—Flora McCambridge, managed to escape with the child.   As she fled she met Captain Campbell of Craigneish, one of Argyll's soldiers, who not only spared the child but said (when she alleged that it was her own) ' It has the eye of the Macdonald ; no matter, it wants clothing,' and cutting off the tail of his belted plaid, gave it to her for a covering for the naked infant.   So she got it away in safety,[2] and concealed herself in a cave, still known as ' Macdonald's Cave,' where the adherents of the clan attended to her wants until the Covenanter's army had left that part of the country.

Before they did so Argyll burnt the castle and razed it to the ground.   The feuds between the two rival clans of Macdonald and Campbell had long existed, and at this time the latter were smarting under the ravages of Montrose.

> Argyll and Lesley were not slack
> Sternly to pay the outrage back ;
> When leagured by that western sea,
> In the strong-walled Dunaverty,
> Those clansmen famishly implored
> Mercy, and found the merciless sword.—KILMAHOE.

---

[1] Sir James Turner's memoirs of his own life and times.
[2] The child grew up to be the Ranald Macdonald who married Anne Stuart, sister of the first Earl of Bute.

Donald Campbell's body was taken to Cambelton to be buried with his ancestors, and his grave was still visible in 1877.[1] The following epitaph, said to have been written by the bloodthirsty Chaplain Neave, was copied by Neil Brodie in 1825 from his tombstone, the last remaining in the old burying-ground :

> A Captain much renowned
> Whose cause of fight was still Christ's right
> For which his soul is crowned.
> So briefly then to know the man
> This stone tells all the story ;
> On earth his race he ran with grace,
> In heaven now rests in glory.

The second Matthew, Captain of Skipness, had three sons, Æneas or Angus, Walter, and Colin. Æneas married in 1671 Jean, daughter of Sir James Stewart of Ardmoleish, Sheriff of Bute, and their marriage contract, attested by his brother Walter Campbell, is in existence. Colin, who joined the chief of their clan in his disastrous attempt in 1645, was hanged at Inveraray, with seventeen other Campbells, by order of the Marquis of Atholl.[2] Either Æneas or Colin must have had a son John, as Walter alludes to this nephew. He was a goldsmith in the Strand and principal of the banking firm which afterwards became the famous bank of Coutts & Co. In George Baillie of Jerviswood's correspondence we find two letters written to him from Secretary Johnstone, in which Campbell the

---

[1] The late J. T. Campbell of Islay in a letter to the writer says : ' I sought the grave at Campbell-town. The churchyard was made into a promenade ; a tombstone with the name had been used as a door-step within living memory, and an old broad-sword taken out of the grave had been sold.'

[2] A small obelisk of chlorite erected close to the church at Inveraray commemorates their death. Mr. Charles Campbell (son of Lord Niel Campbell), who was confined by fever at the gates of Inveraray, was also to have suffered, but the Privy Council, at the intercession of some ladies of distinction, prevented the Marquis of Atholl from carrying this into effect. (Fountainhall's *Chronicles*.)

goldsmith is mentioned. One dated December 1704 says: 'There is an order signed by the Queen for £130 to be remitted to Campbell the goldsmith here as money laid out for her service, which may pass for secret intelligence, as part of it indeed is.' And again in January 1705 he writes: 'I wish at least £50 of that money to come to Campbell could be got.' John Campbell died in 1712, and was buried in the churchyard of St. Paul's, Covent Garden. He left his partner, George Middleton, his sole executor (described as his honest and faithful partner) in trust for his four children, i.e. William, Mary, George, and Elizabeth.[1] George Middleton married Mary Campbell and took George her brother into partnership about 1729. He died in 1748, leaving the bank then solely in the hands of George Campbell. At this time there were only two banking houses west of Temple Bar, one Whig and one Tory. The latter was Andrew Drummond's, and the Whig bank was George Campbell's, patronised, of course, by his chief, the great Duke of Argyll. It was not till 1754 that George Campbell took into partnership James Coutts (son of John Coutts, the banker of Edinburgh), who had married Polly Peagrim,[2] his niece, that same year.

The firm then became Campbell and Coutts. When George Campbell died in 1761, James Coutts took his brother Thomas as a partner and changed the name of the firm to James and Thomas Coutts.[3]

---

[1] Elizabeth Campbell married Mr. John Peagrim of Colchester.

[2] Their only daughter, Frances Coutts, married her cousin, Sir John Stuart of Allanbank.

[3] Thomas Coutts married twice; by his first wife he had three daughters, one married the third Earl of Guildford, another the Marquis of Bute, and the youngest Sir Francis Burdett, Bart., father of the present Lady Burdett Coutts. Thomas Coutts married, secondly, Harriet Mellon, the actress, who became after his death Duchess of St. Albans.

Walter Campbell, 'Captain of Skipness,' the eldest of Matthew's sons, was granted in 1670, by Archibald ninth Earl of Argyll, a new charter of the lands of Skipness which his father had. He also was 'out' in 1685 with Argyll, but, more fortunate than his brother Colin, he managed to escape, and, dropping the sword for the pen, became a notary in the Goosedubs. Notaries in those days were much in request, as most Scotch gentlemen at this time were very poor scribes and had to get all their writings done for them. Walter thus made a fairly good income, to which he added somewhat by at least two of his three marriages, his first wife, Anne, being the daughter of Sir James Stewart of Ardmoleish,[1] Bart., Sheriff of Bute, and widow of Alexander Macdonald of Sana (Islay), and his third wife was the daughter of one Stewart, factor to James, Earl of Bute. In any case he was able before his death in 1702 (aged 72) to settle something on each of his four daughters,[2] as well as on his five sons. Angus the eldest, born 1669, is described as 'a trader in black cattle at Cambelton,' which sounds a more legitimate if less romantic calling than that of some of his forbears. Many men, even of birth and position, went into this trade, and Sir Walter Scott used to tell a story of the Hon. Patrick Ogilvie who was engaged in it, and on being remonstrated with by his brother, the Earl of Seafield, dryly remarked: 'Better sell nowte than sell nations.' Lord Seafield as Chancellor of Scotland had been deeply concerned in bringing about the Union. This same Angus became Deputy-Lieutenant of Argyllshire, and was one of the 'Free-

---

[1] The two brothers Angus and Walter married sisters.
[2] His four daughters married respectively Colin Campbell of Ardentinny (first cousin); Charles McAllister of Tarbert (ancestor of McAllister of Loup), Duncan Lamont of Achnasiloch, and Robert Campbell of Balerno.

M

holders and Heretors within the shire of Argyle,' convened to meet at the Tolbooth of Inveraray on August 11, 1715, 'for the purpose of being made acquainted with an invasion designed by the Pretender, and to concert proper measures for the service of the Government.' In this list Angus is called 'of Skipnidge.'[1] Walter Campbell's four remaining sons, Daniel, John, Matthew, and Robert,[2] became prosperous merchants and proved the truth of the adage 'Union is strength,' as they all acted in concert with each other. John, who in 1691 was trading in America, was Lord Provost of Edinburgh in 1719–20, 1723–24, and M.P. for Edinburgh 1721–2, also 1727–34. He held several government appointments, having been successively Master of the Works, Groom of the Bed-chamber, and Commissioner of Customs for England and Scotland. He died in 1739. He was a strong advocate for the Union and consequently was unpopular with the larger proportion of the community. A song of thirteen stanzas printed soon after George I.'s accession begins :

> If ever I have seen
> Such a parcel of rogues in a nation,
> The Campbells and the Graeme
> Are equally to blame,
> Seduc'd by strong infatuation.

---

[1] Angus was succeeded by his son Colin, Captain of Skipness, born 1690. He raised an independent company in 1725, and was captain in the Earl of Crawford's regiment in 1739. He married his cousin Ann, daughter of Daniel Campbell, but had no issue, so that at his death in 1756 Skipness devolved upon his cousin, the second Daniel of Shawfield. Angus had a daughter Grizel, who married Will Boyd of Portnacross.

[2] Robert's arms are given as follows : The paternal coat of Campbell within a bordere cheque argent and azure for Stewart of Bute, and charged with eight crescents argent for his difference. Crest a dove with an olive branch in his bill proper. Motto, 'Gaudium adfero.'

Another of the stanzas runs thus :

> Tweddale and his club
> Who have given many a rub
> To their honor, their Prince and their nation,
> Next to that heavy drone,
> Poor silly Skipness John,
> Have established the best reputation.

Matthew, a merchant sailor, married in 1710 Magdalene, daughter of Sir Francis Kinloch, second baronet, and died 1721, leaving a daughter Mary, who married Sir Robert . . . . of Gogar. Robert Campbell was a merchant in Stockholm, but Donald, or Daniel, as he was generally called, the second son of Walter Campbell of Skipness, far surpassed all his brothers in business capacity, and proved himself a very canny Scot. By his indomitable energy and general shrewdness, combined, we must add, with a certain amount of what his countrymen call ' pawkiness,' he, from a very small beginning, amassed a large fortune, and from an insignificant position raised himself to one of great importance, not only in Glasgow, where for many years he was the most prominent of its citizens, but also in Westminster, where he had considerable influence. Born in 1670 he began trading in a very small way at an early age, and after serving apprentice to Robert Campbell, a merchant of the Dean of Guild [1] of Glasgow, he started in business on his own account in 1691. The following year he joined his brother John at Boston and traded with the West Indies, whither he went himself in 1694. He became the owner of several merchant ships, and in 1696 he got a grant from the Treasury for losses incurred by ships being taken by the French.

---

[1] In 1605 the inhabitants of Glasgow, in consequence of the losses which they sustained by strangers usurping their commercial privileges, nominated a body of merchants and craftsmen, under a Dean of Guild or Gild, who had always to be a merchant, a merchant-sailor, and a merchant-venturer.

Argyll and Queensberry made the order. From his own letters we find that at this time, and during the following six years, he did a roaring trade, and it is dreadful to read that amongst his articles of commerce were both ' niggers,' whom he bought and sold ! and servants whom he exported to the West Indies, there to be purchased ! [1] Daniel Campbell came home in 1694 in the ' Adventure,' of which he was part owner. On his return he was made a burgess of Glasgow, and his name appears in 1696 amongst those who subscribed for the ' Company of Scotland trading to Africa and the Indies,' his subscription being £1,000. This scheme, which was set on foot by William Paterson (the first projector of the Bank of England), was to plant colonies in Asia, Africa, and America, and to establish trade with these countries. It was enthusiastically taken up by an immense majority of the leading men of Scotland, and the subscriptions 'sucked up all the money of the country.' Notwithstanding the opposition of the English Government, the first expedition sailed in 1698 and was followed by two others, a colony of twelve thousand Scots being planted at Darien, which was to be a general emporium. It proved a most calamitous venture,[2] and the following year the settlement was attacked by Spaniards and ultimately abandoned. Few survived to return to Scotland, and the whole capital was lost. We shall see later on how Daniel Campbell managed to recoup himself, and meanwhile, nothing daunted by this disaster, he engaged in various other commercial

---

[1] In 1702 he was engaged in the Guinea trade, exporting niggers to Nevis. Between 1680 and 1700 about 140,000 negroes were exported by the African Company and 160,000 more by private adventurers. Bryan Edwards estimated the import into the British colonies and the West Indies from 1680 to 1786 at 2,130,000, and this is much less than was commonly supposed.

[2] The Scotch say it might have succeeded had it not been for King William's indifference to their interests and still more for the commercial jealousy of the E. I. Company.

DANIEL CAMPBELL, OF SHAWFIELD.

From a Picture in the possession of Captain Walter Campbell.

enterprises both at home and abroad. In 1701 he and his sailor brother Matthew presented a petition asking to be allowed the privileges of a manufactory 'for distilling brandy and other spirits from all manner of grain of the growth of this kingdom, in order that the nation may be the more plentifully provided with the said commodities, as good as any that have been imported from abroad, and because the distilling will both be profitable for consumption and for trade for the coast of Guinea and America, seeing that no trade can be managed to the places foresaid or the East-Indies, without great quantities of the foresaid liquors.' The brothers Campbell proposed setting up an additional sugar-work in connection with the distillery and engaging 'several foreigners and other persons eminently skilled in making of sugar, distilling of brandy &c., whom, with great travel, charges, and expense, they had prevailed to come to Glasgow.' The petition was granted.

Besides his mercantile transactions, Daniel Campbell increased his fortune by lending money on land securities and acting as banker at a period when there were no banks in Scotland. In those troublous times the Scottish lairds were always in need of ready money to carry them on and were glad to offer their broad acres as security, and in many cases the landowners were unable to pay back the moneys they had borrowed. Even in 1696, when the Bank of Scotland was first instituted, the branches which were opened at Glasgow and elsewhere, proving unsuccessful, were at once given up, and as late as the middle of the eighteenth century all the banking business in Glasgow was carried on by private traders. As early as 1697 we find by his papers that Daniel Campbell was lending money to the Argyll family, and we also find mention of loans to Maccalister of Loup, his cousin, to Stewart of Appin, to Sir Mungo Stirling, to the Earl of Kilmarnock, to James and Adam Montgomerie, and many other lairds. By this means, as well as by his mercantile transactions, the opening of the eighteenth century found him a rich man, and he began to buy property. In 1701 he was still living in the Salt Market, but in 1708 he was the owner of the estate of Shawfield and Rutherglen on the Clyde, which he bought for £2,200; and henceforward was known as Campbell of Shawfield. Four years later he purchased the estate of Woodhall, in Lanarkshire, for £4,384. This was a good investment, for in 1862 it sold for £175,000, after yielding £12,000 annually. Woodhall became the family country seat, and Daniel Campbell was made Deputy-Lieutenant of the county in 1716. He was now much taken up with politics and left some of his commercial affairs to subordinates. He was a steady supporter of the Whig ministry and served in the Scottish Parliament as member for Inveraray from 1702 till 1707.[1]

Before the Union, in order to remove as far as possible the ill-blood caused by the failure of the Darien scheme, the English Government arranged to pay an 'Equivalent,' this being a compensation of £400,000 of ready money sent from England,[2] to be applied partly to the discharge of the public debt, but chiefly as a restitution of the money lost in the African Company, the payment to become due upon the signing of the Union. Daniel Campbell was made one of the twenty-five Commissioners of 'the Equivalent,' and got back his

[1] This was before he bought Shawfield, and he was then described as 'Daniel or Donald Campbell of Ardentinnie, councillor.'

[2] We read in the *Edinburgh Gazette* under August 7, 1707: 'This day the Equivalent money came in here from South Britain in fivteen waggons drawn by six horses, guarded by Scots Dragoons.' This escort was very necessary, as the unfortunate drivers of the waggons were constantly pelted with stones by those who thought their country was being sold.

thousand pounds as well as his pay as a Commissioner. He was a strong advocate for the Union and was one of the Scotch Commissioners for the treaty, and his name appears among the ' Approvers ' in the Parliament of 1706. At the Council-chamber in the Cock-pit he signed the treaty as ' Daniel Campbell of Ardintinnie ; ' he also signed the twenty-five articles in Edinburgh, his seal upon the original document in the registry office having the Skipness cross-oars for crest. He was one of the members returned to represent Scotland in the House of Commons of the first Parliament of Great Britain as member for Glasgow 1707–8, and again during the Parliaments extending from 1716 to 1722, 1722 to 1727, and 1728 to 1734. Daniel Campbell was a very great personal friend of Sir Robert Walpole,[1] and when the latter was expelled from the House of Commons in December, 1711, a charge of corruption having been brought against him,[2] Mr. Campbell retired with him and accompanied him to the Tower. Lady Louisa Stuart, in her introductory anecdotes to the ' Life of Lady Mary Wortley Montagu,' says : ' Whichever way truth may lie, Walpole afterwards proved how keenly he felt the mortifying transaction ; but proved it in a manner creditable to his heart— by showing gratitude, not by seeking revenge. On his being ordered to withdraw while the House voted his commitment to prison, one personal friend only, Daniel Campbell, of Shawfield, a Scotch member, arose, went out with him, and attended him to the gates of the Tower. Sir Robert did not forget this

---

[1] Captain Walter Campbell has a portrait of Sir Robert Walpole which was painted for Daniel Campbell ; it is now at Holly Grove, Windsor Park.

[2] The charge brought against him was that of having, when Secretary for War, accepted two sums of £500 from the contractors for supplying forage to the army, in consideration of taking their contracts, the said contracts being very high, by which means the Government was put to extraordinary unnecessary expense.

when he was minister. Mr. Campbell, a moderate man, asked few favours for himself; but any person in whose behalf he could be induced to say a word had a fairer chance of success than if patronised by the greatest and most powerful of Walpole's supporters.' Daniel Campbell's[1] paramount influence and the consequence it gave him are alluded to in Lord Binning's satirical ballad upon the 'Duke of Argyll's Levee :'

> '——when, lo !
> Great Daniel showed his face.
> At sight of him low bowed the peer ;
> Daniel vouchsafed a nod.
> " I've seen Sir Robert, and 'tis done,
> You've kept me in, by—— ! " '[2]

At this time Daniel Campbell held several offices under Government, all of which tended to augment his income, amongst them that of 'Tacksman of the Revenue.' The Tacksmen and their officers were, of course, not favourites in the country where the feeling in favour of undutied liquors was so strong, and the execution of the revenue laws caused much bad blood.[3] Campbell of Shawfield was not, therefore, popular, and he further incurred the hatred of the inhabitants of Glasgow by furnishing, as it was supposed, the Government with such information of the manner of trading in Scotland as occasioned an Act of Parliament to be passed which struck a heavy blow at their tobacco trade. Ten years after the Union much of this was in the hands of Glasgow merchants, and the

[1] Daniel Campbell was often called 'The Great Daniel,' partly from his stature and build, and partly from the position he achieved.

[2] *Gentleman's Magazine*, February, 1740, p. 87.

[3] Burton in his 'History of Scotland' says: ' The revenue officers, looked upon always as an English force, or, what was worse, renegade Scotsmen in English pay, received little countenance from the local authorities.'

wealth of the tobacco-lords,[1] which was the name given to those at the head of the trade, was very great. Bristol, Liverpool, and Whitehaven, having been up till then the great entrepots, became alarmed, and petitioned the House of Commons on the subject. New officers were appointed, Campbell of Shawfield was made Collector of Customs at Port-Glasgow, and it was said that his evidence ruined this trade in Glasgow.

The culminating point of his unpopularity was reached in June 1725 when he voted in Parliament for the tax of 6*d.* on every bushel of malt. Up to this date the chief beverage of the Scotch was a light ale usually sold at 2*d.* for two quarts, and therefore commonly called 'twopenny.' The Government thought they might raise £20,000 per annum by the tax, and Campbell of Shawfield used his influence largely in favour of its imposition. Where it became evident that this measure would occasion a desperate resistance the tax was reduced to 3*d.*, but in spite of this reduction a very serious riot took place in Glasgow the day that the Act came into force. This rising was called 'Shawfield's Mob,' because the chief violence was directed against him. He seems to have anticipated something of the sort, for not only did he send to General Wade for military assistance, but we are told he removed many of his most valued possessions, and placed them in the houses of his neighbours and friends, and he also took good care to be away from home that day ; this was lucky for him, as Lockhart in his Papers says, ' Had Mr. Campbell himself been in town they had certainly dewitted him.' [2] As it was, the insurgents sacked his fine

[1] Previously to the breaking out of the American war the 'Tobacco Lords' had a privileged walk, where they promenaded in long scarlet cloaks and bushy wigs.

[2] This quotation is interesting as being an example of the newly coined word 'dewitted,' i.e. murdered by the mob. The brothers Jan and Cornelius De Witt were torn in pieces by an infuriated populace in Holland in 1672.

new house and carried off the silver which his second wife had brought with her from West Shields, and after wrecking the contents of the mansion the mob broke into his cellars and inflamed their fury by indulging in the contents. The military were called out, and nine persons were killed and seventeen wounded. As it was but too justly believed that the magistrates sympathised with the mob, Duncan Forbes, the celebrated Lord Advocate, went to Glasgow, accompanied by General Wade himself, who commanded a considerable force, and had them confined in their own prison, and afterwards sent to Edinburgh. The following curious song, entitled 'The Glasgow Campaign,' appeared at this time :—

'To Glasgow, to Glasgow we'll goe,
    With our cannon and mortar we'll make a fine show,
    With three thousand stout men, so gallantly led
    By our Advocate-General and his A.D.C. Wade ;[1]
    There's Daniel the traitor, and John of goud sleeves,
    And Campbell of Carrick and his Highland theeves,
    With loyal Duncan and Diamond so bright,
    Which he got for abjuring the Hanover right.

To chastise these rebels for appearing so keen
    For the House of Hanover in the damned year '15
    Long live the grate Walpole
    May he ——ly then reign ;
    But if Garge gets his eyesight
    He may happen to swing.'

[1] General (or Marshal as he became) Wade is chiefly remembered now in connection with roads in the Highlands. There were absolutely none there till he made them. Troops were employed on extra pay for this work, which took eleven years. On the road between Inverness and Inveraray, near Fort William, an obelisk was erected with these naive words :

'Had you seen these roads before they were made,
    You would lift up your hands and bless General Wade !'

The Lords Justices wrote a letter of condolence to Campbell of Shawfield, assuring him that they would resent what had befallen him as in effect done to King George himself. Allan Cameron, writing to Lord Inverness shortly after, says : 'Weeve had a hot tryal in the Justiciary Court of Glasgow rioters ; the Earl of Hay and Lord Royston with the out most zeal to find the libel relevant to infer the pains of death, the other Lords insisted it could go no further than one arbitrary punishment and carried it except where any person was proven guilty of actually pulling down Campbell's house. . . .' A Bill was passed ordering the community of Glasgow to pay Campbell of Shawfield £9,000 damages, to be raised from an imposition laid upon all the beer and ale brewed in Glasgow.[1] About this time Daniel Campbell made a good deal one way and another out of the forfeited lands of the Jacobites. Katherine, wife of John Walkinshaw of Barrowfield, had petitioned the King to grant the benefit of her husband's forfeiture for her and her children. Daniel Campbell in 1722 presented a memorial to the Lords of the Treasury, stating that he was a very considerable creditor upon the estate, and prayed that the grant might be limited. The result was that Parliament granted Daniel a considerable sum for losses and damage. Soon after this Daniel was anxious to possess the estate of Kilsyth, with the value of which he was thoroughly acquainted.[2] It was forfeited by Viscount Kilsyth at the

---

[1] The following curious minute of the Corporation appeared on May 6, 1746, twenty-two years after the sacking of the house : 'John Cochrane, Master of Work, represented that by advice of the magistrates he had sent to London to sell the broken necklace of diamonds which was found among the rubbish of Daniel Campbell's house with a piece of gold coin, and that the same had been offered to Lady Shawfield, who refused to take it in regard that Shawfield was satisfied by the Parliament as to his damages, and that it was sold for £30, and the piece of gold for £2 10s.'

[2] It yielded a clear rent of 800*l.*

time of the rebellion in 1715 and had been sold by the Commissioners of Enquiry to the York Buildings Company,[1] who had let it in 1721 to one Stark for nineteen years at £800 a year. This was no bar to our friend Daniel! In 1725 he managed to persuade Stark to give it up, paying him a douceur of £700, and he then induced the Company to lease it to him for ninety-nine years at £500 a year (£300 less than Stark had paid), and, moreover, he entered into possession at Whitsuntide 1727, though the lease was only made out from March 1728![2]

In January 1745, Charles Edward, after spending a week in Glasgow, marched with a column of the Jacobite army to Stirling, and stopped a night at Kilsyth House, where his troopers helped themselves liberally to Daniel Campbell's possessions, leaving a message when they moved on that he must repay himself with the Kilsyth rents.[3]

The following was the final stroke of policy by which Daniel was said to have augmented his fortune : he had become Feuar of Smerbie and Clockfinn in Cantire, part of the Argyll estate, and often acted as chamberlain or agent to Duke John, who one day, as the story goes, sent for him and said that, hearing that the islands of Islay and Jura were for sale, he should like his advice as to the desirability of purchasing them. Now this canny Scot knew Islay well, for his mother came from there, and he had lent money on it to the owner and had long envied its possession.[4] However, he sent back an adverse opinion.

---

[1] The company of Undertakers for raising the Thames Water in York Buildings, London.

[2] All this came out in evidence in a case brought before the House of Lords.

[3] Daniel's grandson, Walter Campbell, sold Kilsyth in 1783 to Sir Archibald Edmonstone, Bart., of Duntreath.

[4] In 1769 the rental was about £2,300 ; it now amounts to £30,000 a year. The late Mr. Morrison bought it for £450,000.

DANIEL CAMPBELL, OF SHAWFIELD.
From a Picture in the possession of Captain Montgomerie, R N

The Duke did not buy Islay, but the merchant banker did! This is the story told, but the real facts of the case are these. In the year 1722 the owner of Islay and Jura, John Campbell of Cawdor, M.P., mortgaged these islands to Daniel Campbell for the sum of £6,000, reserving power to redeem them up till the year 1744, and in 1726 he sold them both to Daniel for the additional sum of £6,000. It was true that the Duke asked Daniel to bid for him, but the estates went beyond the limit his Grace gave, so that Shawfield was in his right to buy them for himself. The Duke, however, was apparently aggrieved, which may account for what Wodrow writes: 'In July 1726 Campbell of Shawfield waited on John Duke of Argyll at Edinburgh; his entertainment was not very satisfying.' And in July 1729, Wodrow writes: 'It's given out that the Duke is to drop Dan Campbell, and they say he would not see him at Greenock and at Inveraray. It's talked that Shawfield at London vyes with the Duke and reckons he stands on his own legs.' This shows what an influential position he had attained when he dared to brave

> 'Argyll, the State's whole thunder born to wield,
> And shake alike the senate and the field.'

Shawfield's second marriage with the sister of a well-known peer had probably given him a lift in the social scale, and his eldest son John further helped to aggrandise his family by making two noble alliances, one of which gave his descendants several royal descents, both Scottish and English.[1] The canny old Scot died at Woodhall in 1753, aged eighty-three.[2] By his

---

[1] His granddaughter Margaret, Countess of Wemyss, had sixteen quarters displayed on the escutcheon or hatchment placed over the family mansion at her death.

[2] Captain Walter Campbell has a portrait of him by Ramsay, which is here reproduced.

first wife, Margaret, daughter of John Leckie,[1] of Newlands, merchant and burgess of Glasgow, by his wife Jannet, of L . . . .,[2] who died in 1711, he had three sons and three daughters.[3] His second wife, whom he married in 1714, was Katherine Erskine, eldest daughter of Henry, third Lord Cardross (by Katherine, daughter and sole heiress of Sir James Stewart of Strabrock), sister to the Earl of Buchan and widow of Sir William Denholme[4] (Denham), Bart., of West Shields.[5]   By her Daniel Campbell left one daughter, Catharine Campbell, who

[1] The family of Leckie was settled in the north of Ireland for several centuries, and a branch was early established in the neighbourhood of Stirling, where the ruins of the ancient seat are still visible.   Daniel Campbell's wife was probably the granddaughter of Alexander Leckie of Leckie.   'Joannes Leckie de eodem' was served heir of his father, 'Alexander Leckie de eodem,' January 17, 1648.

Professor Robert Baillie, of Glasgow, in his *Letters and Journals*, writes in 1640 : 'Our countrymen in Ireland being pressed there by the Bishops to countenance the Liturgie and all their ceremonies, did absteeme much from the public worship ; and in privatt, among themselves, their ministers being all banished, did in that place and tyme of persecution, comfort themselves with prayer and reading.   The most of this good people flying over to us, were heartilie embraced of us all, their privatt meetings were overseen.   We let alone till the Laird of Leckie, one who had suffered much by the Bishops, was marked, useing his Irish forme of privie exercise in Stirling.'   Professor Baillie goes on to describe the religious dissensions between the said Alexander Leckie and Guthrie, minister of Stirling, afterwards Bishop of Dunkeld—dissensions which went on till Professor Baillie called in the aid of Argyll, who was the instrument of a 'happie concord.'

[2] One daughter Margaret married Sir Duncan Campbell of Lochnell ; Anna married her first cousin, Colin Campbell, Captain of Skipness, but had no children ; and the third daughter, Janet, married Alexander Macmillan, Clerk to his Majesty's Signet.

[3] John Leckie's signature and that of his wife 'Jannet' appear on an old parchment still preserved, but her surname is illegible.

[4] In the contract of marriage between Daniel Campbell of Shawfield and Dame Katherine Erskine she signs herself 'K. Denham.'

[5] Sir William Denholme was 'out' with the Earl of Argyll in 1685.   In the Wodrow Correspondence there is a letter from Wodrow to Daniel Campbell, written in 1722, excusing himself from any intention of disparaging in his history the conduct of the late Sir William Denholme, Lady Denholme having taken exception to something he wrote of her first husband.

married, in 1737, Thomas Gordon of Earlston, Bart.[1]   Daniel's
three sons died in his lifetime.[2]   The eldest, John, a Commissioner
of Inland Revenue, was born in 1696, and died in 1746, aged
fifty.   He had married first Lady Margaret Campbell, daughter
of the Earl of Loudoun, who descended from a common ancestor
with the Duke of Argyll ; by her he had no children, and he
married secondly, in 1735, Lady Henrietta or Harriot[3] Cunningham,[4] daughter of William, twelfth Earl of Glencairn, and his
wife Lady Henrietta Stewart, by whom he had four sons, the
eldest of whom, Daniel, succeeded, at his grandfather's death in
1753, to the estates of Shawfield, Woodhall, Islay, and Jura.
This second Daniel was a great character in his day, but of a
totally opposite sort to his grandfather.   The first Daniel of
Shawfield had a genius for making money, and accumulated a
large fortune which this grandson helped largely to diminish.
He is described as living in great style.   He kept hounds, was
a conspicuous dandy, his wonderful wardrobe being sold in
Edinburgh in 1854 as 'theatrical dresses.'   And he spent his

[1] Catharine Gordon, *née* Campbell, had three children, only one of whom, a
daughter Catharine, left any descendants ; she married in 1770 General Stewart
of Afton, and had one son, who died unmarried, and four daughters.

[2] Daniel's second son Walter, born in 1700, died in 1733.   He was Receiver
General of Customs, and was described in the dedication of a book by the
Rev. James McRobe, minister at Kilsyth, as 'an honest man, of great integrity
and religiously inclined.'   He married, in 1728, Mary, daughter of Sir James
Campbell of Ardkinglas, and had two daughters.   There is a large full-length
portrait of him in the possession of Captain Montgomerie, R.N., and a half-
length, belonging to Captain Walter Campbell, is now at Holly Grove, Windsor
Park.

[3] In her will she is called ' Henrietta ;' in the sermon preached after her death,
which was printed, her name is given as ' Harriot.'

[4] Lady Henrietta survived her husband many years.   By her will, signed at
Woodhall in 1773, she leaves everything she possessed (with the exception of
a few legacies to her two sons, Daniel and Walter) to Miss Katharine Erskine
Drummond, daughter of Alexander Drummond, late Consul at Aleppo, who had
lived with her from a child.'   Lady Henrietta died in Edinburgh in 1774.

money right and left, even more on others than on himself.
He was a well-informed travelled man, had considerable literary
tastes, bought many valuable books, subscribed to rare
publications, and helped Wodrow to publish his metrical
version of McPherson's 'Fingal.' He was very musical and
played well on the violin, and collected rare old instru-
ments.   When as a young man he made the Grand Tour
he visited St. Petersburg, and there became acquainted with
the famous Princess Daschkow, on whom he seems to
have made considerable impression.   This remarkable woman,
daughter of Count Worontzow, was born in 1744, and was for
many years the friend and confidante of the Empress Catherine II.
of Russia, and is said to have been, when only eighteen years of
age, the prime mover in the Revolution of 1762 which deposed
and murdered the Emperor Peter III. and put Catherine, his
wife, in his stead.   Her husband, Prince Daschkow, who was sent
by Catherine to place Poniatowski on the throne of Poland, died
at Warsaw, having accomplished his task, leaving her a widow at
twenty.   Princess Daschkow then made a journey through Europe
with her two small children, accompanied by Mlle. Kamensky
and M. Worontzow.   When at Aix in Provence she met Daniel
Campbell again ; both spent a winter season there, and made
many excursions together, in company with other English.[1]
They went to Montpelier, Marseille, and Hyères, and in spring
the party proceeded to Switzerland.   Princess Daschkow in her
Memoirs says : ' The day after our arrival at Geneva, I sent to
beg permission to call on Voltaire, accompanied by my friends.

---

[1] Mrs. Hamilton, daughter of Mr. Ryder, Archbishop of Tuam ; Mrs. Morgan,
daughter of Mr. Tisdall, Solicitor-General in Ireland, and Lady Ryder. Mrs.
Hamilton afterwards visited Princess Daschkow in Russia, when the Princess
named a new village built on her estate ' Hamilton,' after her dear friend.

Although very unwell, he assured me of the pleasure he should have in seeing me, and that I was at liberty to bring whom I pleased. On the appointed evening Mrs. Hamilton, Lady Ryder, Mlle. Kamensky, my cousin Worontzow, and Mr. Campbell of Shawfield, went along with me to his house. The night before he had lost some ounces of blood, and, though very ill, desired it should be kept a secret, that we might not be deterred from the projected visit. On entering his room we found him lying back in a great chair, weak, and apparently in pain. I went up to him, and half-upbraidingly insisted that in his present situation our visit must be considered an intrusion, and that the most flattering proof I could receive of his esteem was to be thought capable of appreciating the value of his health so far as to have suspended for some days the pleasure of his society. A few compliments followed, and then we talked about the Empress of Russia. After making a pretty long visit, when I proposed returning home he earnestly requested us to go to his niece Madame Denis's apartment, where he hoped we would indulge him with our company at supper. We agreed, and were not long with Madame Denis before we were joined by her uncle. Voltaire was supported into the room by his valet-de-chambre, and placed on his knees in a great chair, over the back of which he leant and continued opposite to me in this uneasy posture during the whole of supper time.' During his stay at Geneva Daniel Campbell acquired some likenesses of Voltaire. Some of them were by Hubert, who had many opportunities of observing Voltaire's peculiarities, as he frequently played at chess with him. These likenesses no doubt savoured of caricature, and we have, besides Princess Daschkow's assertion that 'Voltaire was afraid of him,' the opinion of Le Vieux Malade de Ferney himself. In writing to

N

Madame Du Deffand in 1772 he says : 'Puisque vous avez vu M. Hubert, il fera votre portrait : il vous peindra en pastel à l'huile, en mezzotinto : il vous dessinera sur une carte avec des ciseaux, le tout en caricature. C'est ainsi qu'il m'a rendu ridicule d'un bout de l'Europe à l'autre. Mon ami Fréron ne me caractérise pas mieux, pour réjouir ceux qui achètent ses feuilles.' M. Hubert was always one of Princess Daschkow's party, and it was thus that Daniel Campbell became intimate with him. When the Princess left Switzerland, Mr. Campbell continued to travel with her and her friends. They engaged two large boats for carrying them down the Rhine. 'Mr. Campbell,' writes the Princess, 'was our spokesman whenever we left our boat, till, by his continual mistakes, I was encouraged to speak German.' At Carlsruhe the party were most hospitably entertained by the Margrave and Margravine of Baden. From there they returned via Düsseldorf and Frankfort to Spa, whence they parted. The Princess set out for Russia, and the others for England, but five years after the Princess and Mr. Campbell met again. She wished to place her young son at the University of Edinburgh under Principal Robertson, the historian, and accordingly proceeded to the Athens of the North, and she tells us in her 'Memoirs' that on arriving at Edinburgh she 'engaged apartments in Holyrood House, the ancient palace of the Scottish sovereigns.' The Princess stayed in Scotland during her son's entire course, and describes this time as 'the most satisfactory and happiest of her life.' She saw a good deal of Daniel Campbell in Edinburgh, and in the summer she visited him at Woodhall, and it was upon this occasion that he is said to have given her the celebrated Shawfield pearls, and she presented him with her portrait, which was sold at Woodhall in 1850. Whilst she was yet in Scotland, Daniel Campbell died,

VOLTAIRE.

From an Etching formerly in the possession of Daniel Campbell, Junr., of Shawfield.

aged forty. He appears to have been a most charming and loveable man, and the following is a sketch of his character which was printed for private circulation at the time of his death.

'A SKETCH OF THE CHARACTER OF
THE LATE DANIEL CAMPBELL, ESQUIRE, OF SHAWFIELD.

"Quando ullum invenient parem ?"

Bring every sweetest flower, and let me strew
The grave where Shawfield lies.

' He was one of the most accomplished gentlemen his country has produced. Nature was liberal to him of her choicest gifts. A happy education, an accurate knowledge of mankind, carried these to a high degree of improvement.

' He was distinguished by the essential qualities of true excellence—untainted integrity, unsullied honour, diffusive benignity, and every social virtue. He possessed the graces in perfection ; not as a pack of hired, servile flatterers, but as the faithful ministers of every gracious office. To make all easy and happy was his art of pleasing : and being a perfect master of the most engaging manner, he could not possibly fail of success. Taste and elegance seemed natural to him ; they appeared in every word and action, they descended to the lowest border of the garment. His household resembled a small but well-regulated republic, where harmony and happiness constantly prevailed. He was the friend of man. His graceful hand placed every character in the fairest point of light ; and no unfavourable reflection could be offered without being reproved by the decorum of his presence. His charity was boundless. Few knew the world better ; none valued it less. His soul melted at the sighs of distress. The hopes of the indigent were

N 2

always exceeded. Under his friendly shade multitudes lived in ease and affluence, and through all his extensive possessions the voice of oppression was never heard.

‘ The fine arts were his chief amusements ; and those authors he chiefly valued who nobly planned the public welfare. He sat in two Parliaments ; and gave such specimens as declared him qualified to have made an eminent figure in the British Senate.

‘ Above all the ineffable sweetness, the flowing sensibilities of his heart, enhanced every accomplishment ; gave a charming lustre to the whole man ; and rendered him, at once, admired and beloved by all who knew him.

‘ His country has not lamented the loss of a more worthy patriot, nor Friendship shed the tear for a more faithful votary.

‘ Is there yet a blank ? It shall be filled up His piety was manly and rational. It exerted itself in supporting an eminent station with whatever was beneficial to society, or ornamental to human nature. Indeed, there was in him something so truly great and good which could not be ascribed to any other cause. Let Folly blush ; but Wisdom triumphs while I write. He entertained the most venerable sense of the sublime truths of religion : his bosom by nature kind, but still more refined with their heavenly dictates, became the parent of all that was generous and exalted.

‘ In the full strength of manhood he resigned this transient life, with that perfect serenity, and firm confidence in a better, which the assured hopes of immortality natively inspire.

‘ These are the rude lines of a great original—The hand of a complete master, alone, can do it justice.

‘ It is enough. The picture is already fully drawn, in more lasting characters, on the hearts of his friends. Upon that sacred tablet, the beautiful features, the tender endearments, of one of the most amiable of men will be preserved, as the most precious treasure, as the only solace of their woe.'

Daniel Campbell was succeeded by his brother, Walter Campbell of Skipness,[1] an advocate. He married first in 1768 Eleonora Kerr, daughter of Robert Kerr of Newfield, grandson of the first Marquis of Lothian, by whom he had ten children. He married secondly Mary, daughter of William Nisbet of Dirleton, with whom he acquired Pencaitland, Saltcoats, and Dechment. By her he had two daughters.[2] He died in 1816, aged seventy-five. Of his eight daughters only three left descendants, namely, Harriet, who married Mr. Hamilton, the present Lord Hamilton of Dalzell being her great-grandson ; Margaret, who became the wife of Francis, seventh Earl of Wemyss, whose grandson is the present Earl of Wemyss ; and Katherine, who married Sir Charles Jenkinson, tenth baronet, nephew of the first Earl of Liverpool.

Walter Campbell sold Shawfield and the Isle of Jura in his lifetime, but left an estate to each of his surviving sons. Robert had Skipness ; Walter, Sunderland (Islay) ; and Colin, Ardpatrick. John, the eldest, who married Lady Charlotte Campbell, daughter of the Duke of Argyll, pre-deceased his father, and his son Walter Frederick succeeded at his grandfather's death to Islay and to Woodhall. It is sad to think that of all the estates acquired by Daniel Campbell only one now remains in the possession of his descendants, namely Ardpatrick, which belongs to James Campbell, R.N., the grandson of the last Campbell of Shawfield.[3] The head of the family

---

[1] His mother, Lady Henrietta Campbell, in her will, dated October 7, 1773, calls him 'my son Walter Campbell, *now of Skipness.*'

[2] Mary, Lady Ruthven, and Hamilton, Lady Belhaven.

[3] Archibald Campbell, Provost of St. Ninian's, Perth, the Bishop-elect of Glasgow, is the eldest son of the last Walter Campbell of Skipness.

is Captain Walter Campbell,[1] C.V.O., Groom-in-waiting to King Edward VII., and Deputy-Ranger of Windsor Great Park, who is the great-great-great-grandson of *The Canny Scot.*

[1] His talented elder half-brother, John F. Campbell of Islay, well known as an author, died in 1885. He was a distinguished Gaelic scholar and an enthusiastic Highlander, and his contributions to folklore are most valuable, his great work on that subject being *Tales of the West Highlands.* He also wrote *Frost and Fire, Natural Engines, Toolmarks and Chips,* and other scientific works, and he invented the sunshine-recorder for indicating the varying intensity of the sun's rays. Mr. Wilson, in his *Notable Men and Women of Argyleshire,* says of him : ' Iain og Ile' (young John of Islay), a man of most lovable nature, preserved, as he deserved, all the affectionate loyalty of the islanders of Islay, although he had lost the estates of his fathers. An obelisk was raised to his memory in June 1887, on the summit of Cnoc-na-Dàb, a hill in Islay near his birthplace.'

A BYGONE BEAUTY

CROKER in his Diary on July 23, 1828, makes the following entry : 'Dined at Sir Henry Hardinge's, where besides Lady Emily we had Lords Brecknock, Lowther and Downe, Sir Herbert Taylor, Robert Farquhar, Messrs. Calcraft, Planta, Holmes, Col. Cradock. Talking of beautiful women, I told the anecdote that I had separately asked the King [George IV.] and Sir Thomas Lawrence, whom they thought the most beautiful woman they had ever seen, and before I gave their answer I asked the present company to guess whom they had named. Sir Herbert Taylor and Holmes both agreed in saying Lady Charlotte Campbell, and it was Lady Charlotte that both his Majesty and Sir Thomas selected. I have never met any one except the Duke of York who had known her in their youth who did not represent her as the most beautiful creature they had ever seen.'[1] The beauty in question, Charlotte Maria Campbell, had indeed every right to those looks for which she was so justly celebrated. Her mother was one of the beautiful Gunnings,[2] and her father—John, fifth Duke of Argyll, himself

---

[1] In Croker's manuscript he says on another occasion : 'Lady Charlotte Campbell was thought by the best-judging of her contemporaries the most beautiful creature ever seen. I saw her in 1801, still magnificent, whole theatres turning round to look at her.'

[2] Kirkpatrick Sharpe goes the length of saying that she was 'handsomer than either mother or aunt,' and adds that 'no picture did her common justice.'

Mackenzie, in his *Reminiscences of Glasgow*, says: 'We remember seeing very frequently the Duke (of Argyll) in Glasgow, who was an exceedingly handsome man, accompanied by his two sisters, Ladies Augusta and Charlotte Campbell ; when Lady Charlotte in particular came to visit some of our haberdashers' shops—

a very handsome man—was son of the beautiful Mary Bellenden. Born on January 28, 1775, she received the name of Charlotte from George III.'s queen, who was her godmother, and that of Maria in memory of her aunt, Lady Coventry.

'The Flower of the House of Argyll,' as she was called, showed early signs of that beauty which became so remarkable. Horace Walpole, writing to Miss Berry (afterwards one of Lady Charlotte's most intimate friends) in January 1791, says *à propos* of the Duke of Argyll's family : 'Everybody admires the youngest daughter's person and understanding.' At this time she was only just sixteen, and had lost her mother six months previously. For some years past the Duchess of Argyll had been obliged to spend every winter abroad, and Lady Charlotte, who always accompanied her, has left a detailed account of these wanderings in her Journal, which shows, for one so young, a very remarkable and true appreciation of all that is most elevating in nature and art. Her love for Italy was then, as it continued to be throughout her long life, a veritable passion. She became an accomplished Italian scholar, and in the French language she was equally proficient. She was celebrated for the grace and agility of her dancing, and she played the harp and sang with great delicacy and expression. We have the testimony of Tommy Moore, who said that of all those who sang his melodies no one gave him such pleasure as Lady Charlotte ; and 'Monk' Lewis,[1] describing a party at his cottage, writes :

then few and far between—in the Trongate or Argyle Street, such was her transcendant beauty that crowds ran after her to get a glimpse of her, and tell that they had really seen her :

> " For ne'er did Grecian chisel trace
> A Nymph, a Naiad, or a Grace,
> Of finer form or lovelier face." '

[1] Lady Charlotte Campbell was the bright particular star which held a powerful influence over the life of Matthew Lewis, and he celebrated her charms in his lyrical

LADY CHARLOTTE CAMPBELL.

From a Painting by Tischbein, at Swallowfield

'Oh ! there was music since *she* was prevailed upon to sing, and the high-born and fairest of Caledonia's daughters breathed the simple melodies of her native hills to many a spellbound heart.'[1]

A full-length life-size portrait of Lady Charlotte, painted at Naples by Tischbein (now in the possession of the writer), gives a good idea of her dawning beauty when she was about sixteen, although the colour has somewhat faded from the face.[2] The tall graceful form and long limbs are veiled in a simple clinging robe of white, with draperies formed by a scarf of pale gold colour recalling the tint of the hair, which is crowned by a wreath of pink roses. The wondrously small foot, with its arched instep, is encased in a white and gold shoe. One of the beautifully moulded arms is uplifted to bend down a branch of the oak tree under which she sits, whilst a fawn nibbles the leaves. The right hand (the length and lissomness of which appear somewhat exaggerated) rests on a roll of music.

When she was about seventeen Lady Charlotte was presented at Court, and we have Lady Hester Stanhope's description of her at that time. She says : 'I remember Lady Charlotte Campbell's first going to Court, and the effect was very much what she describes of Miss Mordaunt [a character in one of

effusions under the title of 'Amoret.' She was also his heroine in *The Monk.* Lockhart, in his Life of Sir Walter Scott : 'When Lewis reached Edinburgh, Lady Charlotte Campbell, always distinguished by her passion for elegant letters, was ready, "in pride of rank, in beauty's bloom," to do the honours of Scotland to the " Lion of Mayfair," and I believe Scott's first introduction to Lewis took place at one of her Ladyship's parties.' It is curious now to read that at this time Scott was much flattered at his literary work being noticed by Lewis, and that he told Allan Cunningham thirty years after that he thought he had never felt such elation as when 'the Monk' invited him to dine with him for the first time.

[1] The late Alfred Bunn, in his *Retrospections*, was present at this party and says : 'The vocal talent of Lady Charlotte and Scottish music will long be talked of together.'

[2] This picture was for many years on the staircase of 29 Upper Brook Street (now ' Brook House '), exactly facing a window.

Lady Charlotte Campbell's novels], that is, somebody said, " She is too thin, very handsome to be sure, but too thin;" and somebody else observed that in a year's time, when she filled out, she would be remarkably beautiful, which turned out to be the case. She had such a hand, and arm, and such a leg ! She had beautiful hair too, gold colour, and a finely shaped nose and fine complexion. In about three years she all at once disappeared from the *beau monde* ; she married her cousin and was still Lady Charlotte Campbell, but always in uneasy circumstances. If I were rich enough I would invite Lady Charlotte here, and she would come, for she has children and would like to shew them the East. How pleasant it would be for me to have such a companion for two or three hours a day ! What a beautiful woman she was ! What an arm and hand ! I have seen the whole Opera House turn to look at it on the front of the box. The last time I ever met Lady Charlotte was walking with her brother in Kensington Gardens. She walked so well ! not mincing like some women, nor striding like others, but with a perfect use of her limbs, unaffected and graceful.[1]   The Duke [George, sixth Duke of Argyll] was like her in that respect,

[1] Lady Charlotte dressed in the extreme of the 'mode' when clinging transparent draperies showed every line of the figure. Gillray drew a portrait of her under the title of ' Modern Elegance,' May 22, 1795. It is thus described by Wright : ' The celebrated beauty is drawn in profile, seated in a reclining posture, while a mirror gives back the reflection of her full face. The features are noble and the figure voluptuous.

> Limbes fondlie fashioned in the wanton moulde
> Of Nature ! Warm in Love's slie wytcheries,
> And scorning all the draperie of Arte,
> A Spider's loom now weaves her thinne attire,
> Through which the rogueish tell-tale windes
> Do frolicke as they liste !'

Once when Lady Charlotte was walking in the streets of Glasgow with her handsome sister-in-law, Lady Jenkinson, such a mob followed them that they had to take refuge in a house and send for an escort to return home.

LADY CHARLOTTE CAMPBELL.
From a Picture by Anna Tonelli at Swallowfield, 1795.

COLONEL AND LADY CHARLOTTE CAMPBELL.

From a Drawing by Edridge, at Swallowfield

and his smile was incomparably sweet. Her features were equally charming with her person. C. told me she is still [1838] a loveable woman, and that the Persian Ambassador left England desperately in love with her.'

Lady Charlotte married, on June 14, 1796, John Campbell, eldest son of Walter Campbell of Shawfield, Woodhall, Jura, and Islay, by his first wife, Eleonora, daughter of Robert Kerr, grandson of the first Marquis of Lothian. The cousinship to which Lady Hester Stanhope alludes was of the most distant kind even for 'Scotch cousins,' and consisted in the fact that the Campbells of Ardentinny (ancestors of the Campbells of Shawfield) were said to be descended from Sir Colin Campbell of Lochow, great-grandfather of the first Earl of Argyll ! [1]

John Campbell—or Jack Campbell, as he was generally called—was at the time of his marriage in the 3rd Regiment of Foot Guards (Scots Guards), and became Colonel of the Argyllshire Militia and M.P. for the borough of Campbelton. He was only twenty-four, and a fine handsome man, and it was a love match on both sides ; [2] but it was a very poor alliance for the spoilt beauty. His father, though well-to-do, had fourteen children and was himself scarcely fifty-five years of age, so he gave his eldest son only a moderate allowance. After their marriage Colonel and Lady Charlotte Campbell at first paid many visits, and then,

---

[1] This is so according to Nisbet and Crawford.

[2] Lady Louisa Stuart, writing from Inveraray in 1804, says : 'Lady Charlotte is a sweet creature, and her character as well as her beauty improves upon a nearer view. I wish she were better bestowed than on that great fellow her husband ; but she loves him tenderly, and he is after his fashion fond of her.' We conclude that Lady Louisa did not admire his build. Jack Campbell was like the rest of his generation, a very tall strong man, of whom it was said :

> 'When Campbell walks the street
> The paviours cry
> "God bless your legs ! "
> And lay their rammers by.'

in 1803, took up their residence at Hartwell, in Bucks, celebrated as being afterwards the residence of Louis XVIII. of France whilst exiled from his throne (from 1807 to 1814), of which at this time Monk Lewis says, ' Nothing can be more beautiful in its kind, rustic colonnades, fruit and flowers in profusion.' Colonel Campbell predeceased his father, dying in Edinburgh in 1809, aged thirty-six,[1] and leaving Lady Charlotte a widow at the age of thirty-four, with nine children very ill provided for. Her impoverished condition induced her to accept, a year after her husband's death, the position of Lady in Waiting to Caroline, Princess of Wales. She had been her friend for some years ; and Lord Teignmouth mentions that Princess Charlotte, accompanied by Lady Charlotte Campbell, was present at an installation of the Knights of the Bath in Henry VII.'s Chapel as early as 1806. In 1813 the Princess of Wales sent Lady Charlotte to the Prince Regent with a letter petitioning him to allow her freer intercourse with her daughter ; but Lady Charlotte says nothing could be more insulting than the manner in which it was received.[2] This year Lady Charlotte was living at 13 Upper Brook Street, and was, she tells us, going out morning, noon, and night. Up till now she had loyally stood by the Princess of Wales, and seems really to have thought her conduct only very foolish and most undignified ;[3] but she now, it is evident, had many misgivings on the subject. In 1814 she made excuses to leave the Princess,

---

[1] Colonel Campbell was buried at Bothwell, near his mother.

[2] We conclude that the insulting manner was solely directed at the sender of the petition, and not at the bearer, as Lady Charlotte tells us that ' few persons ever have or ever can possess greater fascination than the Prince of Wales ;' and we also know that his Royal Highness thought Lady Charlotte the most beautiful creature he had ever seen.

[3] Lady Charlotte also said that the Princess was very fond of scandalising people by things she said. Once she told Lady Charlotte that she had had nine children, and did not explain for some minutes that they were adopted children.

COLONEL JOHN CAMPBELL, OF SHAWFIELD.
From a Miniature at Swallowfield.

and went for several months to Geneva with her youthful family and their governess. It was on this occasion that, stopping *en route* at Calais, Lady Charlotte Campbell tells us : ' Emma, Lady Hamilton—the Lady Hamilton I had seen twenty-five years ago at Naples—sent me a message to say that one who had known me long and well, and dearly loved those I loved, wished to see me again. Poor soul ! I was sorry for her, and a mixture of curiosity and sadness made me desire to see her once more. I went to her apartment—time had marred her beauty, but not effaced it—and when I said " Toujours belle," a smile of pleasure reanimated her fine eyes. My compliment was not altogether untrue, although it was a little more than reality : but such reality is not worth adhering to. Her eyes were filled with tears : she said the remembrance of the past crowded upon her, and excited them. She talked agreeably and spoke of her own fate. In mentioning the child she brings up, she assured me it was not her own, nor could be. When anybody assures me of a thing that may be true, and is favourable to themselves, I always believe them. It may be silly, but I cannot help it.'

Lady Charlotte stopped at Paris for some days, where we are told she was much admired. She tells us herself that she saw more and did more then than she ever saw or did in the same given time. Amongst other things she went to Court, and the King, Louis XVIII.,[1] said to her in English, with marks of

[1] Louis XVIII. had returned to France from his exile in England in April of this year. Lady Charlotte was intimate with the French royalties. The Comte de Beaujolais and his brother stayed with her for some days in 1801, and on leaving, the former said he hoped Lady Charlotte would call the child she was then expecting after him ; and accordingly Lady Charlotte's third daughter was christened Beaujolais, and the name as a female one continues in her family at the present day in the third generation. The Comte de Beaujolais was second brother of King Louis Philippe. He had a *vie orageuse* : he spent five years of his childhood in prison at Marseille, eighteen months of the time in a dungeon on bread and water ; then when he was thirteen he was shipped off to America.

feeling, that he should never forget what he owed to England. Lady Westmorland was the only other English lady present. At Geneva Lady Charlotte took a house called Les Grottes, and was soon in the midst of the clever literary set that was assembled there at this time, and met constantly Pictet, Vernet the painter (his son-in-law), De Saussure, Sismondi, Schlegel, Sir James Mackintosh, Sir Humphry Davy, Sydney Smith and Robert Smith ('Bobus'),[1] Mme. Necker (of whom her cousin, Mme. de Staël, said : 'Elle a toutes les qualités qu'on me donne et toutes les vertus que je n'ai pas '), and last, not least, Mme. de Staël herself, 'whose name,' Lady Charlotte says, 'must, like Aaron's rod, swallow up the rest.' Lady Charlotte had made the acquaintance of Mme. de Staël in the summer of 1812, when she wrote to a niece[2] the following ecstatic letter :

'I have seen her, that wonderful woman who has more knowledge of the human heart in its moral sense than the whole College of Surgeons and dissectors in the physical. I can scarcely tell you what Mme. de Staël is like, for I never saw any one to whom I can resemble her—she is ugly—but that first glance once passed which tells you so, she produces all the effect of beauty for one wishes to love her—she is middle-aged, straight made, neither fat nor thin—has little or no decided shape, but she has grace. Her eyes are very fine : they have the gift of the same eloquence with which her speech is imbued. She remained two hours and a half here. I really thought it only two minutes. She asked innumerable questions, and seised

---

[1] 'Bobus' Smith was the eldest of four brothers. Sir James Mackintosh said that 'of all the men he had ever known, Bobus Smith was the one that had the most robust vigour of intellect. No, he added after a pause, I must not say that, but Mr. Fox was the only man that I would put before him.' Sydney Smith was the well-known Canon of St. Paul's.

[2] Charlotte, daughter of Lady Augusta Clavering.

the sum of what I said before I could utter my answers! Her
tone of voice has no sweetness, but without being loud, it carries
the decision and quickness of the intellect which it interprets.
Mme. de Staël flatters you as another person would tell you a
disagreeable truth ; her flattery therefore carries more sure success
with it because it seems as if it were not flattery. She says
nothing for nothing—nothing merely to shine or be agreeable ;
but during the short period I saw her to-day the conversation
was confined too much to question and answer for me to taste of
that torrent of continued eloquence which her writings as well
as fame report to be so peculiarly her own. In short, I have
only seen enough to make me long to see more of her ; and yet,
by a fatal impression she seems to have received of the poor
Princess, I am much afraid she will not go to her, and this will
necessarily drive her considerably from my society, as it is
perfectly impossible consistent with any degree of gratitude that
I should become an intimate of a person who shews a marked
rudeness to the Princess, which it will certainly be if, after the
latter's inviting her, which I know she will do, they persuade
Mme. de Staël to decline. . . . I think this desultory account of
what I feel about this wonderful personage may amuse you. I
am too much under the influence of the excitement her presence
created to write you a literal distinct history of her person
and speech, but I pour out my detached descriptions, which
perhaps may convey my sensations better than a more regular
account.'

No doubt Mme. de Staël flattered Lady Charlotte right well,
for old sake's sake. Mme. de Staël, eight years before, had
been much in love with Lord John Campbell, Lady Charlotte's
youngest brother, the fact of his being eleven years her junior
proving no bar to her passion. They were together for many

months in Switzerland, 1804-5, after which she wrote to him several letters entreating him to return to her. In one dated '23 Juillet 1805, Coppet,' and directed to

lord John Campbell
in vereray argyll's house,
North britania, Scotland,

she says : ' . . . J'irai vous chercher dès que je le pourrai sans déchirer mes liens naturels . . . ne pouvant plus mener ici la douce vie que je vous devais, celle que j'aurais voulu prolonger tout le reste de mon existence. . . . Vous m'avez rendue parfaitement heureuse pendant nos relations ensemble. . . . Si vous aimer est un crime, je suis bien coupable. Je ne puis me consoler de your escape.[1] J'aurais été pour vous un doux geôlier. Farewell.'

In another letter, writing from Zürich, she says : ' Il me semble, my dear lord, que vous pourriez me donner le bonheur de vous posséder encore un ou deux mois en Suisse. . . . J'ai une maison toute prête pour vous à la campagne près de Lausanne à Ouchy. . . . Est-ce un rêve que tous ces projets, my dear lord, et *votre* cœur les réalisera-t-il ? Ecrivez-moi votre décision ; avec quelle joie je recevrai l'espoir d'une longue continuation de nos relations ensemble ! Adieu, my dear lord, dites-moi que vous m'aimez et que vous croyez que je vous aime *directement.*'

[1] Lord John was travelling in Switzerland in 1803, after the rupture of the Peace of Amiens, when Napoleon ordered the arrest of Englishmen travelling on the Continent. Mme. de Staël asked him to come to Coppet, which he did ; but the Duke of Argyll begging of him to return to Scotland at once, he left for Berne. Marshal Ney was there, and Lord John was about to be arrested, but managed to escape by disguising himself in woman's dress provided by Mlle. de la Chaux, a Swiss lady, a friend of his family. Dr. R——, Lord John's travelling companion, was arrested.

Another says : ' J'étais bien convaincue avant de vous connaître qu'il était possible de me plaire, de m'intéresser, mais non pas de me rendre la vie tout-à-fait douce. Mon âme naturellement agitée n'a trouvé du calme qu'auprès de vous, dire . . . de révolution m'avaient fait mépriser les hommes et vous m'avez rendu ce que j'éprouvais à vingt ans, l'estime et la confiance. Pardonnez-moi donc si j'ai senti je ne sais quel déchirement inexprimable quand le dernier lien de l'espoir s'est brisé—il m'en reste un cependant, c'est que vous acceptez la proposition que je vous ai faite d'un rendez-vous en Allemagne. Auguste[1] meurt d'envie d'être mis en pension à Edimbourg . . . si je vous donne mon fils, n'est-ce pas que j'irais en Ecosse le printems prochain ? et je suis tentée comme Don Quichotte d'obliger tous ceux qui me lièrent à vous, c'est-à-dire que je vous aime et que vous devez m'aimer . . . je vous en prie . . . Quelques lignes à la fin de votre journal ; mettez sur un petit papier *je vous aime,* je me porte bien et s'il le peut *je vous attends là tel jour,* voilà des lignes qui feront plus de bien que toute la puissance consulaire n'en pourra jamais produire. N'est-il pas doux de penser qu'au milieu de l'empire du pouvoir l'empire de l'affection reste, et que l'amitié dispose encore du bonheur ? . . . Si cette lettre vous parvient à tems pour me rejoindre en Allemagne, ah ! my dear lord, attendez-moi—je vous aime tous les jours plus—il y a des trésors dans votre âme que je vous découvrirai à vous-même, et vous redeviendrez heureux en sentant mieux tout ce que vous valez. Ecrivez-moi, écrivez-moi, jamais vous aurez causé un plus doux sentiment à personne.'

In June of the following year she writes again from Coppet : ' Ah my dear lord, il y a un an que j'étais avec vous, un an que

[1] Auguste de Staël-Holstein, Mme. de Staël's son, born 1780.

j'étais heureuse, et ma vie est foudroyée ; jamais, jamais je ne reprendrai ni de l'intérêt ni de l'espérance ; je remplirai mes devoirs, j'élèverai mes enfants, mais il n'y aura plus sur cette terre un but pour moi, il n'y en aura plus. Je mènerais mon fils à Edimbourg l'année prochaine, c'est mon projet, mais si vous veniez ici je ne pourrais pas me défendre de n'y pas être . . . il faut que je vous revoye. . . . Je n'ai plus dans le présent que la contemplation du passé ; je ne vis que pour y songer. Ma santé est abîmée—je ne puis écrire deux pages sans tremblement. Adieu.'

To this love affair the world probably owes 'Corinne,'[1] in which Mme. de Staël gives utterance to a personal experience. Sainte-Beuve, *à propos* of this *chef d'œuvre*, says : 'Comme dans " Delphine " il y a des portraits. On savait de quels éléments un peu divers se composait la noble figure d'Oswald, de même qu'on croyait à la vérité fidèle de la scène des adieux.' It is easy to see that Lord John was in her mind's eye when she describes her hero as a Scottish nobleman, aged 25, who, when travelling abroad for his health after an unfortunate episode with a lady, meets with Corinne, a woman much older than himself, and they become deeply attached to each other. That the scenes are taken from real life is evident even in such detail as the form in which she addresses him, ' My dear Lord ' being a literal translation of the ' Mon cher Seigneur ' in ' Corinne.'

In 1810 Mme. de Staël married secretly Monsieur de Rocca,[2] a distinguished officer, who was a handsome young man, many

---

[1] The idea of Corinne, we are told, first came to Mme. de Staël in 1804. She worked at it during the two consecutive years, and it appeared in 1807.

[2] Monsieur de Rocca died of consumption. Mme. de Staël always said she hoped she would not survive him ; and she had her wish, for she died a short time before him, in consequence of the fatigue she underwent in her journey to Russia, following shortly after the birth of her child.

years younger than herself, and by him she had a son who
died young. Lady Charlotte mentions his paying her a visit,
and says there was an open kindliness of manner in him which
was peculiarly pleasing. When Mme. de Staël paid her first
visit to Les Grottes, Lady Charlotte tells us she took particular
pains to decorate it, but that Mme. de Staël's only observation
upon the pretty villa and its comfortably arranged rooms was—
' Ma chère, vous avez trop de luxe.' Mme. de Staël's own
house at Coppet was a specimen of what she considered a proper
dwelling, and certainly, says Lady Charlotte, ' a more comfortless
and barren-looking abode could not be found.' Lady Charlotte
says Mme. de Staël considered that luxurious surroundings
tended to weaken the mind, and, Lady Charlotte adds, ' literary
genius is seldom united with taste.'

After Lady Charlotte had been some months at Geneva, to
her horror the Princess of Wales put in an appearance there—and
such an appearance ! A ball had to be got up in her honour, and
she went to it dressed, or rather undressed, most injudiciously,
quite à *la Vénus*. Lady Charlotte writes : ' The natives were,
as the Princess would have expressed it, all over shock, and
when she began to waltz the *terræ motus* was dreadful. Waltz
she did, however, the whole night, and amongst others whom
she honoured with her hand upon this occasion was Sismondi.
These two large figures turning round together were quite
miraculous.' The Princess of Wales did not leave Geneva till
she had extracted a promise from Lady Charlotte that she would
rejoin her later at Genoa, and go on with her to Naples and
Rome.

In October Lady Charlotte left Geneva and went to Nice,
where she spent six months, in the Faubourg de la Croix de
Marbre, and was there during the excitement caused by

Napoleon's evasion from Elba. Lady Charlotte writes that on Thursday, March 2, the Prince of Monaco came to see her and told her that Bonaparte had landed at Grasse the previous day and bivouacked close by that night, and the Prince also said that he had been stopped on his way to his little dominions by Bonaparte, who asked him whither he was going. 'A mes terres, sire,' was the reply. 'Et moi aussi, je vais aux miennes,' said Bonaparte. Six days after, the 'Aboukir,' commanded by Captain Thompson, came from Genoa in pursuit of the small frigate in which Bonaparte had escaped—a day after the fair, as Lady Charlotte remarks. A few days later still, Sir Neil Campbell arrived at Nice ; and Lady Charlotte says she was curious to hear what he would say, as she had been under the impression that he was stationed off Elba to prevent Bonaparte getting away, and as a matter of fact he was at Leghorn at the time ; Captain Aidy (*sic*), his subordinate, and his frigate being also away, having gone to fetch Sir Neil. Lady Charlotte, however, adds that Sir Neil entirely exonerated himself, and told her that he did not consider himself Bonaparte's jailer and had no hold over him. He also told Lady Charlotte that, after Bonaparte's evasion, he called upon Princess Pauline Borghese and Mme. Mère, both of whom were at Elba at the time. They professed to know nothing of Bonaparte's movements, but the Princess took the hand of Sir Neil (he being, says Lady Charlotte *en parenthèse*, a very handsome man) and pressed it to her heart, desiring him to feel how it beat with anxiety. 'I could not,' said Sir Neil, 'perceive any symptoms of alarm, and, being in haste, shortened my visit as much as possible.'

Lady Charlotte left Nice for Genoa in April 1815 in the Princess of Wales's frigate, the 'Clorinda,' forty-eight guns, commanded by Captain Pechell,[1] and took with her all her young family and their governess. When she entered the Princess's palace at Genoa, the person who opened the door to her was, she says, 'the one whom it was impossible to mistake, hearing what is reported, six feet high, a magnificent head of black hair, pale complexion, mustachios which reach from here to London. Such is "the stork."'[2] Whilst at Genoa the Princess of Wales seems to have been paid much attention. She was visited by the Queen of Etruria, the King of Sardinia, the Archduke Constantine, and by (which sounds curious) the Pope, who had fled to Genoa when Murat had declared the independence of Italy. Lady Charlotte says the Pontiff sat with the Princess for half an hour, when she and Lady Glenbervie had time to fall in love with the Almoner. Lady Charlotte says : 'The Pope went away blessing all whom he passed, the scullions and cooks coming out in a crowd to kiss his toe, which they did most audibly. When he finally left, he turned and made the most graceful bow I ever saw ;' and she goes on to say, 'his countenance is very fine and his figure most venerable.' From Genoa Lady Charlotte went to Milan with the Princess, where the latter was also very well received, a *cortège* of ladies and gentlemen being appointed to accompany her everywhere. The Grand Duke met her at the entrance of the Court ball and conducted her round. Lady Charlotte says this was the most magnificent fête she ever beheld.

In May 1815 Lady Charlotte finally left the Princess of Wales, having remained with her longer than any other member

[1] Samuel John Pechell, Rear-Admiral, R.N., F.R.S., C.B., K.C.B., born 1785, succeeded his father, Sir Thomas Pechell, as third Baronet in 1826. Lady Charlotte describes him as very good-looking, as also his brother George, who was with him on board the 'Clorinda.' She knew their mother, who was a daughter of Sir John Clavering, and their uncle (General Clavering) had married her sister, Lady Augusta Campbell.

[2] Bergami.

of the English suite, the rest having quitted her the previous March.   Among the names of witnesses moved for in 1820 to be summoned on behalf of the Queen is that of ' the Lady Charlotte Bury.'   This brings us to Lady Charlotte's unfortunate change of name.   Ever since her husband's death she had had a train of admirers, but her nine children and want of money must have proved a bar to her making any second marriage that would be advantageous to her.   When she returned to England in 1815 she was in her fortieth year, but apparently as young in her ways as she had ever been.   Miss Susan Ferrier, the authoress, writes at this time : ' I thought Lady Charlotte looking more like herself, for she would dance and sing and go about and talk blue, and that is hard work in this town ; ' and she (Miss Ferrier) goes on to say : ' Lady Charlotte seems more eaten up with sentiment than ever ; all her sayings and doings are delightful, but how odd they would seem in the ugly part of the creation ! '   A contemporary, writing this year, couples her name with that of the handsome Mr. Locke ;[1] and another says : ' I think Lady Charlotte is a little smitten with the handsome Algernon Percy.   She said to me his voice and looks are supremely interesting, and she talked to him the whole night.'[2] Just at this time there came upon the scene Mr. Edward John Bury, a man of good family,[3] but with no money and the most

---

[1] Sir Thomas Lawrence said to Mme. d'Arblay in 1826 : ' I have seen much of the world since I was first admitted to Norbury Park, but I have never seen another Mr. Locke ! '   Sir Thomas was, at the time he made this speech, painting his beautiful picture of Mrs. Locke senior.

[2] Algernon Percy was a son of Lord Beverley, and was taken prisoner in France with his father.   The latter remained a *détenu* on parole for twenty-one years at Tours and Moulins.   Algernon Percy became Minister at Berne, and died in London of cholera.   He had been engaged to the beautiful Rose Bathurst, who was drowned in the Tiber.

[3] Mr. Bury's father, who died at Bridgwater in 1837, aged eighty, was a lineal descendant of Douglas, Earl of Morton.

extravagant tastes. He undertook to travel in Italy with Lady Charlotte's eldest son, Walter Frederick Campbell, who had lately left Eton and was now seventeen years of age. Mr. Bury was a clever and accomplished man and an artist of a very high class, his paintings being in the style of Turner, and some of them comparing most favourably with those of the great master.[1] His love of Italian art, and all his artistic accomplishments, made him a most agreeable companion to Lady Charlotte, and after some acquaintance she foolishly engaged to become his wife. They were married on March 23, 1818, at nine in the morning, at Lord Burghersh's house in Florence. Admiral Sir Thomas Fremantle [2] gave her away, and she was attended by the Misses Mary and Agnes Berry. Mr. Bury had been ordained, and in 1823 became rector of Titchfield in Hants, a parish which contained at that time only thirty souls, and he does not appear to have done duty there himself. By Mr. Bury Lady Charlotte had two children, both daughters. The eldest died an infant ; the second, Bianca Augusta Romana, married David Lyon, Esq., of Goring Park, Sussex. As far as Lady Charlotte herself was concerned, she seems to have been quite contented with her second choice. Five years after she wrote : ' In my husband I am really bless'd. He has his faults, like us all, but as a husband has as few as possible— inexpressibly careful and tender of me—quite lover-like, never leaving me, and all his tastes and pursuits those which are most refined and most of a nature to keep him constantly at my side ; indeed he has no wish ever to leave me and his child for a moment.'

[1] In an article in the *Quarterly Review* for 1834 the writer says : ' The world has lost a truly great artist by the death of Mr. John Bury, though the modesty of his character prevented him from making any public display of his extraordinary accomplishments during his too short life.'

[2] Grandfather of the present Lord Cottesloe.

At this time Lady Charlotte made a good deal of money by her writings, her novels[1] meeting with considerable success. They were all romantic love tales about the Upper Ten, full of sentiment, but with excellent morals. She also wrote some poetry, the best known of her poetical works being 'The Three Sanctuaries of Tuscany.' An article in the 'Quarterly Review' for 1834 says : 'In verse and in prose Lady Charlotte Bury has painted the "beautiful gloom of Vallombrosa's bowers" with a skill and a grace which must do honour even to her name.' This work was illustrated by some beautiful Turneresque drawings by Mr. Bury. She also published several religious works, amongst which were 'Prayers for every day in the month,' 1826, and 'Suspirium sanctorum, or Holy Breathings,' 1830. Lady Charlotte sent a collection of her poems to Sir Walter Scott in 1799, and in return he sent her a manuscript copy of his own poems, with the following lines :

> Of old 'tis said in Ilium's battling days,
> 　　Ere Friendship knew a price, or Faith was sold,
> The Chief, high-minded, famed in Homer's Lays,
> 　　For meanest brass exchanged his arms of gold.

> Say, lovely lady, know you not of one
> 　　Who with the Lycian hero's generous fire
> Gave lays might rival Grecia's sweetest tone
> 　　For the rude numbers of a northern lyre?

---

[1] Amongst her novels were the following : *Self-Indulgence*, 1812 ; *Conduct is Fate*, 1822 ; *Alla Giornata*, 1826 ; *Flirtation, A Marriage in High Life*, 1828 ; *The Exclusives, The Separation*, 1830 ; *The Disinherited, The Ensnared*, 1834 ; *The Devoted*, 1836 ; *The Divorced, Love*, 1837 ; *Family Records, The History of a Flirt*, 1840 ; *The Manœuvring Mother*, 1842. Nathaniel Parker Willis, the American author, writes : 'Lady Blessington's novels sell for a hundred pounds more than any other author's, except Bulwer's. Bulwer gets £1,400, Lady Blessington £400, Mrs. Norton £250, Lady Charlotte Bury £200, and most other authors below this.'

Yet—tho' unequal all to match my debt,
  Yet take these lines to thy protecting hand,
Nor heedless hear a Gothic bard repeat
  The Wizard harping of thy native land.

For each (forgive the vaunt) a wreath may grow
  At distance due as my rude verse from thine,
The classic laurel crown thy lovely brow,
  The Druid's magic mistletoe be mine !
                    Walter Scott, Edinburgh, 1799.

Sir Walter Scott also paid Lady Charlotte the compliment of placing four lines of hers as a heading to one of his chapters in the ' Heart of Mid-Lothian.' [1]

The only work of hers that has survived is ' The Life and Times of George IV.,' of which a new edition has lately been published. The greater part of this consists of Lady Charlotte's private journal and was never intended for publication. Mr. Bury took possession of it, made a few alterations and additions, introducing some remarks on Lady Charlotte by way of disguise, and published it without her knowledge, adding many letters addressed to her by the Princess of Wales, Sir William Gell, Keppel Craven, Mrs. Damer, most of all by Mr. C. Kirkpatrick Sharpe, the Horace Walpole of Scotland. The disguise was so flimsy that every one at once recognised the real author, and it was then quite easy to fill in all the names that were left partially blank. Five thousand copies of the review in the ' Literary Gazette' of Almack's, which indicated some of the characters, were sold. The publication of this journal naturally gave great offence to many of Lady Charlotte's friends, who never forgave

[1] Sir Walter Scott, writing to George Ellis in 1802, says : ' I am glad you have seen the Marquess of Lorn, whom I have met frequently at the house of his charming sister, Lady Charlotte Campbell, whom, I am sure, if you are acquainted with her, you must admire as much as I do.'

her caustic remarks on themselves and their relations ; and others, notably Mr. Kirkpatrick Sharpe, were furious at their letters being published without their leave. Lady Charlotte was a great letter-writer and wrote a fine large hand, and her letters were often witty and most entertaining.   One of them, addressed to Mr. Kirkpatrick Sharpe, is published in a collection of letters as a good specimen of a quaint and pithy style, though by no means one of her best.

Lady Charlotte was thrown much in the society of many of the leading men and women of the day. In her diaries and letters are constant allusions to Lords Aberdeen, Byron, Brougham, Castlereagh, Erskine, Grey, Liverpool, Melbourne, Moira, and Wellesley ; to Sir Walter Scott, Tommy Moore, Rogers, Thomas Campbell, ' Monk ' Lewis, the brothers Smith (authors of the 'Rejected Addresses '), Lady Blessington, Sydney Lady Morgan, ' L. E. L.' (Miss Landon), the Miss Berrys, Canning, 'Fish ' Crauford, Percival, Luttrell, George Selwyn, Sydney Smith, Sir William Gell, Sir William Hamilton and the beautiful Emma, and hosts of other celebrities ; and with many of these Lady Charlotte was on intimate terms.

Lady Charlotte's latter years were spent entirely in London, where she lived at 5 Audley Square, and also at 81 South Audley Street.   Shortly before her death, which took place on March 31, 1861, she moved to 91 Sloane Street in order to be near her only two remaining children, Lady Arthur Lennox and Mrs. William Russell, one of whom or their daughters were with her every day. Up to the last there were here daily assembled many of her old friends and countless relations, and though her intellect became sadly impaired and latterly her memory totally gone, she always received and welcomed them with that wonderful manner which was so characteristic of her a mixture of queenly dignity

LADY CHARLOTTE CAMPBELL.
By J Hoppner, R A

and gracious urbanity. The writer can see her as she sat very upright in her carved armchair, always dressed in the softest and richest satin (for many years before her death she never wore any other material), with a long sort of mantle trimmed with chinchilla, and her very small mittened hands in a large muff of the same ; and on her head the high mobcap of gauze trimmed with satin ribbons and tied under the chin, made on the same pattern as the one of her beautiful mother, the Duchess of Hamilton, represented in the well-known engraving of Miss Catherine Read's picture.[1]   She was generally surrounded by her Maltese dogs, ' Titania,' ' Oberon,' ' Mab,' ' Margo,' and ' Piccolo,' with her Swiss servant Charles and her maid ' Anachini ' always in attendance. She passed peacefully away at the age of eighty-six, without any pain, simply from a gradual decay of nature ; and as she had been beautiful in her life she was beautiful in death.

Lady Charlotte transmitted much of her beauty to some of her children.   Three at least of her daughters were most beautiful women—the beauty of the Gunnings ' lasted like huckaback,' as Horace Walpole says.   Her seven daughters were : (1) Eliza, married Sir William Cumming, Bart. ; (2) Eleonora, married the Earl of Uxbridge (afterwards Marquis of Anglesey) ; (3) Beaujolais, married the Earl of Charleville ; (4) Adelaide Constance, married Lord Arthur Lennox ; (5) Emma, married Mr. William Russell ; (6) Julia, married Mr. Langford-Brooke; (7) Bianca (Bury), married Mr. David Lyon.   Her sons were Walter Campbell of Islay and John Campbell, the present male representative of the family being her grandson, Captain Walter Campbell, C.V.O., Groom in Waiting to Queen Victoria from 1880 to 1901, and the same to King Edward VII., and Deputy Ranger of Windsor Great Park.

[1] This picture is at Inveraray Castle, but is inferior to its engraving.

In the early sixties a middle-aged spinster lady was living with her maid in poorly furnished dreary rooms in a lodging-house in Brompton Row.[1] She seldom went out, and, with the exception of two or three persons, no one ever came to see her ; a more obscure individual apparently did not exist, and no one at the lodging-house wondered, therefore, that when the time came for her removal to her last home, one hack-cab conveyed all the mourners, and after that every trace of her seemed blotted out of existence.

And yet this lady had been a personage in her way : she held quite a salon in Park Lane, where she delighted the political and literary lights of society by her brilliant conversation and lively wit ; an Emperor was one of her devoted admirers and correspondents, and she had been engaged to be married to two English dukes.

Who was this lady ? If we follow her to that most melancholy spot, the Brompton Cemetery, we read on the plain stone slab which marks her grave only the name 'Catherine Black Campbell,' and even to that name she had no right. She was a natural daughter of George Campbell, sixth Duke of Argyll. Her birth, which took place in April 1806, is wrapped in mystery. She herself said that her mother was the Countess

---

[1] Brompton Row no longer exists ; it was part of what is now known as Brompton Road, and was close to Ovington Square.

GEORGE, 6TH DUKE OF ARGYLL.

From a Pastelle by Hugh Hamilton, at Swallowfield.

of M., and this assertion is so far corroborated by the fact that there was a great deal of scandal about that lady's connection with Lord Lorne (as he then was). Anyhow, whoever the mother was, she left her daughter an annuity which was regularly paid through the Rev. Dr. G. Penfold (of Dorset Square), who knew the secret of her birth and probably had the care of her during her childhood. When she was fourteen years old she was sent to Paris, where she remained till she was twenty.

In 1810 her father married the beautiful Caroline, Lady Paget ; by this lady he had no children, and some years after they separated. The Duke then sent for his daughter Catherine, publicly recognised her as such, and made her the mistress of his house, 29 Upper Brook Street, the corner of Park Lane. She was well received by her father's friends and relations, and at once took her place in society ; which is testified by her voluminous correspondence, all of which she preserved, even to every note of invitation to dinner or *soirée*, and we have before us letters of the most friendly description from many celebrities addressed to her.

The writer has an oil portrait of Miss Campbell painted at Rome in 1832 by Horace Vernet. It represents her with a clear olive complexion, brown eyes, black hair and eyebrows and a slight *duvet* on the upper lip. It must have been an excellent likeness, as it was the image of her in later life. She was of medium height, and had remarkably small hands and feet ; these and her magnificent teeth constituted her best points. Looking at her portrait it is impossible not to come to the conclusion that somehow or other she had a strain of foreign blood in her veins.[1] She had not a look of her father, neither

---

[1] She is painted in the dress of an Italian peasant, which of course adds to her foreign look.

can one trace any resemblance to Sir Joshua Reynolds's beautiful portrait of Lady M. ; but strong physical characteristics often skip a generation, and it would be interesting to trace back Lady M.'s ancestry on both sides.

Miss Campbell was a very clever and agreeable woman and an accomplished linguist, and had many estimable qualities, but she had an ungovernable temper which in later years she vented on her best and dearest friends, taking offence where no offence was intended, and launching out into the bitterest invectives, which she was very fond of committing to paper ; but she had a warm affectionate heart and a generous disposition, and it is fair to say that she had much to embitter a naturally proud and sensitive nature. After living for many years in the lap of luxury, fêted by the great and idolised by her father, she suddenly found herself, by the death of that father in 1839, reduced to comparative poverty. This, added to the accident of her birth, which seems to have been overlooked before, lost her all social position. Her proud temper could not endure this change. She shut up the house in Brook Street, which her father had left her with all its contents, and in a few years retired to the Continent, living there till a year or two before her death, when she came to Brompton to be near her now almost sole remaining friends, Lord and Lady Arthur Lennox, the latter being a niece of Miss Campbell's father. To this lady she left all she possessed, including many boxes of letters and papers. A great portion of these were destroyed soon after her death, but the remainder have been preserved by the writer, and form a most interesting collection of autographs. A packet of letters addressed to Miss Campbell by the Czar Nicholas unfortunately was lent to a lady who died shortly afterwards, and her executors, not knowing what they were, burnt them ! Amongst the papers still existing

HORACE VERNET, PINX.

MISS CATHERINE BLACK CAMPBELL.

are two letters labelled in Miss Campbell's writing, 'The two last.' They were written to her by the Duke of Newcastle[1] shortly before the date fixed for their marriage. The first of these two letters is dated December 30, 1844, and says : 'I long to be with you again, my very very dear Catherine. I trust not again to part without being tied by the bands of wedlock ;' and the Duke goes on to say : 'Look over and consider the marriage service. I will do the same. We shall then be quite *au fait*, for in all else we have tried ourselves pretty well, I think ; and yet, thank God! here we are on the point of making the happiness of each other as I most firmly believe. In great haste, Yr. ever most affec^te. N.'

The second letter is written by the Duke from Clumber shortly after, acquiescing in Miss Campbell's wish to break off their engagement. The Duke appears to have been sincerely attached to her, and after all was over between them, he wrote as follows to a mutual friend—a Swiss lady : 'Aux grandes et belles qualités de Mlle. Campbell je rends, j'espère, une justice parfaite, et je serais des plus ingrats si je la refusais, car j'en ai souvent profité, et je lui dois beaucoup aussi bien à ses pensées et son conseil qu'à des bienfaits réels et substantifs.'

No doubt Miss Campbell bitterly repented her mad folly. Though sick at heart, mortification led her the following year to accept the addresses of another suitor, and she became engaged to George, fifth Duke of Marlborough.[2] She seems, however, not to have cared for him, and broke off her engagement at the last moment. Amongst the papers she left, and which have been preserved, is the licence for 'the marriage of George Spencer Churchill of the parish of Woodstock, a widower, and Catherine

---

[1] Henry Pelham, fourth Duke of Newcastle, born 1785, died 1851.
[2] George Spencer Churchill, fifth Duke of Marlborough, born 1793, died 1857.

Black Campbell of the parish of St. Luke Chelsea between the hours of eight and twelve in the forenoon, given this 22nd of November, 1845.'

In each case Miss Campbell's engagements were broken off by herself, and the marriage so near that the *trousseaux* were in her possession. Both were found untouched after her death, marked with the ducal coronets and the letters N. or M.

STRANGE VICISSITUDES OF A HIGHLAND LADY OF QUALITY IN THE EIGHTEENTH CENTURY

IT seems difficult to realise that as late as the middle of the eighteenth century a lady of unimpeachable character, born of gentle lineage, and nearly allied to some of the highest in the land, could have been incarcerated by her husband in a lonely castle and deprived of proper food and clothing; and yet such was the case with Primrose Campbell, the subject of this sketch.

In later years this lady was wont to say that the vicissitudes of her life would make a good story, but that nobody would believe them. Born in 1710, she was the twelfth child of the Hon. John Campbell of Mamore by his wife the Hon. Elizabeth Elphinstone,[1] and was given the name of Primrose by her aunt and godmother, Lady Elphinstone, *née* Elizabeth Primrose, who was a daughter of Sir William Primrose, Bart., of Carrington (ancestor of Lord Rosebery).

Primrose Campbell's father having joined, though unwillingly, his father Archibald, ninth Earl of Argyll, in his invasion of Scotland, was capitally convicted on his own confession, but the sentence of death was commuted into banishment, and this was

---

[1] The daughter of John, eighth Lord Elphinstone, by his wife Lady Isabel Maitland, whose brother Richard, fourth Earl of Lauderdale, married Lady Anne Campbell, daughter of Archibald, ninth Earl of Argyll.

rescinded in 1689. He died in 1730, leaving his family totally unprovided for. Luckily the four eldest daughters, though they had not only no dowries but 'ne'er a bawbee to bless themselves with,' had all married, perhaps not so much in consequence of their looks as from the fact that they were first cousins of John, the great Duke of Argyll, and of the Earl of Islay,[1] and also that Queen Anne had taken them under her protection. Mary Campbell, the eldest, married James, second Earl of Rosebery, and her son Niel was great-grandfather of the present Earl. Anne Campbell married Archibald Edmonstone of Duntreath, ancestor of the present Baronet of that name ; Isabel Campbell married Captain William Montgomery of Rosemount, of the family of the Earls of Mount Alexander ; and Jean Campbell married Captain John Campbell of Carrick. Primrose, who was twenty at her father's death, was still single, but in 1733 her friends and relations arranged a marriage for her, as a matter of policy, with the notorious Simon Fraser, twelfth Lord Lovat. He was the second surviving son of Thomas Fraser of Beaufort, fourth son of Hugh, ninth Lord Lovat, and at his birth was very far from being heir to the title and estates which he afterwards acquired.

In 1696 Hugh, tenth Lord Lovat, had died without male issue, leaving a widow (Lady Amelia, daughter of the Marquis of Atholl) and four daughters, the eldest of whom was heir to the title and estate, and assumed the title of Baroness of Lovat, but Thomas Fraser and his son, Captain Simon Fraser of Beaufort, claimed to be the next heirs male. This Thomas Fraser was, as we have seen, a cadet of the family of Lovat and had no manner of estate, having only a lease of a piece of land called

---

[1] Their brother, who had married the beautiful Mary Bellenden, became fourth Duke of Argyll in 1761.

Beaufort, belonging to the said family, to maintain himself and his children. Litigation ensued ; and Simon, as an effectual way of ending the strife, attempted to carry off the aforesaid Baroness of Lovat, who was still a child. She was, however, brought back, and eventually married some one else.[1] Nothing abashed, and determined by hook or by crook to get possession of some of the Lovat estates, he seized and forcibly married Amelia, the Dowager Lady Lovat, mother of the aforesaid young lady ! For this act, which was accompanied by great violence,[2] Captain Simon Fraser was condemned to death in 1698, but escaped to France, where he adopted the Catholic religion and offered his services to James II., who employed him to raise recruits in Scotland. After this it became known in France that he had revealed the substance of his commission to the British Ministry, and consequently he was, on his return to that country, put into the Bastile, where he was kept for some years. On recovering his liberty he went to St. Omer and entered into the order of the Jesuits. At the death of Queen Anne Lord Lovat, as he had become, received a full pardon and a grant of the Lovat estates ; and in 1717, his former marriage having been declared invalid, he

[1] She married Alexander Mackenzie, who took the name of Fraser of Fraser-dale.

[2] Having raised a gallows on the green before Castle Downie, where she then resided, to intimidate all who might wish to protect their mistress, he kept her a prisoner ; and then, as we are told in the indictment, 'one night, having dragged out her maids, proposes that she should marry him, and when she fell in lamenting and crying, the great pipe [bagpipe] was blown up to drown her cries, and the wicked villains ordered the minister, Mr. Robert Munro, to proceed, and though she protested with tears and cries, and declared she would sacrifice her life sooner than consent to their proposals, nevertheless the said minister proceeds, and declares them married persons ; and Hugh Fraser and Hutcheon Oig, both of them thieves and murderers, are appointed for her waiting-maids, and though she often swarved [fainted] and again cried out most piteously, yet no relenting. But the bagpipe is blown up as formerly, and the ruffians rent off her clothes, cutting her stays with their dirks, and so thrust her into bed.'

married Margaret, daughter of Ludovic Grant of Grant, and had the reputation of making her an unkind husband. She had barely been dead a year when it was suggested that he should marry Primrose Campbell, and it is not to be wondered that she strongly objected. Besides his moral delinquencies, Simon, Lord Lovat, had the disadvantage of being thirty-two years her senior and was very plain in appearance, becoming in later life a monster of fat, as may be seen in his well-known portrait by Hogarth.[1]

It is said that it was only by the following stratagem that she was finally induced to consent. She received a letter purporting to be from her mother, desiring her to come to her at once to a particular house in Edinburgh where she was lying very ill. She hastened there and found—Lovat. On her reiterating her abhorrence of his addresses, he told her that the house stamped infamy on any female who was known to have crossed its threshold, and thus she was literally forced into marrying him. She was married at Roseneath, and the marriage contract was signed by her mother and brother, her uncle Lord Elphinstone, her aunt the Countess of Mar, the Duke of Argyll, and the Earl of Islay. It is not to be wondered at that Lord Lovat found his bride ' irritable and sullen ; '[2] from the first it is said that he treated her with the greatest brutality, and after the birth of her only child he shut her up in two or three rooms in a lonely turret of his castle, which she was never allowed to leave. A modicum of the coarsest food was sparingly supplied to her, enough to keep body and soul together and nothing more ; she was not allowed to wear her proper clothes, and suffered intensely from the cold. Added to this, he constantly threatened to shoot her should she thwart

[1] Burton, in his *Life of Lord Lovat*, says that, if plain, he was eloquent and pleasing, even fascinating.

[2] As Primrose Campbell she was said to have had a sweet and gentle expression, with delicate features and complexion.

him. For a long time she tried in vain to let her friends know the state of affairs. At last rumours reached them, and they sent a lady to visit her unawares, who was to report what she saw. The wily tyrant, who was an adept at dissimulation, was not to be caught this way. Sir Walter Scott thus tells us what happened : ' Lord Lovat's last wife, though nearly related to the House of Argyll, was treated by him with so much cruelty that the interference of her relations became necessary. A lady, the intimate friend of her youth, was instructed to visit Lady Lovat, as if by accident, to ascertain the truth of these rumours concerning her family. She was received by Lord Lovat with an extravagant affectation of welcome and with many assurances of the happiness which his lady would receive from seeing her. The Chief then went to the lonely tower in which Lady Lovat was secluded without decent clothes and even without sufficient nourishment. He laid a dress before her becoming her rank, commanding her to put it on to appear, and to receive her friend, as if she were the mistress of the house in which she was in fact a naked and half-starved prisoner. And such was the strict watch he maintained and the terror his character inspired that the visitor durst not ask, nor Lady Lovat communicate, anything respecting her real situation. It was, however, ascertained by other means, and a separation took place.' The way in which Lady Lovat effected this was by rolling up a letter in a clue of yarn and dropping it out of a window to a confidential person who conveyed it to her friends.

In 1747, when her husband was in the Tower awaiting execution for high treason, she offered to go to him. This he declined, but in his letter wrote ' the only expressions of kindness and regard she had ever received from him since her marriage.' After the death of her husband, Lady Lovat's jointure, small as it was, being only £120 per annum, was not paid to her for several

years, during which time, being absolutely destitute, she lived
with one of her sisters. She was offered the loan of money by
many friends, and especially by Lord Strichen,[1] who was a kinsman
of Lord Lovat and who had married Lady Anne Campbell, sister
of John, Duke of Argyll (and widow of Lord Bute), and consequently her cousin ; but she declined to borrow from any one.
When at last she received the arrears of her jointure she bought
a flat at the head of Blackfriars Wynd, in Edinburgh, and
furnished it. Here she lived till her death, and on her small
income managed not only to entertain many nephews and nieces,
but gave a permanent home to several relations. Her niece,
Lady Dorothy Primrose, lived with her for many years ;[2] and
Lady Lovat also gave a home to an old cousin, the Hon. Mrs.
Elphinstone, who was always called the Mistress of Elphinstone, or 'the Mistress,' and to one of her grandsons whilst his
father was living at Algiers. This boy, who was thirteen or
fourteen years of age, was probably half crazy.[3] He took a
great dislike to his grandmother, and one day put poison
into the oatmeal porridge which she was accustomed to take at
supper. Feeling unwell that night she did not eat it ; Mistress
Elphinstone took it instead, and notwithstanding all the efforts
of the doctor who was called in, she died from the effects. The
boy, who lamented the result with many tears, being very fond
of Mrs. Elphinstone, was sent to sea and died in obscurity.
Lady Lovat continued to live in her flat in Blackfriars Wynd[4]

[1] Alexander Fraser, Lord Strichen, was a Lord of Session, and sat for forty-
five years on the Bench ; he was uterine brother to the celebrated John, Earl of
Crawford.

[2] She married in 1766 Sir Adam Inglis of Cramond.

[3] Lady Lovat used to say to him when he frowned at any contradiction, 'Aie,
callant, dinna gloom that gate, ye look sae like your grandfather.'

[4] The old Scottish tirling-pin of her housedoor is preserved in the Museum of
the Scottish Antiquarian Society.

till her death, which took place in May 1796 when she was in her eighty-seventh year, having survived her husband nearly half a century. She was aware of her approaching death for some time, and, in anticipation of her obsequies, had her grave-clothes ready and the stair whitewashed.

Lady Lovat's appearance as an old woman is thus described : ' When at home her dress was a red silk gown with ruffled cuffs and sleeves puckered like a man's shirt ; a fly-cap encircling the head with a mob-cap laid across it, falling over the cheeks and tied under the chin. Her hair dressed and powdered ; a double muslin handkerchief round the neck and bosom ; lammer-beads ; a white lawn apron edged with lace ; black stockings with red gushets and high-heeled shoes ; the heels being three inches deep. She usually went abroad in a chair, and any one who saw her sitting in it, so neat and fresh and clean, would have taken her for a queen in waxwork pasted up in a glass case.'

She left one son, the Hon. Archibald Campbell Fraser of Lovat, born in 1736, who was a merchant in London and appointed Consul-General at Algiers in 1766, and who in 1782 succeeded to the family estates at the death of his half brother, General Simon Fraser, to whom, in consequence of his distinguished services, all his father's forfeited lands had been re-granted subject to the payment of £20,983.[1] Archibald Campbell Fraser married Janet, daughter of William Fraser, and sister of Sir William Fraser, Bart., of Leadclune, by whom he had five sons, all of whom predeceased him.[2] He himself died

---

[1] General Simon Fraser was a man of irreproachable character, and he raised the Fraser Highlanders or old 71st Regiment.
[2] The five sons were : (1) John Simon Frederick, M.P., died 1803 ; (2) Archibald, died 1792 ; (3) Henry Emo, died 1782 ; (4) George, died 1781 ; (5) William, died 1801. The *Complete Peerage* says there was a sixth son ; if so, perhaps he was the one who poisoned Mistress Elphinstone.

in 1815, and there being then, it was said, no descendant of Thomas of Beaufort living, the male representation of the family devolved upon Thomas Alexander Fraser of Strichen (the descendant of the second son of the sixth Lord), who was created Baron Lovat in 1837 and was grandfather of the present Lord Lovat; but in 1885 a claimant arose in the shape of one John Fraser, an old miner who hailed from Carnarvon, who told the following romantic story. At the death of Thomas Fraser of Beaufort in 1698, when he was succeeded by his youngest son, Simon (the husband of Primrose Campbell), his eldest son, Alexander, who was said to have died in Wales, was still living and working there as a miner, his story being that, having killed a piper in a quarrel on some festive occasion, he had been obliged to flee from Scotland, and had hidden himself in Wales, working first of all in the mines of Lord Powys (who was a Jacobite), and afterwards for forty years in the mines of Sir Nicholas Bayley, grandfather of the Marquis of Anglesey. He married in 1738, at the age of sixty-five, a Welsh girl of the name of Elizabeth Edwards, by whom he had four sons, and died in Anglesey in 1776, aged, it is said, 103! During the early part of his life in Wales he took every means to disguise his identity, but in his later years spoke openly on the subject, and was called 'Lord Lovat' or 'Lord Fraser.' He died as he had lived, a poor man. His son, John Fraser, called himself, and was called by others, 'Lord Lovat' or 'Lord Fraser,' and in 1817 he appeared in Scotland and laid claim to the title and estates of Lovat, but from his great poverty was unable to prosecute his claim. William Hone in his 'Table Book' says that he also applied to the Lord Mayor for advice and assistance, and that he was in person and face as much like the rebel lord, if one may judge from his pictures, as a person could be. The old man, who said he was about sixty, was very ignorant, not knowing how to read or write, having been born in the mine and brought up as a miner, but he said he had preserved Alexander Fraser's Highland dress and that he had it in Wales.

In the history of the case brought forward to support the claim of John Fraser in 1885,[1] evidence was adduced that a Scotch miner of the name of Alexander Frazier, or Fraser, did come into Anglesea in 1762 in search of mines, and after visiting Parys Mountain, two miles from Amlwch, gave the owner (Sir Nicholas Bayley) so flattering an account of his property as induced him to sink shafts and seek for copper ore ; but the work was soon stopped by an influx of water. Two years after a Macclesfield company, who took a lease of the mines, discovered, within seven feet of the surface, solid mineral which proved to be that vast body which has since been worked with such advantage.

There is no doubt that the claimant is the direct descendant of this miner, but it has yet to be proved that the miner Alexander Fraser was one and the same as Alexander of Beaufort.

[1] A suit was instituted before the House of Lords, but the Committee of Privileges decided that in their opinion ' John Fraser has no right to the titles, dignity, and honours claimed in his petition.'

AN EMPRESS OF FASHION

Come, Paris, leave your hills and dales ;
  You'll scorn your dowdy goddesses,
If once you see our English belles,
  For all their gowns and bodices.

Here's Juno, Devon, all sublime ;
  Minerva, Gordon's wit and eyes ;
Sweet Rutland, Venus in her prime :
  You'll die before you give the prize.
            Epigram written on the Duchesses of Devonshire,
                          Gordon, and Rutland.

HORACE WALPOLE, writing in 1791 to Miss Berry, says : 'One
of the empresses of fashion, the Duchess of Gordon, uses
fifteen or sixteen hours of her four-and-twenty. I heard her
journal of last Monday. She first went to Handel's music in
the Abbey, she then clambered over the benches and went to
Hastings' trial in the Hall ; after dinner, to the Play, then to
Lady Lucan's Assembly ; after that to Ranelagh, and returned
to Mrs. Hobart's faro-table ; gave a ball herself in the evening
of that morning into which she must have got a good way ; and
set out for Scotland the next day. Hercules could not have
achieved a quarter of her labours in the same space of time.' This
energetic lady—Jean or Jane, daughter of Sir William Maxwell,
Bart., of Monreith, N.B., and his wife Magdalen, daughter of
William Blair of Blair—was born in Wigtownshire in 1750. She
was one of a large family of sons and daughters who grew up

distinguished for their beauty and intelligence,[1] but Jane out-stripped them all. Apart from the endowments that Nature had bestowed upon her, there was little in the early life of Jane Maxwell to foretell the brilliancy of her future career. At the beginning of George III.'s reign, the houses, or rather flats, in Edinburgh, in which many of the best Scottish gentry were wont to live and bring up their families, were odorous and inconvenient, and the closes or streets were often so narrow that persons could shake hands with their opposite neighbours from window to window. In one of these dismal places, called Hyndford's Close, our heroine spent a great part of her early days. The house had a dark passage, and the kitchen door was passed in going to the dining-room. In this passage, we are told, the fineries of Lady Maxwell's daughters were usually hung up to dry, while the underclothes were slung from a pole projecting from a window! Miss Eglintoune Maxwell [2] used to be sent with the kettle across the street to fetch water from the fountain-well to make the tea, so says Robert Chambers; and he adds: 'An old gentleman who was their relation told me that the first time he saw these beautiful girls was in the High Street, where Miss Jane was riding upon a sow which Miss Eglintoune thumped lustily behind with a stick! It must be understood that in the middle of the eighteenth century vagrant swine went

[1] The present head of the family, and the direct descendant of Jane Duchess of Gordon's brother, is the talented and learned writer Sir Herbert Maxwell, Bart., M.P.

[2] Miss Eglintoune or Eglantine Maxwell, called after her uncle the Earl of Eglintoun, married in 1772 Sir Thomas Wallace, Bart., of Craigie, and also became celebrated in Scotch society for her 'extraordinary cleverness, genuine wit, and delightful *abandon*.' Robert Chambers says: 'It almost seemed as if some faculty divine had inspired her.' She was, however, fiery-tempered, and when the English censor refused to allow her play, 'The Whim,' to be acted, she went off to France, where, being anything but a Democrat, she nearly lost her life in the French Revolution.

as commonly about the streets of Edinburgh as dogs do in
our own day, and were more generally fondled as pets by the
children of that generation.   It may, however, be remarked that
the sows upon which the Miss Maxwells rode were not the
common vagrants of the High Street, but belonged to Peter
Ramsay of the Inn, and were among the last that were permitted
to roam about.   The two romps used to watch the animals as
they were let loose from the stable-yard, and get upon their
backs the moment they issued from the close.'

Miss Jane's attractions appear to have developed early, for
before she was grown up a song called 'Jenny of Monreith'
was composed in her honour.   'The shape of her face was a
very beautiful oval, but her chin rather too long.   Her hair,
eyes, and eyebrows were dark, her upper lip short, and her
mouth, notwithstanding a certain expression of determination,
was sweet and well defined.'   Such is an account of her looks
given by a contemporary.   Another says : 'Above middle size,
very finely shaped, she had dark expressive eyes, very regular
features, fine complexion, and a most engaging expression.[1]
She was eminent for agility and grace in the performance of
those exercises which display beauty and symmetry, and for the
gaiety, spirit, and brilliancy of humour and wit which so agreeably set off her acute and vigorous understanding.'

'The Flower of Galloway,' as she was called in song and
story, when very young became deeply attached to a young
officer, and he to her.   They had soon to part, as he was ordered
abroad with his regiment, and shortly after news came that he

---

[1] There are several beautiful pictures of Jane, Duchess of Gordon. A lovely
one of her with her son, painted by Romney, was formerly in the possession of
Sir Herbert Maxwell, Bart. One painted by Sir Joshua in 1775 was engraved by
Dickinson. Raeburn also painted her.

had been killed. This was generally believed, and Jenny Maxwell was plunged in grief; but when the young Duke of Gordon appeared as a suitor, she was induced to accept his hand. They met at a ball in Edinburgh in the Old Assembly Rooms, and a story is told of how, on her way thither, Jane Maxwell discovered she had a hole in one of her thread stockings, and stopped *en route* at a friendly shop to have it mended. On leaving, the shopkeeper presented her with a pair of silk stockings, saying, ' When you are Duchess of Gordon you must patronise my establishment.' The shopkeeper knew that the Duke was to be present at the ball, and had implicit faith in the fascinating beauty of Miss Maxwell. The Duke accordingly did fall in love at first sight, and they were married in October 1767, when she was still only seventeen years of age. The marriage took place in Edinburgh at the house of her brother-in-law, Mr. Fordyce, who had married her eldest sister, Catharine, in the beginning of the same year, and after the ceremony the Duke and Duchess went to Ayton, Mr. Fordyce's place in Berwickshire. During the honeymoon the Duchess received a letter addressed to her in her maiden name and written in the well-known hand of her early lover. He was, he said, on his way home to complete their happiness by marriage !

The wretched bride, who was alone at the time, fled distractedly from the house, and according to local tradition was, after long search, found in a swoon by her husband, who read the letter, and it was said that in consequence they never got on well together. The result of this heartrending episode [1] was that the

---

[1] It has been said that this story suggested the ballad of ' Auld Robin Gray.' The authoress, Lady Anne Barnard, was sister of Lady Margaret Lindsay, who married the banker Alexander Fordyce a near relation of Mr. John Fordyce, the Duchess's brother-in-law.

young Duchess threw herself at once into a life of excitement to 'drown dull care,' and after a short time her natural high spirits began to assert themselves, and she soon became celebrated, not only for her beauty, but for her gaiety and exuberant wit.   On the occasion of a visit of Lord Monboddo, the philosopher, and his usual companion, Lord Kames, to Gordon Castle—when the Duchess, we are told, was unusually brilliant in her admirable sallies of ready wit and *jeux d'esprit*—Lord Monboddo said : ' Her Grace has a brilliancy and radiance about her like the rays round the head of an apostle.'   To her beauty and wit the Duchess added a conspicuous tact which made her universally popular with all sorts and conditions of persons, from the highest to the lowest ; and she was especially a great favourite with persons beneath her, owing to her habit of suiting her conversation to her company, and had the power of making all persons within the sphere of her actions pleased with them-selves.   A writer of the day, alluding to this characteristic, says : ' I remember, in 1777, just ten years after the Duchess's marriage and when she was twenty-seven years of age, spending an evening at the Inn at Blair when a large party of country gentlemen came there from the Duke of Atholl's place, where she had been one of the guests.   Her charms were the theme of universal praise for several hours, and on asking one of the visitors what he thought was the secret of her fascination he replied that it was because she gave every one an opportunity of speaking on the subject on which he supposed he could speak well.   " Not all her engaging qualifications," he said,. " made such an impression on my father as a conversation in which he was enabled to bring forward his favourite opinions on planting trees and potatoes, as most beneficial both to gentlemen and the poor ! and his good neighbour was no less captivated by her

JANE, DUCHESS OF GORDON, AND HER SON, THE MARQUIS OF HUNTLEY.

From a Picture by Geo. Romney, R.A., now in the possession of Mr. Charles Wertheimer.

Grace's discourse with him on sheep-farms! You may depend upon it," continued the young man, "that her understanding and manners, independent of her face, countenance, and figure, will secure to her an ascendency in any particular company in which she happens to be placed as well as the general circle in which she moves."' The Duchess's tact was sometimes at fault. Once when she was careering through the country upon some of those electioneering schemes which often occupied her fertile imagination, she called on the Laird of Craigmyle, a very simple-minded man, and having heard that he was making bricks on his property, with her usual tact she opened the conversation by saying, 'Well, Mr. Gordon, and how do your bricks come on ?' Craigmyle, having lately taken to a new leather part of his dress, looked down on his nether garments and said in pure Aberdeen dialect, 'Muckle obleeged to yer grace, the breeks war sum ticht at fust, but they are deeing weel eneuch noo.'

It was the Duchess of Gordon who started in London the custom of dancing at routs, an agreeable change from the interminable card-playing ; and she also introduced Scotch dancing—till then unheard of in the fashionable world—much improving it by adding grace to agility. She was the originator of the Northern Meeting. In the memoirs of a Highland lady edited by Lady Strachey we read : 'The Northern Meeting had been set agoing soon after my birth (1797) by her who was the life of all circles she entered, the Duchess of Gordon.' Both the Duchess and her daughters danced beautifully ; and Sir William Hamilton, describing a ball given by the Duchess in Paris, alludes to Lady Georgina Gordon dancing a gavotte and a minuet with Vestris. It is not therefore remarkable that the life and spirit of the London season were said never to commence till the Duchess of Gordon arrived in town. Once, when she remarked to Henry Erskine that she would not go to some races, as they would be dull, he replied in the following impromptu lines :

> ' Why, that is as if the sun should say
> A cold dark morning this, I will not rise to-day ! '

According to Beattie, the Duchess of Gordon was feelingly alive to every fine impulse, demonstrative herself, and hating coldness in others, the life of every party, the consoling friend of every scene of sorrow, a compound of sensibility and vivacity, of strength and softness ; ' but this was not the view of every one. She was sometimes accused of being unfeminine in her actions, coarse in her wit, and worldly in her ambition.　To the last two indictments we fear she certainly must plead guilty : that she was by no means scrupulous in her remarks cannot be denied, and it would be impossible to quote many of her *bons mots* ; but it must be remembered that the licence of speech, even amongst ladies, was very great in those days, and that Scotland, where she had been brought up, was far behindhand in refinement.[1]　Although many of her sayings are on record of which the keen wit is unquestionable, as also the indelicacy, the Duchess's morality was irreproachable, and there never was a breath raised against her fair name even by her detractors.　Worldly in her ambition she undoubtedly was, and kept the main chance always in view as regarded the aggrandisement of her family.　This may be seen in the matrimonial projects she evolved for her daughters, as

---

[1] Jane Maxwell had not many advantages of education and was married at seventeen, therefore it is not surprising to hear that, on her first arrival in London, she astonished the *beau monde* occasionally by her expressions.　When George the Third inquired how she liked London, the young Duchess answered, 'Not at all, your Majesty, for it is knock, knock, knock all day, and friz, friz, friz all night.' This story is told by Sir Walter Scott, who goes on to say : ' It would appear, however, that the Duchess subsequently grew very fond of London life, and once she said, "I surprised my bed last night before 12 o'clock, laughing at the unusual circumstance." '

JANE, DUCHESS OF GORDON.

well as by the marriages she ultimately arranged for them. The Duke was a man of calm inert nature, with no energy excepting for country pursuits, and he left the entire management of his family to his better half. For her eldest daughter, Lady Charlotte —whom even Cosway's art has succeeded in making only very pleasing-looking, but who had some of the wit of her mother— she fixed upon Pitt as an eligible husband ; and it is said that, difficult as he was to approach in that light, he nearly succumbed, and would have done so had it not been for Dundas, who, trembling for any interference with his influence, pretended that he himself was a suitor for the hand of Lady Charlotte, upon which Pitt instantly retired. Once when Pitt and some of his friends were spending the evening with the Duchess of Gordon and her daughters, and were amusing themselves with capping verses, Dundas remarked to him how fine a woman the Duchess of Richmond was, and what small feet she had for her size. At the time the Duchess did not seem to hear, but when she left to go home, she said ' Though you have not done your game, gentlemen, I must bid you good night, and the next time you are capping verses let me beg of you to take care that you don't put in more feet than belong to them ! ' Apropos of Pitt we are reminded of another well-known story of the Duchess of Gordon. Ferguson of Pitfour, long the Father of the House of Commons and a great friend of Pitt, was most eccentric, and had a servant, John, who was a well-known character. He used to talk a great deal about his master and Mr. Pitt, and Dean Ramsay says he always prefaced his conversation with something in the style of Cardinal Wolsey's ' Ego et rex meus ; ' it was always ' I and Pitt and Pitfour' went somewhere and did some-thing. The Duchess one day wrote to him as follows : ' John, put Pitfour into the carriage on Tuesday and bring him up to

Q

Gordon Castle to dinner.' John showed the letter to Pitfour, who said dryly, 'Well, John, I suppose we must go.' After this same dinner games were started in which every one had to propound a riddle. The Duchess's was as follows :

> My first is found upon the banks of Tyne,
> My second is scarce quite the half of nine,
> My whole a Laird of Aberdeenshire race,
> An honest fellow with an ugly face.

Answer : Pitfour.

The following story of the Duchess of Gordon is very characteristic. A marriage was on the *tapis* between her daughter Lady Louisa Gordon and Lord Brome, whose father, the celebrated Lord Cornwallis, objected on the grounds of madness in the Gordon family. No doubt—though sixteen years had passed since the Gordon Riots, and then, through the great ability and eloquence of the Hon. Thomas Erskine, Lord George Gordon had been acquitted—the horrors consequent on his conduct were still fresh in the public mind. He was generally admitted to be insane, and at this time he had embraced Judaism, wore a long beard almost reaching to the ground, and called himself Israel Abraham George Gordon ![1]

The Duchess, who was very anxious to bring about this marriage for her fourth daughter, who had not the good looks of her sisters, is asserted to have said to Lord Cornwallis, 'I give you my word, Louisa has not a drop of Gordon blood in her veins.' *Se non è vero è ben trovato.*[2] The marriage did take place, and Lady Louisa Gordon became eventually the Marchioness of Cornwallis. The Duchess succeeded in marrying three others of her daughters to dukes. The eldest, Lady Charlotte Gordon,

---

[1] In 1791 he was confined in Newgate for a libel on Queen Marie Antoinette, and died there, aged forty-one.

[2] The Duchess told this story herself to Lord Stowell.

GEORGIANA, DUCHESS OF BEDFORD.

From a Miniature by R. Cosway.

became fourth Duchess of Richmond;[1] Lady Susan married William, Duke of Manchester; and Lady Georgina became the wife of the sixth Duke of Bedford. Lady Georgina, who was very handsome, was engaged to Francis, fifth Duke of Bedford, a man conspicuous for his virtues and talents; but before they were married 'an over-exertion at tennis' caused his death at the age of thirty-one. The Duchess of Gordon was not going to let the Dukedom of Bedford escape her, and after Lady Georgina had left off her mourning for her betrothed, she became engaged to his brother and successor, John, sixth Duke of Bedford, to whom she was married a year later.[2] For her other daughter, Lady Madelina, who was not good-looking, but clever, the Duchess had to be content with a Scotch baronet, Sir Robert Sinclair. At his death, six years after, the Duchess tried to bring about a second marriage for this daughter with the Earl of Aberdeen, the Prime Minister, but the latter chose a wife for himself elsewhere, and three months later Lady Madelina married *en secondes noces* Charles Fysshe Palmer of Luckley Park, Berks.[3] She died in 1847 and is buried with her second husband at Finchampstead. In later years she became so peculiar as to leave no doubt that she at all events had plenty of Gordon blood in her veins!

[1] On the death of her brother, the fifth Duke of Gordon, without issue in 1836, the Gordon estates, by virtue of an entail, came to her son, the fifth Duke of Richmond.

[2] Georgina, Duchess of Bedford, had ten children, of whom two survive: General Lord Alexander Russell and Louisa, Dowager Duchess of Abercorn, now in the ninety-third year of her age and a perfect specimen of a *grande dame*. In July 1902 she had over 210 living descendants. See Addenda.

[3] He was a son of Henry Fish, of Ickwell, Bedfordshire, who assumed the name of Palmer on being left East Court, Finchampstead, by his kinsman, Charles Palmer. Sir John Gordon Sinclair succeeded to East Court at the death of his mother, Lady Madelina Fyshe-Palmer, but sold it shortly afterwards to Mr. John Walter of Bearwood, in whose family it now remains.

According to William Beckford,[1] the Duchess once thought of him as a possible son-in-law, and he gives a most whimsical account of her visit to Fonthill. ' I never,' says he, ' enjoyed a joke so much. At that time everybody talked of Mr. Beckford's enormous wealth—everything about me was exaggerated proportionately. I was in consequence a capital bait for the Duchess of Gordon—so she thought; I thought very differently. She had been told that even a dog-kennel at Fonthill was a palace—my house a Potosi. What more on earth could be desired by a managing mother for a daughter ? I got a hint from town of her intention to surprise me at Fonthill. . . . I resolved to give her a useful lesson. Fonthill was put in order for her reception, with everything I could devise to receive her magnificently—not only to receive her, but to turn the tables upon her for the presumption she had that I was to become the plaything of her purposes. The splendour of her reception must have stimulated her in her object. I designed it should operate in that manner. I knew her aim—she little thought so. My arrangements being made, I ordered my major-domo to say, on the Duchess's arrival, that it was unfortunate Mr. Beckford had shut himself up on a sudden— a way he had at times—and that it was more than his place was worth to disturb him, as his master only appeared when he pleased, forbidding interruption, even if the King came to Fonthill. I had just received a large lot of books ; nothing could be more opportune. I had them removed to the rooms of which I had taken possession. The Duchess conducted herself with wonderful equanimity, and seemed much surprised

---

[1] The celebrated author of *Vathek*, written when he was twenty-one, was a son of William Beckford of Fonthill Abbey. He married in 1783 Lady Margaret Gordon, who died three years after.

IN LANDSEER, pinx

LADY LOUISA RUSSELL, DUCHESS OF ABERCORN.

and gratified at what she saw, and the mode of her reception—just as I desired she should be, quite on tip-toe to have me for a son-in-law. When she got up in the morning, her first question was, "Do you think Mr. Beckford will be visible to-day?" "I cannot inform your Grace—Mr. Beckford's movements are so very uncertain. Would your Grace take an airing in the Park—a walk in the gardens?" Everything which Fonthill could supply was made the most of, whetting her appetite to her purpose still more. "Perhaps Mr. Beckford will be visible to-morrow?" was the Duchess's daily consolation. To-morrow, and to-morrow, and to-morrow came and went—no Mr. Beckford. She remained seven or eight days, magnificently entertained, and then went away, very angry, without seeing him!'

The Duchess of Gordon mixed much in French society and was very fond of going to Paris. When she was there in 1802 with her daughter, Lady Georgina Gordon, she received flattering marks of attention from Napoleon, of whom she was a great admirer. Lady Malmesbury writes to Hookham Frere in 1803 : 'The Duchess of Gordon is returned from Paris raving about Bonaparte and talked such real treason that if it would not give her too much consequence, she ought to be sent to the Tower.' It was said that the Duchess wished for Eugène Beauharnais as a husband for Lady Georgina. She had not much knowledge of the French language, and Madame Le Brun in her 'Souvenirs' says : 'Je me souviens qu'un jour que j'allai dîner chez la Duchesse de Gordon, elle me montra le portrait de Bonaparte en me disant : "Voilà mon Zéro." Comme elle parlait fort mal le français, je compris ce qu'elle voulait dire, et nous rîmes beaucoup toutes deux quand je lui expliquai ce que c'était qu'un zéro !' Sir Walter Scott, alluding to another of the Duchess of Gordon's visits to Paris—in 1815—writes that it was reported that she said to the box-keeper at the theatre : 'Ne laissez pas entrer aucun Anglais dans ma boîte.'

Although the Duchess was so much taken up with the world, and was such a lover of society, she was by no means frivolous. We hear of her, both in Edinburgh and at Gordon Castle, occupying herself with elevating pursuits, reading much and bestowing great pains on the education of her daughters. In Edinburgh, where the Duchess and her family were wont to take up their residence in the winter and spring, she was the leader of society. She tried to get all the literary and other men of note to her parties there ;[1] and when Burns first went to the Athens of the North in 1787, at which time he was little known, she invited him to her house and did all she could to help him. 'There is a great rumour here,' wrote one of his friends in Ayrshire, 'concerning your intimacy with the Duchess of Gordon. I am told that "Cards to invite fly by thousands each night."' Later on the Duchess asked Addington, the Prime Minister, to meet Burns at Gordon Castle, and it was on leaving after this visit that the poet wrote the song of 'Bonnie Castle Gordon.'[2] Beattie, with whom she became very intimate, shows by his letters, in spite of their rather exaggerated adulation, that he respected the understanding of the woman to whom he wrote. His happiest hours were passed at Gordon Castle, and

[1] The *European Magazine*, in noticing the Duchess of Gordon's death, said of her : 'She aimed to gain the esteem and render herself worthy of all the most eminent *literati* of her country. She was the correspondent of Lord Kames, of Dr. Beattie, of Dr. Robertson, of Mr. Hume, and other eminent writers of that day, and in her extensive correspondence she displayed a depth of reading, a solidity of judgment, and a taste in composition, which, if her letters should ever reach the public, would place her high in the estimation of the literary world.'

[2] The Duchess of Gordon occupies a prominent place in the picture which Mr. C. Hardie, A.R.S.A., painted to commemorate the centenary of Burns's introduction to Edinburgh society.

he was with the Duchess when he wrote the following 'Lines to a Pen :'

> Go and be guided by the brightest eyes,
>   And to the softest hand thine aid impart
> To trace the fair ideas as they arise,
>   Warm from the purest, gentlest, noblest heart.

Sir William Forbes in his Life of Beattie says : ' So tenderly solicitous was she (the Duchess) at all times to soothe his sorrows and dissipate those gloomy ideas that preyed upon his mind, that he found consolation and relief in the free interchange of thoughts with which her good nature delighted to indulge him ; and he was never more happy than in the society he found in Gordon Castle. . . . He was charmed by her beauty, the brilliancy of her wits and her cultivated understanding.' ' This culture, or the increase of it,' Miss Margaret Forbes tells us in her recent Life of the poet, ' the Duchess partly owed to her intercourse with Beattie. He took much pleasure in directing her reading, and was often astonished at the rapidity with which she grasped the salient points of a book. He used to say he frequently gave her a book one day and was astonished to hear her discussing it the next at table with her guests, when he knew she had been so occupied as not possibly to have had time to read it except overnights.'

She was a keen politician of High Tory principles, and was most energetic as a Government Whip, particularly at the celebrated election for Westminster in 1784, when Sir Charles Wray was opposed to Charles James Fox, who had for his female champion the celebrated Georgiana, Duchess of Devonshire. The poll continued open for forty days, and every nerve was strained on either side. At this time the Duchess of Gordon lived in Buckingham House, Pall Mall (now the War

Office), the splendid house of the then Marquis of Buckingham,[1] and every evening numerous persons attached to the Administration gathered in her saloon, as well as many doubtful members, with whom she used all her art to confirm their allegiance to Pitt.[2]   The Prince of Wales spent a part of almost every evening in her society, and when it was determined by his friends to appeal to the House of Commons concerning his debts, she acted as mediator between him and Fox, Sheridan, Lord Loughborough, and Pitt alternately, it is said, advising, consoling, and reproving the Prince.   At the time of the King's illness, approving of Pitt's plan, the Duchess, we are told, reprobated with much indignation those who, having professed themselves the King's friends, joined the opposite party when they knew it was likely to be in the ascendant ; and she was not sparing in her animadversions on their fickleness.   She accosted with very great and just severity a well-known peripatetic, and exposed his conduct in a strong and humorous satire.

In one of the Duchess's letters to Beattie quoted by Miss Forbes in her book ' Beattie to his Friends,' her Grace says : ' I have been constantly going for days into the country, and Mr. Pitt has been mostly of our society—never was so merry and pleasing a companion.   In one of our evening conversations poetry was the subject ; my favourite " Minstrel " I talked of as I felt, and was delighted to find a certain Beattie and Milton being his first favourites.   During the course of the evening he repeated the most of it.   When we meet I will show

---

[1] She also, at a later period, gave political parties at No. 6 St. James's Square and at No. 15.

[2] There was no limit to her efforts in this respect.   Major P. L. Gordon, in writing about Sir James Mackintosh, says : ' The Duchess of Gordon told me that she had in vain tried all her persuasive powers, and they were not small, to detach Sir James from his party.   I took the liberty to observe to her Grace that I was well acquainted with him, and knew that his politics are his principles.'

you his favourite lines. There is an elegance in his taste, and a wise kind of folly in his social hours of conversation, that raises him more in my estimation than even his political talent. But come and be convinced, you would be delighted with him ; there is a rectitude of mind, and steady firm principle of honour, in every word. Do come soon.'

The Duchess's energy was almost unparalleled ; we have seen one example of it, here is another. In 1794, when there was a scare of a French invasion, her son, the young Marquis of Huntly, offered to raise a regiment from the Gordon tenantry, and letters of service were granted him for this purpose. Upon hearing that at first the recruits were coming up but slowly, the Duchess set off from London, in the midst of winter, for the Highlands (no small feat in those days), and, chiefly owing to her personal exertions, within four months a corps of volunteers a thousand strong was raised, which developed into the regiment known as the Gordon Highlanders. Her *modus operandi* was as follows. She attired herself in a regimental jacket with a plaid of the Gordon tartan—

> ' O' a' the tartans east or west,
> I like the Gordon tartan best '—

and putting a cockade and a diced border on her Glengarry, she then mounted her palfrey and went the round of the country, especially frequenting the fairs where the rustic youths most congregated, and offered a kiss to every one who would take the King's shilling ! Afterwards, when the Duchess was relating this feat in the salon of a Whig magnate, a young man of high degree said to her, ' I wish I had been present, I would have taken the kiss and the shilling myself.' ' But,' said she, ' you would not have understood what I said in broad Scotch.' ' Oh,

yes, I would ; I understand Scotch, however broad.' 'Well,
I will try you,' said the Duchess, 'and if you tell me what I
mean I'll give you a kiss.' 'My canty carle, come pree mi mou.'
This her Grace said with great rapidity, and the Englishman
exclaimed, 'Oh ! that's French, not Scotch !' 'You have lost
your kiss, my Lord,' replied the Duchess ; 'what I said was Scotch,
and means " My handsome fellow, come taste my mouth." '[1]
The regiment of the Gordon Highlanders was gazetted as the
100th, but afterwards as the 92nd. It was embodied at Aberdeen
on June 24, and the Duchess's young son, the Marquis of
Huntly, was appointed lieutenant-colonel commandant. Though
only twenty-four years of age, he had already seen a good deal
of service, and was captain in the 3rd regiment of Foot Guards
when he was twenty-two. The first move of the Gordon
Highlanders was to the camp at Netley Common, and soon
after they were sent to the Mediterranean, where they remained
for several years. On Lord Huntly's passage home the vessel
he was in was taken by a French privateer ; he himself was
plundered of everything and put on board a Swedish ship, in
which he arrived at Falmouth in September 1796, greatly to
the relief of the Duchess, who had not seen him for so long.

> Cock o' the North, my Huntly bra',
> Where are you with my Forty-twa ?
> Oh ! wae's my heart that ye're awa'.
> *Carle now the King's come*—SIR WALTER SCOTT.

The Duchess's untiring energy was not confined to politics
and pleasure. She exerted herself much on behalf of the poor

---

[1] The Duchess at all times spoke with a Scotch accent. Mrs. Delany writes :
'Lady Bute brought the Duchess of Gordon here on pretence of showing me my
herbal—really to show me her beauty ! I fancy I got the better bargain for she is
beautiful indeed. She is very natural and good-humoured, but her Scotch accent
does not seem to belong to the very great delicacy of her appearance.

on her husband's estates. At the time of her marriage Lord Kames addressed a letter to her impressing upon her the great responsibility of her position, and he lived to see the day when he could 'thank God that his best hopes had been realised' in regard to the manner in which 'his dear pupil' had given effect to his views. In a letter which she wrote at a later period to her devoted and attached friend, Henry Erskine, the Duchess says : 'For years I have given premiums for all kinds of domestic industry—spinning, dyeing, &c.—and most years had some hundreds of specimens of beautiful colours from herbs of the field.[1] But there is an evil I cannot remedy without a large sum of money. The children are neglected in mind and body—cold, hunger, and dirt carries off hundreds. The cow-pox would save many ; no doctors for thirty miles makes many orphan families. . . . I wish to add to the comforts of the aged and take the children, teach them to think right, raise food for themselves, and prepare them to succeed to their fathers' farms, with knowledge of all the branches of farming, &c.'

Mrs. Grant of Laggan, writing in 1802, says : 'The Duchess had a seat at Kinrara, near Laggan, where she spent the summer months. Unlike most people of the world, she presented her least favourable phases to the public ; but in this her Highland home all her best qualities were in action, there it was that her warm benevolence and steady friendship were known and felt.' Again, in 1809, she says : 'I called on the Duchess yesterday, she and I having a joint interest in an orphan family in the Highlands which created a kind of business between us. She

---

[1] George Gordon, of Fodderletter in Strathaven, who was both a chemist and a botanist, discovered that by a simple preparation of a species of lichen found among the rocks of the Grampian Hills a purple dye could be procured. This dye, which was called 'Cudbear,' was largely used in the Highlands for dyeing the home-made cloth.

had a prodigious levee, and insisted on my sitting to see them out, that we might afterwards have our private discussion. I saw Lord Lauderdale, who made me start to see him almost a "lean and slippered pantaloon," who, the last time I saw him, was a fair-haired youth at Glasgow College . . . more gratified was I to see Sir Brooke Boothby, though he too looked so feeble and so dismal. Being engaged to dinner, I could stay no longer. The Duchess said that on Sunday she never saw company, nor played cards, nor went out. In England, indeed, she did so because every one else did the same, but she would not introduce those manners into this country. I stared at these gradations of piety growing warmer as it came northward, but was wise enough to stare silently. She said she had a great many things to tell me and I must come that evening, when she would be alone. At nine I went and found Walter Scott, Lady Keith (Dr. Johnson's 'Queenie'), and an English lady, witty and fashionable-looking, who came and went with Mr. Scott. No people could be more easy and pleasant. . . . I think Mr. Scott's appearance very unpromising and commonplace indeed ; yet tho' no gleam of genius animates his countenance, much of it appears in his conversation, which is rich, various, easy, and animated.' This same lady writes from Stirling to another correspondent (John Hatsell) in 1808 : 'I was sitting quietly at the fireside one night lately, when I was summoned with my eldest daughter to attend the Duchess of Gordon. We spent the evening with her at the inn, and very amusing and original she certainly is. Extraordinary she is determined to be wherever she is and whatever she does. She speaks of you in very high terms, which, you know, always happens in the case of those whom the Duchess " delighteth to honour." As the highest testimonial of your merit that she can give, she says you were one of the great favourites of Mr. Pitt, and then she pronounced an eloquent eulogium on that truly great man. Her Grace's present ruling passion is literature— to be the arbitress of literary taste and the patroness of genius— a distinction for which her want of early culture and the flutter of a life devoted to very different pursuits, has rather disqualified her. Yet she has strong flashes of intellect, immediately lost in the formless confusion of a mind ever hurried on by contending passions and contradictory objects, of which one can never be obtained without the relinquishment of others. Having said all this it is but fair to add that in one point she never varies, which is active—nay, most industrious benevolence. Silver and gold she has not, but what she has—her interests, her trouble, her exertion—she gives with unequalled perseverance.'

In one of the Duchess's letters to Beattie she says : ' Have you no commands for me ? My amusement is to get commissions and places for unprovided countrymen.' And we find her accordingly getting an appointment for Beattie's son through Dundas and for his nephew through Lord Chatham.

During the last few years of her life the Duchess had many domestic sorrows, of which perhaps the keenest was the loss of her dearly loved youngest son, Lord Alexander Gordon, who died at Edinburgh in 1808, after a severe illness, in the twenty-third year of his age. His death had a great effect upon her, and she became a changed woman, fully realising the hollowness and vanity of the world, and bitterly and genuinely regretting the worldliness of her past life. She survived her son four years, and died in London on April 11, 1812, aged sixty-two, in great composure and peace, having spent her last weeks in prayer.

A DUKE 'BORN IN A BARN, AND DIED IN A BARN'

CROKER, writing to his wife in 1819, says that the fourth Duke of Richmond, who died in a barn, was also born in a barn. His mother, Lady Louisa Lennox (a daughter of Lord Lothian, and wife of Lord George Lennox) was taken ill when on a fishing party, and there was only time to carry her to a neighbouring farmyard, where the future Duke was born in 1764.

He became a gallant soldier and one of the most fearless of men, but is chiefly celebrated for his duel with the Duke of York, for the memorable ball which he and his wife gave at Brussels in 1815, and for his tragic death in 1819.

The history of the duel is as follows : In May 1789, at a masquerade given by the Duchess of Ancaster, the Duke of York joined Lord Paget, who was walking with the Duchess of Gordon, and in the course of conversation H.R.H. said that Colonel Lennox had heard words spoken to him at d'Aubigny's Club to which no gentleman ought to have submitted, and added, 'The Lennoxes don't fight.' This observation being repeated to the young soldier, who, though barely twenty-five years of age, was a colonel in the Coldstream Guards, he shortly after took the irregular mode of publicly asking the Duke (who was his commander-in-chief), at a field day, what were the words he had alluded to and by whom they were spoken. To this the Duke gave no answer and ordered him to his post. After the parade

JOHN HOPPNER R A *pinx*

CHARLES, 4TH DUKE OF RICHMOND.

was over he sent for Colonel Lennox, declined to give his authority, but said before his officers that 'he desired to derive no protection from his rank as a Prince and his station as commanding officer, and that, when not on duty, he wore a brown coat and was ready as a private gentleman to give the Colonel satisfaction.' Colonel Lennox then wrote a circular letter to every member of d'Aubigny's Club requesting to know whether such words had been used to him, begging for an answer within seven days, and adding that no answer would be considered equivalent to a declaration that no such words could be recollected. The seven days having expired and no member answering, Colonel Lennox sent a written message through Lord Winchilsea to the Duke of York, calling upon him to give him the usual satisfaction. This was acceded to ; and accordingly the Duke attended by Lord Rawdon, and Colonel Lennox by Lord Winchilsea, met on Wimbledon Common on August 26. The ground was measured at twelve paces ; the signal given. Colonel Lennox fired, and the ball grazed His Royal Highness's side curl, but the Duke did not fire himself. Lord Rawdon then said he thought enough had been done. Colonel Lennox pressed that the Duke should fire, but he positively declined, and so this duel terminated.[1] Some time after a person named Theophilus Swift wrote a pamphlet on the subject, taking the Duke of York's side, whereupon Colonel Lennox called on Mr. Swift and demanded satisfaction, and another duel took place in a field near the Uxbridge Road. Colonel Lennox was attended by Sir W. A. Browne, and Mr. Swift by Colonel Phipps. Ten paces were measured by the seconds, and it was settled that Colonel Lennox should fire first, the result being that he shot

---

[1] Lord Rawdon always said that by delaying the signal for firing, and thus rendering Colonel Lennox's aim unsteady, he had saved the life of the Duke (*Cornwallis Memoirs*).

Mr. Swift through the body ; but the latter ultimately recovered from his wound. Colonel Lennox soon after exchanged from the Duke of York's Regiment into the 35th Regiment of Foot [1] quartered at Edinburgh. On joining, the officers gave him a grand entertainment, and Edinburgh Castle was illuminated to mark their sympathy and approval of his conduct. He was greeted in the streets with clapping of hands and other demonstrations of applause, and was certainly the most popular man in Edinburgh at the time. He had the freedom of the city conferred upon him by the magistrates, and the corporation of Goldsmiths made him an honorary member of their body and presented him with a beautiful snuffbox. The same year he married Lady Charlotte Gordon, eldest daughter of the fourth and sister of the last Duke of Gordon. After this he served in the Leeward Islands, and arrived in St. Domingo in 1794 at the time of the breaking out of the yellow fever, to which forty officers and six hundred rank and file fell victims in two months.

In 1806 he succeeded his uncle as fourth Duke of Richmond, and in 1807, when the Portland Administration came into power, he was appointed Viceroy of Ireland, where he remained for six years and won all hearts by his genial manners.[2] Sir Arthur Wellesley was appointed Chief Secretary,[3] and the great intimacy

[1] He exchanged with Lord Strathavon.

[2] The Hon. Mrs. Swinton, in her *Reminiscences of Lady de Ros*, quotes a letter of Mr. Ogilvie to his wife, the Duchess of Leinster, written in 1809, in which he says: 'No Lord-Lieutenant ever reigned so much in the hearts of the people of every rank and religion, and no man ever was more respected at the same time. He understands them and manages them beyond anybody I ever saw, and the Duchess is also a very great favourite.'

[3] Sir Arthur only accepted this post conditionally, 'that it should not impede nor interfere with his military promotion or pursuits.' Accordingly, that same year he went in Lord Cathcart's expedition against Denmark and successfully bombarded Copenhagen. During these operations Lord Rosslyn rode occasionally a favourite mare which, soon after the return home, produced a colt, which in consequence was called 'Copenhagen' and eventually carried the Duke of

CHARLOTTE, DUCHESS OF RICHMOND.

From a Miniature by R Cosway

between the Iron Duke and the Lennox family[1] dates from this time.

The following, written by Lady Sarah Napier to Lady Susan O'Brien when staying with the Duke and Duchess of Richmond at the Viceregal Lodge in 1811, describes the family party in pleasing colours : 'We are ourselves now in the very great world, for we are a week with the Richmonds, where, in spite of the just attention they pay to being retired during the poor King's illness, still a Lord and Lady Lieutenant's house must be publick. At least, comparatively so to me, but as I am permitted to be a privileged person and wear the individual cap and gown I do at Castletown, I feel no inconvenience for coming here, for I do not care if strangers say, " How can the Duke have that queer old blind woman in the corner ? " and I do care very much that the affection of my dear nephew should induce him to have me here, surrounded by his delightful girls, who absolutely vie with each other who shall attend most to me, and the Duchess is kindness personified to me on all occasions. There are seven girls in this house, and I rejoice to hear from all quarters that those who are known meet with universal approbation from true judges ; . . . their minds are as well regulated as their manners, and their adoration of their father is the most delightful thing, for it produces a reciprocal good, as he enjoys their society and

Wellington throughout Waterloo. Copenhagen died in 1835 at Strathfieldsaye, where his grave is much visited.

[1] The Iron Duke stood sponsor to the Duke of Richmond's youngest son, Lord Arthur Lennox, and he was also his guardian. The writer has a letter of his, giving him good advice on his entering the Army ; in it the Duke says : 'The only chance that you have of being either respectable or comfortable in life is to be economical, not to waste your money, and above all not to run into debt. You will have to submit to many privations, and it is best that you should accustom yourself to them at an early period, as you may rely upon it that neither your brother nor I can or will defray any extravagant expense incurred by you. I think it best to say this to you thus early. . . .'

seems to depend on it for the comfort of relaxation at his leisure moments. . . . It is impossible not to dread the Duke's removal from a country which he is absolutely formed to govern with the even hand of perfect justice tempered by humanity.'

Soon after his return from Ireland the Duke of Richmond, having six sons and seven daughters, settled in Brussels for purposes of economy in 1813. He rented a house in the Rue de la Blanchisserie [1] from Simon, the celebrated coach-builder, who built the six gala coaches used by Napoleon at his coronation.[2] There, on the night of June 15, 1815, the eve of Quatre-Bras (not on the 17th, as is so often erroneously stated), the Duke and Duchess of Richmond gave their memorable ball, immortalised by Byron in the beautiful stanzas in ' Childe Harold.' The Duke of Wellington had received news of Napoleon's movements, and at first it was decided that the ball should be put off; but on second thoughts he not only desired it should take place, but issued orders that the general officers should attend, thinking it highly important that the people at Brussels should be kept in ignorance of the real state of affairs as long as possible. The officers were told to leave the ball quietly at ten o'clock to join their divisions *en route.* We cannot do better than here quote the words of the late Lady de Ros,[3] the Duke of Richmond's daughter, and are induced to do so the more in consequence of the late Sir William Fraser [4] having given to the world sundry assertions anent the

[1] Hence always called by the Duke of Wellington ' the Washhouse.'

[2] Simon himself being a tenant of a M. Van Asch. Jacques Vanginderachter, also a coachbuilder, purchased the house in 1807 from Van Asch, and his son turned it into a *brasserie,* which it has continued to be till quite lately, when I believe it has been demolished.

[3] Taken from the Hon. Mrs. Swinton's deeply interesting *Life and Remini-scences of Georgiana, Lady de Ros,* published by John Murray in 1893.

[4] Sir William Fraser, Bart., of Leadclune, and not Sir William Fraser, Kt., the well-known biographer of Scotch families.

ball which are totally opposed to the vivid recollections of both
Lady de Ros and her younger sister, Lady Louisa Tighe. The
constantly repeated asseverations of Lady de Ros, who was one
of the most clear-headed and accurate of persons, and who was
present at the ball, should surely prevail against the theories of
Sir William Fraser, who merely visited the scene fifty years after.
Sir William Fraser's contention was that the ball did not take
place in the room on the ground floor of the Duke's house,
but on the first floor of the coachmaker's depôt at the rear of
the house, used, when he visited it in 1888, as the brewer's
granary.[1] In corroboration of this he quoted a letter of Lady
de Ros's in which she said that 'the house had belonged to a
coachmaker, and the warehouse in which he kept his carriages
was converted into a long narrow room in which the ball took
place.' The conversion to which Lady de Ros here alluded was
not a conversion at the time and for the purpose of the ball,
but a conversion made before the Duke of Richmond took
possession of the house ; and Lady de Ros and her sister were
positive that the ball took place in the house in which they lived,
and on the ground floor. Lady de Ros says : ' My mother's
now famous ball took place in a large room on the ground floor
on the left of the entrance, connected with the rest of the house
by an ante-room.[2] It had been used by the coachbuilder, from

---

[1] This granary, which is approached by fifteen steps, is only ten feet high, the
floor is painfully uneven, and it is supported by six strong square posts which have
never been painted and which run down the centre of the granary. Scarcely a
place which would have been chosen for a ball !

[2] This statement is borne out by the accompanying plan of the ground floor of
the Duke's house, which plan was drawn during his tenancy ; and a professional
civil engineer, who compared it with the premises in 1889, wrote to us as follows :
' The declaration of Sir William Fraser is not accurate. . . . I have compared the
plan in *Murray's Magazine* with the present house. The ball-room, the front hall,
and the billiard-room can easily be recognised, as you will see from the following
plan. All that is erased exists no more. Lady de Ros visited the spot and could

whom the house was hired, to put carriages in, but it was papered before we came there, and I recollect the paper—a trellis pattern with roses. My sisters used the room as a schoolroom, and we used to play battledore and shuttlecock there on a wet day.[1] The accompanying plan of the ground floor of our house was given me by my brother William and corresponds exactly with my recollections and those of my sister, Lady Louisa Tighe. When the Duke arrived rather late at the ball I was dancing, but at once went up to him to ask about the rumours. He said very gravely, " Yes, they are true ; we are off to-morrow." This terrible news was circulated directly, and while some of the officers hurried away,[2] others remained at the ball and actually had not time to change their clothes, but fought in evening costume.[3] I went with my eldest brother (A.D.C. to the Prince

see nothing of the house, and being told that it had ceased to exist, accepted the statement ; but this can be explained by the fact that houses were built between the wall of the ball-room and the present *alignement* of the Rue de la Blanchisserie.'

[1] This room was also used by the Duke of Richmond's family for theatricals. Lord William, who got up these entertainments in 1817, writes : 'The scene of our histrionic efforts was the room immortalised by Byron . . . it was a long gallery, with an alcove at the end admirably suited for a temporary stage. . . .'

[2] Captain Bowles (Coldstream Guards), afterwards General Sir George Bowles, wrote : 'After the Prince of Orange, who had whispered to the Duke of Wellington a few minutes, had left the supper table, the latter remained about twenty minutes, and then rose to go, and asked the Duke of Richmond if he had a good map. The Duke of Richmond said he had, and took him into his dressing-room. The Duke of Wellington shut the door, and said, " Napoleon has humbugged me, he has gained twenty-four hours' march on me." The Duke of Richmond said, "What do you intend doing ?" He answered, " I have ordered the army to concentrate at Quatre-Bras, but we shall not stop him there, and if so, I must fight him here " (at the same time passing his thumb-nail over the position of Waterloo). The Duke of Richmond was to have had the command of Reserve if it had been formed.' The late Lady Louisa Tighe told the writer that she remembered that the Duke of Wellington, finding that there was no table large enough in her father's room for him to see the map comfortably, moved into the Duchess's bedroom and spread the map on the bed.

[3] Major Henry Percy, A.D.C. to the Duke, who took home the despatch

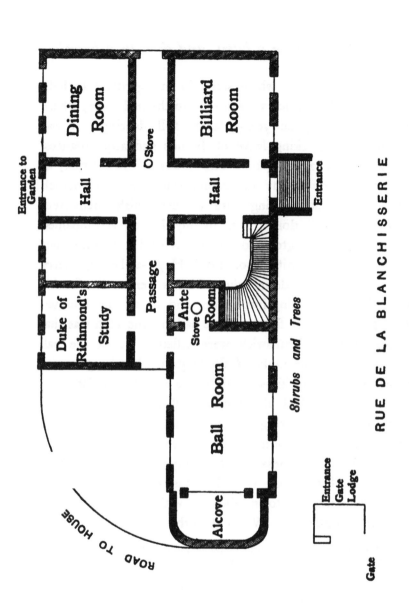

RUE DE LA BLANCHISSERIE

Plan of the ground floor of the Duke of Richmond's house at Brussels, showing the room in which the Waterloo Ball took place.

of Orange) to his house, which stood in our garden,[1] to help
him to pack up, after which we returned to the ball-room, where
we found some energetic young ladies still dancing. It was
a dreadful evening, taking leave of friends and acquaintances,
many never to be seen again. The Duke of Brunswick, as
he took leave of me in the ante-room, made me a civil speech
as to the Brunswickers being sure to distinguish themselves
after "the honour" done them by my having accompanied
the Duke of Wellington to their review! I remember
being quite provoked with poor Lord Hay—a dashing merry
youth, full of military ardour, whom I knew very well—for his
delight at the idea of going into action, and of all the honours
he was to gain ; and the first news we had on the 16th was that
he and the Duke of Brunswick were killed. . . . At the ball
supper I sat next to the Duke of Wellington, when he gave me
an original miniature of himself painted by a Belgian artist. . . .
On the 18th we walked about nearly all the morning, being
unable to sit quiet, hearing the firing and not knowing what
was happening. The wounded officers who were brought into
Brussels kindly sent us messages about my brothers being safe.
The first sight of the poor wounded was sickening, and each
litter, as it came into the town, filled us with intense anxiety to
know whom it contained. We went to the Marquise d'Asche's[2]

announcing the victory, actually arrived in London in the same clothes in which
he had danced at the ball and fought at Waterloo.

[1] This was a little *pavillon* which was in the garden, half hidden by the
chestnut trees, and according to Mr. Vanginderachter, the late proprietor (a
brewer), was pulled down to construct the small 'Hôpital privé des Sœurs Hospi-
talières' which now stands in the Rue des Cendres (No. 7), *the said street having
only been in existence since* 1835.

[2] At Queen Victoria's Jubilee, the King of the Belgians, having heard of Lady
de Ros's wonderful memories of 1815, begged to be allowed to call upon her, and
was deeply interested in her reminiscences of Brussels. In reading the list of the
guests at the famous ball, the King remarked upon the names appearing of four of

house (at the corner of the Parc and the Rue de la Pépinière), from whence we saw Lord Uxbridge and Lord Fitzroy Somerset, the Prince of Orange, and others brought in. . . . My father, with my brother William, who had been prevented from taking part in the action by an accident, rode to the army,[1] but the Duke of Wellington would not let them remain.[2] In the evening of the 18th the brilliant victory was known in Brussels, and most thankful we were that our immediate belongings had been mercifully protected,[3] and that war was at an end, although the losses were fearfully great. The next morning we heard that the Duke had arrived in Brussels, so I walked with my father at about 10 A.M. up to the Parc, his house being in the Rue de la Montagne du Parc, and my father went into the house to inquire for the Duke, who sent word he would join us, which he accordingly did, and took a turn with us. He looked very sad, and when we shook hands and congratulated him, he said, " It is a dearly bought victory. We have lost so many fine

his attendants, one of whom, Count d'Asche, was the grandson of this lady. The family of the Marquis d'Asche is a very ancient one. In their arms appears the famous *écaille*, which means that they trace back to the time of the Crusades, and some of them went to Palestine under Godefroi de Bouillon.

[1] It is recorded that, as the Enniskillings were on the point of advancing across the Wavre road to charge, an individual in plain clothes on their left called out, ' Now's your time ! ' This was the Duke of Richmond, who even rode into the squares of infantry while under the fire of the enemy.

[2] Lord Stanhope, in his *Notes of Conversation with the Duke of Wellington*, quotes that when Lord Fitzroy Somerset said to the Duke, ' You always were very particular in sending away from dangerous positions men who had no duty to perform there,' the Duke mentioned having done so, the morning of Waterloo, to the Duke of Richmond, and having said to him, ' You are the father of ten children ; you have no right to be here ; you should go—and you may go now—but a quarter of an hour or twenty minutes hence you could not go—it would no longer be right.' '.Had the firing not then begun ?' ' It was only just beginning, but it was already quite clear we should have a terrible day. It did not do him much good, poor fellow !—he died by a more distressing death, but, however, he lived a few years longer.'

[3] Lord March and Lord George Lennox were in the battle.

fellows." My father asked him to dinner, but he refused. The reason of his coming early[1] into Brussels was that he had given up his bed at Waterloo to poor Sir Alexander Gordon, who was dying of his wounds. The Duke tried to sleep on the floor, but after being called up to speak to Sir Alexander he could not go to bed again, and began to write his despatch ; however, Sir Alexander's groans were so distressing that he could not get on with it, and so he rode into Brussels, where he was busy with despatches all day long, and left on the 20th.'

The winter of 1815 was spent by the Duke of Richmond and his family in Paris, and in 1816 and 1817 they were at Cambrai during the occupation of the British army, when they often stayed with the Great Duke at Abbaye, Mont St. Martin.

In March 1818 the Duke of Richmond was appointed Governor-General of Canada and assumed his duties there in June.[2] In 'Old Quebec' by Gilbert Parker and Claude Bryan, the authors say : 'The Duke of Richmond, a chivalrous but uncompromising advocate of the extreme views of his party in England, almost atoned for the political narrowness of his administration by the stimulus he brought to the social life of the capital and the sincerity of his belief that by personal influence he could harmonise contending factions. Under his magnificent patronage, Château St. Louis became once more the scene of lavish hospitality. Dinners, dances, and theatricals

---

[1] Lord Stanhope in his *Reminiscences* writes that the Duke told him he 'rode off there at four in the morning.' On Lord Stanhope saying ' Was your Grace up at four the day after the battle ? ' he replied ' Yes, and even earlier. Between three and four they came to tell me that poor Gordon was dying, and I went immediately to see him, but he was already dead.' Lord Stanhope then added, ' At what o'clock did you dismount on the evening of the battle ? ' ' About eleven, I think.'

[2] The Duke was accompanied by two of his sons, William and Frederick, and by four of his daughters, Ladies Mary, Charlotte, Louisa, and Sophia.

were the order of the day—with pomp and circumstance the Duke made progress through his dominions everywhere, speaking, entertaining, endeavouring to conciliate.'

The following year he commenced a tour of inspection of the outposts under his command, and left Quebec in a Government ship. The first station he visited was Mount Henry (now Sorel), on the south bank of the St. Lawrence, about 120 miles from Quebec, and it was there, between June 23 and 28, that the lamentable accident took place which caused his tragic death. The Duke had with him his favourite dog Blucher, and a fight took place between this animal and a pet fox belonging to a private. The Duke in separating them was bitten by the fox in his hand, but the wound was but a slight one and he paid no attention to it. So little was then thought of the affair that there is no mention of it in the Journal of his daughter, Lady Louisa Lennox, who was at Mount Henry at the time ; but Lady Louisa told the writer that she perfectly remembered her father ' coming into the sitting-room at Mount Henry with a silk handkerchief over his hand, and that he said the fox in the yard had bitten him.'[1] We read in Lady Louisa Lennox's Journal, in the entry for June 28, as follows : ' This morning we left Mount Henry, where we had spent four very pleasant days. Went in the " Malsham " to Montreal. We got out at the foot of a rapid below Montreal and walked about a mile to the hotel. The Mansion House is really very comfortable.'

From Montreal the Duke went up the country, accompanied

[1] Mrs. Richard Trench writes in her journal in October 1819, *à propos* of this tragic affair : ' One circumstance only it may not be wholly unprofitable to keep in mind. The bite was inflicted by an irritated animal—a fox, which had been confined, escaped to the woods, was retaken, and became enraged at being again subject to confinement.

only by Colonel Cockburn, D.Q.M.G., and Major Bowles, Military Secretary. By the time he reached Kingston the wound had completely healed, and when his two sons, Lord William and Frederick, joined him at Niagara, the circumstance had almost been forgotten. After a visit to Drummond's Island, the Duke returned to Kingston, where he remained for a week, during which time he was in the highest spirits, playing racquets and cricket with the officers of the garrison. The Duke was said to be the finest formed man in England, and his playing at cricket was praised as an exquisite display of grace, strength, and skill.

And now we come to the last week of the Duke's life. Wishing to inaugurate a new township to be called in his name, Richmondville, he left Kingston on August 20, accompanied by Colonel Cockburn and Major Bowles, and it is from the Diary of the latter that we have the following particulars : 'The Duke,' writes Major Bowles, 'travelled sometimes on horseback and sometimes on foot, and on the 21st we reached Perth. The next morning (the 22nd) he walked for three hours round the Settlement. On returning, a violent shower of rain wetted most of the party through, but his Grace refused an umbrella and rather enjoyed the circumstance. He changed his clothes the instant he returned to the Inn, appeared in perfect health, and we dined a large party. The following day (the 23rd), it being determined to remain at Perth, we again walked for two or three hours to look at the Settlement, and the Duke went to bed apparently perfectly well, having arranged to proceed early the following morning towards Richmond. On being called, he complained to his servant that he felt unwell and had not slept in consequence of a pain in his right shoulder and throat, and we observed that he did not make his usual breakfast. I recommended him to rub his shoulder with spirit of turpentine, which he agreed to do. We proposed remaining on another day at Perth, but this he declined, and we accordingly set out for Beckwith. His Grace rode, excepting here and there where the road was bad. I remarked, however, that he was unwell, and he agreed to remain three hours at a house halfway, where he laid down, slept well for an hour and a half, ate some chicken broth, and appeared better. He drank frequently weak brandy and water, and was particularly thirsty. On the 25th his servant observed that on attempting to wash his face, the Duke had a sort of spasm and he complained to him of a pain in his throat. He ate very little breakfast, and said he would lay down till we were ready to set out. We endeavoured to prevail on him to return to Perth, but he preferred going on. It was then arranged we should make two days of the journey to Richmond instead of one, and we accordingly halted for a few hours during the heat of the day at a cottage, where the Duke slept a short time and drank some tea. Thinking his indisposition proceeded from cold, I persuaded him to drink a large glass of hot wine and water after going to bed, which he did.[1] The next day (the 26th) his Grace was up the first of the party. He said he had slept well, and wished to set off immediately. I observed that he had not washed or shaved himself, but it being a small cottage and the distance to Richmond only three or four miles, I was not surprised, thinking he intended to postpone it until his arrival in that place.[2] He drank a little tea, but complained of a difficulty

---

[1] Another account says that when his servant brought the negus he looked at it, shuddered and turned away, but said, 'I dare say it is very good, my good Baptiste, but I have changed my mind ; take it away, and bring me pen, ink, and paper.'

[2] The Duke said overnight to his servant Baptiste, 'When I am to wash in the morning do not bring me water, but dip a towel in water and bring it me squeezed dry.'

in swallowing. I did not observe anything particular in his appearance, altho' I thought he looked unwell. The Duke walked very strong and made his way through the swamps to Richmond without difficulty, but observed to me that on seeing a person jump or run into a wet place he had a sort of spasm in his throat for which he could not account. On our arrival at Richmond he said he preferred seeing the Stores, Village, &c., before he breakfasted, and this he did. We then returned to the Inn and went to dress. Before I was ready the Duke came into my room and asked the name of the Surgeon. I immediately sent for the only medical man in the Settlement. On his arrival he examined the Duke's throat and recommended his using a gargle of Port wine, vinegar, and sugar, and taking a little medicine. On going away he told me he thought the Duke would be quite well the following day. The Duke used the gargle frequently, but always with difficulty, and he made me observe that even taking the cup in his hand gave him a spasm : he said it was very extraordinary, but he could not help it ; he treated it rather as a joke, and in other respects appeared perfectly well. He talked on a variety of subjects and appeared in good spirits. He then wrote for an hour, and having finished a letter brought it open to me and said as nearly as I can remember,— "Now, my dear Governor, do not think me a fool, but here is a letter which, if anything happens to me, you must deliver to Mary." [1] I was much alarmed at his manner, which, though mild, was particularly serious, and I endeavoured to laugh him out of what appeared to me a nervous fit. He then again alluded to his throat, and said that as a sudden spasm might carry him off, he thought it right to be prepared. He then

[1] Lady Mary Lennox, his eldest daughter, who afterwards married General Sir Charles FitzRoy, K.C.B.

talked on the subject of the letter and on some other subjects, on which he was very solicitous, and said that having done so, and having written, he felt better. I again endeavoured to rally him, but on my making a remark that he would certainly deliver his letter himself, he said very earnestly, " No, my dear Governor, you will deliver that letter." I then noticed one of the glands of his throat appeared a little swelled. He persevered in constantly endeavouring to swallow small quantities of water, but the spasms were evident. I felt his pulse, which was about 72 and quite regular. Three or four officers belonging to the Settlement dined with us. The Duke was in good spirits, drank wine with most of the party, and made a joke of the spasms, remarking to me, laughing, that it was fortunate he was not a dog or he should certainly be shot as a mad one.[1] The evening passed as usual, and the Duke went to bed about 11, being determined to proceed the next day to the banks of the Ottawa, as he wished to keep his appointment at Montreal.

'At daylight on the 27th the Duke sent for me. I found him in bed. He said he had passed a very disturbed night, had awoke several times with a feeling of the nightmare, and an idea that something dreadful had happened ; that he would not attempt to go to sleep in that bed again for the world ; that he knew it was absurd, but he could not help it. I was much alarmed at his manner, although he was perfectly collected and even more than usually kind and mild. He wished to set off immediately ; I endeavoured to dissuade him, but in vain, and after a short time left him to dress and prepare for our departure. On returning to the Inn I found the Duke walking up and down the

[1] The Duke, four years before, had ridiculed the terrors of hydrophobia, and said there was no such thing, and that he had been bitten a hundred times and had never seen a case.

house in a very disturbed state with Colonel Cockburn. He was abusing himself for allowing the spasms, and his looks and manners struck me as extraordinary ; he desired us to go to breakfast, and whispered to me to take no notice of him when he came in, as it would increase the spasms which he knew the sight of the tea would occasion. He soon came in, and attempted to swallow some tea, but got down very little. We endeavoured to prevail upon him to give up the idea of proceeding that day, but he was determined to go on. It was then arranged that his Grace and myself should travel part of the way in a canoe, and we accordingly walked down a mile to the place of embarkation.' On coming to a ravine the Duke's spasms redoubled, and his companions experienced so much difficulty in getting him across it that they suspected brain fever was coming on. At length the river was reached, where he was to enter the canoe which was to take him down about seven miles. He asked eagerly if there was no other means of conveyance. He was answered ' No, except by walking,' to which he was now quite unequal. He appeared much agitated and very reluctant, but at length said, ' Tie a hand-kerchief over my eyes, and lead me to the boat ; I cannot get in myself.' This was done, and the moment he got in, he threw himself flat on his face and held tight by the sides. He could not breathe without great apparent difficulty, but, writes Major Bowles, ' he endeavoured to control himself and forced a smile whenever I looked at him.' The boat had not gone many yards, however, when, from the splashing of the oars, the Duke's agonies became greater than he could bear, and he cried out, 'Take me on shore instantly or I must die.' They put back in consternation, and the moment he was landed he broke from them and flew through the woods, leaping over fences and other obstacles with the strength and agility of a hunted criminal flying for his life. His affrighted attendants soon lost sight of him, and were in extreme distress till they again saw him flying like a maniac, without his hat and covered with mud and perspiration. Colonel Cockburn and Major Bowles caught him up with great difficulty ; when they did so they directed his steps towards a farm a few miles distant, but it was all they could do to get him over three or four small drains which lay in their path. When they reached the farm the Duke ran into an open barn, which, being a little further from the river, he said he preferred to the house ; and throwing himself upon some straw, said, ' Here Charles Lennox meets his fate.' 'This was early on the 27th. Colonel Cockburn then,' writes Major Bowles, ' left to endeavour to procure some assistance. The Duke could not long lay down, but walked about slowly, holding my arm. He then became more tranquil and conversed most seriously and earnestly ; . . . he was perfectly convinced he could not recover, and dictated messages and remembrances to his family and friends. During this period I had ventured to propose a short prayer, to which he instantly agreed ; and after a few moments' reflection he prayed most earnestly to be enabled to support whatever trials were deemed good for him with patience and resignation, professing at the same time his perfect willingness to quit this world, his confidence of being acquitted of ever having done an intentional injury to any human being or having ever acted dishonourably by any one, and his hopes that his smaller offences would be forgiven. He forgave every one from the bottom of his heart who had ever injured him, and his whole conduct and demeanour on this occasion proved the piety, the fortitude, and the purity of his heart. During the most violent agonies not a murmur escaped him. His only anxiety was for his family. He only hoped it was not presumption to pray that his sufferings might

be shortened ; he professed the most perfect confidence in his
future happiness, and his hopes of finding his father and his
uncle to receive him.   On the arrival of Colonel Cockburn and
the surgeon the Duke consented to be blooded, and about 2
pints were taken from his arm.   This at first appeared to relieve
him, but the paroxysms soon returned and became more violent
every moment.   Towards evening he was able to swallow about
20 drops of laudanum in some peppermint water, and afterwards took a grain of solid opium in a little chicken broth.
During his fits of delirium he fancied himself with Lord
Wellington in battle, cheered his men, rallied them &c. with all
the fire and impetuosity of a hero ; then thought himself fighting in defence of Quebec, wounded and dying, and desired to be
buried under the Ramparts.   At other times, evidently alluding
to the cause of his sufferings, begged to have " that nasty beast
taken out of the room," and said " Will nobody throw the animal
overboard ? "   On one of these occasions I brought the Duke's
dog Blucher to him in my arms, and said " Here is the animal ;
I will have him taken away and destroyed."   The Duke looked
up and said " Oh ! no, not my faithful Blucher ; give him to me."
He kept him by him till he died, and preserved his affection for
him till the last moment of his recollection, and in the midst
of violent pain would call out to him in his natural tone of
voice.   One of his last directions was, " Give Blucher to Mary :
it will make her cry at first, but turn him in when she is alone
and shut the door."

'When composed, the Duke would say to himself in an
undertone, "Richmond, for shame ! Is this your courage ?"
At another time he said, " Charles Lennox, rouse yourself, you
have faced death before."   His kind and affectionate manner never
forsook him for a moment ; he kept his hand almost always in

mine, and knew all those about him till nearly 12 o'clock at night, when he fell into a sort of stupor. About 7 the next morning the quantity of saliva collected in the throat and mouth caused a remarkable appearance of foaming at the mouth. An hour later his sufferings were terminated without a struggle, leaving his companions in a state of horror and distress better imagined than described ; yet they had no time for indulging in grief. A coffin was at once made with such materials as they could procure, and in eight hours after his decease was placed in the same boat from which he had fled, and conveyed to Montreal. His body was from there removed to Quebec, and, after lying in state in the Château, was buried beneath the Communion table of the Cathedral.'

The following were the Duke's last messages as dictated to Major George Bowles : 'Tell March that I know he will regret being Duke of Richmond, but that I am satisfied I leave my titles and estates to one of the most honourable men in England. Tell him that I know he will take care of his brothers and sisters. Give my love to dear Car.[1] God help them both. Tell my mother[2] that I know she possesses the soul and spirit of a Roman matron with all the polish of 1819. She will rejoice that her son died in honor, although he could not have his wish of doing so on the field of battle. Give my love to George and tell him I know he will do well. Give my kind love to the Duchess, and desire her to remember me to the Regent and to the Duke of York. Louisa Lennox will, I know, do well. Let

[1] Lord March's wife, Lady Caroline Paget, the beautiful daughter of the Marquis of Anglesey, whom he had married in 1816.

[2] The Duke's mother was a daughter of Lord Lothian ; she survived till 1830 She accompanied her husband, Lord George Henry Lennox, in many of his campaigns. She was ninety-four when she died, and was described as clever and sharp to the last ! She was a great-great-granddaughter of the great Duke of Schomberg, and sixth in descent from King James I.

Charlotte follow her example, and little Sophia bring up the train.   Love to dear little Georgy.   I leave Harriet Emma to her, Blucher to Mary.   Arthur will, I think, make a good sailor.[1] Love to William and Jane.   Give Cockburn my pencil.   I give you my watch.   My will is at Goodwood—I think March knows where.   Mary will take care of Baptiste—he is an honest fellow. Let my funeral be moderate—in the Lower Province or the Ramparts at Quebec.   Remember me to Anglesey and Jane Paget, to Peel, to the Duke of Wellington, to Steele, to Sir Charles Vernon, Lord O'Neil and John O'Neil, to Sneyd, Huntly, and Harvey.   Tell my sisters[2] I bid God bless them.   Tell Sarah[3] that with my latest words I forgive her and General Maitland from the bottom of my soul, and they and their family have my blessing.   Give my love to Bathurst, to my sister, to Apsley and Georgina Bathurst.   Tell Ready[4] I know he will deeply regret his old master.   I die in charity with all the world and in perfect confidence of mercy from the Almighty.   I think I was injured by one man, and him I forgive from the bottom of my heart.   A message to Lady E. Berkeley not to repine at her husband's death and to set a good example on this subject to my family, who will need it.'

[1] Lord Arthur Lennox, the Duke's youngest son, did not go into the Navy, and the Duke of Wellington gave him a commission in the Army.

[2] The Duke had three sisters, to whom the King's warrant was granted that they should enjoy the same rank as if their father had succeeded.   The eldest, Lady Mary Louisa Lennox, died unmarried in 1843, aged eighty-three ; the second, Lady Emilia Lennox, married her cousin, the Hon. George Berkeley, and had five children : Sir George Berkeley, Grenville Berkeley, Anne Berkeley (who married, first Sir Thomas Hardy, Nelson's friend, and secondly Lord Seaford), Georgina Berkeley (who married Admiral Sir George Seymour), and Mary Berkeley (who married the Duke of Grafton).   The third sister of the Duke of Richmond, Lady Georgina Lennox, married Earl Bathurst.

[3] Lady Sarah Lennox had married, without her father's consent, Colonel Maitland, who was very poor, though extremely handsome.

[4] Ready was his coachman.

The Duke was only fifty-two years old at the time of his death. By his wife, Lady Charlotte Gordon, who died in 1842, he had fourteen children, twelve of whom survived him. They were : (1) Lady Mary, who married Sir Charles FitzRoy, K.C.B. ; (2) Charles, who became fifth Duke of Richmond ; (3) Lord George ; (4) Lady Sarah, who married General Sir Peregrine Maitland, G.C.B. ; (5) Lady Georgina, who married William, twenty-third Baron de Ros, and died in 1891, in her ninety-seventh year ; (6) Lady Jane, who married Lawrence Peel, son of Sir Robert Peel, Bart. ; (7) Lord Henry Adam, who was drowned in 1812 ;[1] (8) Lord William Pitt ; (9) Lord Frederick, Captain 7th Foot, who died in 1829 ; (10) Lord Sussex ; (11) Lady Charlotte, who married Lord Fitzhardinge ; (12) Lady Louisa, who married the Right Hon. William F. Tighe, and died in 1900, in her ninety-seventh year ; (13) Lord Arthur ;[2] (14) Lady Sophia, who married Lord Thomas Cecil, and died in 1902, in her ninety-third year, was the last of his children, but about sixteen of his grandchildren, of whom the writer is one, are still living.

[1] Lord Henry, a most amiable and promising youth, was a midshipman on board the 'Blake.' When that ship was coming to anchor at Port Mahon, in Minorca, he fell into the sea whilst going aloft to assist in furling the sails. One of his comrades swam to save him, but he was found lifeless, having probably received a fatal blow in his fall. His remains were interred in Fort St. Philips, amidst the tears of those present and deeply lamented by Captain Codrington and all on board.

[2] The following is a copy of a letter written by Arthur, Duke of Wellington, to Lady Georgina Lennox in October 1819 :

'Dearest Georgy,—I have not written to you since the accounts were received of the dreadful misfortune which has occurred, but I am sure you will give me credit for having felt it and for you as I ought, and for the motive of my silence. I am anxious, however, to have a line from you to tell me how you are, as well as to have some account of the Duchess and Jane. Pray remember me to them both most kindly. You will have heard that I am to have the charge of Arthur [Lord Arthur Lennox]. Will you ask the Duchess whether she approves of what I propose to do for him, or whether she wishes to have him educated for any other line or profession. I proposed that of Woolwich as being immediately under my own hand. God bless you, dearest Georgy. Believe me ever yours most affy., W.

THOMAS SCOT, THE REGICIDE

Many and various descents have been assigned to Thomas Scot, one of the most conspicuous of the regicides. In the work entitled 'The Compleat Collection of the Lives of those Persons lately executed, by a Person of Quality (W. S.), London, 1661,'[1] Thomas Scot is said to have 'been born in Buckinghamshire of no noted family.' Lipscombe says 'it is probable that he was descended from Thomas Scot, a Yorkshire-man, who married Margaret, daughter of Robert Pakington, and widow of Benedict Lee of Burston, Bucks;' while Burke in 'Landed Gentry,' under 'Scott of Carbrooke,' quotes Blomefield, who in his 'History of Norfolk' states that he was son of Thomas Scott the elder, of Watton, co. Norfolk, who left the Manor of Rockells in Watton by will in 1672[2] to his grandson Thomas Scott, son of the regicide.

Now none of these is correct, and on examining sundry wills, visitations, marriage licences, &c., it seems clear that Thomas Scot the regicide was son of Thomas Scot of Chester-

[1] This was a reprint of *Rebels no Saints*, published in 1660 with the 'Lives' added.

[2] If this were the case, 'Thomas Scott the elder, of Watton,' must indeed have been an elderly man when he made his will in 1672, as the regicide is described as an old man in 1660!

THOMAS SCOT, THE REGICIDE.
From a Miniature

ford, Essex, and of Cambridge and London, by his wife Mary Sutton,[1] grandson of Thomas Scot of London and Ellen, daughter of William Brumsted, Esq., of co. Cambridge, and great-grandson of another Thomas Scot. Further back than this we cannot trace the regicide's ancestors with certainty, but there seems every probability that his family was a branch of the ancient family of Scot of Scot's Hall, Kent. William Scot,[2] great-grandson of Sir William Scot, Lord Chief Justice in 1346, settled at Stapleford Tawney, Essex, and died in 1491. He married Margery, daughter and heiress of Thomas Swynborne of Yorkshire ; and their son, John Scot, married Margaret Drax, and in a Visitation of Essex the arms of the Scots of Essex quartering Swynborne and Drax are attributed to the regicide, and also the arms that are emblazoned on the monument to the regicide's wife in Westminster Abbey are those of the Stapleford family of Scot.

Thomas Scot the regicide was educated at Westminster, under the head-master Lambert Osbaldeston, with Sir Arthur Haslerigg (or Haselrig), Sir Harry Vane, and other notorious anti-monarchists ; and Ludlow in his ' Memoirs ' says that Thomas Scot went on to Cambridge. The regicide's connection with the county of Bucks was through his marriage, he having married first, in 1626,[3] Alice, daughter and heiress of William Allanson, citizen and salter of London, and described as ' descended out of Yorks.' This William Allanson was a rich man, and owned

[1] When the regicide was instrumental in displacing Mr. Fourness, the vicar of Great Marlow, one Daniel Sutton was 'entruded' in his place—not unlikely a relation, and probably of the family of Sutton of Littlebury, Essex, of which was Thomas Sutton, founder of the Charterhouse.

[2] Younger brother of Sir John Scot (of Scot's Hall, and Constable of Dover, Ed. IV.) and of Thomas and Michael Scot.

[3] He was married at Chesterford Essex, June 27, 1626. (Colonel Chester's *London Marriage Licences*.)

breweries in Bridewell Precinct and Stockwell Green and had 'messuages and land at Great and Little Marlow,' and probably lived at the latter place, where his first wife was buried. He died in 1633, and left these lands to his son-in-law, Thomas Scot, whom we find accordingly described as ' of Westthorpe, Little Marlow, co. Bucks.'[1] He is said to have been an attorney or solicitor at Aylesbury, but he certainly was also a partner in the breweries of his father-in-law, and must have taken some share in the business. We find him continually called by his enemies 'the Brewer's Clerk,' and in some imaginary conversations published in 1660, entitled 'The Private Debates, Conspiracies, and Resolutions of the late R., imported to publick view,' one Ledsum says to Thomas Scot : 'For Godsake, Master, be not so dismayed, but comply and keep your offices. Alas ! what will become of your poor servant else ? I must be again confined to the narrow gains of Bottle-ale.'

In 1640, by order of the 'Long Parliament' which met in November, lands in Aylesbury belonging to Sir John Pakington were taken from him for the use of the people, and trustees were appointed ; Thomas Scot was one of them, and three years later he was one of the committee left at Great Marlow after the surrender of the town.. It was not, however, till the following year that Thomas Scot began to make any mark. He then married his second wife, Grace, eldest daughter of Sir Thomas Mauleverer, Bart., by Mary, daughter of Sir Thomas Wilbraham. She died the following year, aged twenty-three, and was buried in Westminster Abbey in the vault of the Mauleverers. Upon a pillar adjoining the Chapel of St. Michael, in the north

---

[1] See Whitaker's *Leeds* ; and he is also thus designated in a private manuscript belonging to the Sykes family.

transept, is a small monument erected to her memory and inscribed as follows :

GRACE, ELDEST DAUGHTER TO SIR THOMAS MAULEVERER OF ALLERTON-
MAULEVERER, IN YORKSHIRE, BAR^T, BORN IN THE YEARE 1622,
MARRIED UNTO COLLONEL THOMAS SCOT A MEMBER OF THE
HON^BLE HOUSE OF COMMONS, 1644, AND DIED THE 24 OF FEB, 1645.

Below are these lines :

> He that will give my *Grace* but what is hers
> Must say her death hath not
> Made only her deare Scot,
> But virtue, worth and sweetnesse, widowers.

Thomas Scot's alliance with Sir Thomas Mauleverer seems to have still further advanced his republican tendencies, and about this time he abandoned the profession of the law and entered into the Parliamentarian Army as a major ; and the following year, when a vacancy occurred in the Long Parliament for the borough of Aylesbury, he and Simon Mayne were returned to represent it, and Whitelock tells us ' Scot and Fountaine that same year brought Colonel Fleetwood, one of the new Knights, into the House with great triumph, though the election was but yesterday.'

Scot soon began to make himself disagreeable to Oliver Cromwell, and continually opposed him. In November 1647, at the celebrated rendezvous at Ware, when, as Carlyle says, ' Cromwell and the General Officers had to front the Levelling Principle, in a most dangerous manner, and trample it out or be trampled out by it on the spot,' Scot and Lilburne were foremost in raising the mutiny. Three of the mutinous soldiers were condemned to death, but were given ' the mercy of the dice,' and the two whom the lot reprieved shot the third.[1]

[1] Carlyle says : ' The name of him is Arnold ; long memorable among the Levellers

Lilburne was committed to the Tower, and Scot put into the marshal's custody at Ware. It seemed probable that Scot himself would lose his life for his share in this insubordination. The regiments of Fleetwood, Whalley, and Barkstead, in their petition to Fairfax, ask that 'inquisition be made for the blood of Colonel Rainsborough and Scot;' and the 'Mercurius Melancholicus' for November 1647 says that 'Shuttle-cock Major Scot, the goodly Cabinet of Treason and Religion, is like to pay Scot and lot in a halter for all the good services he has done the State; O may the heads of all such saints triumphant be so exalted!' This 'exaltation,' however, was destined to be deferred, and we find that Scot was very soon discharged.

Thomas Scot was one of those who advocated putting the King to death, and was only twice absent from the so-called High Court of Justice. He assisted in giving judgment, and signed and sealed the warrant for the King's murder. Soon after this the Parliament, having resolved to constitute a Council of State to carry on the executive part of the government, authorised five of their members to agree upon the persons they thought fit for this purpose. Thomas Scot was one of these five; afterwards he was himself constantly one of the Council of State, and in the work already alluded to, 'The Compleat Collection,' it is said of him: 'He acts in the nature of a Secretary of State and is made the only person to manage the intelligence as well foreign as domestick both publick and private, and thinks himself little other than a petty Prince, in which condition he continued till the year 1653.'[1] If Thomas Scot did think himself a petty prince, it did not prevent him from

[1] Scot was returned for Aylesbury in the second Parliament called by Cromwell; in the Parliaments of 1654, 1656, and 1658 he represented High Wycombe. About 120 Republican members were excluded.

being bitterly opposed to Cromwell calling himself Lord High Protector and assuming somewhat of the state of a king.

When the second Parliament of the Protectorate assembled in 1656, Scot, Haselrig, Ashley Cooper, Chute, and others were refused admittance; Carlyle calls them 'stiff republicans—intolerability of the Single Person their one Idea, which in fact they carry with them to the gallows at Charing Cross, when no Oliver any more is there to restrain it and them! Poor windy angry Haselrig, poor little peppery Thomas Scott!'

'The Compleat Collection' says: 'When Oliver Cromwell took the government upon himself Scot did nothing observable, but that government ceasing and Richard Cromwell being settled in the scornful seat of his father, Mr. Scot begins to show himself.' Richard Cromwell would not let Scot take his seat in the House until he signed an engagement not to disturb his government, to which he reluctantly submitted. This does not, however, appear to have deterred him from becoming a very active instrument in dethroning that foolish pretender, and he was a chief councillor at Wallingford House with Lambert, Fleetwood, &c., for the re-establishment of the Rump Parliament.

One of the witnesses against Scot at his trial gave evidence that he had heard Scot say, while Richard's Parliament was sitting, 'I have cut off one tyrant's head, and I hope to cut off another.' On the retirement of Richard Cromwell, Scot rose to greater consequence than ever, and was considered 'one of the firmest pillars of the State.' General Monk's commission as commander-in-chief was signed by him in January 1659 as President of the Council of State appointed by the Parliament. As late as November 1659 he was appointed one of the Council of State and Custos Rotulorum of the City of West-

minster ; but on November 29, 1659, Mr. Josiah Berners, in
writing to Mr. John Hobart, says : ' I hear Mr. Nevle [Neville]
Scott &c. are left out of the new Comittee of the Militia for
Westminster &c. because they utterly disowned the Comittee
of Unsafetie's lettre and order, and voted that they, being
appoynted by Parliament, according to their trust they ought
not nor would obey any orders from or give accompt unto any
but the Parliament or their Councill of State &c.   It's strange
to see these seraphelists can act without law, against Parliaments
and against morality, as if God had not as much comanded the
duties of the second table to be kept as the first.   Surely they
hope for another John of Leyden to be sett upp againe, though
not so good as their late Oliver, and, like Knipperdolen,
to be lifted uppe by and under him.'   On January 1, 1660,
when General Monk left Scotland for England, Thomas Scot
and Luke Robinson were sent as commissioners from the
Parliament to meet him, ostensibly to congratulate, and with
private directions to try and make him take the oath of
abjuration.   Scot had kept up a long correspondence with
Monk, and in some of the letters received from the General
the latter declared his resolution to live and die with the
Parliament without a King, single person, or House of
Lords.   And Ludlow says that Scot and Robinson were much
courted by Monk, who pretended to be wholly directed by their
advice ; but evidently Scot had now begun to mistrust him, if
we are to believe the account given by Dr. Skinner in his ' Life
of General Monk.'   He says : ' All the way from Leicester to
St. Albans, Scot and Robinson took up their quarters in the
same house with Monk, and when they withdrew to their own
apartment they always found or made some hole in the door or
wall, to look in or listen (which they had practis'd so palpably

that the General found it out and took notice of it to those about him, reflecting on their baseness and evil suspicions), that they might more nearly inspect his actions and observe what persons came to him, and also be in readiness to answer the addresses and to rush with those that brought them. But here they were so plainly and severely reprimanded by those gentlemen that came, that Scot in great passion reply'd tho' his age might excuse him from taking a part, yet as old as he was (before this present Parliament should be entangled by restoring the excluded members, or by new elections) he would " gird on his sword again and keep the door against them." '

Dr. Gumble, one of Monk's chaplains, in describing the General's march to London, tells the following anecdote about Thomas Scot : ' One story I cannot but relate which I was an eye-witness to : in the coach and six horses wherein Mr. Scot and Mr. Robinson came down to meet and attend the General, these two, Scot and Robinson, sitting at each end of the coach, upon some great shaking and descent in the road, their heads beat one against the other, and Scot's head fell into a very great bleeding which to stanch they were forced to call for a chyrurgeon of the Army, and to make some stop in their journey for his application. This was then observed as a preface to some great disaster, Mr. Scot's future execution.' [1]

Skinner also relates a ludicrous episode concerning Scot which occurred later on in the march. At Barnet General Monk, for the first time since he left Leicester, managed to throw off his ' two evil angels ' and got a house to himself. Scot, receiving in the middle of the night news of some muti-

---

[1] They met Monk between Leicester and Nottingham. The General, writing to the Speaker, says that when he wrote they had 'nott yett met because the wayes are soe unpassable they cannott reach beyond Leicester in a coach.'

nous behaviour of the soldiers in the suburbs of London, got alarmed and, not stopping to dress himself, went through the town to the General's quarters 'in the Dishabit of his night-gown, cap, and slippers,' urging General Monk to march forward instantly. Monk, however, took the news very calmly, refused to move, and persuaded Mr. Scot to return to his bed and put his fears under his pillow. Soon after Monk's return Scot and others of the fiercest Republicans, fearing that proceedings tended to the restoration of the King, tried to induce Monk to assume the government himself.

Scot finished his parliamentary career with the following declarations : 'Tho' I know not where to hide my head, yet I dare not refuse to own that not only my hand but my heart also was in it ;' and after defending the murder of the King, he con-cluded : 'I desire no greater honour in this world than that the following inscription may be engraven on my tomb : "Here lieth one who had a hand and a heart in the execution of Charles Stuart, late King of England."' He then left the House, followed by all those attached to his principles, and retired into the country. On the calling of a new Parliament, however, in April 1660, notwithstanding that the House consisted, with few exceptions, of persons friendly to the royal family, Thomas Scot had still sufficient influence to be again returned a member, though he never sat.

Ten days after Charles II. landed at Dover, a proclamation was issued to command the regicides to surrender themselves within fourteen days under the penalty of being excluded out of the Act of Indemnity. Amongst those excepted absolutely as to life and estate was Thomas Scot. He accordingly at once attempted to escape to the Continent, and got on board a vessel, but was 'intercepted by some pirates' who, after plundering him, set him on shore in Hampshire. He made a second attempt and landed in Flanders, where he was seized by an agent of the King's ; but Don Alonzo de Cardenas, Governor of the Netherlands, who, when Ambassador for the King of Spain to the Commonwealth, had received civilities from Scot, set him free. Scot then surrendered himself to the English agent, hoping to be entitled to the Act of Indemnity, and he was brought over to England to take his trial. He was first taken to the Tower, and then conveyed to Newgate. In July of this year (1660) the regicide's third wife, Anne, petitioned ' to enjoy, though even as a close prisoner, the company of her husband who from a place of freedom has given himself up in confidence, which his Majesty only can say was not unfounded,' and her petition was granted.

Scot was indicted at Hicks's Hall, Clerkenwell, on the 9th, and tried on October 12. He combated every legal objection made to his defence, but was found guilty and condemned to be hanged, drawn, and quartered. Whilst under sentence he conducted himself with great intrepidity. When his wife mentioned her intention of soliciting Sir Orlando Bridgeman (the Lord Chief Baron of Exchequer) to be a mediator with the King for his life, he said : ' Perhaps Sir Orlando may think I shall confess guilt, and that I cannot do, for, to this day, I am not convinced of any, as to the death of the King.'

About three or four in the morning of October 17, the day of his execution, he was visited by many friends, and by his wife and children, and they all prayed. In 'The Tryal of the Regicides' it is said that as soon as Mr. Scroope [1] had ended praying, Scot turned about, and opening his arms, he embraced his wife and one

---

[1] Colonel Adrian Scroope, who suffered the same day as Thomas Scot.

of his daughters. Scot and Mr. John Jones [1] were drawn upon the same sledge through Fleet Street to Charing Cross, where they were hanged, drawn, and quartered, the sentence being literally carried out.[2] Evelyn writes in his Diary on this day : 'Scot &c. suffered for reward of their iniquities at Charing Cross in sight of the place where they put to death their natural Prince, and in the presence of the King his son whom they also sought to kill. I saw not their execution but met their quarters mangled, and cut and reeking as they were brought from the gallows in baskets on the hurdle.' Their heads were all set up on poles upon the tops of the City gates. Scot's was on the gate of London Bridge, and his quarters were set up on the gates of the City.[3]

Scot began to make a speech from the ladder immediately before his execution, justifying his conduct from his apprehension of the approach of Popery, but the sheriff stopped him and advised him to occupy the little time left to him in prayer. Accordingly Scot did then make a very long prayer, expressing assurance of future happiness and blessing God that He had engaged him in a cause not to be repented of, mentioning with much fervour a manifestation of the divine presence in his cell that morning. The prayer is given *in extenso* in ' The Tryal of the Regicides.'[4]

In the British Museum there is an old ballad which was found pasted on the lining of a trunk. It is headed ' A relation

---

[1] Mr. John Jones, member for Merionethshire and brother-in-law of Oliver Cromwell. According to *The Tryal of the Regicides* it was Gregory Clement who went in the same sledge as Thomas Scot, and John Jones with Adrian Scroope went together an hour after.

[2] This was a most horrible and barbarous custom, as the bodies were cut down ' being half dead,' and mutilated before the head was cut off.

[3] The writer has a curious contemporary sketch of it as it then appeared.

[4] It is said that in the middle of Scot's prayer he was stopped by the hangman, who stooped down to take drink which was reached up to him on the ladder.

of the grand infamous traytors who were executed Oct. 1660
&c.' Part of it runs thus :

> Next Wednesday foure came
> For murder all imputed,
> There to answer for the same,
> Which in judgement were confuted,
> Gregorie Clement, Jones and Scot
> And Scroope together for a plot
> Likewise were executed.

To be sung to the tune of 'Come let us drink, the time
invites.'

The emoluments from Thomas Scot's offices must have been
very considerable. He purchased the Archbishop's palace at
Lambeth for the sum of £7,073 0s. 8d. conjointly with Matthew
Hardy. They did not agree as to their division of it, and
presented a petition to Parliament, which was referred to a
committee in November 1648. Scot, ultimately becoming
possessed of that part which contains the chapel, demolished its
beautiful windows, and, it is said, made his dining-room at the
east end. Furthermore it is said that this fanatic broke open
Archbishop Parker's tomb, sold the leaden coffin, and cast his
bones into an outhouse. In the 'Athenæ Oxonienses,' however,
this is stated to have been the act of Hardy.

Thomas Scot had a large family. By his first wife, Alice
Allanson, he had five sons and three daughters ; and by his third
wife certainly one daughter and a son, if not more.

(1) William, born 1627, described 'of Marlow,'[1] to whom his
grandfather, William Allanson, left 'a messuage at Kennington.'
He married Joanna, daughter of Brigge Fountaine of Sall,
Norfolk, and sister of Sir Andrew Fountaine—and they had one
child, Elizhia. After the Restoration William fled into Holland,

---

[1] Visitation (Bucks), 1633-4.

and appears to have acted as a spy in the pay of the Dutch.   He
is constantly alluded to in the Calendar of State Papers under the
name of ' Celadon,' and we read that ' Long John ' gave William
Scott of Rouen a place of 1,000 dollars or guilders a year.
Apparently he returned to England in 1667, when he is
described as of St. Mary Overy.

(2) Thomas Scot, born 1628, became a colonel in the Parliamentarian army, and was even more violent than his father.   He
took part in the conquest of Ireland, and after the terrible massacre
at Wexford was granted the manor of Longrange in that
county as payment of arrears due to him.   He married Martha,
daughter of Sir William Piers, Bart., of Tristernagh, and had
eleven children, most of whom married in Ireland and had
numerous descendants.

(3) Francis Scot had lands at Storrington in Sussex, left
him by his grandfather Allanson.   Among the certificates in
General Monk's Order-Book is one stating that Mr. William
Carre had informed him in 1659 that ' Francis Scott, sonne of
Tho Scott, had vowed to kill him.'

(4) Colonel Richard Scot, to whom his grandfather left his
brewery at Bridewell Precinct, went to Jamaica.   His first grant
of land there was in 1675, and two years later he settled the
plantation called ' Y.S.' (' Wyess ') in the parish of St.
Elizabeth.   He became joint owner of land there with Julines
Herring, and when the latter died (in 1690) Richard Scot
married his widow.   He was M.P. for St. Elizabeth from 1677
till 1688, and seems to have been a prosperous man.   His stepdaughter,[1] Bathshua Herring, married in 1726 Peter Beckford,
the Speaker of the House of Assembly in Jamaica, who had

[1] His own two daughters, Anne and Julines, married, the one Richard Mill, and
the other Francis Moore.

inherited the immense wealth of his father, the Hon. Colonel Peter Beckford, commander-in-chief in Jamaica.

(5) John Scot also went to Jamaica and died there. In Brooks's MS. in Heralds' College it is said that he was buried on the ' Y.S.' estate, and that on his tombstone was the following : ' Here lies the remains of John Scott, who had a hand and heart in the execution of Charles Stewart.' Verily these fanatics seemed to glory in their iniquities !

The regicide's eldest daughter, Elizabeth, born 1630, married Richard Sykes, lord of the manor of Leeds and of Ledsham Hall, Leeds, of the same family as the present Sir Tatton Sykes, Bart. He is described as ' a good man and pious, and of admirable natural parts, was a good justice in bad times and favourable to the Royalists that were then under a cloud.' They had four daughters : one married Thomas Wilson, grandfather of Christopher Wilson, Bishop of Bristol, and one married Ralph Thoresby, the celebrated antiquary.[1] The latter thus describes his marriage : ' Mr. Thomas Wilson recommended his wife's sister Anna, the comely and virtuous daughter of Mr. Richard Sykes. I was very solicitous for Divine directions and prayed fervently for guidance in a matter of so great concern to me both in respect of this world and of a future. And it pleased God to hear and answer, so that we were joined together in Holy Matrimony in the parish church of Ledsham, by Mr. Hammond, the Vicar, Feb. 25th 1684, a day of mercy never to be forgotten by me or mine, having since that happy moment enjoyed her endeared society thirty-five years (in which space it pleased God to give us six sons and four daughters), and I have by experience found her to be the greatest blessing, she being

---

[1] There is a portrait of Ralph Thoresby at Sledmere, probably by Parmentier, and also a pedigree of his family, of whose ancient descent he was very proud.

eminent for piety and devotion, meekness, modesty, and sub-
mission (tho' there has rarely been occasion to try this, except in
matter of baptising and education of our children, after I changed
my sentiments as to Conformity), and singular prudence in a
provident management of the family concerns.   Notwithstanding
our designed privacy, we were met (on our return from our
marriage) by about 300 horses.   But our joy was presently
turned into mourning for the death of the king, which was
bewailed with many tears for the gloomy prospect of Popery.
The License was taken out in King Charles the second's time
and we were married the very next week, yet King James II.
was then upon the Throne.'   At the landing of the Duke of
Monmouth, Richard Sykes was imprisoned for a short time, and
his son-in-law, Thoresby, was summoned to appear before the
sheriff, but Thoresby says : 'Nothing save Non-Conformity
being objected against me I was immediately dismissed ;' and
he adds : 'The danger that our holy religion was in from the
enemy made me more sensible of and I hope penitent for a
practice I had unwarily (since my marriage into a family which
though very pious was more averse to the public Establishment
than ours had ever been) and insensibly stepped into, viz. reading some pious piece of practical divinity at home to my family
when I should have been joining with the congregation in public.
For this, though good at other times, has neither so good success
nor promises made to it in Scripture.   I therefore more constantly joined in the public prayers and worship as judging the
Church of England the strongest bulwark against Popery and a
union of Protestants absolutely necessary.'

The regicide's second daughter, Mary, married William
Rowe, one of the trustees and manager of the sale of crown
lands, who is mentioned by Ward in 'Athenæ Oxonienses' as

one of the six captains sent by the Rump Commission in 1649 to Woodstock to survey lands belonging to the King.

His third daughter, Alice, married Edward Pearse of St. Margaret's, Westminster, a Nonconformist minister and author, of whom there is a notice in Calamy's account of the ministers ejected after the Restoration.

Anne Scot, the regicide's fourth daughter, was probably the child of his third wife, Anne. She went to Jamaica with one of her brothers, and there married twice. First she became the wife of Colonel Thomas Ballard of St. Iago de la Vega and of New Hall, Jamaica, who was a captain in the regiment commanded by General Venables in the expedition to St. Domingo in 1655, and, after the Restoration, a member of the King's Council. He died in 1690, and she then married in 1692 (as his second wife) the Hon. Colonel Peter Beckford,[1] commander-in-chief in Jamaica, from whom were descended the Dukes of Hamilton, Newcastle, and Leeds, the Earls of Devon, Carnarvon, Effingham, and Suffolk, and Lords Howard de Walden, Bolton, Penrhyn, Rivers, and Dorchester.[2]

The regicide's third wife, Anne, whom he must have married after 1645, outlived him. We do not know her surname, but she was of a Royalist family, and in 1660 sent a petition to the King to say she was in great distress, as, besides her husband's estates and goods being seized, her 'unnatural brother withholds her portion.' What became of her we know

---

[1] There were other intermarriages between the Beckfords and Scots, and the relationships are most puzzling. After Anne Scot married the Commander-in-Chief Beckford, her granddaughter (by her first husband), Mary Ballard, married in 1713 Thomas Beckford, one of her stepsons ; and in 1726 Peter Beckford, the Speaker, her other stepson, married the stepdaughter of her brother Richard Scot.

[2] The two latter titles have lately become extinct, but that of Dorchester has been revived.

not ; but her son, Thomas Scot, called after his father like his elder brother (between whom there must have been nearly twenty years' difference), settled in Dover. This town had long been a stronghold of dissent, and the inhabitants were almost unanimous on the side of the Parliament. The Rev. S. Statham in his interesting ' History of Dover ' says that ' Dover was one of the first places in Kent to declare against Charles I., and the Castle was captured by several of the townsmen and handed over to the Parliamentary authorities as early as 1642. The demand made upon them for ship-money in all probability accentuated their dislike to the King's government, and another reason was the anti-Popish feeling, always strong in Dover, which had received a considerable impetus in 1621 by the arrival of numerous Protestant refugees from France, driven from their own country as a result of the Protestant rebellion under the Duc de Rohan which broke out that year. In 1642 the inhabitants of Dover threw themselves with fervour into the arms of Parliament, and in a published list of suspected persons in Kent (made by the Parliamentarians) under twenty are given in Dover. Thus young Thomas Scot found himself in the midst of congenial souls. Among them were the family of Dell, who had come from Aylesbury, where they had been friends and neighbours of the regicide Scot. One of the ' Five eminent Ministers ' ordered by the fifty-nine commissioners (of which the regicide was one) to give King Charles I. ' spiritual assistance ' before his execution was William Dell. This William Dell had been chaplain to General Sir Thomas Fairfax in 1646,[1] and afterwards to Oliver Cromwell, and in 1652 was Master of Gonville and

---

[1] William Dell brought the Articles of Oxford to the Parliament in June 1646, when a gratuity was publicly presented to him. He was the author of innumerable religious works, and a great many of his sermons were published and are constantly offered for sale in catalogues.

Caius College, Cambridge. In 1660 his daughter Susanna married Thomas Scot, and they continued to live at Dover. He became a 'Dutch and Russia merchant' trading with Hamburg, and was the founder of Lathom's house of business and bank, and built the house. In 1690 and 1691 he was Mayor of Dover. He was the father of Hester Scot, who married in 1699 Michael Russell, and their son was the first Sir Henry Russell of Swallowfield.

THE TWO LORDS WHITWORTH

AND SOME OF THEIR KITH AND KIN

THE title of Whitworth is now extinct, as the only two peers of this name, Charles Baron Whitworth and Charles Earl Whitworth, died, the one in 1725 and the other in 1825, without legitimate issue. They were both remarkable men, and both were celebrated for the number and importance of their embassies; and it is somewhat singular that each of them should have been sent to the Court of Russia, not only for their ability, but because it was hoped their personal influence with the two Empresses Catherine [1] would assist their diplomatic relations, and that in both cases the plan was eminently successful.

The Whitworths were an old family. Shortly after the Conquest Robert de Whitworth held the Manor of Whitworth, near Rochdale, and there have been Whitworths in that neighbourhood ever since, their name appearing constantly in the Surveys of both Lancashire and Cheshire. John Whitworth, grandfather of the first Lord Whitworth, was an anabaptist, and one of the church surveyors employed by the Commonwealth.[2] He died in 1688 and was buried at Adbaston, Salop.

[1] Catherine I., Empress of Russia, born about 1683, died 1727; Catherine II., born 1729, died 1796.

[2] Some surveys of lands for the Dean and Chapter of Chester were returned in

His son Richard, we are told, 'raised his fortunes by being steward or land agent to several gentlemen in Staffordshire, and settled at Blowerpipe (or Blorepipe), near Adbaston, about 1680.' He was steward to Charles Gerard, first Earl of Macclesfield, and to his two sons, Gerard, second Earl, and Gerard Fitton, third Earl, and also to their sister, Lady Gerard of Bromley. It was in connection with this family that Richard Whitworth was the involuntary cause of the celebrated duel between the Duke of Hamilton[1] and Lord Mohun,[2] in which both combatants were killed. The Duke and Lord Mohun married nieces of Charles, second Earl of Macclesfield, and the latter left the chief part of his estates, including Gawsworth, to Lord Mohun, passing over the Duchess of Hamilton, who was the daughter of his elder sister.[3] The Duke brought an action against Lord Mohun, and this Chancery suit had been going on for years. The feelings of the two parties were mutually much embittered in the course of the proceedings, and the animosity was increased by the divergence of their political opinions. On November 13, 1712, the two litigants met by appointment in Lincoln's Inn, at the chambers of Mr. Orlebar, a Master in

the Registry Office in September 1649 signed by him; and again in 1653 we find his name affixed to an indenture between the High Sheriff and the Constables when Cromwell nominated Colonel Charles Worsley for Manchester.

[1] James, fourth Duke of Hamilton and first Duke of Brandon, K.T., K.G., one of the handsomest men in Scotland, born 1658, married secondly Elizabeth, daughter of Digby, fifth Lord Gerard, of Gerard's Bromley, by Lady Elizabeth Gerard, youngest daughter of Charles, fifth Earl of Macclesfield.

[2] Charles, fifth Baron Mohun, of Boconnoc in Cornwall, married first Miss Charlotte Mainwaring, daughter of Thomas Mainwaring by his wife, Lady Charlotte Gerard, eldest daughter of Charles, fifth Earl of Macclesfield.

[3] It is said that Lord Macclesfield passed over the Duchess because the Duke of Hamilton had refused to perform an engagement to which he had bound himself respecting his wife's fortune and guardianship. Lady Gerard also so highly resented the Duke's action in this matter that she left all she had to her brother, the aforesaid Lord Macclesfield, and she left her daughter, the Duchess, five shillings.

Chancery. On the examination of Mr. Whitworth, Lady Gerard's steward (now an old man), on behalf of Lord Mohun's case, the Duke raised an objection to the witness, saying he had lost his memory and had ' neither truth nor justice in him ; ' upon which Lord Mohun replied : ' I know Mr. Whitworth is an honest man, and he has as much truth and justice as your Grace.' No further recrimination passed ; another business meeting was arranged for the Saturday following ; the Duke, on retiring, made a low bow to Mohun, who returned it. There were eleven persons present, and none expected any evil consequence ; but the next day Lord Mohun sent General Macartney with a challenge to the Duke, which was accepted, and accordingly they met the following morning at eight o'clock at the Ring in Hyde Park. Colonel Hamilton of the Scots Guards was the Duke's second, and General Macartney was Lord Mohun's. All four drew swords ; it was a most sanguinary affair, the Duke and Lord Mohun fighting with peculiar determination and ferocity.[1] They thought nothing of self-defence, but from the first made desperate lunges at each other, and each received four serious wounds. Lord Mohun died on the spot, the Duke's weapon finally going right through him up to the hilt, so that the surgeon's hands met in the wound from opposite sides.[2] The Duke had the tendons of his sword-arm cut, which occasioned such loss of blood as alone would soon have caused death, even if he had not received the stab in the left breast, which was the last inflicted. This stab, by one account, was given by Lord Mohun, who shortened his sword when the Duke fell over him ; but according to the positive oath of Colonel Hamilton and the

---

[1] There is a small drawing of the duel in *Crowle's Illustrated Pennant* in the British Museum.
[2] This thrust was effected by the Duke with his left hand.

general opinion, it was a case of foul play, and dealt by General Macartney. Dr. Garth affirmed, on his word as a medical man, that it was utterly impossible for Lord Mohun to have given the Duke the death wound, which must have been inflicted by some one standing above him. So strong was the presumption of the truth of this, that the General absconded ; but a circumstance of no small weight in his favour was, that though nine or ten park-keepers came up as well as the Duke's steward, Colonel Hamilton did not have him seized, but allowed him to walk quietly away. When the Duke, who was on his face on the ground, was lifted up, he walked about thirty yards and then sank down and expired on the grass. His body was taken to his house in St. James's Square while the Duchess was still asleep. Lord Mohun's body was taken to his house in Marlborough Street, when the only remark made by his widow [1] was an expression of great displeasure that the men had lain the body on her state-bed, thereby staining with blood the rich and costly furniture.

Dean Swift, in writing to Mrs. Dingley about this duel, says : ' Before this comes to your hands you will have heard of the most terrible accident that hath almost ever happened. This morning at nine my man brought me word that Duke Hamilton had fought with Lord Mohun. I immediately sent him to the Duke's house, but the porter could hardly answer him for tears, and a great rabble was about the house. The dog Mohun was killed on the spot, and when the Duke was over him, Mohun, shortening his sword, stabbed him in at the shoulder to the heart.

---

[1] Lord Mohun's second wife, Elizabeth, daughter of Dr. Thomas Lawrence (physician to Queen Anne), and widow of Colonel Edward Griffith. Lady Mohun married as her third husband Colonel Charles Mordaunt, a nephew of Lord Peterborough, who was greatly her junior. She sold all Lord Mohun's Cornish and Devonshire estates in 1717 for £54,000 (a very cheap bargain) to Governor Thomas Pitt.

I am infinitely concerned for the poor Duke, who was an honest, good-natured man. I loved him very well, and I think he loved me better.' A tremendous sensation was occasioned by this duel, owing to the circumstance of the Duke of Hamilton being regarded as the head of the Jacobite party, while Lord Mohun was a zealous champion in the Whig interest. What seems to have originated in personal animosity was considered by the Tory party as a dastardly attempt on the part of their political opponents to inflict a vital wound on the Jacobite cause. The Duke had just been appointed Ambassador Extraordinary to Paris, with powers to effect an arrangement for the restoration of the exiled Stuarts at the death of the Queen ; and it was also understood that Lord Arran, the Duke's eldest son, should receive in marriage the hand of the Princess Louisa Stuart, youngest daughter of James II.[1] Queen Anne was devoted to the Duke, and when she bestowed on him the Garter (he having already the Thistle), and it being remarked to her that the case was without precedent, she replied that ' such a subject as the Duke of Hamilton has a pre-eminent claim to every mark of distinction which a crowned head can confer.' Miss Strickland tells us the Queen was stupefied with grief at his loss, and when the news of his death reached Scotland every one went into mourning.

The night before the duel the Duke wrote the following letter to his eldest son : [2]

' London : November 14th, 1712.

' My dear Son,—I have been doing all I could to recover your mother's right to her estate, which I hope will be yours.

---

[1] This princess died a few months after the duel.

[2] James, Marquis of Clydesdale (after fifth Duke of Hamilton, K.T.), married Lady Anne Cochrane, one of the three beautiful daughters of the Earl of Dundonald ;

I command you to be dutiful towards her, as I hope she will be just and kind to you ; and I recommend it particularly to you if ever you enjoy the estate of Hamilton and what may, I hope, justly belong to you (considering how long I have lived with a small competence, which has made me run in debt), I hope God will put it into your heart to do justice to my honour and pay my just debts. There will be enough to satisfy all and give your brothers and sisters[1] such provisions as the state of your condition and their quality in Scotland will admit of. May God preserve you, and the family in your person. My humble duty to my mother,[2] and my blessing to your sisters. If it please God I live, you shall find me share with you what I do possess and ever prove your affectionate and kind father whilst

' HAMILTON.'

A proclamation was issued offering £500 from the Government and £300 from the Duchess of Hamilton for the apprehension of General Macartney, who, however, escaped and established himself at Antwerp. At the accession of George I. he returned to England and surrendered himself. He was

and his son, the sixth Duke of Hamilton, married the beautiful Elizabeth Gunning. The following curious anecdote occurs in a manuscript account of this family :
' In 1726, when James, fifth Duke of Hamilton, was installed Knight of the Thistle at Holyrood Palace by the Earl of Findlater as King's Commissioner, the regalia being locked up in the castle, they wanted the sword of state for that purpose, and, as the story went, they had recourse to the Earle of Rothes's, which was not only gifted by General Macartney to him, but the same with which he should have so basely stabbed the Duke his father.'

[1] The Duke's daughters were : (1) Lady Catharine Hamilton, who died a fortnight after her father ; (2) Lady Charlotte Hamilton, who married Charles Edwin of Dunraven, and, dying in 1777 s.p., left a large fortune to the seventh Duke of Hamilton ; (3) Lady Susan Hamilton, married Anthony Tracy Keck, Esq., of Great Tew. The Duke's younger sons were Lord William Hamilton, who married Frances, daughter and heiress of Francis Hawes of Purley Hall, Berks ; and Lord Anne Hamilton, so named after Queen Anne, his godmother.

[2] Anne, Duchess of Hamilton in her own right, married Lord William Douglas ; she died in 1716, aged eighty.

tried in the King's Bench in June 1716. The jury, by direction of the court, acquitted him of the murder, but found a verdict of manslaughter, of which he was discharged by the formality of a cold iron immediately made use of to prevent appeal. At this trial Colonel Hamilton deviated from what he had sworn before, and only averred that he saw Macartney's sword over the Duke's shoulder. Colonel Hamilton was obliged to sell his company in the Guards, and to leave the kingdom to avoid a prosecution for perjury, and died October 17, 1716.[1]

Richard Whitworth, the involuntary final cause of this terrible catastrophe, did not long survive it. He had married in 1674, when he was thirty-six, Anne Mosley, aged nineteen, niece of Sir Oswald Mosley, Bart.,[2] and by her he had six sons and one daughter.[3] Of three of the sons we know little beyond their names and professions, and presumably they left no descendants. These are Gerard (called after Gerard, Earl of Macclesfield), who took orders, had a living in Kent in 1724, and was chaplain to King George I.;[4] John, born 1680, a captain of Dragoons; and Edward, born 1686, who went into the Navy and became captain of a man-of-war. The three other sons were Charles (the eldest), Richard, and Francis. Charles was born in 1675, and baptised on October 14 at Wilmslow Church, Cheshire, of which his maternal grandfather was rector. He was educated at Westminster School under the head-mastership of the celebrated

[1] Justin McCarthy says : 'Probably Macartney and Mohun and Hamilton and the Duke of Hamilton are best remembered in our time because of the effect which that fatal meeting had upon the fortunes of Beatrix Esmond.'

[2] She was daughter of the Rev. Francis Mosley by his wife Catherine Davenport, daughter of John Davenport of Davenport.

[3] The daughter, Anne Barbara Whitworth, married Tracy Pauncefort of Witham, ancestor of the present Lord Pauncefote.

[4] In 1720 Gerard Whitworth (whose name appears also to have been Charles) was elected a Fellow of the College of Manchester, and on March 13, 1722-3, we find an account of his preaching before the King in his chapel at Whitehall.

CHARLES, LORD WHITWORTH, (ÆTAT 62) 1752.
From a Painting at Swallowfield

Dr. Busby, and went on to Trinity College, Cambridge, where he became a Fellow (B.A.) in 1699. Macky in his ' Characters' speaks of him at this date as being ' of great learning and good sense, very handsome in his person, of a fair complexion, and of perfect address.'[1]

Directly after leaving Cambridge, under the direction of George Stepney, the statesman and poet,[2] he entered upon that diplomatic career in which he became so distinguished, it being said of him that, after Stepney, he understood the politics of the Empire better than any Englishman during the reign of Anne. In November 1701 Mr. Stepney writes to Mr. Secretary, Sir Charles Hedges, recommending Mr. Whitworth as Minister at Ratisbonne, and says : 'He having been about with me through several Courts of Germany, has thereby acquired some knowledge both of their affairs and language.' The answer duly came from Mr. Secretary Vernon, who succeeded Sir Charles Hedges, announcing that her Majesty approves of Mr. Whitworth and 'supposes an allowance of 40s. per diem will be a competent encouragement for him at present.' And accordingly Mr. Whitworth was sent to represent England at the Diet of Ratisbonne in February 1702.

In 1704 he was appointed Envoy Extraordinary to Moscow with the view of negotiating the adhesion of Russia to the Grand Alliance, and also of securing advantages for English merchants in Russia, which post he held with the greatest credit for six years. He arrived in Russia in time to see Petersburg springing from the ground, Peter the Great having laid the

---

[1] The three portraits of this Lord Whitworth, one at Knole and two at Swallowfield, do not give any idea of good looks, but they were taken when Lord Whitworth was fifty years of age.

[2] George Stepney appears as one of the minor poets in Johnson's *Lives of the Poets*. Burnet says he had ' admirable natural parts.'

foundations the previous May.   Menshikow was then all-powerful ; Mr. Whitworth was very unfavourably impressed with him.   He says : 'Menshikow [or Menzikoff] is of very low extraction,[1] extremely vicious in his inclinations, violent and obstinate in his temper.   However,' he adds, 'by his assiduity and diligence he has gained such favour with the Czar that no subject ever had the like.'   The nation was suffering from Peter's sweeping and tyrannical reforms.   Between 1705 and 1708 there were two terrible revolts which shook the empire, and the insurgents seized Astrachan, the third city in the kingdom.   Mr. Whitworth says this was due to the brutal manner in which the officials enforced one of the Czar's despotic edicts.   The women had always been used to wear a long loose gown buttoned down the front, and the ukase ordered them to wear petticoats.   'The Governor of Astrachan,' he adds, 'placed officers at the doors of the churches, who cut off the women's loose garments, and pulled out beards of venerable persons by the roots.'   In 1710 Mr. Whitworth left Russia, and Peter the Great gave him, on parting, his portrait set in diamonds.

Early in 1711 the Emperor Joseph of Austria died of small-pox, and Queen Anne sent a message to both Houses to say she had come to a resolution to support the interests of Austria and to use her utmost endeavours to get the King of Spain made Emperor ;[2] and the English Ministry followed this up with a proposal to make peace by yielding Spain and the West Indies to King Philip.   With these instructions Mr. Whitworth was now sent to Vienna, and many of the Duke of Marlborough's despatches of this year are addressed 'To Lord Ambassador

---

[1] Voltaire says Menzikoff was a pastrycook's boy.

[2] Queen Anne, we are told, was anxious to write her wishes in favour of Charles with her own hand, but was hindered by the gout, and Bolingbroke penned the despatch for Whitworth.   (Sichel's *Bolingbroke*, p. 316.)

Whitworth.' Finally, Marlborough in November 1711 writes to him from the Hague as follows :

'I propose to go to the Brill to-morrow to be at hand to make use of the first opportunity of a wind to embark, but must not leave this place without repeating to Y. E. my hearty thanks for your constant and useful correspondence, which I am per-suaded the Ministers at home must be very sensible of, and you may depend I shall omit no opportunity of doing you justice to them. You will hear from other hands of the measures that are taking for putting an end to this ruinous war. I do not enter into particulars because I am to have no share in the negotiations, but I can assure you no man living can be more desirous than I am of a good and speedy peace, and I shall be more than satisfied with the thoughts of having in any way contributed towards it. I pray the continuance of your friendship and that you will believe me with great sincerity &c., M.'

Later on in the same year Mr. Whitworth was again sent to Russia, having been appointed Ambassador Extraordinary to the same Court in consequence of a serious difficulty that had arisen between England and Russia, and which threatened a rupture between the two countries. The case was this : In May 1707 the Czar sent M. de Matvéiff[1] to London to endeavour to exert personal pressure over Marlborough and Godolphin with a view to secure the possessions he had conquered in the Gulf of Finland, and to offer them large presents ; and in the draft Peter added with his own hand : 'I do not think that Marlborough can be influenced in this manner, because he is enormously rich, but you may promise a few 100,000 or so, or more.' Matvéiff could get nothing settled satisfactorily. He wrote back to the Czar : 'The Ministry here is more subtle even than the French in finesse and

---

[1] His name also spelt Matueof and Matvéieff.

intrigue, their smooth and empty words being nothing but loss of time.'   In July 1708 (o.s.) Monsieur de Matvéiff was recalled to Russia, and, after attending Queen Anne's levee and taking formal leave of her, was arrested in Charles Street, St. James's, by bailiffs at the suit of Thomas Morton, laceman, of Covent Garden, his creditor for £50, and taken with much indignity to a sponging house called the Black Raven.   From there the Muscovite ambassador sent to one of the Secretaries of State to inform him of how he was being insulted.   Only Mr. Walpole, an under-secretary, could be found, who came to him (as the Czar afterwards observed) to be witness to his disgrace, for instead of being discharged he was only allowed out on bail. He resisted manfully, and seriously wounded several of his captors.   As soon as he was liberated he left England and went to Holland, from whence he sent a very serious complaint to the Czar, who threatened to declare war with England and meanwhile stopped all intercourse of trade with this country.   The Prussian and other foreign ministers as well, looking upon themselves as concerned in this affair, demanded satisfaction for the outrage.   The explanation forthcoming was not deemed satisfactory,[1] and it is said that Peter wrote a most curious letter to Queen Anne asking her to return him by bearer the head of Morton, together with the heads and hands of any of his abettors in the assault that her Majesty might have incarcerated in her dungeons !   The Queen sent the Czar back an answer that she had not the disposal of any heads in her kingdom but those forfeited by the infraction of certain laws which Mr. Morton and his *posse* had not infringed.   An angry corre-

---

[1] The case was tried in the Court of the Queen's Bench before the Lord Chief Justice Holt, who referred the point to a scrutiny at which all the other judges were to assist.

spondence continued for two years, when the troublesome affair was at length terminated by her Majesty deputing Mr. Whitworth to deliver a letter from her to the Czar in a public manner, and at the same time to do all in his power to pacify the enraged potentate. There can be little doubt that Mr. Whitworth stood high in the favour of Queen Anne, who writes to the King of Prussia on April 18, 1711, 'that she has ordered Charles Whitworth, Esq., who is going as her ambassador to his Russian Majesty, to stop at Berlin to explain her sentiments to the King of Prussia upon the present conjunction and to confer upon the measures most fitting to be taken for the tranquillity of the Empire and for the support of the interests of the common cause in this situation of public affairs the most ticklish that ever was.'

Mr. Whitworth made a solemn entry into Moscow, accompanied by a vast concourse of Russian officials and two regiments of Russian Guards which were sent to meet him, and after he arrived at the Court he made a speech to the Czar and presented the Queen's letter, which stated that she had had the law repealed so that his Imperial Majesty's ambassadors could never be subjected to further insults.[1] The Czar then made a short answer, in which he said he accepted this as a satisfaction ; and after a conference which Mr. Whitworth had a few days later with the Russian Ministers, the difference ended to the mutual satisfaction of the two Powers.[2] The Czar, by way of marking his sense of Mr. Whitworth's conduct in the affair, gave orders to Soltikof to entertain him for three days with the greatest magnificence, the officers of his Majesty's household serving at table. Mr. Whitworth's negotiations were rendered easier by the

[1] This was really done, and ever since then the persons of ambassadors and their suites have remained sacred from arrest.

[2] We are told that Peter was specially pleased at Mr. Whitworth commencing his speech, ' Très-haut et très-puissant *Empereur.*'

friendship of the Empress, with whom he had had tender relations in her earlier days when he little could have realised that
she would have such an extraordinary career. Born about 1683
in Livonia, she was the child of a small Catholic yeoman, Samuel
Skovronsky—some accounts say the natural child—by a country
girl. She was adopted by a Lutheran pastor of the name of
Gluck at Marienburg, where she was employed in attending on
the children. In 1701 she married a Swedish dragoon named
Johan, who disappeared entirely directly afterwards. The following year, when Marienburg was taken by the Russians, Catherine,
or rather Martha, as she was then called, attracted by her youth
and beauty the notice of General Bauer, who took her under his
protection. Not long after Prince Mentzikof purchased her as
a servant for his wife and transferred her to Moscow, where she
lived with him till the beginning of 1704, when the Czar Peter
took her for himself and seven years later married her, after she
had been received into the Greek Church and re-christened
Catherine Alekycevna. The marriage was publicly solemnised
at St. Petersburg in 1712, at seven o'clock in the morning. The
Czar had settled that one of her brothers, whom he had unearthed
from Lithuania and ennobled for the occasion, should, with Prince
Romodanowski, walk on either side of him in the procession.
Now this Prince was the highest noble in Moscow, and, after the
Czar, was the greatest personage in the empire ; and when this
order was notified to him, he said, ' On which side of the Czar
am I expected to place myself ? ' On being told that the
brother-in-law of his Majesty would take the right, he replied,
' Then I shall not attend.' This answer reported to the Czar,
the latter said, ' You shall either attend or I will hang you !'
' Say to the Czar,' replied the haughty boyar, ' that I entreat him
first to execute the same sentence on my only son, who is but

fifteen ; it is possible that, after having seen me perish, fear might make him consent to walk on the left hand of his sovereign, but I can depend on myself never to do that which can disgrace the blood of Romodanowski.' The Czar yielded, but to revenge himself on the independent spirit of the Muscovite aristocracy he built Petersburg. Catherine's bridesmaids were two of her own little daughters ! In the evening there was a ball, during which the Czar drew Mr. Whitworth and Comte Vitzthum [1] aside and jocosely informed them that the wedding was a fruitful one, as, though he and his spouse had only been married a few hours, they had five children.[2] At this same ball the Czarina sent for Mr. Whitworth to dance with her. As they began the minuet she squeezed his hand and said in a whisper, ' Have you forgot little Kate ? '

Mr. Whitworth, when he was sent as Ambassador, had also been deputed to ascertain the state of Russia, so that in the event of his endeavours to avert a war being unsuccessful, he might be able to report to his Government upon the resources of the Emperor. Accordingly he wrote ' An Account of Russia as it was in the year 1710,' which was printed by the Strawberry Hill Printing Press in 1758.[3]

In 1714 Mr. Whitworth was appointed English Plenipotentiary at the Congress of Baden [4] and Minister Plenipotentiary

---

[1] Comte Vitzthum was Minister of Augustus II., King of Poland.

[2] She bore him eleven children in all, of whom two only, Anne and Elizabeth, survived him.

[3] Lord Whitworth's despatches and correspondence are contained in the voluminous *Sbornik*, or Collections of the Russian Imperial Historical Society, vol. lxi.

[4] Lord Bolingbroke writes, April 27, 1714 : ' Mr. Whitworth will be immediately despatched into the Empire : I prevailed last night that he should not be ordered directly to Baden, which might have exposed him to make a very mean figure, the French and Imperialists being locked up there, as they were at Rastadt. . . .'— *Bol. Pol. Corr.* vol. iv. pp. 122-28.

to the Diet of Augsburg and Ratisbon ; in 1716 Envoy Extraordinary and Minister to the King of Prussia ; and in 1717 Envoy Extraordinary to the Hague, from whence he sent the British Government many communications respecting Jacobite conspiracies.   During his stay at the Hague he had become acquainted with the de Salengre family.   They were of ancient and noble lineage, originally from Hainault, but in the time of the religious persecutions under the Duke of Alva (1567–73) they left their country and settled in Holland.   Albert Hendrick de Salengre, seigneur de Grisoort in Holland, married Gertruida Jacoba Rotgans, sister of the celebrated Dutch poet of that name, and Lord Whitworth married their daughter, Magdalena Jacoba de Salengre.   The marriage took place at the Hague on June 24, 1720, 'the ceremony being after the English fashion.'[1]

In 1721 Mr. Whitworth was appointed Minister to the King of Prussia, and this same year King George I. remunerated his long public services by creating him Baron Whitworth of Galway in Ireland.   In 1722 he was appointed Ambassador and Plenipotentiary to the Congress of Cambray.[2]

Lord and Lady Whitworth came to England in 1722–3, and that same year he was returned to Parliament for Newport, Isle of Wight.   Lady Whitworth's brother, Albert de Salengre, who was Councillor of the Princess of Orange and Commissaire

---

[1] Baron de Pollnitz in his Memoirs, published 1739, mentions that Lady Whitworth gave a smart rebuke to Cardinal Corsini, afterwards Pope Clement XL, for trying to meddle with their household affairs at the Cambray Congress.   It appears that the Cardinal, who was very penurious, had a fancy to regulate every plenipotentiary's household.   One day he took it into his head to give his economical rules to Lord Whitworth, but he did not find her ladyship very complaisant, and, said she, ' M. le Marquis, we make use of the Italians to regulate our concerts, but as for the table, pray give us leave to consult the French.'

[2] His chaplain on this occasion was Richard Chenevix, afterwards Bishop of Waterford and great-grandfather of Richard Chenevix Trench, Archbishop of Dublin.

CHARLES, LORD WHITWORTH, AND HIS NEPHEW
(afterwards SIR) CHARLES WHITWORTH.
From a Painting by Jack Elys at Swallowfield.

des Finances des Etats Généraux, came with them to England. Although he was only twenty-nine years of age, he was a most distinguished author, and on arriving in England was made a member of the Royal Society. Immediately after his return to Holland he was attacked with smallpox and died at the Hague in July 1723, to the great grief of Lord and Lady Whitworth. Two years later Lord Whitworth himself died at his house in Gerrard Street, aged fifty. He probably died of apoplexy, as we know that he had been treated by the celebrated Dr. Arbuthnot for ' vertigo.'[1] .This doctor, writing to Swift in November 1723, says : ' I know how unhappy a vertigo makes anybody that has the misfortune to be troubled with it, and I will propose a cure for you, that I will pawn my reputation upon. I have of late sent several patients in that case to the Spa, to drink thereof the Geronstere water, which will not carry from the spot. . . . But because the instances of eminent men are most conspicuous, Lord Whitworth, our Plenipotentiary, had this disease (which, by the way, is a little disqualifying for that employment) ; he was so bad that he was often forced to catch hold of anything to keep him from falling. I know he has recovered by the use of that water to so great a degree, that he can ride, walk, or do anything as formerly.'

Lord Whitworth was buried in the south aisle of Westminster Abbey on November 6, 1725, and a funeral sermon was preached upon his death at Wostram by George Lewis. Lord Whitworth's widow survived him eight years. She married secondly, at the Hague on October 9, 1729, François Marie de Villers de la Faye, Comte de Vaulgrenant (of Burgundy), who was Ambassador of France at Turin. She died at Malles-sous-Pizzighettone, near Cremona in Lombardy, in 1733.

[1] In Johnson's Dictionary one of the examples given of the use of the word ' vertigo,' taken from Dr. Arbuthnot's Works, is as follows : ' The forerunners of an apoplexy are dulness, vertigos, tremblings.'

Lord Whitworth had no children, and by his will, dated at Berlin, March 1722–3, which was proved by his brother Francis Whitworth, the latter was made his heir. Lord Whitworth thus passed over his brother Richard, probably because he did not approve of his Jacobite principles. 'The Honourable' Colonel Richard Whitworth, as he was generally called, was Colonel of the 'Queen's Horse.' When he was fifty he married a lady of means, Penelope, widow of North Foley, Esq., of Stourbridge, and daughter of William Plowden of Plowden. He owned land in Northamptonshire and a house in Conduit Street, but it was said that he lost a great part of his property through having to pay a heavy fine which was levied upon him by the Government for high treason, in consequence of his saying he would rather raise a regiment for the King of France than for the King of England. No doubt he was a Jacobite at heart. His wife's family were staunch supporters of the Stuarts ; and he may have imbibed these principles also from his own mother, whose brother, Sir Oswald Mosley, had received Prince Charles Edward at his house at Ancoats during one of his secret visits to England.

Colonel Richard Whitworth's only son, Richard, born in 1745, was a most eccentric character. He was M.P. for Stafford, and published in 1769 a political work called 'The Injured Ghost of Liberty.' Towards the close of the eighteenth century he raised at Adbaston, near where he lived, a body of volunteers, sailors as well as soldiers. The sailors were trained on a large ship with guns, which he had on a lake or canal which he made near his house.[1] He never married, but he was once engaged to Miss Pigott of Edgmond, Shropshire. This lady, after visiting him at Batchacre Park, broke off the engagement in

---

[1] The writer has a curious mezzotint of the said Richard in camp at Winchester with his dog Neptune.

HARDY, *pinx.*

COL. RICHARD WHITWORTH, M.P.
In Camp at Winchester, 1778.

consequence of his eccentricity. The death of Miss Pigott's father, which took place in May 1770, was memorable in this wise. When he was upwards of seventy, Mr. Pigott's son Robert agreed with Mr. Codrington to run their fathers' lives one against the other, Sir William Codrington being a little over fifty ; and the wager was laid for £500.[1] Mr. Pigott was already dead when the bet was made, quite unknown and unexpected by either party. To show the then utter impossibility of it being known at the time of the bet, we are told that Mr. Pigott died at 2 A.M. in Shropshire on the day on which the bet was made after dinner at Newmarket! Mr. Pigott was induced to resist payment; and Lord March (afterwards the well-known Duke of Queensberry), who had taken Mr. Codrington's bet, was compelled to bring his action, which he gained, Lord Mansfield deciding that the impossibility of a contingency is no bar to its becoming the subject of a wager, provided the impossibility is unknown to both the parties at the time of laying it.[2] The case was tried in the Court of King's Bench in June 1771.

'Dick' Whitworth, as he was commonly called, died in 1811, aged seventy-six, greatly lamented by the poor, to whom he was most kind and generous.[3] He left his property to Lord Aylmer, who had married his cousin Catharine Whitworth ; then to Mr. Edmund Plowden of Horton Hall (who, however, died before Lord Aylmer) ; and then to his cousin, Mr. Pauncefort, to him and his sons for ever. Sir Charles W. Pauncefote Duncombe sold it.

[1] The wager was that if Sir William Codrington died first, Lord March was to pay Mr. Pigott 1,600 guineas ; and if old Mr. Pigott died first, Mr. Pigott junior was to pay Lord March 1,500 guineas.

[2] *Burrow's Reports.*

[3] Among other benefactions he gave a house and land at Adbaston for the support and education of the poor.

Francis Whitworth, whom Lord Whitworth made his heir, was born in 1684. He was elected member for Minehead in 1723, and altogether was in Parliament for nineteen years during the Administration of Sir Robert Walpole, and appears to have been a supporter of the Ministry. In 1724 he bought the manor and castle of Leybourne Grange, near Malling in Kent. In 1725 he succeeded to the estate of his brother, Lord Whitworth, in 1728 was appointed a Gentleman Usher of the Privy Chamber, and in 1732 Surveyor-General of the King's Woods and Forests, and Secretary of Barbadoes. He died in 1742, aged fifty-eight. He had married Joan, daughter and heir of William Wyndham of Clowerworth, Gloucestershire, by his wife Rebecca, daughter of Sir Nicholas Strode of Chevening and Westerham, Kent, and left one son, Charles, born in 1714–5. After leaving college this young man seems to have gone out in London society a good deal, and later on gave himself up to political life. The following letter, which mentions a private festivity in which he took part, seems worth publishing to show the contrast of the luxury of the present day with what was considered ' handsome ' for a duke's table in those days. It is written by a son of Lord Wentworth to his father in 1733. ' Dear Papa,—We were last night at the Duke of Devonshire's, it was a ball, there were 8 couple, viz. Lady Caroline Cavendish and Lord Sunbury, Lord Hartington and Lady Mary Montague, Lord Conoway [*sic*] [Conway] and Lady Harriet [her sister], Mr. Walpole and Lady Lucy [sister], Mr. Conoway and Miss Wortley, a Mr. Webster and Lady Dorothy [sister], Mr. Whitworth and Lady Betty Cavendish, me and Lady Betty Montague, and we had a very handsome supper, viz. at the upper end cold chicken, next to that a dish of Cake, parch'd almonds, Sapp biskets [*sic*], next to that a dish of tarts and cheese cakes, next to that a great custard, and next to that another dish of biskets, parch'd almonds and preserved apricocks, and next a quarter of lamb.' This same young man writes again : ' Your lordship order'd me before you went out of town to go to Major Fouberts[1] an inquire ab^t. the price of learning to ride. Went this morning and he say'd the price was 6 guineas enterence and 3 g^s. a month. There was about 7 people riding, my L^d. Holderness, my L^d. Dalkeith, my Lord Deerhurst, Mr. Roper, Mr. Wallop, Mr. Whitworth, and Mr. Ashburnham.'

Mr. Whitworth became a prominent and most useful man. He sat in Parliament for thirty-one years during the Administrations of Pelham, Newcastle, Pitt (Lord Chatham), Lord Bute, Grenville, Rockingham, Grafton, and North. He was chairman of the Committee of Ways and Means for ten years, and was knighted in 1768. Amongst other measures that he brought forward was one for improving the paving and lighting of London, and he was the author and compiler of many useful books of the day. He was Lieutenant-Governor of Gravesend and Tilbury Fort for twenty years, and had a house at Greenwich. On returning to it from London one day in 1767 a footpad stopped his carriage at the end of Peckham Lane and demanded his money, but instead of complying Mr. Whitworth let down the glass and fired at him with a blunderbuss. The coachman drove on, and the footpad was found dead.

Sir Charles Whitworth appears to have got into straitened circumstances, for in 1776 an Act was passed to enable him

---

[1] A Monsieur Foubert came to England from France on account of his religion in the reign of Charles II., and started a Riding Academy in Regent Street on the site of the mansion of the Countess of Bristol. He is mentioned by Evelyn in his *Diary* and by Sir John Reresby in his *Memoirs*. Major Foubert was his son, and taught the young nobility mathematics as well as riding.

to sell his property in Somersetshire, called Blachford, and he also sold Leybourne Grange [1] and removed to Stanmore. He died at Bath in 1778, aged sixty-four, and is buried at Walcot Church, where there is the following epitaph : ' Here lies, in expectation of a joyful resurrection, Sir Charles Whitworth, Kt., whose eminent qualities it would be impossible, were they to be enumerated, to comprise on this tablet. Suffice it to say that his whole life was a constant and cheerful display of every public and private virtue. He served his country in five successive Parliaments, and departed this life on the 21st of August, 1778.'

Sir Charles married in 1748 Martha Rose, daughter of Richard Shelley, Esq., son of Sir John Shelley, third Baronet, by his wife Mary, daughter of Sir John Gage, Bart. Lady Whitworth survived her husband eight years, and died in Great Ormond Street in 1786.[2] By her Sir Charles had nine children, all of whom were christened at Leybourne : (1) Margaret, born 1750, was Maid of Honour, and died unmarried in October 1812, aged sixty-two ; (2) Catharine, married Lord Aylmer, by whom she was mother of Rose Aylmer, immortalised by Landor ; (3) Charles (afterwards Earl Whitworth) ; (4) Mary, married T. Lloyd ; (5) Francis (Sir), Colonel R.A. ; (6) Richard, R.N. ; (7) Priscilla, married first Sir Bellingham Graham, Bart.,[3] and secondly Viscount Lake ; (8) Robert ; (9) Anne Barbara, married Sir Henry Russell, Bart.[4]

Colonel Sir Francis Whitworth, Sir Charles's second son, was

---

[1] Leybourne Grange was sold to James Hawley, M.D., F.R.S.

[2] Sir Charles Russell has a family group by Hogarth in which Lady Whitworth appears, as well as her father, mother, and sister.

[3] She was grandmother of the present Sir Reginald B. Graham, who has a lovely picture of her by Romney.

[4] Anne Barbara Whitworth was also painted by George Romney a few years after her marriage, and this beautiful picture is now at Swallowfield in the possession of Sir Charles Russell, Bart., her great-grandson.

Lady Russell and Son
From the original at Swallowfield by George Romney
painted in 1786-7

born in 1754, and entered in 1768 as a cadet in the Royal Military Academy at Woolwich. In 1771 he received his commission in the Royal Artillery, and in the following year embarked for Gibraltar, where he remained some years till recalled to fill a staff commission in that corps. Soon after the commencement of the war with France, having been promoted to a company, he was detached with it to the West Indies, where, under General Bruce and Sir Charles Grey, he very eminently distinguished himself in the eventful campaigns of that period, and ultimately succeeded to the command of the Artillery. He was aide-de-camp both to Lord Cornwallis and to Lord Chatham when they were Masters General of the Ordnance ; and in the expedition to the Helder he embarked with Sir Ralph Abercromby, and in the various situations which the events of that campaign produced, his active exertions were most eminently conspicuous. Shortly after his return to England it became necessary for the general good of the country that an incorporation should be made of the corps of Royal Irish Artillery with that of England. In this most delicate service, with which he was intrusted by Lord Cornwallis, then Lord Lieutenant of Ireland, he had the principal share in arranging the union of the two corps, which was ultimately effected notwithstanding the obstacles opposed to it. Sir Francis died at his house in Bruton Street, Berkeley Square, in January 1805, in his forty-ninth year, and was buried at Plumstead. A contemporary account says of him : 'Early introduced into life, no man was perhaps more indebted to nature for those excellences which are calculated to gain the esteem and favour of the world—no man enjoyed them to a greater extent. Handsome in his person,[1] graceful in action, and accomplished in manners, he

---

[1] Sir Charles Russell has an oil-painting of him by Linnell, copied from a miniature by Engleheart.

early attracted the esteem and admiration of his associates. In his further progress in life these endowments were but in him secondary, for to them was added a disposition and temper peculiarly kind and conciliatory, which he universally and successfully exerted for the interests and happiness of the society in which he lived.'

Sir Charles Whitworth's two remaining sons were both drowned. Richard, born 1755, was a lieutenant in the Royal Navy, and during the American war was on the 'Roebuck,' commanded by Sir Andrew Snape Hammond, in the squadron under Admiral Graves off the Chesapeake. Young Whitworth volunteered to carry in a small vessel to Lord Howe the intelligence of the arrival of the French fleet off the coast. In the evening his vessel was seen making a press of sail to get through the French fleet, and it must have been lost, for it never again was seen or heard of. This took place in 1777, when he was in his twenty-second year.[1]

Robert Whitworth, Sir Charles's youngest son, was drowned the following year in the Thames. He was a ' King's Scholar,' aged sixteen, at Westminster, and went out in a small boat with three other youths, the sons of Mr. Fenton and Dr. Warren. The boat capsized opposite Vauxhall, and Dr. Warren's son alone was saved. Robert Whitworth was buried on May 13, 1778, in the south cloister of St. Peter's, Westminster Abbey.

Charles Whitworth (afterwards Earl Whitworth), the eldest son of Sir Charles Whitworth by his wife, Martha Rose Shelley, and grand-nephew of Charles, Lord Whitworth, after whom he was named, was born in 1752 at Leybourne Grange, Kent, and baptised there on May 29. He was educated at Tonbridge School under James Cawthorn, the poet, and Towers, the trans-

---

[1] Sir Charles Russell has an oil-painting of him.

lator of Cæsar and other classics. On leaving this academy he entered the Army, with a commission in the 1st Regiment of Foot Guards, in 1772, and attained the rank of lieutenant-colonel in 1783 ; but that *mauvaise langue* Wraxall says he was more distinguished during this period of his career by success in gallantries than by anything else. He was conspicuous for his good looks, fine presence, and charming manners, so it is not surprising to hear that when John Frederick, third Duke of Dorset, the Ambassador at Paris, who was his intimate friend, introduced him into French society he should have had great *succès* with the ladies of the Court ; but, more than this, he made a very favourable impression upon the Queen (Marie Antoinette), who not only distinguished him by flattering marks of her attention, but interested herself in promoting his fortune, and, when he quitted the Army and aspired to enter the Corps Diplomatique, recommended his interests to the Duke of Dorset, who, not without great difficulty, at length obtained for him, in the year 1786, the appointment of Minister Plenipotentiary to the Court of Stanislas Auguste Poniatowski, King of Poland. Warsaw was then the centre of intrigues, but Colonel Whitworth at once justified the interest shown in him, and gave great satisfaction during the two years he remained there, which included the troublous period immediately preceding the second partition. Recalled from Warsaw early in 1788–9, he was in the following August selected and nominated Envoy Extraordinary and Minister Plenipotentiary to the Court of Russia, where he remained nearly twelve years. We are told he was 'well received by the Empress Catherine,' and the words of the poet [1] thus described his arrival :

> Suppose him then at Petersburgh ; suppose
> That pleasant capital of painted snows ;

[1] Lord Byron intended them as a description of Colonel Whitworth.

Suppose him in a handsome uniform ;
   A scarlet coat, black facings, a long plume,
Waving, like sails new shiver'd in a storm,
   Over a cocked hat in a crowded room,
And brilliant breeches, bright as a cairngorme,
   Of yellow kerseymere we may presume,
White stockings drawn, uncurdled as new milk,
O'er limbs whose symmetry set off the silk ; [1]

Suppose him sword by side, and hat in hand,
   Made up by youth, fame, and an army tailor—
That great enchanter, at whose rod's command
   Beauty springs forth, and Nature's self turns paler,
Seeing how Art can make her work more grand
   (When she don't pin men's limbs in like a jailor).

The courtiers stared, the ladies whisper'd, and
   The Empress smiled ; the reigning favourite frown'd—
I quite forget which of them was in hand
   Just then, as they are rather numerous found,
Who took by turns that difficult command
   Since first her Majesty was singly crown'd ;
But they were mostly nervous six-foot fellows,
And fit to make a Patagonian jealous.

Catherine, I say, was very glad to see
   The handsome herald, on whose plumage sat
Victory ; and, pausing as she saw him kneel
   With his despatch, forgot to break the seal.

Her Majesty look'd down, the youth look'd up—
   And so they fell in love—she with his face,
His grace, his God-knows-what.

[1] The writer has a charming mezzotint of Captain Whitworth, engraved by Robert Laurie from a portrait by A. Graff, which depicts him at this age and in uniform with a cocked hat ; and we may add that Lord Whitworth was celebrated for the symmetry of his leg.

Col. Charles Whitworth, *afterwards* Earl Whitworth.
From a Miniature by Graff

He, on the other hand, if not in love,
    Fell into that no less imperious passion,
Self-love—which, when some sort of thing above
    Ourselves, a singer, dancer, much in fashion,
Or duchess, princess, empress, ' deigns to prove '
    ('Tis Pope's phrase) a great longing, though a rash one,
For one especial person out of many,
Makes us believe ourselves as good as any.

And Catherine (we must say thus much for Catherine),
    Though bold and bloody, was the kind of thing
Whose temporary passion was quite flattering,
    Because each lover look'd a sort of king.

All the ambassadors of all the Powers
    Inquired, ' Who was this very new young man,
Who promised to be great in some few hours ? '
    Which is full soon (though life is but a span).
Already they beheld the silver showers
    Of rubles rain, as fast as specie can,
Upon his cabinet, besides the presents
Of several ribbons, and some thousand peasants.

Juan, who found himself, he knew not how,
    A general object of attention, made
His answers with a very graceful bow,
    As if born for the ministerial trade ;
Though modest, on his unembarrassed brow
    Nature had written ' Gentleman.'   He said
Little, but to the purpose, and his manner
Flung hovering graces o'er him like a banner.

Allowing for poetical licence, there seems no doubt that
Colonel Whitworth, or ' Milord Witford,' as he was then called

at Petersburg, seized the Empress's fleeting fancy ; and even after Zouboff became chief favourite (in 1789) he maintained his influence over her through one of her ladies, the beautiful Princess or Countess Gerebtsoff (or Jerebzoff),[1] Zouboff's sister, who became desperately enamoured of the handsome Ambassador, and continued so for many years, to his cost, as will be seen later. The Empress frequently passed her evenings in the society of Platon Zouboff,[2] Princess Gerebtsoff, and 'Milord Witford,' and they played whist at ten roubles the rubber, also rocambole, piquet, and Boston, always for very low stakes. The Empress was on these occasions surrounded by her English grey-hounds, the original pair having been given her by Dr. Dimsdale, whom she sent for from London in 1768 to inoculate her.[3] The head of the race of greyhounds she called 'Sir Tom Anderson,' and his spouse 'Duchess Anderson' !

In 1791, in consequence of Pitt's foreign policy, Mr. Whitworth went out of favour with the Czarina, and she said to him one day ironically, 'Sir, since Mr. Pitt is determined to drive me out of Petersburg, I hope he will permit me to retire to Constantinople.' Peace between Russia and the Porte was concluded at Galatz in August 1791, partly owing to the threats of England. Better terms for Turkey might have been obtained had not Pitt been thwarted by Mr. Adair, who was sent to Petersburg

---

[1] It is also written Jerebstof.

[2] Masson says : ' Les dernières années de sa vie (Catherine) Zouboff se trouvait à la lettre Empereur de toutes les Russies.'

[3] The Empress was the first, or almost the first, in her empire to be inoculated. A boy of seven, called Morkoff, who had been inoculated first of all, in order to inoculate from him, was ennobled, and was given the surname of Ospiennzi (ospa = smallpox). The family of this name, now occupying a high position in Russia, owes its fortune to this ancestor. Dr. Dimsdale received the title of Baron and a pension of £500.

by Fox for that purpose.[1] The Empress, to mortify the allied Powers, placed Adair on her right hand in the place of honour, and on the conclusion of the peace gave presents exactly of the same kind to both him and Mr. Whitworth, but of greater value to the representative of Mr. Fox. Mr. Whitworth took his revenge in the following manner. The Empress asked him, 'Est-ce un homme très considérable ce Mr. D'Ada?' 'Pas trop, Madame,' answered Mr. Whitworth, 'quoique son père était grand *Saigneur*.' (Alluding to the fact that Adair's father was a surgeon.) Gradually the Ambassador more than recovered his position, probably through the influence of the Zouboffs. Baroness de Bode (*née* Kynnersley) writes in 1795 of having been from Petersburg to Finland with 'a most agreeable party of pleasure, consisting of Sir Charles Whitworth' (the Ambassador had been made a K.B. in 1792 for his share of Jassy), 'his nephew Aylmer,[2] Count Zouboff's sister and her son, and his tutor, a French abbé, all the party agreeing vastly well together.' Mme. de Bode appears to ignore the well-known *liaison* which existed between Mme. de Gerebtsoff and the English Ambassador.[3] Mr. Childe-Pemberton, in his Memoirs of the Baroness de Bode, says à *propos* of this : 'The Zousboff were in

[1] This furnished a stanza to a squib which appeared in the *Anti-Jacobin* called A Bit of an Ode to Fox.' Adair is introduced in the character of a goose :

> ' I mount, I mount, into the sky :
> Sweet bird, to Petersburg I fly,
>   Or, if you bid, to Paris.
> Fresh missions for the *Fox and goose*
> Successful treaties may produce,
>   Though Pitt in all miscarries.'

[2] Matthew, fifth Baron Aylmer. At the death of Lord Whitworth, he assumed by royal permission the surname of Whitworth before that of Aylmer, and the arms of Whitworth in addition to those of Aylmer.

[3] Mme. de Gerebtsoff maintained that Lord Whitworth had promised he would marry her if ever she got a divorce from her husband.

consequence of it Anglophile in their tendencies and tastes, and Mme. de Gerebtsoff is said to have so far indulged her love of English fashions and of Sir Charles, as to substitute at his instigation the unheard-of innovation of late dining, according to the vogue of London, for the practice, then invariable at St. Petersburg, of dining at the early hour of 2.30.'[1]   Mme. Vigée le Brun tells how she and her daughter, being engaged to dine with that lady, arrived at 2.30, but that 'une heure, deux heures se passent . . . vers six heures ma pauvre fille et moi, nous étions tellement affamée . . . je me sentais tout-à-fait mourante.   Ce ne fut qu'à sept heures et demie qu'enfin l'on vint nous dire que l'on était servi ; mais nos pauvres estomacs avaient trop souffert.   Il nous fut impossible de manger—thanks to Sir Charles Whitworth.'

The Empress at last gave way to the solicitations of the British Minister and agreed to support the league against France. She also promised to join the English fleet with a squadron of twelve ships and eight frigates, and to provide at least 60,000 men in return for a large sum of money.   This treaty was 'justly regarded as a triumph for Whitworth's diplomacy,' though, unfortunately, just before the date fixed for its final ratification by both countries, the Empress Catherine II. died suddenly of apoplexy (February 1795).   Her son and successor, the Emperor Paul I., commonly called 'the mad Czar,' who hated the memory of his mother in consequence of the manner in which she had always treated him, set to work from the moment of his accession to reverse all Catherine's policy and to annul all her decisions.   One of his first acts, therefore, was to

---

[1] The Empress's hour for dining was earlier than this. Waliszewski tells us that 'up to the time of the Swedish war, dinner was at one o'clock ; afterwards the hour was put off till two, at which it remained.'

refuse to sign the treaty put forward by Sir Charles Whitworth, though the latter did later on manage to carry it through.

Among Paul's autocratic reforming ukases at this time was one forbidding the wearing of frock-coats, pantaloons, or round hats, the latter being his particular aversion. Whenever a round hat was seen it was snatched off by the police ; and Sir Charles says that he saw large numbers of persons of all grades bare-headed in the streets, the stock of privileged headgear not being equal to the demand. Sir Charles used his influence to get the ukase modified so far as it affected strangers, and the police were ordered merely to detain the wearer of a round hat till he proved he was not a Russian. There was a special decree passed by the Czar for the dress of Englishmen—namely, a three-cornered hat, a long queue with a curl at the end of it, a single-breasted coat and vest, buckles instead of latches at the knee-breeches and shoes.

Individually Paul was friendly to Sir Charles, who was included in many of the dinners and *petits soupers* given at the time of the coronation ; and at the Court balls, where it was not etiquette for the Ambassador to dance, we hear of him playing at piquet with the Empress. The now dethroned King of Poland, Stanislas, who lived at Grodno on a pension allowed him by the three sovereigns who had divided his kingdom, arrived in Petersburg at Paul's invitation, after thirty years' absence, to take part in the coronation, Stackelberg, formerly Ambassador to Poland, being nominated to act as his chamberlain. In the King's Journal he makes frequent mention of 'M. de Withwort,' who entertained, and was entertained by him.[1] Mme. Vigée le Brun in her 'Souvenirs' says she used constantly to meet

---

[1] Stanislas's dinners and suppers were most *recherché*, his *maître d'hôtel*, Fremeau, being famed. The ex-King was evidently a gourmet. Sir Charles Whitworth tells us of a supper given by Stanislas in honour of Princess Dolgo-rouki's birthday for which he (Sir Charles) provided 'the first oysters' which were

'Lord Wilford' at 'les petits soupers du Roi de Pologne,' where the Marquis de Rivière made up the *partie carrée*, and she says : 'Après le souper il s'établissait constamment une causerie charmante.' Sir Charles had staying with him his nephew, Mr. Lloyd, who also partook of Stanislas's hospitality. At Gaczyna, formerly the residence of Grégoire Orloff (one of Catherine's lovers), which was the Emperor's favourite residence, Sir Charles Whitworth was the only diplomat besides Count Dietrichstein invited to the Empress's fête ; Sir Charles stayed in the Palace with the King of Poland as the guest of the Emperor. He mentions an affecting incident which took place while he was there : when Stanislaus presented the Empress on her fête-day with a magnificent *objet d'art* which had formerly belonged to Marie Antoinette, the Princesse de Tarente (granddaughter of Louise de la Vallière), who was present, was much overcome and burst into tears. She was deeply attached to that unfortunate Queen and was herself in prison during the Reign of Terror. One of Robespierre's satellites said to her, " Si vous dites : Je hais la Reine, vous aurez votre liberté.' She answered, ' Je l'ai toujours aimée, aujourd'hui je l'adore.' At Moscow, during the coronation festivities, Sir Charles dined with King Stanislas and met Cobentzel, the Austrian Ambassador, Prince Repnin and his wife and daughter, and Princess Radziwill *née* Przezdziecka, and another night the King dined with Sir Charles, the remainder of the party being M. Tremo, Baron de Steding (Swedish Ambassador), the Chevalier Itorla (Portuguese minister), Count Dietrichstein, Baron de Leykam, and Mr. Lloyd. When Stanislas went to Kamienny-ostrow, which the Emperor had occupied during Catherine's life, and which he now gave to the

much appreciated. This supper appears to have been lively, and after it the Duke de Crussol sang a song in honour of the King of Poland.

LAWRENCE *pinx*

CHARLES, EARL WHITWORTH.

King of Poland as his summer residence, he sent for Sir Charles the first day to sup with him as well as Count Golowkin, M. Waleki, Cobentzel, Count Chreptowiez, and Prince and Princess Dolgorouki. Sir Charles says they all went *en chaloupe*, followed by another full of musicians. Early the next year the *ci-devant* king died somewhat suddenly of apoplexy brought on by his long-continued worries.

In 1798 Sir Charles 'obtained the adhesion of the Czar to an alliance with Great Britain, with the object of putting a stop to the encroachments of France ;' but on the British seizure of Malta, Paul grew furious and abruptly dismissed the English Ambassador. He wanted to become Grand Master quite as much from the desire of appearing in a picturesque dress before his latest fancy, Princess Lapoukine, as from any political consideration, and he actually sat on his throne several times in this costume.

Mrs. Richard Trench tells the following ridiculous story in her 'Remains': 'One assigned cause for Sir Charles Whitworth's disgrace with the Court of Russia is curious. The Emperor had given orders no empty carriage should pass a certain part of the palace. Sir Charles, ignorant of this, had left his coach to speak with a workman, and desired it might drive on and meet him at a distance. The sentinel stopped the carriage, the servants insisted on driving on, a scuffle ensued. The Emperor, ever on the watch about trifles, inquired into the cause of the dispute, and, on learning it, ordered the servants to be beat, the horses to be beat, and the coach to be beat (Xerxes lashing the sea). Sir Charles Whitworth, by way of washing off this stain, ordered the servants to be discharged, his horses to be shot, his carriage, after being broken into a thousand pieces, to be thrown into the river. The Emperor, indignant at this mark of offended pride, insisted on his recall.'

On his return from Russia Sir Charles was created, on March 21, 1800, a peer of Ireland by the title of Baron Whitworth of Newton Pratt, in the county of Galway, and soon after he was sent as Plenipotentiary Extraordinary to Copenhagen on a special mission, the seizure of a Danish frigate having induced strained relations with that Court. The mission was backed by a strong squadron. After a considerable time elapsed in discussion, an adjustment at last took place in August 1800, and Lord Whitworth returned to England.

Soon after his arrival in London he presented himself to the Duchess of Dorset, whom he did not know before. She was the widow of his friend John Frederick, Duke of Dorset (who had died the year previously), and was thirty-three years of age, the daughter of Sir Charles Cope, Bart., of Brewerne, by Catherine, sister of Lord De La Zouche, and was rich as well as good-looking,[1] 'a capable woman,' says Wraxall, 'with a taste for power and pleasure.' Lord Whitworth was now forty-eight years of age, and a very handsome man, described as noble-looking and commanding in person, and combining the most dignified deportment with the most conciliating manner. So far as his looks are concerned, this account is certainly justified by the canvas of Sir Thomas Lawrence, who painted him more than once.[2] After a short courtship they became engaged, and were married by special licence at Dorset House, Whitehall, on April 7, 1801. The Duchess's income was thirteen thousand a year, and she held the borough of East Grinstead for life, and eventually Dorset House and Knole, and another nine thousand a year passed into her hands.[3]

[1] There are two portraits of her at Knole: one by Madame Le Brun, and a full-length by Hoppner. Isabey also did a lovely one of her.

[2] One of these portraits is at Knole, one at Swallowfield, and one at the Louvre.

[3] In a letter from Lady Wellesley to her husband, she says: 'The race of the Duchesses is run, and Dorset is the winner,' alluding to the fact that two other Duchesses, Leeds and Newcastle, were in the running!

ARABELLA DIANA, DUCHESS OF DORSET.
WIFE OF CHARLES, EARL WHITWORTH.
From a Painting by Isabey, now in the possession of S Neumann, Esq.

Meanwhile, according to some accounts, the Princess Gerebtsoff had succeeded in procuring her divorce, and was on her way to England. At Leipzig she read in a newspaper that Lord Whitworth's marriage to the Duchess of Dorset was expected to take place shortly. She hurried forward, but when she arrived in London she learnt that she was too late. The fair Russian was very irate, and her protestations became so great that Lord Whitworth had to buy her off with £10,000.[1]

In 1802 Lord Whitworth, having been previously sworn of the Privy Council, was appointed Ambassador and Plenipotentiary to the French Republic, and in November proceeded to Paris, accompanied by the Duchess and her children, Mr. Talbot (the secretary of Embassy), Mr. Mandeville (secretary), Mr. Hodgson (chaplain), and Dr. Maclaurin.

Colonel Whitworth, Lord Whitworth's brother, and Captain the Hon. Edward Pierrepont, also formed part of Lord Whitworth's staff. The Embassy was in the Caraman mansion, Faubourg du Roule, and Maria Edgeworth, in writing to Mrs. Sneyd from Paris in November 1802, says: 'It is a singular circumstance that Lord Whitworth, the new Ambassador, has brought to Paris the same horses and the same wife, and lives in the same house, as the last Ambassador did eleven years ago' (she alludes to the Duke of Dorset).

On November 10, writing from Calais, Lord Whitworth says: 'We arrived here this day at three o'clock after a pleasant passage of four hours and a half. We were received on our landing by an immense concourse of people, and with much huzzaing. The guns were fired and flags displayed. When we

---

[1] This lady died at an advanced age, having amassed an immense fortune. Another account of her visit to London is quite different, and says she came with her husband !

arrived at our Inn, where I found a Captain's guard mounted, I was complimented by the constituted authorities, consisting of the Mayor, the Commissary-General Margand, the Juge de Paix, &c., then came General Barbasande at the head of the officers of the garrison, and after them the " poissardes " with a present of fish—in short nothing was wanting. After dinner we were formally invited to assist at the theatre, in order, as it was said by the Mayor, that the public might have an opportunity of seeing what had been so long and ardently desired, an English Ambassador in France. We could not resist an invitation on such grounds, and we were received with great enthusiasm. " God save the King " was struck up and played for a quarter of an hour, but almost drowned by the applause of the whole house, who followed our example of standing up while it was playing, in the good old English fashion.'

Six days later Lord Whitworth writes from Paris announcing his arrival and describing his visit to Talleyrand. He says : ' Were it permitted to judge of his disposition by the manner in which he received me, and by the terms in which he answered the assurances I gave him of the conciliatory tendency of my instructions, I might look forward to some degree of satisfaction in my intercourse with him. I communicated to him a copy of my credentials, and upon my requesting that he would take the First Consul's orders on the subject of my presentation, he told me that he did not apprehend that there would be any opportunity until the regular day of presentation, which is in something less than three weeks.' The First Consul did, however, see Lord Whitworth one day sooner than the usual reception day, the ceremonial being as follows. The First Consul sent three of his carriages : one, with six horses, conveyed Lord Whitworth and a Prefect of the Palace ; the other two carriages, drawn by four horses, conveyed Mr. Talbot and the gentlemen attached to the Embassy; and Lord Whitworth's own carriage, drawn by six horses, followed empty. 'In this order,' says Lord Whitworth, 'I set out on Sunday last for the Tuileries, and was conducted to the Audience Chamber, at the upper end of which stood the First Consul with the Second[1] and Third[2] Consuls on his right and left,—the Ministers, Generals, &c., behind him, and the Corps Diplomatique in a circle in front. I was led through the open space thus formed, by M. Talleyrand, Minister for Foreign Affairs, and two Prefects of the Palace to the First Consul, and in presenting my credentials made use of the following expressions: " J'ai l'honneur, Général Premier Consul, de vous présenter la lettre de creánce du Roi mon maître en qualité de son Ambassadeur Extraordinaire et Plénipotentaire auprès de la République française. Je vous prie d'ajouter foi aux sentiments qui y sont exprimés. Vous n'y trouverez, Général Premier Consul, que le désir sincère du Roi mon maître de maintenir avec vous les relations de paix et d'amitié." After the First Consul had received the credentials, and delivered them to M. Talleyrand, he replied: " Je suis très sensible à ce que vous venez me dire des sentiments du Roi, et je vous prie d'assurer Sa Majesté que je désire ardemment avec elle, non seulement la paix, mais la meilleure intelligence. J'espère que lorsqu'on me connaîtra mieux, on me rendra la justice d'être persuadé de ma sincérité. Je répète toujours, c'est de la paix entre nos deux grandes nations que dépend le bonheur du monde." He then asked me a few questions about my journey, and I fell back in the circle, where the English gentlemen who were to be presented were placed. In a few minutes he came round, and after conversing for a short time on indifferent subjects, I

[1] Cambacérès.   [2] Lebrun.

presented, one after the other, six-and-thirty persons.   He
spoke a few words to each, and when he had done, on my
apologising for having given him so much trouble, he addressed
himself to the English collectively, and said: "Messieurs, je suis
charmé de vous voir ici ; je désire que vous vous y amusiez,
et qu'en retournant chez vous, vous emportiez l'assurance de
l'estime de cette nation pour la vôtre, et que leur bonne
intelligence est nécessaire à la tranquillité du monde. . . ."
We then proceeded to the apartment of Madame Bonaparte,
where I was presented by the Prefect.   She received us very
affably, but with a great deal of embarrassment.   From thence I
was conducted home, where I found an invitation to dine at six
o'clock at the First Consul's.   I accordingly went there with
Mr. Merry.[1]   At this dinner were present Madame Bonaparte,
the family of the First Consul, and her own, with several ladies
attached to her person, the Foreign Ministers and their wives,
and about two hundred and fifty others.   After this dinner,
which did not last above half an hour, the First Consul repeated
in conversation the substance of what he had said to me
more formally in the morning, and talked a considerable
time of indifferent matters, with the greatest ease and affability.
I yesterday, in compliance with what was signified to me as the
established etiquette, made a visit to the Second and Third
Consuls, sending previously to them to fix a time, and then
to the individuals of the First Consul's family—to Joseph,
Lucien, Louis, his mother, and a sister.   I left my name with
them as well as with the Ministers of the country, &c. &c.
A few days later the Duchess of Dorset was introduced to
the First Consul and Madame Bonaparte at St. Cloud.   She was
received with every possible mark of civility and attention.   The

---

[1] The British Agent.

Prefect-in-Waiting (the Master of the Ceremonies of this country) was ready to receive her on stepping from the carriage, and conducted her upstairs into the apartment where the circle was awaiting the arrival of the First Consul. The fauteuil next to Madame Bonaparte was kept vacant for her. . . . I have already begun my round of dinners. The Duchess has received and returned a visit to M. Talleyrand, and, furthermore, intends to accept the invitation, which she has received conjointly with me, to dine with M. Talleyrand. This will be a great diplomatique dinner, and of course no person admitted but such as the Duchess of Dorset can meet with propriety. The same might not be, perhaps, the case at other times or in other places ; but we have thought that the line which we are disposed to draw with regard to society should not extend to the house of the Minister for Foreign Affairs, with whom it is my duty to be chiefly in relation, and the more particularly when the lady who presides in his house bears his name, and is in fact married to him, as far as the sanction of the Romish Church can make such a marriage lawful.'[1]

After numerous preliminary conferences with Talleyrand on the subject of the retention of Malta by the English Government, Bonaparte sent for Lord Whitworth on February 17, and a long and important interview took place, which was unsatisfactory to both. Napoleon talked incessantly for upwards of two hours, flying from one subject to another, and scarcely ever gave Lord Whitworth an opportunity of saying a word ; the latter, however, did not attempt to press his arguments, as he saw the First Consul was losing his temper. In giving an account of this interview, Lord Whitworth says : 'The First Consul received me in his cabinet at the Tuileries with tolerable

[1] Talleyrand married Mme. Grandt.

cordiality, and after talking on different subjects for a few minutes he desired me to sit down, as he himself did on the other side of the table, upon which he placed his elbows and began. He told me that he felt it necessary, after what had passed between me and M. de Talleyrand, that he should in the most clear and authentic manner make known his sentiments to me in order to their being communicated to his Majesty. He said that it was a matter of infinite disappointment to him that the Treaty of Amiens, instead of being followed by conciliation and friendship, had been productive only of continual and increasing jealousy. He now enumerated the several provocations which he pretended to have received from England. He placed in the first line our not evacuating Malta and Alexandria as we were bound to do by the treaty. In this he said that no consideration on earth should make him acquiesce, and of the two he had rather see us in possession of the Faubourg St. Antoine than Malta. He then adverted to the abuse thrown out against him in the English public prints, but this he said he did not so much regard as that which appeared in the French papers published in London.[1] . . . He now went back to Egypt, and told me that if he had felt the smallest inclination to take possession of it by force he might have done it a month ago, &c. . . .'

A few days later Lord Whitworth tells us he had a most interesting conversation with Joseph Bonaparte in which he deplored in very strong terms the calamities which the question

---

[1] A few days after Lord Whitworth received by the *petite poste* a copy of the *Courrier de Londres*, containing a most violent attack against the First Consul and his family, and the following words were written in a disguised hand on the margin of the paper : ' Il faut qu'un ministère ait bien peu d'honneur et de bonne politique pour payer de pareilles infamies, et lorsqu'en même tems on envoie un ambassadeur à Paris, c'est une lâcheté ;' and Lord Whitworth believed that this was written by the First Consul.

of Malta was likely to draw down upon France, and said that the determination of the First Consul was fixed, and that all the reasoning of his friends was unavailing. Three days later, on Sunday, March 13, occurred the celebrated scene between Napoleon and Lord Whitworth. The generally received version of what took place is that Napoleon got so violent that Lord Whitworth expected to be struck, and that in that case the Ambassador was prepared to run his sword through the body of the First Consul ; but we have not only Napoleon's but Lord Whitworth's account of what occurred, which shows this to be considerably exaggerated. Barry O'Meara says : ' I asked him [Napoleon] his opinion of Lord Whitworth. " Un homme habile, un intrigant," said he, " a man of address—un bel homme—your Ministers had no reason to complain of him, for he answered their purposes well. The account which was published by your Ministers of his interview with me was plein de faussetés. No violence of manner or impropriety of language was used by me. The ambassadors could not conceal their surprise when they read such a mass of misrepresentations, and publicly pronounced it to be false. His wife, the Duchess of Dorset, was greatly disliked by the English in Paris. They said publicly that she was *sotte* with pride. There was much disagreement between her and many English ladies about presentation at Court. She refused to introduce any who had not previously been presented at St. James's.'

Lord Whitworth's account written to Lord Hawkesbury [1] is as follows :

' Paris : March 14, 1803.

' Until yesterday, Sunday, I saw no one likely to give me

---

[1] Lord Hawkesbury, then Minister for Foreign Affairs, afterwards Earl of Liverpool and Prime Minister, died early in 1827.

any information as to the effect which his Majesty's message had had on the temper of the First Consul. I was, however, on that day a witness of, and in some degree a sufferer by, its violence. At the Court which was held at the Tuileries, and the which I attended for the purpose of introducing some English gentlemen and ladies to Madame Bonaparte, he accosted me, evidently under very considerable agitation. He began by asking me if I had any news from England. I told him that I had received letters from your Lordship two days ago. He immediately said, "So you are determined to go to war." "No, Premier Consul," I replied, " we are too sensible of the advantage of peace." " Nous avons," said he, " déjà fait la guerre pendant quinze ans." As he seemed to wait for an answer, I observed only, " C'en est déjà trop." " Mais," said he, " vous voulez la faire encore quinze années et vous m'y forcez." I told him that was very far from his Majesty's intentions. He then proceeded to Count Marcoff and the Chevalier Azzara, who were standing together at a little distance from me, and said to them—" Les Anglais veulent la guerre, mais s'ils sont les premiers à tirer l'épée, je serai le dernier à la remettre. Ils ne respectent pas les traités. Il faut dorénavant les couvrir de crêpe noir." I suppose he meant the treaties. He then went his round, and was thought by all those to whom he addressed himself to betray great signs of irritation. In a few minutes he came back to me, to my great annoyance, and resumed the conversation, if such it can be called, by something personally civil to me. He then began again : " Pourquoi des armements ? contre qui des mesures de précaution ? Je n'ai pas un seul vaisseau de ligne dans les ports de France, mais si vous voulez armer, j'armerai aussi ; si vous voulez vous battre, je me battrai aussi. Vous pourrez peut-être tuer la France, mais jamais l'intimider." " On ne voudrait," said I, " ni l'un ni l'autre. On voudrait vivre en bonne intelligence avec elle." " Il faut donc respecter les traités," replied he ; " malheur à ceux qui ne respectent pas les traités l Ils en seront responsables à toute l'Europe." He was too agitated to make it advisable to prolong the conversation ; I therefore made no answer, and he retired to his apartment repeating the last phrase. It is to be remarked that all this passed loud enough to be overheard by 200 people who were present. I was fortunate enough not to be betrayed into anything imprudent or which could be misconstrued ; I am persuaded that there was not a single person who did not feel the extreme impropriety of his conduct and the total want of dignity as well as of decency on the occasion. I propose taking the first opportunity of telling M. de Talleyrand that I go to the Tuileries to pay my respects to the First Consul and to Madame Bonaparte, but if I am to be attacked there in that public manner by the First Consul, on topics which are made to be discussed in the Cabinet, I must refrain from presenting myself there until I have assurances that the same thing will not happen to me again.'

Sir Walter Scott says : ' It would have been more prudent in Napoleon to have left the conduct of the negotiation to Talleyrand . . . the character of the English Ambassador was as unfavourable for the Chief Consul's probable purpose (to browbeat down all arguments) as that of the nation he represented. Lord Whitworth was possessed of great experience and sagacity. His integrity and honour were undoubted ; and, with the highest degree of courage, he had a calm and collected disposition, admirably calculated to give him the advantage in any discussion with an antagonist of a fiery, impatient, and overbearing temper.'

The following description of what took place on this occasion was written in 1852 by the Rev. J. Sanford who was present, and coincides with those given by Lord Whitworth and by Napoleon. He says : 'I send you an account of the very memorable scene which occurred at Madame Bonaparte's drawing-room on the 13th March, 1803. I believe I am the only living witness, as those who were near the person of Lord Whitworth were members of the Corps Diplomatique, Cobenzl, Marcoff, Lucchesini, all dead. Many years after, I became intimately acquainted with the Marchese Lucchesini at Florence, when I had an opportunity of referring to that remarkable conversation. It was announced that Madame Bonaparte was to receive on the following Sunday, and it was reported that she was to have maids of honour for the first time ; a little curiosity was excited on this score. The apartment of Madame B. was on the opposite side of the Tuileries in which Bonaparte held his levées. I was acquainted with Lord Whitworth, who told me to place myself near to him, in order to afford facility for presentation, as Madame B. would occupy an armchair to which he pointed and on each side of which were two tabourets. As all foreigners had been presented to General B. at his levée, his presence was not expected. The rooms, two in number, were not very large ; the ladies were seated round the rooms in armchairs ; a passage was left, I suppose for Madame B. to pass without obstacle. When the door of the adjoining room was opened, instead of Madame B. the First Consul entered, and as Lord Whitworth was the first Ambassador he encountered, he addressed him by inquiring about the Duchess of Dorset's health, she being absent from a cold. He then observed that we had had fifteen years' war ; Lord W. smiled very courteously, and said it was fifteen years too much. We shall probably, replied General B., have fifteen years more ; and if so, England will have to answer for it to all Europe, and to God and man. He then inquired where the armaments in Holland were going on, for he knew of none. Then for a moment he quitted Lord Whitworth, and passed all the ladies, addressing Mrs. Greathead only, though the Duchess of Gordon and her daughter, Lady Georgina, were present. After speaking to several officers in the centre of the room, which was crowded, he returned to Lord W. and asked why Malta was not given up. Lord W. then looked more serious, and said he had no doubt that Malta would be given up when the other articles of the Treaty were complied with. General B. then left the room, and Madame B. immediately entered. As soon as the drawing-room was over, I observed to Lord W. that it was the first Cabinet Council I had ever witnessed ; he laughingly answered, by far the most numerously attended. Lord W. then addressed the American Minister who was very deaf, and repeated what had passed, and I perceived that he was very much offended at what had occurred. In justice to the First Consul, I must say that the impropriety consisted in the unfitness of the place for such a subject ; the tone of his voice was not raised, as was said at the time. He spoke in the same tone as when he inquired for the Duchess of Dorset.'

Lord Whitworth had one other interview with Bonaparte on April 3, concerning which he says : ' The Corps Diplomatique were assembled at one o'clock for the purpose of paying their compliments to the First Consul. He was, however, occupied from that time till five in the evening in inspecting the knapsacks of about eight thousand men assembled in the court of the Tuileries ! When that ceremony was performed he received us, and I had every reason to be satisfied with his manner towards me.'

From this time the communications between the two govern-

ments were formal and constrained and limited exclusively to
the question concerning Malta. Lord Whitworth agreed to
lower England's claim of retaining that island in perpetuity to
that of holding it for ten years, provided the First Consul made
no opposition to the cession by the King of Sicily to the English
of the island of Lampedusa if that King could be persuaded to
cede it for a valuable consideration. Bonaparte, however, would
not listen to any modification of the Treaty of Amiens. In the
Times of May 7 we read as follows : 'The painful task which
we have for some days considered as almost inevitable, falls upon
us this day ; and it is our duty to announce, that all the efforts
and forbearance of ministers, all that patience and conciliation for
which they have been so unjustly blamed, have not been able to
avert the calamity of WAR. General Andreossi has applied for
his passport to Lord Hawkesbury, in order that he may take his
departure for Dover immediately, and may reach Calais by the
time Lord Whitworth arrives at Dover.' On the night of
May 12 Lord Whitworth left Paris, and on the 18th Britain
declared war against France.

Lord Whitworth had made all arrangements for leaving a
week sooner,[1] but at the last moment, and after their friends had
taken leave of them, at twelve o'clock at night when Lord
Whitworth and the Duchess were waiting for their passports,
Mr. Huber being with them, a servant came into the room to
say that some one wished to speak to Mr. Huber. On descend-
ing to the street the latter found Regnault St. Jean d'Angély
in his carriage, who said that he came from Joseph Bonaparte

[1] We read in the *Times* of May 9 : 'The information given in our paper of
Saturday of the unexpected stay of Lord Whitworth at Paris, produced an extraordinary and immediate sensation in the City. The Committee for managing the
Stock Exchange would not suffer business to proceed till the truth of our intelligence could be ascertained. At their instance the Lord Mayor addressed a note

to make, through Mr. Huber,[1] a proposal to the Ambassador which, if he agreed to, might bring the business to a conclusion in the course of a few hours, and this was that Malta should be put into the hands of the Emperor of Russia. Lord Whitworth says : ' Mr. Huber came upstairs to communicate to me this proposal, and I can take no great merit to myself for having immediately and without the smallest hesitation declined it.'

On the declaration of war all Englishmen in France between the ages of eighteen and sixty were constituted prisoners of war and ordered to be detained for twelve years, and unless *détenus* gave their parole to abide in certain towns assigned to them, they were confined to prison.[2] The two packet-boats sent from Dover for the remainder of the English Embassy were seized and the crews imprisoned. In the midst of the commotion and distress caused by this state of affairs, it is amusing to read in a letter from Mr. Talbot to Lord Whitworth sent from France with a French flag of truce, that although the members of the Embassy were detained *nolentes volentes*, 'the parcel containing the Duchess's dress for the King's birthday is embarked and will leave Calais that evening.'

The *Times* tells us that at Lord Whitworth's departure a number of persons, whom curiosity or a juster interest had

to Lord Hawkesbury soliciting information. To this note the Chancellor of the Exchequer, Henry Addington, wrote a vague reply cautioning the Lord Mayor against receiving impressions through any unauthorised channels.'

[1] Mr. Huber was a connection of Necker. He belonged to a Swiss family long settled at Lyons.

[2] Lord Elgin, late Ambassador at the Porte, who was in a bad state of health, was one of these *détenus* at Pau. He was arrested, and confined in the Château de Lourdes, a few leagues from Barèges. Lady Elgin applied to the First Consul for his release, to which he would only agree on condition that a French General (Boyer) on parole in England should be given up in exchange. To this the English Government could not consent ; so after some weeks, during which Lord Elgin was treated with great severity, he was allowed to return to Pau.

assembled together, were affected even to tears ; and his lordship certainly quitted the unfortunate capital of France amid the regrets of the people.

For the next ten years Lord Whitworth remained in retirement, the greater part of his time being spent at Knole, where he was most popular and esteemed by all around him, both high and low. When the country was threatened with invasion, he raised and clothed at his own expense 600 men, called the ' Holmesdale Battalion of Infantry,' and he frequently repaired to their headquarters at Maidstone.

In March 1813 he was made Lord of the Bedchamber, in June created a peer of Great Britain by the title of Viscount Whitworth of Adbaston, co. Staffordshire, and at the same time appointed Lord Lieutenant of Ireland in succession to Charles Lennox, fourth Duke of Richmond. Two years later he was promoted to the Grand Cross of the Bath and created Baron Adbaston and Earl Whitworth of Adbaston.

In Ireland Lord Whitworth's reign was, says Mr. O'Connor Morris, ' much troubled by disturbance and agitation, the result of the tithe collection, which was made sometimes with hardship, while its incidence was unfair, the poorer tenants being more severely mulcted than the wealthier sheep and cattle farmers. The peasant soldiers in this campaign against tithe were known as ' Caravats ' and ' Shanavests,' while in the King's County the opponents of the system adopted the abominable practice of ' carding.' Hence it was necessary to renew the Insurrection Act. Meanwhile the agitation for complete Catholic emancipation was proceeding. It was in Lord Whitworth's time that the famous duel took place between O'Connell and D'Esterre, when the latter was killed, the scene of the duel being Bishop's Court, now the residence of Lord Clonmell, but then the property of Lord Ponsonby.

Lord Whitworth's tenure of the Viceregal office was saddened by the terrible domestic catastrophe which occurred a fortnight after this duel. The young Duke of Dorset, who had been as his own son ever since he was seven years old, on leaving Oxford at the end of 1814 joined Lord Whitworth and his mother in Dublin. On February 13, 1815, he went to pay a few days' visit to his friend and schoolfellow Lord Powerscourt, and the day after went out with Lord Powerscourt's harriers round Killiney, mounted on a well-trained Irish mare and accompanied by Lord Powerscourt and Mr. Wingfield. Having been out for several hours without finding anything, they were actually on the point of returning home when a hare sprang up and the chase commenced. They had gone but a short distance, when the Duke, who was an excellent horseman, rode at a wall. The mare cleared it, but alighting among some large stones on the other side, turned headlong in the air and came down upon her rider, who had not lost his seat, and he was thus crushed with his back on a large stone and the mare on his chest. She at length disentangled herself and galloped away. The Duke sprang upon his feet, saying he believed he was not much hurt, and attempted to follow her, but soon fell into the arms of a Mr. Farrel who had come to his assistance, and to whose house he was conveyed. Lord Powerscourt, leaving his brother to look after the Duke, rode full speed to Dublin to get a surgeon, but before Messrs. Crampton and Macklin could reach him, life was extinct. He lived about an hour after his fall and suffered no pain.

The young Duke is described as having been endowed with great judgment and penetration, possessing, with the accomplishments of a perfect gentleman, all the qualities of an honest man, gentle and engaging manners, and warm and steady in his affections. The Dean of Christ Church lamented his departure from the University as 'the loss of an example of all that was amiable and proper.'[1] At Harrow the Duke was fag to Lord Byron, and had been, Lord Byron tells us, 'his frequent companion in many rambles.' In the 'Hours of Idleness' there is a poem addressed to the Duke, written while they were both at Harrow, on the eve of Lord Byron's leaving. It commences with the following lines :

> D–r–t ! whose early steps with mine have stray'd,
> Exploring every path of Ida's glade,
> Whom still affection taught me to defend,
> And made me less a tyrant than a friend ;
> Though the harsh custom of our youthful band
> Bade *thee* obey, and gave *me* to command.

After giving him much good advice, Lord Byron goes on to say :

> Yes ! I have mark'd thee many a passing day,
> But now new scenes invite me far away ;
> Yes ! I have mark'd within that generous mind
> A soul, if well matured, to bless mankind.
> Ah ! though myself by nature haughty, wild,
> Whom Indiscretion hail'd her favourite child ;
> Though every error stamps me for her own,
> And dooms my fall, I fain would fall alone ;
> Though my proud heart no precept now can tame,
> I love the virtues which I cannot claim.
>
> .   .   .   .
>
> Fain would I view thee, with prophetic eyes,
> Exalted more among the good and wise ;
> A glorious and a long career pursue,
> As first in rank, the first in talent too ;
> Spurn every vice, each little meanness shun ;
> Not Fortune's minion, but her noblest son.
>
> .   .   .   .

[1] Mr. Gregory, writing to announce his death to Mr. Peel, says : He was surely a most inimitable young man in every good quality.'

H DRIDGE, *pinx*

GEORGE JOHN FREDERICK, 4TH DUKE OF DORSET.

The hour draws nigh, a few brief days will close,
To me, this little scene of joys and woes ;
Each knell of Time now warns me to resign
Shades, where Hope, Peace, and Friendship all were mine :
Hope, that could vary like the rainbow's hue,
And gild their pinions as the moments flew ;
Peace, that reflection never frown'd away,
By dreams of ill to cloud some future day ;
Friendship, whose truth let childhood only tell ;
Alas ! they love not long, who love so well.
To these adieu ! nor let me linger o'er
Scenes hail'd, as exiles hail their native shore,
Receding slowly through the dark-blue deep,
Beheld by eyes that mourn, yet cannot weep.

   .   .   .   .

D–r–t ! farewell ! I will not ask one part
Of sad remembrance in so young a heart ;
The coming morrow from thy youthful mind
Will sweep my name, nor leave a trace behind.
. . . but let me cease the lengthen'd strain,—
Oh ! if these wishes are not breathed in vain,
The guardian seraph who directs thy fate
Will leave thee glorious, as he found thee great.

Moore also wrote some lines of sympathy to the Duchess on the
occasion of his death :

> We saw the hope you cherished
>   For one short hour appear,
> And when that hope had perished
>   We gave you tear for tear.

The Duke's family honours devolved, at his death, upon his
cousin Charles Germaine (son of Viscount Sackville), who became
fifth Duke of Dorset, but died in 1843 unmarried, when the
title became extinct and the representation of the family devolved

upon the two stepdaughters of Lord Whitworth—Lady Mary, married first to the Earl of Plymouth and secondly to Earl Amherst, and died without children in 1864 ; and Lady Elizabeth, married in 1813 to George John, fifth Earl De La Warr. She died 1870, leaving five sons and three daughters : (1) Charles Richard, sixth Earl De La Warr, d.s.p. 1873 ; (2) Reginald, seventh Earl De La Warr, father of the present Earl ; (3) Mortimer, created Baron Sackville ; (4) Lionel, present Lord Sackville ; (5) William Edward ; (6) Mary, married first to second Marquis of Salisbury and secondly to Edward, fifteenth Earl of Derby ; (7) Elizabeth, married ninth Duke of Bedford ; (8) Lady Arabella Diana, married 1860 to Sir Alexander Bannerman, Bart.

At the close of the year 1815 Lord Whitworth's health began to give way ; and in February 1817 Mr. Gregory writes to Peel that he is anxious about him, and says : ' Every public consideration, every private feeling make Lord Whitworth an object of most anxious solicitude.   He has made an excellent rule of not dining with any one, yet he is more in representation with his own dinners, drawing rooms, &c.' [1]   In October of that year Lord Whitworth left Dublin and took up his residence at Knole.   Lord Talbot,[2] writing thence some little time after, says : ' I returned to-day from Knole, where you will be glad to hear I found our amiable friend as well in health and spirits as I ever saw him.   He rides 2 or 3 hours without fatigue, eats a hearty dinner, and sleeps perfectly well ; you will scarcely believe that he again weighs 13st. 2lbs., his former weight.   'Tis to me

---

[1] ' Lord Whitworth entertained with great splendour.'—*Mr. Gregory's Letterbox*.

[2] Earl Talbot succeeded Lord Whitworth as Lord Lieutenant of Ireland in 1817, and was himself recalled in December 1821 and replaced by Lord Wellesley.

the most delightful part of my existence that I pass with him. To know Lord Whitworth is to love him.'

In 1819, after the restoration of the Bourbons, Lord Whitworth with the Duchess revisited Paris; and though he went in no official capacity, his visit was generally supposed to combine a mission of observation. While there he visited both Louis XVIII. and the Princes. In the following October he and the Duchess went again to Paris on their way to Naples, and at the latter place they were received with great distinction. In 1820 they were again settled at Knole, and in June the following year Lord Talbot writes: 'I have just left our friend Lord Whitworth and the Duchess. Of the latter I will only say I never saw her better. Of the former, he is well, but quantum mutatus ab illo! I am happy to think he is perfectly cheerful, with a comfortable flow of spirits, good appetite, and enjoying the comforts of life, the sight of his friends, &c., but he is much reduced, and he seems to want energy and his usual vigour of body. Yet I do not apprehend any change, and if the summer ever gets like itself, I should hope he will rally sufficiently to make a successful stand against the rude attacks of winter. I thought we did him good—Slade, the Verulams, Drummond and I, the party.'

Lord Whitworth's last public appearance was in July 1821, when he assisted at the coronation of George IV. as 'Assistant Lord Sewer.'

In March 1824 Lord Talbot writes: 'Our friends in Grosvenor Square are particularly well; indeed Lord Whitworth is better than I have seen him for many years. He is lively, upright, riding out in all weathers, and looking younger than ever.[1] I dined in company with him at Lord Camden's yester-

---

[1] Lord Whitworth was now seventy-two years of age.

day, to meet the Duke of York.' Five months later he writes
that Lord Whitworth was sadly feeble and had gone to Sandgate.
And in May of the following year Lord Whitworth died, after
an illness of only three days, from an attack of indigestion
following on gout.

Lord Talbot thus announces his death to Mr. Gregory :

'May 15, 1825.

'It is with a bleeding heart that I communicate to you
(although you have probably heard it before) the departure from
this world to a better, of our dear friend Lord Whitworth.
"He was taken ill on Wednesday and expired on Friday evening.
He had suffered much, but expired without a struggle. He
was conscious up to the last and was not aware of his situation."
Thus writes Plymouth from Knole.

'I will not attempt the description of my feelings on this
painful occasion. They are such as will be common to you and
to his friends. A greater private loss cannot be imagined.
Honest, upright, and sincere, he was a pattern to his equals ;
benevolent, humane, and affectionate, his loss will be felt by all
classes. In him I lose a second father, a friend in whose honest
judgement I always could depend, and a Minister in whose
indulgence my failings always found a lenient judge. May we,
my dear Gregory, be allowed to meet him and others who have
preceded us, in regions of happiness, never again to be separated.
May God bless you and yours, and believe me always your truly
attached and affectionate

'TALBOT.'

Lord Whitworth was buried at Sevenoaks Church, where,
on the north wall, there is a 'magnificent monument' to his
memory, the work of J. S. Carew. All the country round, far

EDRIDGE, *pinx*

CHARLES, EARL WHITWORTH.

and wide, bore testimony to his high deserts by the crowds that
sorrowed at his grave. It was said at the time that 'in all the
private relations of life Lord Whitworth was most exemplary,
charitable and generous to the poor, benevolent to all classes,
affable to his equals, and was justly considered a pattern to
English noblemen.'

Lord Whitworth left the Duchess his universal legatee, his
personalty being under £70,000. She did not survive him
three months ; she died August 1 following, and was buried on
the 10th at Withyam, near East Grinstead.[1]

---

[1] The *Annual Register* says that besides 160 of the tenants, 22 horsemen
attended the remains of this lady, and that the expenses of the funeral amounted
to £2,000.

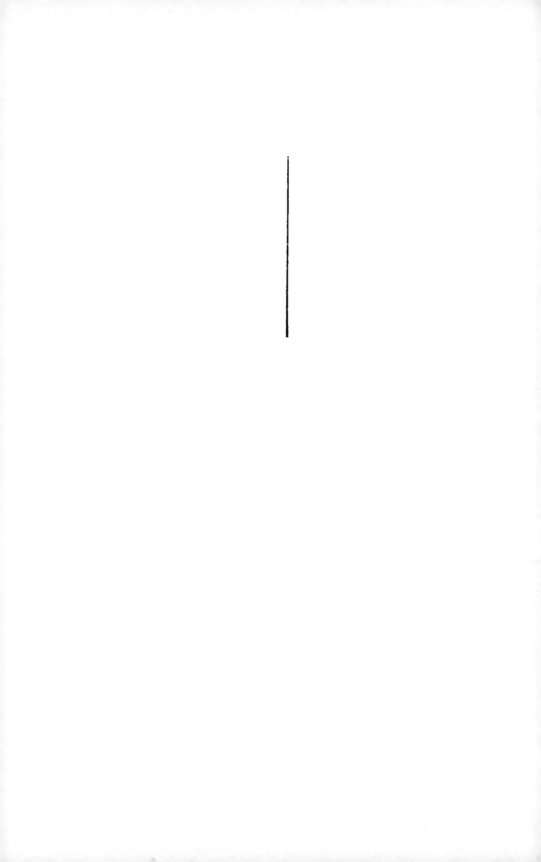

Illud enim in Nostris nunquam delebile Nomen
  Imponet Fastis quo super astra voles.
Gloria Virtutum Comes indivulsa sequetur,
  Teq; feret meritis Fama sonora tubis.
Quisquis es ? hæc tacita tecum si mente revolves
  In tumulis etiam tædia nulla feres.

EPITAPHIUM.

Maximus exiguo jacet hoc sub marmore Præsul,
  Quam parva ingentem contegit urna virum !
Doctrina clarus, nulli pietate secundus ;
  Exemplar seræ posteritatis erit.
Inter opes hic vixit inops ; dum viveret Astris :
  Hinc transmisit opes pauperis ore, manu.

Obiit die 6 Mensis *Julii.* Anno MDCLXXXIV.

PAGE 103, LINE 1.

The family of Geraghty of Connaught is of ancient Irish descent, of the same race as the O'Conors, Kings of Connaught. The name is derived from 'Oireachtach,' signifying 'The Man of the Territory,' Henry Mac Oiraghty was Bishop of Achonry 1296, and David Mac Oiraghty, Archbishop of Armagh, died A.D. 1343. The name was gradually anglicised MacGeraghty or Geraghty. The arms are : Arg. on a mount vert, an oak tree proper in chief, two falcons volant gules ; Crest, on a mount vert an oak tree proper, broken towards the dexter.

In the 'Will-books' there is a brief entry of the brothers and sisters of Richard Geraghty. Of the sisters, one, Elinor Geraghty, made her will March 16, 1719, and another, 'Sarah, was wife of Bryan Gunning, Esq., of Castle Coote, co. Roscommon.'

PAGE 123, LINE 1.

The Duchess of Hamilton went on the 'Catherine' royal yacht and the Duchess of Ancaster on the 'Mary,' and they sailed from Harwich.

There 'are two engravings of these yachts by P. L. Cano, after paintings done on the spot by T. Allen.

PAGE 146, LINE 22.

Letter from Andrew Stuart, one of Lady Betty's guardians, to Baron Mure, also her guardian, June 24, 1774 : 'Dear Baron, For some time past, you could hardly expect to hear from me until the marriage ceremony was over, especially if you had any notion of the hurry there has been to get the marriage settlements &c. ready with the utmost expedition. To give you some notion of that hurry, as also of the nature of the business that was in agitation here, I send you enclosed a letter I received on Tuesday last from sollicitor Hamilton, wherein he states it as nearly impossible they could be got ready for Thursday. In consequence of this letter I posted out to the Duchess's house at Richmond on Wednesday, showed the letter to the partys concerned, and submitted to their consideration whether it would not be better to delay the marriage for a day or two, otherwise the settlements might not be ready. We had a pleasant discussion of this business in presence of Lord Stanley.[1] He could not reconcile himself to the thoughts even of one day's delay ; so he came to town on Wednesday, and we went together to the houses of the men of law urging them in the most earnest manner to have all their papers ready, so as the marriage might be completed yesterday. I remained at Wedderburne's till the first draught of them was finally settled on Wednesday night at eleven o'clock. Then a variety of hands were employed all night in extending the settlements on parchment ; yesterday at two o'clock they were got ready for signing. Lady Betty and Lord Stanley signed them in London between two and three, the company assembled to dinner at the Duchess of Argyle's, at Richmond, between four and five ; the marriage ceremony was performed there between seven and eight ; and soon after the young married couple set out for Lord Stanley's house at the Oaks. . . . I can only say that, in modern times, there are few instances of more ardent lovers than this young heir of the Derby roll. He was highly sensible of Lady Betty's merit and personal attractions, and you never saw any lover more impatient of delays than he has been.

---

[1] Succeeded his grandfather as Earl of Derby in 1776.

We had a very agreeable day yesterday at the marriage ceremony ; everything concluded in the most proper manner, and with the most hearty good-will and approbation of all concerned, at the same time without any parade or affectation. The only persons present besides the Duchess' own family were Lord Archibald Hamilton,[1] who came to town on purpose to give Lady Betty away ; Lady Charlotte Edwin, two sisters of Lord Stanley's, General Burgoyne, and myself.

It is my real opinion that it will turn out a happy and fortunate marriage in every respect. . . . It has given me both health and spirits to see our fair pupil, who is so deserving in herself, so well settled in the world. It is one of the most desirable connexions that could have been made in Britain, &c.'

Page 171, Line 13.

Volume I. of 'Transactions of the Glasgow Archæological Society' contains 'An inventory of articles which escaped the hands of the mob on the occasion of the sacking of Shawfield's Mansion,' contributed by J. Dalrymple Duncan, F.S.A. This inventory was exhibited at a meeting of the Glasgow Archæological Society in 1887 ; it was then the property of William Turner, Esq., of Glasgow. Mr. Duncan says, 'This is an extremely interesting document, and not only indicates how considerable Campbell of Shawfield's wealth was, but also throws a good deal of light on the dress and manners and customs of the day. It would be interesting to know if Shawfield took into account in any way the large amount of articles which were thus restored to him in settling the amount of the compensation awarded him by government, £6,400 for damages to the house and £2,600 for minor items. Some of the things were saved by neighbours, Peter Murdock (afterwards Provost of Glasgow) and James Spreull, and restored to him.'

Page 175, Line 8.

The peerage of Glencairn has been dormant since the death, without issue, of John the fifteenth Earl in 1796. The title was claimed by Sir Adam Fergusson, Bart., of Kilkerran, by Sir Walter M. Cunningham, and by Lady Harriet Don. In 1797 the Lord Chancellor dismissed the

---

[1] Succeeded his nephew Douglas, as Duke of Hamilton, in 1799.

claims of the latter two, and adjudged that Sir Adam Fergusson had clearly proved his being heir-general of the Earl of Glencairn from the first creation, but had not established his right to the title. The present heir-general of the Earls of Glencairn is the Right Honourable Sir James Fergusson, Bart., of Kilkerran.

PAGE 182, FOOTNOTE 1.

The following appeared in the Geological Magazine in 1885 : John Francis Campbell of Islay, F.G.S., the bearer of a name well known among geologists some years ago, was born in Edinburgh in 1821. . . . By birth he was heir to a large patrimonial estate. This inheritance was, however, lost to him through adverse circumstances shortly after he came of age ; and the magnanimous spirit in which through life he bore this reverse of fortune gained him the abiding esteem of the large circle of friends, whose regard his generosity of heart and many attractive qualities must in any case have secured. . . . He found occupation successively as private secretary to his chief, the Duke of Argyll ; Secretary to the Board of Health, to the Mines Commission, and to the Lighthouse Commission, the two latter employments stimulating him in those studies of geology and solar physics which engaged his attention and effort even in the last years of his life. During the years 1861–1880 inclusive he held in succession two posts in the Queen's household. Having withdrawn from the Court at the latter date, he occupied himself till the close of his life with scientific study, travelling, and the social life of his home. His many journeys in former vacations had taken him several times into Iceland and Scandinavia. On one occasion (1873-4) he passed from Archangel through Russia to the Caucasus, returning *viâ* Constantinople and Southern Europe. He also visited Japan, China, Java, Ceylon, Syria, and Palestine, and twice resided in Egypt. In all these wanderings his instinctive powers as a practical linguist were very valuable to him ; his ready skill as a draughtsman not less so. . . . His mind was acute, ingenious, and indefatigably active ; but he had never subjected it to received methods of scientific training. . . . His mental stores, whether gleaned in the field of folklore and myth or in that of experimental science, were original, not derived from other workers. His invention of the ' heliometer,' an instrument in use at Greenwich, and which was mentioned with honour by Professor Balfour Stewart at the meeting of the British Association in 1883, is probably the only distinction that will survive him. But he was not only entirely uninfluenced by any desires after a lucrative result of such work as he did, but comparatively indifferent to the fame which it might have brought him. He loved knowledge for its own sake ; his desire was for ' more light.' His best praise will dwell in the hearts of his many friends ; all who knew what his own heart was —those who have shared his refined and genial hospitality, or benefited by his ready generosity, counsel, and help—will never lose their warm remembrance of his truly noble spirit and kindly bearing. . . .'

PAGE 185, LINE 3.

In Sir Walter Scott's ' Border Minstrelsy,' ' The Mermaid,' a ballad by John Leyden, is dedicated to Lady Charlotte Campbell in these words :

> ' To brighter charms depart my simple lay,
> Than graced of old the maid of Colonsay,
> When her fond lover lessening her view,
> With eyes reverted, o'er the surge withdrew ;
> But happier still, should *lovely Campbell* sing
> Thy plaintive numbers to the trembling string.
> The mermaid's melting strains would yield to thee,
> Though pour'd diffusive o'er the silver sea.

> ' Go boldly forth—but, ah ! the listening throng,
> Rapt by the siren, would forget the song !
> Lo ! while they pause nor dare to gaze around,
> Afraid to break the soft enchanting sound,
> While swells to sympathy each flattering heart,
> 'Tis not the poet's, but the Siren's art,' &c.

PAGE 192, LINE 1.

Madame de Staël and Lord John Campbell had met in 1803. We find her writing from Cappet on July 3 in that year to M. Meister as follows : " Lord John Campbell et M. Robertson, deux Anglais auxquels je m'intéresse beaucoup, ont une lettre de moi pour vous, monsieur. . . . Si la lettre que j'ai donnée à mes Anglais vous est remise, je vous prie

de les recevoir avec intérêt et de leur donner tous les renseignements néces-
saires à leur départ.'

In a previous letter that she had written to " M. Henri Meister,
homme de lettres,' about Lord John and Mr. Robertson she said: ' Tous
les deux ont ce charme dans les manières que nous avons perdu en France
et qu'il est si doux de retrouver. Mais ils sont timides et parlent mal le
français.'

Page 224, Line 9.

In writing to the Hon. Mrs. Boyd in 1783 Beattie says : ' Your
sentiments of the Duchess are perfectly just. I have had the honour to
know her long, and I think I know her well. A perfect character I
have never yet met with, but of her I will venture to say that the more
it is known the more it will be admired, and that nothing but prejudice,
or envy, or ignorance, or pure malice, can be insensible of its worth.'

Page 227, Line 29, Footnote 2.

Since this was written, Louisa, Duchess of Abercorn, has passed away.
She died on March 31, 1905, aged ninety-two, at Coates Castle, Sussex,
and was buried at Chenies, Bucks, by the side of her brother, Lord
Wriothesley Russell.

The following extracts from the ' Daily Mail' are worthy of record :

' For many reasons this famous old lady was one of the most interesting and remarkable personages in the British peerage, and, indeed, in the
world. Born in 1812, the second daughter of the sixth Duke of Bedford,
she had lived in five reigns and had over two hundred descendants, of whom
at least 160 are still living. As her grandfather was born in 1710 three
lives covered the remarkable period of 195 years.

' Practically half the peerage will go into mourning because of her
death. She was married in 1832, five years before the accession of Queen
Victoria. She had seven sons and seven daughters, and eighty-five great
grandchildren. Twenty-two of her descendants fought in the recent war
in South Africa. . . .

' On July 9, 1903, 145 direct descendants assembled in the gardens of
Montagu House, Whitehall, to celebrate the completion of her ninety-
first year. Such a gathering is without doubt unique, not alone for the

number of those who thus honoured the parent of them all, but for the distinguished character of the gathering. The list of those attending presents a remarkable record of illustrious names, not only those of highly placed social leaders, but of many who had achieved distinction in statesmanship, letters, travel, and both branches of the profession of arms.

'Before taking her place in this great family group the Duchess was photographed with the Master of Dunglass—the grandchild of her grandchild. Then she presided over this unparalleled court of honour, and the photograph of the scene has become famous. She was the granddaughter, the daughter, the wife, the mother, and the grandmother of dukes, and their titles represented all the three countries which comprise the United Kingdom. These are the Duke of Gordon, the Duke of Bedford, the first Duke of Abercorn, the present Duke, the Duke of Marlborough, and the Duke of Leeds. She was half-sister to Lord John Russell.'

PAGE 229, LINE 24.

In March 1803, Maurice Dupin (the father of George Sand) wrote to his mother as follows : . . . 'René a donné ces jours-ci un très-beau déjeuner où étaient Eugène Beauharnais, Adrien de Mun, Milord Stuart, Madame Louis Bonaparte, la Princesse Olgarouky, la Duchesse de Gordon, Madame d'Andlaw, et Lady Georgina, laquelle passe dans le grand monde pour un astre de beauté. Il ne lui manque pour mériter sa réputation que d'avoir une bouche et des dents. Mais sur cet article Eugène et elle n'ont rien à se reprocher. La duchesse ne demanderait pas mieux que de la lui faire épouser, mais le cher beau-père Buonaparte n'entend point de cette oreille-là. En sortant de table, nous allâmes nous promene, au Jardin des plantes, les uns en voiture et en boghei (? buggy), les autres dans la calèche à quatre chevaux de la Duchesse. Nous vîmes tout dans le plus grand détail. Eugène distribuait des louis à tort et à travers, comme un autre eût donné douze sous. Il nous faisait les honneurs, et c'est tout au plus s'il ne disait pas au lieu du jardin du roi, le jardin de mon père. À la suite de la promenade, la Duchesse de Gordon donna à la Râpée un dîner dont ni Eugène, ni René, ni Auguste, ni moi, ne fûmes priés.'

The Duchess of Gordon and Lady Georgiana were present at the memorable Court on March 13, when Napoleon's interview with Lord Whitworth took place, and they left Paris four days after.

PAGE 237, LINE 19.

Once when the Duchess had promised to obtain the post of 'Gauger' for someone whom she wished to oblige, she heard by letter early in the morning that a vacancy in this line had just occurred, and instantly dressed and went off to Pitt's house. On the door being opened she asked the astonished servant whether Mr. Pitt was at home. On learning that he was, she desired her name should be sent to the Prime Minister. The servant said that Mr. Pitt would not be visible till twelve o'clock. 'But,' said the Duchess, 'I must see him at once ; show me his room.' The servant reiterated that it was impossible—that Mr. Pitt was in bed, and that it would be more than his place was worth to do so. ' Then,' said the Duchess, 'I'll go by myself,' and accordingly she forced her way past the servant, flew upstairs, and, knocking at the door of Mr. Pitt's bedroom, without waiting for an answer went in and seated herself on a chair by his bedside. Pitt, who had the most rigid notions of propriety, was dumbfounded, but the lady soon let him know why she had come. He then told her that he had promised this appointment to a member of the House of Commons who had been a great supporter of his Government, and that therefore, deeply as he regretted it, he could not give it to her. ' But I must have it,' said the Duchess, ' and out of this chair I do not move till you say I shall.' ' You may have the next for your friend,' said the Prime Minister. 'I must have this one,' replied the Duchess. Pitt knew she would be as good as her word and would not go till she got what she wanted, so he had to give in, and the Duchess secured the appointment for her *protégée*.

PAGE 239, LINE 23.

I remember the Duke of Richmond in Ireland, when, as Colonel Lennox, he was an object of universal admiration to the young of both sexes. His duel with the Duke of York seemed to have something in it chivalrous, displaying a recklessness of all selfish considerations. He was supposed to excel in all manly exercises, and that was a higher praise in those days than it is in these more intellectual times.

PAGE 257, LINE 13.

' The body lay in state for two days, an impressive service was held in the English Cathedral, and the body of one who had been Canada's most splendid governor since the days of De Tracy and Frontenac was deposited in the Cathedral vault ' ('Old Quebec ').

PAGE 264, LINE 14.

We find in a MS. letter dated August 3, 1647, from 'Washburne,' and signed 'G. R.' (George Russell), the following : 'The King whom always the greatnesse of his spirit and resolution holds undaunted, beires it firme above the injurie of threatening, and remaines unhorrified, however Major Scot, an independent member (yet deserving something to hang on), lately, and in the presence of the King, being asked by Major G. Browne what good end they would make in the House, made a desparate sudden resolution, they could never make a good end, till they took off the King's head that stood there, to whom Major Browne replyed : "I had thought, sir, you had come to have kissed the King's hand." "Sir," said Major Scot, "I had rather followed him to the gallows," and I think he spoke the sense and intention of the armie. The Major General immediately addresseth himself to his majestie, made him knowing of that desperate language, takes Scot by the shoulder, saying, "Sir, this is the man." The King whom ever highest Providence, and his own innocence with miracle protects, slights the madnesse and malice of so poysonous a tongue.'

PAGE 302, FOOTNOTE.

Mrs. Richard Trench, writing in 1799 from Dresden, says : 'I went to Graff's, an excellent portrait painter. He is famous for catching the expression of the countenance, but he leaves nature pretty much as he finds her.' Graff was born in 1736 and died in 1813.

INDEX

PRINTED BY
SPOTTISWOODE AND CO LTD., NEW-STREET SQUARE

Lightning Source UK Ltd.
Milton Keynes UK
UKHW02f2029020818
326691UK00009B/591/P